Praise for *The Essence of the Bhagavad Gita*

"It is doubtful that there has been a more important spiritual writing in the past 50 years than this soul-stirring, monumental work. Through a mind blessed with special clarity, Swami Kriyananda has brought us his most vivid memories of the explanations by Paramhansa Yogananda of the Bhagavad Gita, allowing us to hear with greater vibrancy than ever before the Melodies of the Divine. At last the "Lord's Song" is not a mystery to our mind, but music to our ears! What a gift! What a treasure! My personal gratitude to Swami Kriyananda shall be everlasting."

—**Neale Donald Walsch**, author of *Conversations with God*

"Where did we come from, why are we here, and where does this life lead to? Swami Kriyananda is the most experienced philosopher that could help us understand how the Bhagavad Gita answers these questions. Through [this book], people will . . . discover their divine nature and potential."

—**Bikram Choudhury**, Founder, Bikram's Yoga College of India and author of *Bikram's Beginning Yoga Class*

"Swami Kriyananda writes with the same spirit of compassion and intelligence displayed by his teacher, Paramhansa Yogananda. In this extraordinary book, he honors this lineage, showing with great mastery how this message is more relevant and compelling than ever."

—**Dean Ornish, M.D.**, Founder, Preventive Medicine Research Institute and author of *Reversing Heart Disease*

"Great souls, great minds, and even greater wisdom combine here to open doors to the evolution of consciousness and spirit. Not in recent times has there been a work in which the very Presence of the illumined teachers have been rendered so present and available. This book is a gift to our time from once and future times. The very reading of it quickens the soul as it enlightens the path that humanity may take."

—**Jean Houston**, author of *JumpTime* and *A Passion for the Possible*

"This profound vision of the great yogi Paramhansa Yogananda opens a new window that lets the wisdom light of the Bhagavad Gita, the words of the Blessed One, shine as a source of sublime peace in the hearts of many."

—**Tulku Thondup Rinpoche**, author of *The Healing Power of Mind*

"Yogananda's insights are stunning, unexpected, and profoundly wise. This is the Bhagavad Gita as we've never seen it before. Highly recommended!"
—**Linda Johnsen,** author of *Daughters of the Goddess: The Women Saints of India*

"Very inspiring! [This book] reveals the vision of a yogi. Swami Kriyananda's words are fresh, lucid and yet very sublime. They flow joyously like the Ganges toward the ocean of God-realization."
—**Swami Nikhilananda,** Regional Head, Chinmaya Mission, Delhi, author of *The Art of Forgiveness*

"This is not just another ordinary explanation of the Bhagavad Gita. It stands on par with the grand commentaries of this classic as given by the three great masters, Shankaracharya, Madhvacharya and Ramanujacharya. This book contains not just the essence of the Bhagavad Gita but also the essence of Hinduism. . . . We can only be grateful to Swamiji for having given this jewel of Wisdom and Discrimination to us. He has written many books but this is possibly the "chudamani" or crest jewel of his life."
—**Mata Devi Vanamali,** Vanamali Ashram, Rishikesh, author of *The Play of God: Visions of the Life of Krishna*

"This book is a tribute to India's great spiritual contributions to the world as explained by great Guru Paramhansa Yogananda to his brilliant disciple Swami Kriyananda, for the benefit of millions of spiritual seekers."
—**Swami Gokulananda,** Head, the Ramakrishna Math, New Delhi, author of *Swami Vivekanand—The Ideal of the Youth*

"Again, we experience the heartfelt knowledge of Paramhansa Yogananda, this time bringing to life the compassion of Sri Krishna and the Bhagavad Gita. Through Swami Kriyananda's deep relationship and passion for both his Guru and the Gita, the teachings of this Sacred Scripture dance from the ancient to the golden present showering us with Divine Wisdom and inspiration on countless levels."
—**Nischala Joy Devi,** author of *The Secret Power of Yoga: A Woman's perspective on the Heart* and *Spirit of the Yoga Sutras*

"God's song is sweet from all lips. But it's ineffably sweet when sung by a master like Yogananda to a disciple like Kriyananda who, in turn, sings it for modern students in the current style."
—**Hart De Fouw**, author of *Light on Life: An Introduction to the Astrology of India*

"This book is galvanizing! I've taught many patients in my medical practice simple yoga and meditation exercises to reduce their stress and anxiety levels. Frequently, they'll come back to me wanting to learn the philosophy and spiritual teachings that are behind these Yoga techniques. At last, I have the perfect book to recommend. Beautifully written and filled with hope, these Gita commentaries are spiritually awakening yet eminently understandable for the neophyte. Even advanced yoga students will find this book deeply insightful and spiritually thrilling."
—**Peter Van Houten, M.D.**, co-author of *Yoga Therapy for Overcoming Insomnia*

"Swami Kriyananda has done it again! He has captured in one book the essence of one of the world's most inspiring books, the Bhagavad Gita, as interpreted by one of the world's greatest spiritual Masters, Paramhansa Yogananda."
—**Rev. Justin Epstein**, Unity Church

"Swami Kriyananda had the privilege of spending more than 60 years attuning his consciousness to that of his great guru Shri Paramhansa Yogananda. Hence he could recollect . . . the words of his great master and give fresh insight into the Master's own masterpiece, making matters simpler, clearer, logical, and appealing to [all], both in the East and West. He has also succeeded in making relevant cross-references to contemporary thoughts and scriptures of other religions including Christianity, Islam, and Judaism."
—**D.R. Kaarthikeyan**, former Director, CBI and National Human Rights Commission, former Director General, Central Reserve Police Force, India

". . . this commentary is a must for anyone on the spiritual path. One feels Swami-ji alongside, as a friendly guru through this book."
—**Ashok Arora**, Advocate, Supreme Court of India

The Essence of the Bhagavad Gita

"I asked the Divine Mother whom I should take out with me to help me with editing, and your face, Walter, appeared.

"To make extra sure, I asked Her twice more, and each time your face appeared. That's why I am taking you."

—Paramhansa Yogananda

The Essence of the Bhagavad Gita

Explained by Paramhansa Yogananda

*As Remembered by His Disciple
Swami Kriyananda
(J. Donald Walters)*

Crystal Clarity Publishers
Nevada City, California

Designed by Crystal Clarity Publishers
Cover illustration is an oil painting by the American artist
Dana Lynne Andersen
Commissioned for this book, and titled: *The Divine Vision*.

ISBN-10: 1-56589-219-4
ISBN-13: 978-1-56589-219-4

Printed in Canada

1 3 5 7 9 10 8 6 4 2
First Edition

Crystal Clarity Publishers
14618 Tyler Foote Road
Nevada City, CA 95959
800.424.1055 or 530.478.7600
Clarity@crystalclarity.com
www.crystalclarity.com

Library of Congress Cataloging-in-Publication Data
Kriyananda, Swami.
The essence of the Bhagavad Gita / explained by Paramhansa Yogananda
as remembered by his disciple Swami Kriyananda.
p. cm.
ISBN-13: 978-1-56589-219-4 (hardcover : alk. paper)
ISBN-10: 1-56589-219-4 (hardcover : alk. paper)
1. Bhagavadg§t~---Criticism, interpretation, etc. I. Yogananda,
Paramhansa, 1893-1952. II. Title.
BL1138.66.K785 2006
294.5'924046--dc22
                                              2006001655

*Dedicated to
the millions of people who,
my Guru predicted,
would find God through this book*

CONTENTS

FOREWORD

WE ARRIVED IN INDIA FOR A THREE-WEEK VISIT the day Swami Kriyananda began writing this book. He had been struggling for several weeks with the problem of how to approach it.

"My first thought," he told us, "was to write a slim volume, as in fact I called it in the first introduction I wrote. I had long been wanting to tackle the whole Gita, but that project, though it held paramount importance for me, also frightened me, both because of its magnitude and because of its supreme importance. The prospect that your coming," he said to us, "might possibly disrupt my line of thinking was what 'put me over the edge,' in the sense that it brought me to a resolution of my dilemma! I felt I *must* begin work, or else lose whatever clarity I'd arrived at for the project already."

Actually, it was only a week or more after our arrival that he came to realize that, instead of writing the "brief overview" he'd first intended, he had actually launched (or *been* launched!) on writing the whole Gita.

Throughout our visit, Swamiji, while playing the loving host—chatting with us for hours, going out with us to shops and to dinner—spent all his free time working on this manuscript. In answer to our concern that he must be finding our presence a distraction from this work, he replied, "On the contrary, it is helping me! I find the whole project so awe-inspiring that I felt almost overwhelmed by it. Your presence helps me to approach it simply, one day at a time. Getting feedback from you has helped also, even if it doesn't clarify ideas I have already fairly clearly in my mind, for at least it keeps my feet on the ground, mentally, while I wrestle with concepts so subtle that I *must* find ways to make them relevant to everyone." After our departure, others came to visit Swamiji. He kept up the same schedule, and assured them all that their presence, far from distracting him, helped to "ground" him by relating what he was writing to actual needs and realities.

Unbelievably, he finished this work—comprising as it did, in its first draft, six hundred pages—in less than two months! To everyone, himself included, it seemed a miracle.

"Fortunately," he told us, "I have a very clear memory, and can recall vividly the days I spent in Master's company, reading his entire manuscript, and helping him with its editing. I said to him at the time, 'Sir, this is the most wonderful thing I have ever read!'" We too, in reading this manuscript, feel that it is the greatest thing we have ever read. One day, Swamiji said to us, "I feel as though Master were working as I write—not only through me, but *with* me."

To us, this book—of the some eighty-five books Swami Kriyananda has written in his life—is his masterpiece. That it is inspired will be evident to the reader without our saying so. What author, otherwise—especially one who has always labored hard to make all his thoughts simple and clear—could have finished such a book as this in less than two months?! He himself said to us, "I actually thought I would have to devote ten years of my life to writing this book." Add to that his present age—he is now in his eightieth year—and what we are discussing amounts almost to a "labor of Hercules." He told us, "My one fear was that I might not live long enough to see this work completed."

It was in May, 1950, while he was still twenty-three years old, that his guru, Paramhansa Yogananda, asked him to come over to his retreat to begin work with him on the job of editing his commentaries on the Bhagavad Gita. Swamiji had been staying five miles away, at the monks' retreat, working on "editing" (he always puts the work he was doing then in quotes, reflecting how young he was at the time!) the Master's work on *The Rubaiyat* of Omar Khayyam. The Master had kept Swamiji with him during the first days of his dictation of his Gita commentaries. He had then sent him to work alone, however, while he himself concentrated all his time on his commentaries. Now he was ready to begin working with Swamiji (whom at that time he called "Walter") on the editing of his new manuscript.

The Master had told his monk disciples in January of that year, when he took "Walter" with him to the desert, "I prayed to Divine Mother and asked Her whom

I should take with me to help with the editing. Your face
appeared, Walter. That's why I am taking you."

In May, after completing the manuscript, he asked
his young disciple to come over and help him with the
editing. For two months they worked together. The day
"Walter" came over, his guru exclaimed ecstatically, "A
new scripture has been born! Millions will find God
through this work. Not just thousands— *millions*! I have
seen it. I know!"

During this period he told his disciple, "Your job in
this life is lecturing, writing, and editing." Later he
added, "By editing my words, you yourself will grow
spiritually." He added, as he had said to him already
several times, "You have a great work to do."

It seems clear, in retrospect, that Yogananda knew
from the beginning that Kriyananda was destined to edit
his Gita commentaries. Yet, despite many indications
that the Master knew Kriyananda would do this work,
he could not say so at the time: Another editor, much
senior to "Walter," was working on it. Meanwhile,
Kriyananda was given many other things to do. He was
placed in charge of the monks by his guru. He wrote
letters for the Master; he ended up doing much reorgan-
izing within his guru's organization, went on widespread
lecture tours, taught, and guided the activities of centers
throughout the world. Many years were still to pass
before all his guru's predictions about his life's work
would be fulfilled.

Yogananda must surely have seen that his Gita commentaries would not come out that year, as he wanted them
to do. The urgency he expressed for their immediate

publication must have been prompted by his knowledge that, if they did not come out during his lifetime, their publication would be delayed for many years. In fact, they finally came out only in 1995—forty-five years after their completion.

During that time, Kriyananda fulfilled all his guru's other predictions. The "great work" the Master had foretold included writing some eighty-five books, composing over 400 pieces of music, and founding seven communities in which, today, some 1,000 people live lives of dedication to God. In addition, he took some 15,000 photographs, many of which have appeared in his published works.

In 1990, after forty years of writing spiritual books, composing spiritual music, and lecturing to and teaching thousands around the world, he felt guided to take up the task of editing his master's words. From then on, he created such books as *The Essence of Self-Realization* (a book of his guru's sayings); *The Rubaiyat of Omar Khayyam Explained* (an edition of Yogananda's writing on the subject); *God Is for Everyone* (a rewrite of Yogananda's book, *The Science of Religion*); and a final book of his guru's sayings, *Conversations with Yogananda*.

In the year 2003, Swamiji felt his guru's call to found a new work in India. He lives now in the land of his guru's birth, has a daily (prerecorded) television program on two nationwide stations, has written a correspondence course (*Material Success Through Yoga Principles*), and has written several other books, besides. His chief ambition for many years, however, has been to write this book.

"When the first version of this book was finally published," he told us, "in 1995, I was disappointed. I remembered well the material my Guru had dictated in 1950. But how different it was, now, from that original! It lacked the simple beauty and clarity I remembered. It gave repeated evidence of drastic overediting. I longed to offer at his feet a new version of the work he himself had done when I knew him. I don't have access to the original, but fortunately he has blessed me with a very clear memory. Could I, just possibly, reconstruct from memory what he did? Certainly I could not recall the actual phrasing, but it astonished me how much I did recall of the context. Perhaps . . . perhaps! Well, I could at least try!"

And so, finally, in October 2005, he felt the time had come to at least begin the work on Paramhansa Yogananda's Gita commentaries for which his guru had begun to train him during the winter and spring months of 1950—fifty-five years ago. What began as an "overview" soon became a stanza-by-stanza commentary. He skimmed lightly over the published version, primarily as a jog to his own memory, since the labored explanations were not as he remembered them. It was more helpful to him to tune in to the consciousness of Yogananda, which lay beyond what he read.

For us, it was a great blessing to be present in India during the first weeks of this project, which he had finally undertaken. He told us, "Master's thoughts poured effortlessly into my mind, helping me to fill page after page with deep insights and inspiration."

With a radiant look on his face, Swami Kriyananda often worked late into the night. Sometimes he began work

again in the early hours, long before dawn. With quiet
humility and deep inner joy, he told us who were with
him. "I am filled with such bliss as I write, it is hard to
think of anything else! I feel the deep delight my Guru
takes in this work."

Here, then, is a book that is a living tribute to two of
India's great spiritual contributions to the world: the
wisdom of the Bhagavad Gita, and the importance of
the guru-disciple relationship. Through a long life of
dedication to, and attunement with, his guru, Swami
Kriyananda has—we deeply feel—presented the vibrant
truth and power of his master's original explanation
of this beloved scripture. Yogananda has guided his
disciple's life and thoughts for nearly sixty years in such
a way as to enable him to fulfill that commission, given
so many years ago.

It seems to us that this great scripture, known for ages
as simply the Bhagavad Gita (the "Lord's Song"), had to
wait for this age of renewed consciousness that matter
is energy, and that the need of religion in this new age is
a teaching based both on revelation and on common
sense.

As it says in the Bhagavad Gita (10:11), "Out of pure
compassion, I, the Divine One who dwells in all, set
alight in their hearts the blazing lamp of wisdom." May
you, too, find God's light within you through this great
new revelation of ancient, timeless scripture.

Jyotish and Devi Novak
December 14, 2005

Explanatory Note

THE NUMBERS OF THE CHAPTERS IN THIS BOOK have no particular correlation to the eighteen chapter numbers in the Bhagavad Gita itself. In the text that follows, all chapter references are to the Gita, and not to the thirty-one chapters of this commentary.

Thoughts on Pronunciation and Spelling

Sanskrit words that are generally written with a *"jn"* but pronounced with a slightly nasal *"gy"* are treated more phonetically in this book. The following is an excerpt of a conversation I had with my Guru, Paramhansa Yogananda, in 1950. He was going over some of his writings with me when we came upon the word, *gyana* (wisdom). "Jnana," he remarked, "is how scholars usually write it. I can't see why. It isn't *pronounced* 'J-nana.' And how else are you going to pronounce it, if you find it transliterated in that way? This is a simple example of scholarly pedantry." *Gyana* is more correct, though in pure Sanskrit there is a nasal sound, which scholars have tried (futilely) to catch, with their "*jnana.*"

"Another transliteration scholars prefer," my Guru continued, "is to write 'V' instead of 'B.' Instead of Bibaswat they write 'Vivaswat.' Instead of 'Byasa' they write 'Vyasa.'"

In many languages, actually, there is only a slight difference, hardly discernible to foreigners, between the "b" and the "v," but the "b" sound, for Sanskrit, comes closer to the correct one.

PREFACE

Why This Book?

THIS BOOK, WHICH COMES AFTER THE PUBLICATION of Self-Realization Fellowship's (Yogoda Satsanga Society's) *God Talks With Arjuna,* has been written in answer to a publicly expressed need for a simpler and clearer version.

The first version was not published until forty-five years after its writing was completed. It is exhaustive and comprehensive. Can a thing be comprehensive, however, and yet not be complete? Certain teachings, and even certain stories, important to me in the original, do not appear in the first published version.

I should state that I worked personally with Paramhansa Yogananda during the major portion of his writing of this work. He had told the monks in 1950, before he went out to his desert retreat to begin this labor, "I asked Divine Mother whom I should take out there with me to help with the editing, and your face appeared, Walter [the name by which he called me].

To make extra sure, I asked Her twice more, and each time your face appeared. That's why I am taking you."

I read the original manuscript, and worked on it with him (though not extensively). The copy I worked on still exists in SRF's archives; it contains my handwriting. I was in my early twenties then, however, and a "greenhorn" without proper experience as an editor. Now that I have reached nearly the age of eighty, I might be described as somewhat seasoned in this field—especially with some eight-five books to (what I hope are) my credit.

What he dictated was fluent, easy to understand, and beautiful. I remember exclaiming to him at the time, "This is the most wonderful work I have ever read!" For many years (since 1995, with SRF's publication) it has been my deepest desire to present a version that was closer to the original. The actual manuscript, however, is not available to me.

Fortunately, I have an exceptionally clear memory, which I have drawn on in writing other books, most recently *Conversations with Yogananda*. I have also been teaching these truths for nearly sixty years, as a devoted disciple of my Guru, and have the teachings, so to speak, "under my belt." Although I had, of course, to refer to their book, I only skimmed over it lightly. This book is in no way a paraphrase or copy of theirs.

What it represents is my earnest endeavor to reproduce the book I read fifty-five years ago, and loved with all my heart. His was a great work. I have tried to reproduce his book in such a way that I think (and certainly hope) has been pleasing to my Guru, with at least some of its impact of immediacy. His insights are the most amazing, thrilling, and helpful of any I have ever read on the Bhagavad Gita.

INTRODUCTION

T HESE PAGES CONTAIN AN EXPOSITION OF THE hidden meanings in the Bhagavad Gita as they were explained by my great Guru, Paramhansa Yogananda, and (before him) by his line of gurus.

The reader today is confronted by an almost bewildering array of translations and commentaries on the Bhagavad Gita. The very universality of that scripture invites people to see it in terms of their own diverse approaches to truth. Those who by nature are primarily active find wise guidance in the Gita for how to act in such a way as to free themselves of emotional involvement in this world. Those whose natures are primarily rational find in the Gita supreme guidance on the impersonal attitudes needed for living with wise and calm non-attachment. Those of devotional inclination find in the Gita the inspiration to love only God. And those, finally, who seek God through calm meditation find in this scripture deep teachings on right attitudes in meditation.

Truth is one. People try to slice it like a pie, but even the slices of a pie narrow to a single center. What the Gita shows is that, however many aspects there are of truth, all of them radiate outward from a single center.

Yogananda emphasized in his writings, and especially in his commentaries on the Bhagavad Gita, that man is a triune being: physical, mental, and spiritual. All parts of human nature need to be developed, lest any one of them obstruct the others.

My Guru once mentioned to me, with regard to one-sided approaches to the Bhagavad Gita (of which there are many), "Even Swami Shankara, profound though his commentary was, denied the importance of physical reality. What he wrote was overbalanced on the spiritual side. He was right in saying that all things are only an appearance, but it should be added that *in this realm of* appearances *maya* does have its own reality. Everything is a dream, but even dreams, *as dreams*, are real."

The Bhagavad Gita teaches every important aspect of the spiritual path: during activity, *Karma Yoga* (the yoga of right action); during thinking and discrimination, *Gyana Yoga* (the yoga of wisdom and discrimination); when feeling and experiencing emotion, *Bhakti Yoga* (the yoga of devotion). There is a central teaching, however, in the Bhagavad Gita, which unites all paths even as subsidiary streams unite in a larger river.

"That river," Yogananda said, "is the energy flowing in the spine. The subsidiary paths of yoga offer guidance to people of different basic temperaments: the active, the discriminating, the 'heartful.' The central river to enlightenment, however, is shown by *Raja Yoga*, the royal yoga: the pathway of the spine.

"Raja Yoga," he continued, "takes one straight up the central pathway of the spine into the inner silence of divine communion. It is the teaching of this yoga, finally, that makes the Bhagavad Gita truly a scripture for all mankind. It is why Krishna stated in the Gita, 'O Arjuna, be thou a yogi.'"

One thing that sets Paramhansa Yogananda's commentary apart from others is its all-inclusiveness. He himself said to me after he'd finished writing his commentaries, "I now understand why my Guru told me not to read other commentaries on the Bhagavad Gita. He didn't want my mind influenced by human opinions. Instead, what he wanted, and what I did, was tune in to Beda Byasa, the author of the Gita. It was Byasa himself who wrote this great scripture through me."

Over the years since then, I have come to understand more clearly how that great sage, who lived thousands of years ago, might have been able to cross the yawning chasm of time that separates his day from ours. I knew even then that my Guru had not intended a merely poetic image, as if to imply that all he had done was honor the *spirit* of Beda Byasa. Rather, what he did was tune in to the ever-living consciousness of that great sage.

I was able to accept this much without difficulty. The question remained in my mind, however: Did Byasa literally dictate this commentary to Yogananda? Or was the communication effected by some other means?

Superconscious communication is never confined to mere verbal expression; deep intuitions are conveyed, always, that words alone could never express. In *Autobiography of a Yogi* Yogananda tells of how his great guru, Swami Sri Yukteswar, appeared to him after his own death. His guru, on that occasion, described many details of the astral and causal universes. In Chapter 43 of that book, "The Resurrection of Sri Yukteswar," Yogananda states, "My mind was now in such perfect attunement with my guru's that he was conveying his word-pictures to me partly by speech and partly by thought-transference. I was thus quickly receiving his idea-tabloids."

Masters have direct, inner ways of communicating with one another. I witnessed the effect of such communication many years ago in Sydney, Australia. I had published my edition of Paramhansa Yogananda's book, *The Rubaiyat of Omar Khayyam Explained*. The Theosophical Society of Sydney had invited me to speak about this book to their members. After the lecture, a man in the audience raised his hand and asked about a particular quatrain, and my Guru's interpretation of it.

"It seems to me," he said, "that what Yogananda wrote here doesn't relate clearly to the words of the quatrain itself."

"I understand your problem," I replied, "for I faced it several times in editing this book. I would meditate on the quatrain, however, and on my Guru's explanation of it, and always I saw the connection, no matter how obscure it at first seemed."

At this point a lady in the audience raised her hand and stated, "I am from Iran, and I am familiar with ancient Persian. I am also familiar with the particular quatrain to which this gentleman has referred. His problem is that he is trying to compare the *translation* by Edward FitzGerald to Paramhansa Yogananda's commentary. I agree, that connection is tenuous. I've compared his commentary, however, with the original Persian, and I have found that the two, the words of Omar Khayyam and those of Paramhansa Yogananda, correspond exactly."

As I've suggested, superconscious communication is rarely verbal, and is never entirely so. It is instantaneous, conveying deep, direct intuitions that could never be expressed in words alone. Ordinary minds are hemmed in by the intellect, which must ponder the pros and cons of every issue. Most people find it difficult to understand this higher level of communication. The further doubt is natural for them: "If Yogananda's words were inspired by superconsciousness, why have they required editing?" The simple answer is, these are two very different levels of communication. Communication by words is slow and cumbersome, especially if one tries to express himself clearly and exactly. Words have also an endless potential for being misunderstood.

I myself am very familiar with the writing process, having spent more than seventy years trying to hone my ability to convey my meanings in written form. I think of Coleridge's poem, "Kubla Khan"—a *tour de force* of great beauty from which, when I was young, I memorized many passages. This poem however, for all its wonderful rhythm and imagery, in actual fact conveys no message at all! It was a marvelous example of a drug-induced, false inspiration. I, for my part, have tried always to write meaningfully. Generally speaking I have found, in spite of my most conscientious efforts, that even when the writing has flowed as it were on its own, the job still needed editing. I've had to edit every book I've written, though sometimes very little. Editing is rather like plumbing: fitting words, phrases, and sentences together in such a way as to make the ideas flow smoothly.

Bringing spiritual truths down to the material plane is rather like bringing a diaphanous cloud down to where its vapor becomes a surging, wind-tossed ocean. The very process of descent hems in the process of creativity. When the creative flow is powerful, one cannot give primary attention to perfecting his outward mode of expression. I can understand very well why great masters rarely phrase their words with the care demanded by a careful and elegant stylist. It is for their disciples, usually— if any are competent—to "pick up the pieces." Indeed, as my Guru himself indicated to me, this would be the way I myself would grow, spiritually.

God Himself created the universe in a comparable manner, by manifesting His consciousness down through the layers of ideas, energy, and subtler levels of matter until the grossest minerals were manifested.

Before dictating, Paramhansa Yogananda would turn his eyes up to the spiritual eye in the forehead. Then, speaking slowly to give his secretary, Dorothy Taylor, the time she needed to type out what he was saying, he spoke as the guidance came to him from within. Seldom did I see him descend from that high divine level to make a comment—or, from time to time, to check what he was doing against another published interpretation by Swami Pranabananda, a liberated disciple of Lahiri Mahasaya. I imagine that that swamiji's book served him as a means of making sure there wasn't some important detail he might have omitted from what was flowing through him.

When the work was finished, he exclaimed to me again and again, with ecstatic exhilaration and joy, "A new scripture has been born!"

"Millions," he added, "will find God through this work. Not just thousands: millions! I have *seen* it. I *know*!"

I was privileged to read the manuscript, and to help my Guru during the editing process, with which he himself took serious pains. Unlike most philosophical works, this book was, as I expressed it in my autobiography, *The Path*, "fresh and alive, each page a sparkling rill of original insights. With the sure touch of a master teacher, profound truths were lightened occasionally with graceful humor, or with charming and instructive stories, or highlighted with brief touches of new, sometimes startling information. . . . Best of all, the truths expressed in the book were constantly clarified . . . with illustration after illustration."

As my Guru also put it: "This book came entirely from God. It is not philosophy (the mere *love* of wisdom): It *is* wisdom."

Again he exclaimed, with a beatific smile, "A new scripture has been born!"

Chapter One

What Is the Bhagavad Gita?

THE BHAGAVAD GITA MEANS, "THE SONG OF God." It is indeed a song: a work of art, as well as a deep statement of truth. I would, indeed, call it the perfect scripture. I make that statement as a Westerner, raised in the Christian tradition, though now a devout believer in *Sanaatan Dharma*.

The "Gita," as it is lovingly called in India, is the most widely known and best loved scripture in India. Concise, profound, poetic, and deeply inspiring, it has been fittingly called "The Hindu Bible," for it is the definitive statement of the ancient religion of that oldest of all countries on Earth.

The truths taught in the Bhagavad Gita are stated with extraordinary clarity. Interestingly, however, because of their very clarity they open up vast vistas of insight. Hence the value of commentaries on it, of which there have been a large number. There are levels of meaning in the Gita for which the Gita is also an allegory. I base the contents of these pages on the commentaries by my great Guru, Paramhansa Yogananda. I was with him in 1950, as I said in the Introduction, at his retreat in Twenty-Nine Palms, California, while he dictated a major part of those commentaries.

Paramhansa Yogananda began his writing by stating that the Bhagavad Gita presents the quintessence of India's ancient teachings, of which the oldest and most complete are the voluminous *Vedas*. To understand the Vedas is not easy. As Swami Bharati Krishna Tirtha, the Shankaracharya of Gowardhan Math in Puri, stated, many of their words have changed their meaning over the many centuries since they were first written down. (And they were only written down after the arrival of a lower age, when people could no longer recite the words from memory. The invention of writing was not a sign of civilization's advancement, but of a decline in human awareness that made it necessary to record thoughts in writing.)

Bharati Krishna Tirtha stated that many words of deep meaning have acquired, in time, more superficial meanings. Words do, of course, change. The word, "knave," he pointed out, once meant simply a young man, not a bad one. Indeed, "knave" comes from the German *knabe*, which means "boy." Similarly, then, the word "*go*" in ancient Sanskrit meant "light," not "cow" as it does today. Western scholars, taking words like this, have made a hash of the inner meaning of the Vedas.

Only people of deep spiritual understanding can penetrate to the heart of those ancient scriptures. The Brahmin caste, who are supposed to be (but seldom are) deeply versed in the scriptures, often proclaim their traditional scriptural knowledge with names suggestive of their supposed degrees of Vedic scholarship: *Chatturveda* (four Vedas); *Trivedi* (three Vedas); *Dubey* (two Vedas).

A summary of the Vedas is contained in the *Upanishads*. Even these great scriptures are obscure—especially for modern minds.

The quintessence of the *Upanishads*, again, is contained in the Bhagavad Gita. The timeless glory of Sanaatan Dharma, "The Eternal Religion," which is the ancient and true name of what we know as Hinduism, is most succinctly and movingly revealed in this timeless spiritual masterpiece.

CHAPTER TWO

WHAT IS SANAATAN DHARMA?

SANAATAN DHARMA COMPRISES THOSE TIMELESS truths which are rooted in eternity. They predate the forming of the world, and cannot be confined to any one earthly religion. Sanaatan Dharma embraces, indeed, all of manifested existence. Its manifestation in India is unlike other religions in that it was not a teaching by any one master, but expresses the essence of age-old, revealed wisdom.

Christians consider themselves to possess the only divine revelation, which they name The Holy Bible. This belief shows a misunderstanding of the very word, "revelation." The Bible, which is a mere *statement* of truth, cannot convey the *experience* of truth, which alone is the real meaning of *revelation*.

Wisdom does not contradict itself. All great masters attain the same vision of truth: one and eternal, which we call God. Divine vision transcends sectarian differences; it is this direct vision of timeless truth which forms the basis of Sanaatan Dharma. That truth reminds

man of who and what he is: a divine soul, forever indestructible. The true purpose of scripture, then, is to show
man how to find eternal freedom in God.

Jesus Christ said it for all truth seekers: "Be ye therefore perfect, even as your Father which is in heaven is
perfect." (Matthew 5:48) Perfection is the goal of every
true religion. Perfection is a state of existence, not of
mere belief. The Bhagavad Gita, from this point of view,
is a revealed scripture, but it emphasizes the need for
inner revelation, without which no words can suffice to
explain wisdom. Great masters in every religion, having
perceived God (the Supreme Being) directly, have
emphasized again and again in every language that the
Supreme Spirit is the essence of everything there is.

Many true masters have pointed out that there
are countless paths to divine attainment. Indeed, the
paths may be described as numbering as many as there
are human beings in this world. For everyone must begin
his search for enlightenment from his own point of
understanding. His understanding is determined by his
human characteristics, which the Bhagavad Gita
expounds. Briefly, they are devotion, right action,
meditation, and wisdom (or discrimination). The names
of the great world religions—of which Buddhism,
Christianity, Hinduism, Judaism, and Islam are the main
ones—can be misleading if they are not seen to express
the spiritual "needs" of their times. Truth needs to be
explained according to the understanding of the people
for whom it is taught.

Buddha came at a time when the people had come to
depend on Vedic rituals to the point where they expected

divine favors by merely repeating rituals and word-formulae, without any effort devoted to personal purification for self-transformation. Their belief might be classed as mere superstition. Buddha did not speak against the Vedas as such: He spoke against people's excessive dependence on their outward practices.

Jesus Christ came when the Jewish people thought that only by obedience to religious rules—again, without self-purification—would they please God.

Mohammed came to a people who were steeped in superstitious idolatry—again, without belief in the need for self-purification.

Within Hinduism itself, great masters have come repeatedly with the mission of correcting misunderstandings and distortions of the subtle truths of Sanaatan Dharma. Swami Shankaracharya came to correct the misunderstanding prevalent among Buddhists of his time that there is no God. God exists, he declared, but He has no eternal form: He is *Satchidananda*—ever-existing, ever-conscious, ever-new Bliss (as Paramhansa Yogananda translated the term).

In every religion there are various "moods," as they might be called: deeply meaningful to certain people, less so to others. There is the sad longing for eternity expressed in the Gregorian chants. There is the simple, pure kindness expressed in Buddhism. There is the joyful, powerful, but intensely personal devotion in Hindu chanting. There is the Jewish dedication to living in harmony with God's law. We see in Islam also a heroic surrender to the will of God. All these might be described as coming, in a sense, under the heading of what Yogananda called the "romance" of religion: the heady spirit in which the devotees try to live divine truths, without necessarily knowing what truth, itself, is.

The paths to God vary widely according to the natures of individuals, and only superficially according to their different religious beliefs. Thus, Christians and Buddhists with a devotional nature direct their devotion differently, but the upward flow of energy from the heart is the same. Those with an active, serviceful nature may serve in the name of Jesus Christ, Buddha, or some other great teacher, but the principle of service, rather than being centered in one's little self, is the same. People with a discriminating nature develop calmness and dispassion according to their religious systems, but in all cases the wisdom in the attitude they develop is one of calmness and dispassion.

In every case, devotional people of the different religions resemble one another more closely than they do members of their own religions who follow the dissimilar paths of service or of discrimination. Christian monks feel a greater natural affinity with Buddhist or Hindu monks than with fellow Christian householders. The prayers and music, the serviceful attitudes toward others, and calm attitudes of dispassionate wisdom more easily cross the apparent barrier of different religious beliefs within each group than even the differences between them and their fellow religionists.

One extraordinary aspect of the Bhagavad Gita is its universality. Whatever the needs of any particular time or people, this great scripture addresses them all from the highest point of view.

In Hinduism as a whole, indeed, no aspect of the truth is rejected. The Hindu teachings emphasize the universal way of living for high spiritual attainment. The Hindu teachings concern themselves much less with beliefs than with practices. They portray the struggles common to each ego on its long upward journey from ignorance to the light of Self-realization.

Thus, the teaching of the Gita is not specifically Hindu: It is all-embracing. Not only is it completely non-sectarian, but it shows people how even their worldly experiences can help them in the end, spiritually— perhaps after many lifetimes—by weaving the threads of diverse human experience into the vast tapestry that comprises the story of each soul's journey to ultimate perfection in God.

For this journey contains innumerable twists and turns. There is but one guideline that can give it right direction: the polestar of one's own innate divinity. The Bhagavad Gita points in this universally true direction.

CHAPTER THREE

THE ALLEGORY OF THE GITA

THE STORY ON WHICH THE BHAGAVAD GITA IS
based is a brief episode in the longest epic in the
world, the *Mahabharata*. The Gita presents two
main characters of that epic, Arjuna and Krishna, as
they move between two great armies, ranged for battle
on the field of *Kurukshetra*.

Arjuna symbolizes the devotee—the person, that is to
say, who seeks divine salvation and union with God.
Krishna symbolizes God Himself, the divine Self within
every human being. Hence, in the Indian teachings,
Self-realization is described as the true goal of all spiritual striving, whatever one's religion. The two
concepts, Self-realization and the knowledge of God,
are synonymous.

In the story of the *Mahabharata*, Arjuna invites Krishna
to be his charioteer. The Bhagavad Gita is the story of the
dialogue which takes place as Krishna drives Arjuna in
his chariot between the two armies, in response to
Arjuna's request to observe the two armies directly.

9

Arjuna, his brothers the Pandavas, and all the forces on their side symbolize the champions of virtue. The enemy are the Kauravas, cousins of the Pandavas, led by Duryodhana, who has usurped the throne. The confrontation is, as we have said, allegorical—a fact which is suggested by, among other things, Arjuna's very request. He is the leading general of his army. Would the general of an army request something so apparently foolish as to be driven between the ranks of the opposing armies, so close to the enemy, and on the very eve of hostilities? Surely, in practical terms, his request was absurd!

As Krishna and Arjuna pass between the two hosts, Arjuna voices his doubts about the righteousness of the forthcoming war. "It would mean destroying my own kinsmen!" he exclaims. "How can I commit such a sin?" Krishna replies to this very understandable doubt, dispelling it. He then proceeds to expound the essence of the teachings of Sanaatan Dharma itself.

Obviously, this account is allegorical. The opposing armies represent the opposition within every unenlightened human being between his upward- and his downward-inclining tendencies. The upward tendencies are his good qualities; the downward ones are those which induce him to seek delusion, or evil. The war of Kurukshetra does not take place literally on any battlefield, though the field of Kurukshetra actually still exists in India. That historic site, and the story that grew out of the war, represent the eternal conflict within man himself.

At the same time, the truths propounded in the Gita are applicable at all levels of life: material, mental, emotional, and spiritual.

Paramhansa Yogananda makes the point that every great scripture is multi-leveled, addressing human needs at every level from a standpoint of divine wisdom. Thus, Krishna's teaching is also true in a literal sense, for it urges the need for courage in righteous warfare. For righteous causes do, of course, exist.

Krishna turns a righteous outward cause, however, into a description of the eternal conflict within all men between high aspiration and ego-indulgence. In a deeper sense, the war of Kurukshetra is the unending struggle in the mind between good and evil. Its end lies only in final liberation. Krishna himself makes clear the allegorical nature of his timeless dialogue with Arjuna. In a later chapter of the Gita he states, *"This body is the battlefield."*

Arjuna, seeing the enemy up close, confronts the distressing fact that many of those he is about to fight are members of his own family! After all, the Pandavas grew up side by side with their cousins, the Kauravas. They studied under the same teacher, Dronacharya. As children, they played together, argued and squabbled together—after the manner of growing boys everywhere. The bonds they formed, though not all of them friendly, were nevertheless deep and strong.

The first chapter of the Gita is not, as most commentators have considered it, a mere description of the leading warriors on both sides of a coming conflict. They are the opposing forces within human nature itself. Their very names, traced to their Sanskrit roots, become the names of psychological qualities.

Those opposing Arjuna, therefore, are his cousins, well known to him, even loved by him. The *Mahabharata* is the full story behind this impending war, telling how the material desires and the ambition of Arjuna's oldest cousin, Duryodhana, head of the Kauravas, forced the conflict by refusing the Pandavas their throne, which was theirs by right. Now Arjuna, seeing these two related families geared up for mutual destruction, laments the need to fight at all. "Surely," he cries out to Krishna, "it would be a sin to slay my own kith and kin! Would it not be more just for me to surrender our kingdom?"

This war is no mere conflict of ambition, however. It is described in the *Mahabharata* as a righteous war between good and evil. Were Duryodhana, who usurped the throne, to remain the king, the people would suffer under his unrighteous rule. The war of Kurukshetra, which is to begin on the morrow, will pit high principles against proud ambition, and soul-aspiration against qualities in human nature that keep the ego in bondage to delusion.

Krishna comforts Arjuna in his distress. Death itself, he assures him, would be preferable to a life spent in unrighteousness. At stake here is not mere physical life or death. Pitted against each other are the life of the spirit and the abandonment of those qualities which lead to soul-bliss. Death of the body, Krishna reminds Arjuna, is nothing: the mere doffing of a garment. It doesn't affect a person's consciousness, which continues throughout eternity. To reject spiritual principles, however, means to embrace spiritual death. "Fight!" Krishna urges his disciple. The war is not one of mortal, physical combat, but of courageous inner struggle toward the victory of soul principles over spiritual sloth and material ease. This is the first and central message of the Bhagavad Gita.

Krishna goes on to say that there are several paths to God, according, not to people's beliefs, but to each person's own temperament. He delineates the right attitudes for the devotee, the various delusions that can prevent him from finding God, and the way to overcome them. In one supreme chapter is explained, in a highly metaphorical manner, the supernal experience of God.

Although the battle setting is allegorical, the advice given in this scripture may be taken as valid for every level of life, including righteous warfare. A true scripture, Paramhansa Yogananda stated, addresses human needs in their entirety.

The story of the *Mahabharata* is also, in fact, historical, and although many of the characters in it are fictional, others actually lived on Earth. In historical fiction today it is common to include known historical figures, to lend verisimilitude to the story. Byasa (or Vyasa), the author of the *Mahabharata*, differed from this technique primarily in making his main characters the historical characters, while his lesser ones served to demonstrate the great array of characteristics in human nature. His main characters lived, as I say, historically. They include the Pandava brothers (Yudhisthira, Bhima, Arjuna, Nakula, and Sahadeva), some of the Kauravas, and a number of others. The rest of the characters Byasa fictionalized, and presented episodes in their lives in such a way as to conform to the allegory he was weaving like a tapestry.

The over-all theme of this great epic is the soul's first separation, aeons ago, from God: the soul's long voyage through the barren land of delusion; and its final return, after countless trials and tribulations, to the Great Source of all life. This is the story through which every soul must pass, once it enters upon the outward path of life and once it chooses to follow the inward path of divine awakening.

The war of Kurukshetra describes the soul's final struggle to become liberated from the clutches of *maya*, or delusion. The war itself, though also a historical event, illustrates the struggle with which every spiritual aspirant, sooner or later, is faced.

CHAPTER FOUR

ALLEGORY IN SCRIPTURE

THE MIXTURE OF FACT AND FICTION FOR ALLE-gorical purposes is common in scripture. It suggests the same blend in life itself: the dreamlike quality of life on earth mixed with the deep truths of the soul. An example of this literary device may be seen in the Book of *Exodus* of the Bible, and the Jewish people's escape from years of bondage in Egypt. Their escape is a historical fact. In *Exodus*, however, the details of that escape are elaborated on, and contain much allegory. *Exodus* describes the Jews, for example, as wandering for forty years in the Sinai desert. Surely they cannot have literally spent forty years in that search. A simple glance at the map of the area shows a desert far too small for such a long trek—unless, indeed, the whole people were under a dense cloud of delusion. To believe that it took the Jews forty years to cross it demands too great a stretch of the imagination! The time can only have been so stated deliberately in order to suggest a deeper meaning behind the quest for the Promised Land.

Wilderness, in spiritual writings, is often used allegorically to describe the inner silence, enjoyed in soul-communion. In that silence, no cultivated flowers of sense-pleasure bloom. The forty-year journey through the Sinai desert describes the long quest required to attain spiritual enlightenment.

In *Exodus*, all who had been born in captivity had to die before the new generation could enter the Promised Land. The meaning, here, is that every characteristic that was born in the "captivity" of ego-consciousness needs to be transcended. Only soul-qualities, developed in the expansion of divine communion, are able to enter the Eternal Kingdom. The Promised Land described in the Bible is union with God: the land of Cosmic consciousness.

Delusive qualities, born of ego-consciousness, are rooted in the consciousness of separateness from God. The ego is not the true Self. All of us are made in the image of God. The Bible, in the first chapter of the Gospel of St. John, tells us that we are all the sons of God. If we define ourselves as being different from Him, we must transcend this self-definition before we, as pure souls, can enter into the divine realm. Such egoic qualities as selfishness, hatred, passion, greed, personal ambition, covetousness, jealousy, and anger are weights that prevent the balloon of awareness from soaring up into the sky of Spirit. St. John therefore tells us also, "No man hath seen God at any time." Never, in other words, by human, egoic consciousness can the Divine be perceived. The divine truth is far above human realities. As the Bible states also, "My thoughts are not your thoughts, neither are your ways my ways, saith the Lord."*

The Promised Land is the reward bestowed, eventually, on all who seek God earnestly. *Exodus* contains an esoteric hint which reinforces this truth. The Promised Land is described as a "land of milk and honey." The Bible tells us, "And the Lord said, I have surely seen the affliction of my people which are in Egypt . . . , and I am come down to deliver them . . . and to bring them up out of that land unto a good land and a large, unto a land flowing with milk and honey."†

Indeed, certain aspects of the spiritual path are subtler than ordinary knowledge—that is, than what can be comprehended by anyone who lacks personal experience of inner realities. Those aspects are familiar, however, to yogis and to others who meditate deeply. These truths are hinted at in both the Bible and the Bhagavad Gita.

Let us consider momentarily this specific anecdote in the Bible. In deep ecstasy it so happens that the tongue turns automatically upward toward the brain. At the tip of the tongue there is a positive magnetism which, when united with its negative complement in the nasal cavity, "short-circuits" (in a manner of speaking) the flow of energy in the body and keeps it in the brain. With this physical union is formed a kind of "nectar," described by yogis as the inner counterpart of outer sexual union. The Hindu scriptures describe this nectar as having the taste of a blend of clarified butter, or *ghee*—milk in its purest form—and honey. The Hindu Vedas named this

* Isaiah 55:8.
† Exodus 3:7,8.

"nectar," *soma*. An entire scripture was named *Soma Veda*. This *soma* nectar is able to sustain the body for long periods of time while the soul remains rapt in ecstasy, known in the yoga teachings as *samadhi*.

The Promised Land, then, is no mere earthly location. Israel symbolized the soul's true land: Cosmic consciousness.

It must be stated here that the Jews were not, as a whole race, the chosen people of God. For of course there were and always have been good Jews and bad Jews: the same mix that one encounters everywhere on earth of saints and sinners. The Jews in this story symbolize the sincere aspirants in every country and religion who forsake sense-slavery, and commit themselves to realizing the kingdom of God within. As Paramhansa Yogananda often put it, "God chooses those who choose Him."

The story of Moses and the exodus of the Jews from Egypt contains other mystical symbols as well, yogic in nature since they relate to truths more often considered part of the yoga teachings. Moses, for example, is described as raising the serpent power of *Kundalini*: "And the Lord said unto Moses, Make thee a fiery serpent, and set it upon a pole; and it shall come to pass, that every one that is bitten, when he looketh upon it shall live. And Moses made a serpent of brass, and put it upon a pole, and it came to pass, that if a serpent had bitten any man, when he beheld the serpent of brass, he lived."* Here two kinds of serpent energy are described: the downward moving force, which draws the consciousness toward

* Numbers 21:8,9.

worldly and sensual indulgence; and the upward flow, which liberates one's consciousness from delusion.

The "pole" described here is the spine. Many swamis in India carry a *danda*, which is a staff they use to remind themselves to remain ever centered in the spine. This "pole," so described in the story of Moses, is made of brass. The serpent upon it is fiery, suggestive of the inner light which ascends with spiritual wakening. Only when this light, or Kundalini energy, is uplifted can the "poison bite" of delusion be healed.

Thus, Jesus Christ said also, "And as Moses lifted up the serpent in the wilderness, even so must the son of man be lifted up." (John 3:14) Jesus was not speaking of his coming death on the cross. That was an event which no one, as yet, could anticipate. It had to be a later commentator, therefore, who suggested this meaning. What Jesus was saying, rather, was that *human consciousness* must be lifted up, even as Moses lifted up his own consciousness in the "wilderness" of inner silence, by raising the power of Kundalini in the spine.

The present author once asked Paramhansa Yogananda whether Moses was a spiritual master. "Yes, certainly," Yogananda replied in an affirmative tone of voice. "The Bible says he 'lifted up the serpent [that is, the Kundalini power] in the wilderness.'"

These brief excerpts from the Bible are offered here to prepare the reader, especially if he is Jewish or Christian, for similarly deep teachings in the Bhagavad Gita. Even Hindus, after pondering the universality of those teachings, may find it easier to relate to the deeper aspects of this great Hindu scripture.

CHAPTER FIVE

THE GENESIS OF THE STORY

T HE KEY FIGURE OF THE MAHABHARATA, AND therefore of the Bhagavad Gita, is Lord Krishna, whose actual life is shrouded in legend. That he was a real person in history is certain; the basic facts of his life are known. The legends, however—his boyhood days, for example, among the gopis and gopals (cowherd girls and boys) of Brindaban—should be taken as allegories.

There is, for instance, the story of when his foster mother, Yasoda, wanted to tie him up, as a little child, to keep him from getting into mischief. (He loved to steal fresh cheese from the kitchen!) She took a length of string which she thought was quite long enough for the job. Inexplicably, it proved too short. She fetched another length and tied it to the first string. This extension, too, proved insufficient! Several more lengths were added. No matter how long the string was, it was not enough to do the job. At she last understood her mistake: The Infinite cannot be tied by anything! How can the human mind encompass God's vastness? Humbly, then, Yasoda prayed to Bala (the little boy) Krishna, "Lord, please let me tie You so that I can finish my chores!" Sweetly then, on being so prayerfully addressed, the divine child let her have her way.

Obviously this story is allegorical. Even if it had really happened, it would be allegorical in the sense of containing deep meaning. When all of the boyhood stories about Krishna are added up, it becomes clear that they were meant to instruct devotees rather than to report actual, historical events.

The entire epic of the *Mahabharata* is, similarly, one long allegory. For the purposes of this present volume it would be confusing to condense the over-all story of that extremely long and complex epic, which describes the descent of Spirit into the ego and the delusion of separateness—from God, from other egos, and from everything—and the struggle to rise again into oneness with Spirit. Suffice it here to give a brief overview.

The Pandavas were the children of Pandu: the oldest three, the offspring of Pandu and Kunti; the two youngest, of Pandu and Madri. The main characters in the epic actually lived. Beda Byasa wove his allegory around actual people and events in history. Lesser characters, however, had no historical counterparts. They represent psychological qualities in man.

Pandu represents the discriminating intelligence, or *buddhi*. He is described as being white in color (his name derives from *pand*, or "white"). White is intended metaphorically to signify purity; a pure intelligence demonstrates clear discrimination.

Kunti, the mother of the first three Pandavas, represents "the power of dispassion." Her three sons, born of Pandu, are Yudhisthira (divine calmness), Bhima (control of the life force, or *prana*), and Arjuna (self-control).

Madri, the mother of the two youngest Pandavas, who are twins, represents "the power of attachment to dispassion."

To understand why there were two mothers for the five Pandavas, it is necessary to be familiar with the symbolism involved here. Each of the Pandavas stands for one of the five chakras, or spinal centers. The yoga teachings explain—as is explained at length in *God Talks With Arjuna*—that the path of divine awakening is, as I've indicated, the spine. Energy enters the body through the medulla oblongata at the base of the brain. From this point the sperm and ovum, after uniting, begin the process of creating the embryo. Energy, which then solidifies as matter, passes through the nerves (after creating them) into the brain, down the spine, and out to form the body. When the consciousness withdraws from the body at death, the energy withdraws first from the extremities to the spine, then up the spine, and at last emerges through the medulla oblongata again, leaving the body.

In ecstatic meditation, the yogi (or saint, as he would be called in other religions) withdraws his energy and consciousness by the same route. Deep meditation is a process of "dying" consciously—with the possibility, however, of returning to the body after meditation and resuming its normal activities. As St. Paul declared in the New Testament of the Bible (Paramhansa Yogananda often quoted this passage), "I die daily."

As the yogi withdraws his energy and consciousness from the senses into the spine, he seeks to raise them up the spine to the brain. A curious difference occurs in the brain between the superconscious yogi, or saint, and the unenlightened worldly person. The medulla oblongata has two poles, a negative and a positive. The negative pole (the *agya chakra*) is in the medulla itself. The positive pole—reflecting the medulla—is the *Kutastha*, the spiritual eye between the eyebrows.

The unenlightened man sinks back, at death, into the negative sleep state. He must swim the waters of *lethe*, as the ancient Greeks called it: the waters of forgetfulness. After a time he may, if he is not wholly materialistic, awake in the astral world and for a time enjoy its beauties to varying degrees, before material desire draws him back to earth again, to reincarnate in a physical body. Questions of the degrees of enjoyment in the astral must be shelved for a later discussion. For now, we are concerned with the spinal highway to enlightenment.

The yogi who can fix his concentration on the spiritual eye leaves his body consciously, whether in deep ecstasy or in death. Is the spiritual eye, one may ask, merely symbolic? No, it is actually beheld, and is, in fact, a reflection of the light in the medulla, through which the energy moves down the spine in three *nadis*, or subtle channels of life force, called the *sushumna*, the *vajra*, and the *chitra*. The *brahmanadi* is the "spine" of the causal body, so called because it is the primal channel through which Brahman—the divine consciousness— descended into the body. The spiritual eye, when seen clearly, is universally the same: a field of dark blue light surrounded by a golden halo, in the center of which is a five-pointed star. The golden aureole represents the astral world; the blue field inside it, the causal world and also the omnipresent Christ consciousness; the star in the center, the Spirit beyond creation.

Paramhansa Yogananda pointed out that man is made, as the Bible says, in the image of God, because that five-pointed star resembles the body of man: With parted legs, and the arms stretched out to the side, the head at the top, man has the very shape of that star. Symbolically (it should be added) a five-pointed star with the fifth point turned downward is inauspicious.

The spine is the primary channel through which the energy flows. The energy's upward flow is blocked by certain plexuses in the spine, from which energy flows out into the nervous system, and through that system into the body, sustaining and activating the different body parts. When the yogi in deep meditation withdraws his energy from the outer body to the spine, and then up the spine to the brain, he finds that passage blocked by the outward flow of energy from those plexuses (called centers in English translations of the yoga treatises; in their Sanskrit original they are called chakras). The energy at each chakra must be withdrawn into the spine in order to continue its upward journey.

Each of the Pandavas in the *Mahabharata* represents one of the spinal chakras—from the base up to the medulla oblongata. In the allegory, Draupadi represents the Kundalini power. Draupadi, through a concatenation of circumstances (not necessary to be described here), becomes the wife of all five of the Pandava brothers. What, then, is Kundalini?

As the energy enters the body and descends the spine, it becomes locked, so to speak, at the lowest pole (its opposite pole being the *anahata chakra* in the heart). In order for the energy to be raised in the spine, Kundalini must first be "awakened"—that is to say, its grip on matter-consciousness must be released. The strength of that hold is determined by the degree of material attachment in the mind. Non-attachment to matter frees the energy to rise up the spine. As it then passes through each chakra, it finds itself blocked as if by a "closed" door. The blockage is caused by energy's outward flow through those plexuses. The rising Kundalini must spiritually "awaken" each chakra. As the portal of that chakra is opened, a fresh surge of awareness and spiritual power is released, enhancing one's clarity of awareness.

In the *muladhara*, or coccyx center (the lowest chakra in the spine), the awakened energy, as it moves upward after being awakened by Kundalini, is symbolized by the youngest of the Pandava sons, Sahadeva.

The next chakra upward, the *swadisthana* or sacral center, is symbolized in its upward-moving energy by Nakula, the older of the twin brothers. These two twins are the offspring of Pandu and Madri, Madri representing "the power of attachment to dispassion."

From the second chakra, once awakened, the energy flows up through each of the higher chakras, the awakened energy of which is symbolized by the sons of Pandu and Kunti—Kunti representing "the power of dispassion." The difference between the qualities of Madri (the power of attachment to dispassion) and Kunti (the power of dispassion) is the degree of ego-involvement. In attachment to dispassion there is more of the lower thought, "*I am* dispassionate"; in dispassion itself there is the abstract quality, without a personal sense of "doership."

As the energy flows upward from the *swadisthana*, or sacral center, it is again impeded in the *manipura*, or lumbar center opposite the navel. This chakra is symbolized by Arjuna. The next chakra upward is *anahata*, the heart (or dorsal) center, which is symbolized by Bhima. Finally, the last and highest chakra in the spine is *bishuddha*, the cervical center, symbolized by Yudhisthira.

Each chakra, when it has been awakened, bestows with that awakening a certain spiritual insight. Sahadeva, the upward-moving energy in the lowest chakra, bestows the divine power of resistance (to temptation). Nakula, the rising energy in the next chakra, bestows the power of adherence to virtue. These two qualities are the *yamas* and *niyamas* listed by Patanjali in his eight-limbed path to enlightenment: the power to avoid wrong action, and the power to cling to right action. These two powers form an essential foundation for any serious spiritual development.

Arjuna, the "Prince of devotees" as he is called by Krishna in the Gita, resides in the *manipura* or lumbar center, and represents fiery self-control. This self-control develops when the yogi is able to follow the proscriptive and prescriptive rules of the spiritual path.

Bhima, the second-oldest brother, represents the heart quality and, also, control of the life force. In the *Srimad*

Bhagavatam, another deep scripture by the same author, Beda Byasa, the devotee is told during meditation to visualize his heart as a lotus. He should mentally turn the petals upward, to enable their energy to flow up toward the brain. The desires of man are centered in the heart. The yogi must direct every ray of desire-energy upward in divine aspiration to the spiritual eye between the eyebrows.

The highest of the spinal chakras is the *bishuddha* or cervical center, just behind the throat. When the energy gathered at this point is directed upward, the mind acquires divine calmness and expansion. Here is represented Yudhisthira, the oldest of the Pandava brothers.

The young twins, offspring of Pandu and Madri, representing the ego wholesomely directed toward inner freedom, provide support to the aspiring yogi for his spiritual practices. The three older brothers, sons of Pandu and Kunti (the power of dispassion), provide dynamic strength and inspiration for inner, spiritual upliftment.

Thus, it is important from the beginning to understand that the Bhagavad Gita (and the *Mahabharata* on which it is based) provide deep spiritual guidance and inspiration. It is much more than a scripture of pious maxims, but a deep, practical guide to the attainment of union with God.

Were it even, however, a mere guide to goodness and to how to live spiritually in the work-a-day world, it would already be a great and important scripture. What makes the Bhagavad Gita so outstandingly helpful on the spiritual path is that it offers guidance on many levels, as we shall see in the pages that follow.

CHAPTER SIX

WHY COUSINS? WHY ENEMIES?

THE DESCENT OF SPIRIT INTO MATTER IS EXPLAINED allegorically with great care in the *Mahabharata*. Here we bypass much of the elaborate symbolism of that descent, since it predates the story of the Bhagavad Gita. Instead, we shall begin at that point where we ourselves, as human beings, enter upon the scene. For this great scripture is a work, not of history, but of human spiritual development. Man's actual need, as explained in the Bhagavad Gita, is not to understand how he got into delusion, but rather to understand how he can get *out of* delusion.

Dhritarashtra, the father of the Kauravas or Kurus, has Ambika (Negative Doubt) for his mother. He is born blind, as one is, spiritually, when his understanding comes to him only through the senses. Pandu, the father of the five Pandavas, is born of Ambalika, co-wife with Ambika, who represents the positive, discriminating faculty.

These, the two wives of Bichitrabirya (the divine ego, or sense of divine individuality), are the balancing opposites to one another: Negative Doubt pitted against the Positive Faculty of Discrimination. Dhritarashtra (the blind mind) through his first wife, Gandhari (symbolizing the power of desire) begets Duryodhana and his ninety-nine brothers. (Dhritarashtra's second wife, Vaishya, symbolizes the attachments that are formed in consequence of desires; these give birth to Yuyutsu, who represents the eagerness to do active battle in order to protect one's selfish desires.)

Duryodhana, the first son of Gandhari, represents ego-inspired desires. Paramhansa Yogananda in his Gita commentaries called him King Material Desire. All the sense tendencies are subordinate to the ego's supreme desire to feed its own importance.

Pandu is Ambalika's son. Ambalika, remember, represents the positive discriminating faculty. Thus, Pandu symbolizes the active application of that positive faculty: that is to say, the positive, discriminating intelligence.

The Kurus, or Kauravas, children of Dhritarashtra (the blind mind), are first cousins to the Pandavas (the children of Pandu). Theirs is a cousinly relationship, for they are offspring of the same human consciousness. They are also enemies, however, for their interests are in diametric opposition to one another's.

The field of battle is, as I said, the spine. Here the war rages between the downward-moving tendencies (on the one hand), which take one's consciousness outward into the world of the senses, and those tendencies (on the other hand) which lift man's consciousness toward his true source in Spirit. That these two forces flow in opposite directions in the spine can be observed in many common realities of life.

Many of the words people use show these differences. Probably there are equivalents in all languages to the expressions in English, "I feel uplifted"; "I feel high"— or, "I'm feeling downcast"; "I feel low." In Italian (to take one example) these expressions translate as, "*Mi sento su*, [I feel up, or high]" and, "*Mi sento giù* [I feel down]." These words owe their existence to simple facts of human nature: When the energy and consciousness rise in the spine, one feels happy; when the energy and consciousness move downward, one feels depressed or unhappy.

When one's feelings impel him to indulge in material desires, his energy flows downward in the spine, and then outward from it—into, and through, the senses. Spiritual inspiration uplifts both energy and conscious-ness in the spine, directing them toward the spiritual eye. In either case the energy is the same, and influences the self-same consciousness. Negative characteristics, such as hatred, jealousy, anger, and lust, form part of the same "family" of consciousness as those qualities which, being positive, lift the awareness heavenward. Such positive characteristics, or qualities, include love, kindness, forgiveness, compassion, and self-control.

Most people have a mixture of positive and negative qualities. They identify, in their egos, with both groups.

The Bhagavad Gita presents a fascinating picture of human nature. It shows that every individual is a nation unto himself, his "population" consisting of all his qualities, both good and bad. Verily, every human quality may with perfect justification be likened to an individual. In essence, none of us is his characteristics: We merely manifest our character traits. As Paramhansa Yogananda wrote in *Autobiography of a Yogi*, "Thoughts are universally and not individually rooted." Different characteristics develop in us according to the way we act and react repeatedly in this world in response to people and circumstances. No one, in his true nature, is *essentially* angry or jealous or lustful. He allows these qualities to develop in himself by identifying his ego with things that happen to him in his life.

If his ego feels threatened, and he considers that he must meet that threat with aggressive courage, he may gradually develop both those qualities: aggressiveness and courage. If, on the other hand, he considers himself unable to meet the threat successfully, he may gradually develop a fearful outlook, or become jealous, or acquire a resentful attitude. Over time, the innumerable experiences he encounters in life, and *the way he encounters them*, may develop in him innumerable "complexes." In other words, certain aspects of his nature may insist on attack, while other aspects plead, tortoise-like, for a self-protective withdrawal. Still others may mutter helplessly in the background about "the slings and arrows of outrageous fortune," while still others spread a whispering campaign of malicious gossip to get "the world" to side with them, while another whole group of mental citizens may stand, figuratively speaking, on soapboxes pleading for tolerance, forbearance, amused acceptance, or calm non-attachment.

"Circumstances," Paramhansa Yogananda commented, "are always neutral. They appear positive or negative according to the corresponding reactions of the heart." The possible reactions to virtually every circumstance are legion in number. Every reaction may (and does, for most people) seem passing and not binding on one's self or on one's nature. People—to give an example—may say something unkind about someone, then chuckle lightly as if to imply, "See? my unkind words haven't affected me personally!" Action, however, never takes place in a vacuum. Every act, every *thought*, has its specific consequences.

There is another aspect to human nature, which forces passing thoughts to become imbedded as firm characteristics. This is the power of habit. Thus, in the *Mahabharata*, and in that relatively brief excerpt from it called the Bhagavad Gita, there is the fascinating role played by Drona, who is known also as Dronacharya (*acharya* meaning "teacher").

Dronacharya was the guru, or teacher, of both the Kurus and the Pandavas. His role in the epic was to teach them the martial arts, including that most important skill of his time: archery.

The bow, in the *Mahabharata*, symbolizes the spine. When a bow is strung, the string resembles the spine itself; the arched front looks somewhat like the front of the body. The arrow, as it is loosed from the bow, symbolizes the power of concentration. In this respect one can visualize also the eyebrows as the two curving halves of a bow, wherein the point between them stands for that part of the bow where the arrow is firmly placed.

Dronacharya's best pupil was Arjuna. There is a story about Drona's proposing a test for his students. He asked them, each in turn, to strike off the head of a bird seated on the highest limb of a tree. Each pupil, as he approached the teacher, was asked by him, "What do you see?"

Each reported the many things within his range of vision. A typical answer was, "I see the bird, the tree, the passing clouds." Dronacharya knew, in each case, that the archer would miss the head of the bird. In fact, so it proved.

Finally, Arjuna stepped up for his turn. "What do you see?" asked Drona.

"I see the head of the bird," replied the young warrior.

"Nothing else?" asked the Guru.

"Nothing else!" came the answer: "only the head of the bird."

"Loose your shaft!" said Dronacharya proudly, certain of Arjuna's success. Arjuna alone passed the test.

Dronacharya was, as I have indicated, the guru of both the cousinly families. In the war of Kurukshetra, however, he fought on the side of the Kurus. Why, one wonders, would he do that? Wasn't Arjuna his best and favorite pupil? There is a subtle reason for that choice.

Psychologically, what happens in any struggle between high aspirations in oneself and one's worldly tendencies is that habit sides with worldliness. Our need is to replace our bad habits with good ones. Good habits, however, yield to a higher power, which is what gives us our true strength.

The power to concentrate, shown by Arjuna, and all
other good qualities needed for spiritual development,
depend initially on good habits. What gives those good
qualities their real strength, however, transcends habit: It
is a strength that comes from superconscious inspiration.
Thus, it isn't so much our good habits that guarantee our
spiritual victory as the inflow of divine grace, guidance,
and intuition. Meanwhile, the power of habit itself
usually ranges itself on the negative side. Indeed, even
good habits need to be transformed by divine inspiration;
otherwise, if one lacks a higher understanding, he may
slip back again into bad habits.

Drona sided with the wrong side. This means we
should not depend on our good habits alone to see us
through psychological and spiritual tests. Habit born of
past actions may give us good karma, but karma itself
must be transcended in dedication to the truth.

Meanwhile, all our qualities assume the characteristics of
individual personalities, as we become steeped in them by
a repetition of the acts that involve us in them. Because of
habit, they become entrenched as true "citizens" of our
own nation of consciousness. Each person, as I said, is a
nation unto himself. Thousands or millions of "citizens"
mill about, each one bent on fulfilling his own desires and
ambitions. Sigmund Freud hardly scratched the surface of
human psychology with his investigations. He worked
primarily with abnormal psychology, but in truth every
human being, so long as he lives in delusion, is a mass of
conflicting qualities, or complexes. Freud saw only the
conflict between personal desire and the expectations of
society. In reality the case is infinitely more complex.

CHAPTER SEVEN

THE SPINE: PATHWAY TO SALVATION

THINK OF A BAR MAGNET. WHAT DIFFERENTIATES it from other bars of metal—of iron, in particular— is that its molecules are turned in a single direction, producing a north-south polarity. In most bars, the molecules, each with its own north-south polarity, are turned every which way, in effect canceling one another out. It is when the molecules are oriented in one direction that, with many of them acting together, they acquire magnetic power. Magnetism is *generated*, not created. Its presence is latent in every piece of metal—indeed, on subtler levels of manifestation, in everything. Thus, people can be magnetic; their magnetism can cause others to feel toward them a strong attraction or repulsion.

There are many kinds of magnetism. Our individual qualities resemble the iron molecules in the sense that, if they are focused on a single goal, they can produce seemingly miraculous results. On the other hand, when they are directed haphazardly they can render us ineffective. Magnetism is the key to success in everything.

People will often say, "I keep trying to be good. Why, then, do I constantly fail?" or, "I work so hard to become competent in my own field of endeavor; why can I not succeed?" or, "I try so hard to overcome my bad habits; why do they keep on coming back, like weeds?" To all of these questions the answer, while perhaps unfortunate, is, "You have created failure magnetism in yourself: You need to get enough of the citizens among your inner population to support you; then only will you be able to make the over-all change you desire. The good side of the problem is that, when you succeed in converting enough mental citizens to the side of goodness, they will outnumber the unruly ones and will gradually win them over, resulting in your rapid spiritual progress."

We must transform our faults into virtues. Angry outbursts, uncontrollable at first, need to be rechanneled into positive behavior. Incarnations—many of them, perhaps—may be required for complete self-transformation. Nevertheless, a journey of thousands of miles must begin with a single step. Never should one become discouraged. Discouragement itself is simply a characteristic to be fought and conquered by the steady, indomitable pressure of resolute courage. If one thinks, "I simply don't have that kind of courage," know that you *can* develop it, in time. Every human trait is born in the mind. There is nothing man can achieve or even conceive that is inaccessible to any other human being.

The Bhagavad Gita, however, teaches more than the need to overcome our individual faults and weaknesses. It also gives practical methods for sweeping every obstacle out of the way. One such method is described in Chapter 4, Verse 35, where Krishna tells Arjuna of the importance of the guru, or spiritual savior. A guru is more than a mere teacher. The power of the guru can transfer his magnetism to that disciple who tunes in to his consciousness. Thus, his magnetism can help to transform every fault in the disciple into its opposite virtue, by rechanneling the energy in the disciple's spine—in a sense realigning the "molecules" of tendencies and helping them, ever increasingly, to flow upward. A river, when its flow is strong, dissolves any eddies lingering along the bank, and causes those eddies and any debris swirling in them to enter the river's powerful flow down to the ocean. In similar fashion, a strong upward flow of energy in the spine can dissolve all the "*vrittis*," or eddies of feeling, and carry them up to the spiritual eye. Hence Patanjali's definition of yoga: "*Yogas chitta vritti nirodha* (Yoga is the neutralization of the eddies, or whirlpools, of feeling in the consciousness)." The subtle help of a true, or *Sat*, guru can help the disciple to transform his own tendencies and direct them all toward God.

None of this can be accomplished, however, without the disciple's active cooperation. This process, too, can be hastened scientifically by yoga techniques, and particularly by the great, ancient science of *Kriya Yoga*. The Bhagavad Gita emphasizes repeatedly the importance of yoga, and hints more than once at this highest of all yoga sciences. Indeed, the scientific aspect of enlightenment underlies every teaching in the Gita. We have already hinted at that aspect.

When an unmagnetized bar of metal is placed next to a bar magnet, it gradually develops a magnetism of its own, as its molecules realign themselves, similarly, in a north-south direction. Such is the real power of the Satguru, or savior, an essential aid to which my Guru referred constantly. He completely endorsed the Indian tradition that one must have a guru to find God. The part played by the guru is not to make his disciples over in his own image, but, by sharing his magnetism with them, to uplift their consciousness. That influence helps to realign the "molecules" of energy in their own bodies, and most particularly in the spine, toward the "north" of the spine at the spiritual eye and in the top of the head (the *sahasrara*).

Apart from the guru's help, the other thing needed for Self-realization is, as I have said, cooperation with him in the help he gives. This above all is what is intended by working spiritually on oneself. Self-transformation can be accomplished not so much by laboring painstakingly to purify and spiritualize every flaw, but above all by directing all one's energy toward the spiritual eye. That upward flow of energy is like a river, in this case flowing upward (not downward) to the "mouth" of the spiritual eye, where the soul merges at last into the sea.

None of this is to belittle the need for making painstaking efforts to transform oneself. Indeed, the Bhagavad Gita begins by recognizing the state of constant warfare in all human beings between vice and virtue.

When one considers, however, the vast undertaking one faces in overcoming even one deep-seated flaw, the task seems endless. Think how long it takes for an alcoholic to overcome even that one trait. Once he conquers that one weakness, it is an occasion for cele- bration. The number of faults every man needs to conquer seems almost overwhelming.

Think of that bar of iron. It contains billions of mole- cules, probably. They cancel one another out by the fact of being turned every which way. Now then, supposing one could labor minutely on each molecule: Think how long it would take to turn them all in a north-south direction. By the time one had reached only a short distance in the process, and was ready to start on the next level (so to speak), it is quite within the bounds of possibility for the first molecules to be turning already in random directions again. There would not yet be the magnetism to hold them to the right direction.

CHAPTER EIGHT

THE SCRIPTURE BEGINS

THE BHAGAVAD GITA BEGINS WITH DHRITARASHTRA, the blind king, Duryodhana's father, wanting to know how the battle has been faring at Kurukshetra. Dhritarashtra is, as we saw earlier, blind. His blindness represents that aspect of mind which can perceive reality only through the senses. The war of Kurukshetra is not fought literally on an earthly battlefield, but takes place *within* every individual. Dhritarashtra consults Sanjaya, who represents introspection. Introspection alone can tell the blind mind which side is winning.

Sanjaya has the spiritual power to see things at a distance. Thus, through him Dhritarashtra, who naturally wants to know what is happening on the battlefield *even while it happens*, poses his question. He does so, however, in a most interesting manner. He doesn't ask (as one would expect him to do), "Which side is winning?" Rather, what he asks is, "Which side has won?"—past tense.

Paramhansa Yogananda pointed out that this question, asking for introspection on something already past, gives a clear hint that the entire Bhagavad Gita is focused on the field of consciousness, not of martial battle. On an earthly battlefield it is natural to ask, "Which side is winning?" One expects immediate news as to which way the tide of battle is flowing, which ranks are standing firm, which are yielding to aggressive pressure, and which are making inroads into the enemy ranks. In a psychological battle, on the other hand, it is only *after* the struggle that the question arises: "Which side was victorious?"

Stanza 1, Chapter 1, of this great scripture states:

"Dhritarashtra posed this question to Sanjaya: 'On the battlefield of Kurukshetra, where my sons and those of Pandu were ranged against one another, eager for battle, what was the outcome?'"

This apparently simple inquiry constitutes the basis of the Bhagavad Gita. Victory over delusion is absolutely crucial to man's true happiness and freedom. It is very difficult to discern what is true victory, however; what is merely a hollow victory; and what, though it wears the appearance of victory, will prove in the end to have been a crushing defeat.

My Guru told me this story: "A certain man in ancient India was being bothered by a demon. He decided to use a Vedic mantra to banish this pest. Taking a handful of powder, he uttered the mantra over it, infusing (as he thought) the powder with mantric power. He then cast the powder on the demon. The demon only laughed. 'Before you could even recite your mantra,' it mocked,

'I got into the powder myself. How, then, could your mantra harm me?'

"So you see," my Guru continued, "the very mind with which you would banish delusion is already steeped in the very delusion you want to banish! It is not always easy, even, to know right from wrong. Introspection helps, and is, indeed, essential. Even more important, however, is the intuitive guidance of a wise guru, especially from within."

What lamp has man to guide him through the long night of ignorance? "A blind understanding!" was Omar Khayyam's reply. The blind mind must consult introspection, but introspection must be treated cautiously, for it is already tainted by the very ignorance it seeks to dispel.

There are certain guidelines that can help one to understand which side has been the winner in any psychological battle. One guideline is an inner expansion of happiness or, better still, of joy. Another is an expansion of consciousness. A third and even more important one is an expansion of sympathy. Fourth, but equally important as all the others, is inner calmness.

The mind plays many tricks to convince man that he has found these treasures. Happiness and joy are guidelines to right behavior, but delusive emotions can masquerade as both of these. One key to the fact that their nature is delusive is that they convey a sense of excitement, instead of a deepening calmness.

An expansion of consciousness may seem to accompany any increase of power, or dominion, or even knowledge. Yet these accomplishments often give one, instead of an expansion of consciousness, a swelling sense of self-importance, of self-involvement, and a swelled head.

An expansion of sympathy can be binding if it provokes one to hold expectations of others, to become possessive toward them, or to become centered in their emotional demands rather than in wisdom.

Even calmness can be delusive, if it begets indifference.

How is one to know what course in life is right or wrong? The first rule is, "Do what works." That is why the question, "What was the outcome?" is more important than, "What are they doing?" Only from the outcome of a course of action can it be known with any certainty whether the act was justified or not. The maxim, "The end justifies the means," is true only as long as the end is visualized *in theory*, in advance. Once it has been actually reached, however, it will show whether the means to it were right or not. Wrong means to an imaginary good end will produce, at last, disharmony and failure.

"A blind understanding!" Alas, it isn't easy for man, as he stumbles along life's way. Only time can tell for certain whether a course of action was right or not. Therefore the Gita says here, in effect, "What are the results?"

Basically speaking, a right course of action will produce harmony, good health, a balanced state of being, and an ability to keep moving sensibly toward whatever fulfillment one seeks with discrimination.

Where there is joy, and an expansion of consciousness, sympathy, and inner calmness, one will always experience a rising energy in the spine. The opposites of those states—sorrow, contractive awareness and feeling, and restlessness—are always accompanied by a descending energy in the spine. A person's very posture indicates any changes in the flow of energy, for when his energy is "up" he sits straight, with his shoulders back, his chest high; he even tends more naturally to look upward. But when his energy is "down" he slumps forward, his shoulders sag, he holds his chest in as though there were a hollowness there, and he tends to look downward.

"What did they?" asks Dhritarashtra. One way of measuring the degree of any inward victory or defeat is to test it by the above indications. Do you feel you've succeeded, under enemy fire, in remaining calm? If your answer is, "Well, I'm calmly committed to really slaughtering them, next time!" we must conclude, "You didn't do all that well!" Or perhaps we can say, "The answers aren't all in yet."

One way to tell if you've handled a situation well is to judge by other people's reactions. Even their reactions, however, are unreliable. What people *like* is no guide to what is *right*, and most people are guided by their likes and dislikes, by self-interest, by what pleases or displeases *them*. This is one reason why introspection (Sanjaya) is the wisest source of understanding. Provided one is sincerely committed to finding the truth, and above all, God, if by introspection one canvasses the reactions of his own mental citizens, he will have a clearer understanding of what he ought or ought not to have done, and of how he ought to behave in future.

Ranged against his upwardly directed aspirations are innumerable downward-moving tendencies which he himself created by past wrong actions, and developed into bad habits. A few stanzas later (Stanza 10) the statement is made that the forces for error are "innumerable,"* whereas the forces of righteousness are "few in number." Countless are the ways one can slip into error, even as the outside of a large circle has room for taking many approaches to the center. Uplifting virtues are few, for they lead into, and are already close to, the center of our being. Hatred can be defined in terms of countless objects capable of being hated, whereas kindness springs from the inner self, and bestows its beneficence impersonally on all.

Thus, when Dhritarashtra says to Sanjaya, "What did they?" or, "What was the outcome?" the sincere truth seeker is being told, "Judge your thoughts and actions by their effects—on yourself, first; then on others. Are they peace-inducing? Are they as universally beneficial as possible? Do they help to expand your understanding and sympathies? Have they brought greater harmony to your environment?—or have they produced disharmony? Do they inspire you and others? or have they brought less hope, generally—even despair?"

These questions are not always easy to answer. Anger in a righteous cause can be productive of good. Indeed, such anger, if it is spiritual, is not anger at all but only a strong flow of energy toward the promotion of justice. Thus, calm fervor may sometimes look like anger, yet in fact be anything but that. Kindly smiles, on the other hand, may sometimes look virtuous, when in fact they

* This word has been wrongly translated in certain texts as "unconquerable." Inasmuch as the Pandavas win in the end, that statement would be proved false. "Innumerable," however, is the translation my Guru gave.

are designed only to tempt others—and perhaps oneself!—to do evil.

This first stanza forms the basis of the entire Gita. Much remains to be understood, however, before one can safely say he is following the upward path to goodness, truth, and divine love in God.

Chapter Nine

Sanjaya Speaks

S ANJAYA (INTROSPECTION) THEN DESCRIBES THE scene he beholds with his distant vision. Beginning with the army led by Duryodhana (Dhritarashtra's son), Sanjaya tells how Duryodhana, on beholding the Pandava forces ranged against him, repairs anxiously to Drona, his preceptor (Habit, or *samskaras*: past tendencies), and seeks his encouragement and reassurance.

The Bhagavad Gita takes us immediately to meditation as the shortest route to God. Naturally, when the devotee first sits for meditation all his old worldly tendencies, stirred up by material desire, rouse themselves in protest. Duryodhana (King Material Desire) notes fearfully the enemy's power, which stands ranged against his army. Dhristadyumna (the calm inner light), the son of Drupada (extreme dispassion), is a brother student of his under Drona, and is the first one to range the Pandava forces in battle array. Dhristadyumna it is who finally slays Drona (not in his role of guru, but as the influence of past habit). Dhristadyumna is also described, however, as the "skilled" disciple of Drona, for the calm inner light is seen only after repeated meditative practice, resulting in the meditative habit.

Duryodhana is not prepared to see ranged against him so many disciples of Drona, his guru, whom he hopes to see lead his forces of material desire to victory.

It should be emphasized that the Bhagavad Gita plunges right from the beginning into the inner life of meditation, which, it becomes clear bit by bit, is for everyone. This is not a scripture of pious platitudes. It urges people from the very beginning to seek deep soul-communion through direct, inner experience of God.

Duryodhana goes on to lament his perception that many other great warriors are ranged against him, warriors as fear-inspiring as the Pandava brothers, Bhima and Arjuna. Fearfully he lists some of those who are most prominent among them.

Next, he seeks courage by listing the warriors on his own side. They consist of Drona (habit), Bhishma (the essential self, or ego), Karna (attachment), and others too numerous to list in this exposition, which only concerns the Gita itself, not the *Mahabharata*. Duryodhana then says, "Our forces, protected by Bhishma, are difficult to count (because so numerous), whereas their forces, defended by Bhima, are easy to count." Encouraged by his superior forces, Duryodhana exhorts his troops to gather round Bhishma and protect him. As long as one's essential sense of individuality is safe—such is the belief of King Material Desire—their cause is secure.

Meditation, however, takes one's consciousness into inner realms where the grip of separate consciousness begins to loosen. The breath itself becomes calm, and the energy begins to withdraw from the senses. Then (in Stanza 12) **"Grandsire Bhishma, with a view to encouraging Duryodhana, blows his conch with a loud, lion-like roar."** The meaning here is fascinating: Bhishma's "conch" is the breath. When Ego feels its consciousness of individuality slipping away in deep meditation, and even more so in approaching breathlessness, it suddenly thinks, "Wait! What about me?!"

Ego is the linchpin; it holds material desire in place. Ego may be described as the center of the vortex around which all material desires revolve. Sudden recollection of one's accustomed "reality," the body, and of the desirableness of the material world, causes subconscious habit to activate the sense of "I-ness." At that moment, the strong inhalation of breath is suggested by the "loud, lionlike roar" of Bhishma's conch, which returns the meditating devotee to outward consciousness.

Swami Sri Yukteswar likened the mind of man to a little bird that has been kept in a cage for twenty years. If you open the door of the cage, the bird will cower at the back, fearful of the "threat" seeming to beckon: the vast open sky, where it was designed by nature to fly. After a time the bird may hop tentatively outside the cage, but it will hurry back almost immediately, fearful of this experience of freedom for which habit has made it unprepared. Only gradually, by longer and longer sorties, will the little bird stand at last outside its cage, rustle its wings, and after a further pause fly up freely into the sky.

Stanza 13 describes the response of the other Kuru
soldiers to Bhishma's conch: drums, tabors, cow horns,
trumpets. These signify not only the sense-transmitted
noises of the surrounding world, but the inner reawakening of physical sounds: the thumping of the heart, the
rush of blood in the veins within the ears, and other
familiar bodily sounds.

In answer to the lure and agitation of material
sounds, the inner world calls then to the devotee, insis-
tently, with alluring music: the sound of a honey bee,
for example, emanating from the *muladhara chakra*,
or coccyx center, when the energy is stimulated at that
point to rise upward in the spine; Krishna's flute, the
sound emanating from the *swadisthana chakra* or
sacral center; the sweet sound of a harp, emanating
from the *manipura chakra* or lumbar center; the deep
bell sound of the *anahata chakra*, or heart center; the
soothing, expansive sound—like soft wind in the
trees, or like distant thunder—emanating from the
bishuddha chakra or cervical center; and above all
pranaba, the mighty sound of AUM (of which more
will be written later).

This mighty sound pierces the heart of Material Desire
and his supporting army, causing great consternation.

At this point, Arjuna ("he whose flag bears the
monkey emblem") lifts up his bow and addresses a
request to Krishna, his charioteer. The bow, as we have
seen, symbolizes the spine. The monkey is a symbol of
restlessness; raising the "monkey emblem" signifies that
Arjuna has brought his restless mind under control, and
is able to commune consciously with the Lord (Krishna).

"O Changeless Krishna," he says (as I mentioned earlier), **"please direct my chariot between the two armies, that I may see them ranged against one another and know better with whom I must fight."**

We see here also, quite clearly, that the Gita is allegorical. For what army general, on the very eve of battle, would be so foolish as to ask to be driven *between* the two armies for a better glimpse of the enemy? The most that a general would ask, if he wanted such a view, would be to be taken onto a high hilltop or some other point from which he could see without exposing himself to the danger of enemy arrows, spears, and other projectiles.

There is a beautiful story of how Krishna came to be Arjuna's charioteer. Arjuna and Duryodhana went separately to Krishna to try to enlist his help in the forthcoming war. Krishna was asleep, so they waited patiently, Duryodhana seated by Krishna's head, Arjuna at his feet. When Krishna awoke, he found them both there. To be fair, therefore, he gave them a choice: either the help of his entire army, or himself, inactive in battle and giving only advice.

Arjuna was given first choice, since on waking Krishna had seen him first. Arjuna chose Krishna, even though he would be inactive on the battlefield. Duryodhana, the materialist, was well content with having a whole army, of which he himself would in any case be the general.

Krishna became Arjuna's charioteer. Symbolically, what the chariot represents is the human body, the horses representing the five senses (in fact, there are five subtle senses also: hearing and the *power* of hearing; seeing and the *power* of seeing, and so on). Arjuna invited the Lord to guide the chariot of his life, holding the reins of his senses and steering his course through the coming battle. Thus, the devotee also must try always to see God alone as the Doer of all his actions.

Driving the chariot of spiritual endeavor between the two armies signifies the withdrawal of energy into the spine, and the awareness which comes to the meditating devotee that there are actually two forces within him, vying together to draw him in opposite directions: both downward and upward. The purpose of meditation, according to yoga practice, is to raise the energy in the spine, in so doing to transfer all the lower energies into higher energies in the spine, and finally, then, to focus them at the point between the eyebrows, uniting them ultimately with the highest pole in the body at the top of the head (the *sahasrara*).

Arjuna, as Krishna and he pass between the armies, is filled with grief as he realizes that he must fight against, and actually kill, people so closely related to him: his cousins, uncles, grandfather, fathers-in-law, and also his friends and his esteemed preceptor. His mighty bow slips from his grasp, signifying that he can no longer hold a firm meditative pose.

"How can I fight these people, all of them dear to me? Even if they desire to slay me, I cannot commit the great sin of fighting against them." He goes on in this vein, pleading the cause of *ahimsa* (harmlessness) to justify his own unwillingness to proceed with the war. Dropping his bow and sitting back in his chariot, his eyes bedimmed with tears, he cries at last, **"I will not fight!"** The first chapter of the Gita and the beginning of the second portray his discouragement.

CHAPTER TEN

THE NATURE OF DEATH—ALLEGORICAL AND LITERAL

S RI KRISHNA, IN THE SECOND CHAPTER, RESPONDS on two levels of truth. First, he speaks of the occasional need to engage literally in a righteous war, as is this one. The country under Duryodhana has known hardship and suffering. Under its rightful rulers, the Pandavas, it would know peace. Not only are most wars of self-defense righteous, but, here, the welfare of the populace is concerned.

Mahatma Gandhi's belief of the rightness of ahimsa (non-violence) is both valid and not valid. One should always, certainly, hold an *attitude* of ahimsa. That is to say, one should never wish harm on anyone or anything. As Swami Sri Yukteswar said, however, "This world is inconveniently arranged for a literal practice of ahimsa." Sri Yukteswar's advice concerned the killing of mosquitoes. Many insects are harmful to human life, and should therefore be kept under control. It would be difficult, moreover, if not impossible to avoid treading on and killing small insects; when driving one's car to avoid killing the insects flying against one's windshield; when cooking, not to kill harmful bacteria; even when inhaling, not to destroy tiny, invisible creatures. The scriptural proscription against doing harm refers, Sri Yukteswar explained, to one's *attitude.* One should not *wish* harm to anything, but one may be obliged to kill harmful creatures. Indeed, to protect them at the expense of human life would be a sin, for man's body is more highly evolved spiritually than that of any lower animal.

If a lunatic were to enter your neighborhood and start shooting at people, assuming there was no other way of restraining him it might be karmically right, as well as necessary, to kill him. Better one deserved death than many that are undeserved.

There are times, as I said, when war is right, because necessary. Krishna, representing the voice of God, had declared at Kurukshetra that the side of the Pandavas was right and just. For Arjuna to refuse his duty as a warrior in that war would have been, not a virtue, but a sin.

Krishna then reassures Arjuna that the soul in any case never dies. It is a part of God, and is therefore indestructible. He then portrays reincarnation as a fact. The soul doesn't continue its existence only in a higher world, but returns to this world, body after body, until it achieves liberation.

Krishna then goes on, however, to explain a deeper side of death and rebirth. For the Bhagavad Gita is, above all, an allegory of soul-evolution. (Actually the soul doesn't evolve, for it is ever perfect. It is the *jiva,* or ego—the soul attached to the body—which evolves toward liberation. To speak of the soul evolving, therefore, is a convenience, merely, referring to the ego's spiritual, as opposed to its physical, evolution.)

Krishna says, "The energy invested in a fault cannot be destroyed: It can only be transmuted." The same energy that went into hating people, being angry with them, trying to hurt them, and lusting after the pleasures of this world cannot ever be destroyed. The energy invested in them becomes simply, as I said, redirected toward spiritual pursuits.

The fear of worldly people, which Arjuna phrased in noble language though he was in fact speaking possessively of his own inner "citizens" (from ego-consciousness, that is to say), is that in giving up their worldly habits, they will lose something precious to them. Krishna is saying, "Arjuna, nothing is ever lost. What you relinquish on the material plane you will rediscover a thousand times more wonderfully in God."

Thus, in 2:11, Sri Krishna said to Arjuna, **"With words of love you have been grieving over those who deserve no lamentation. The wise mourn neither for those who live on earth nor for those who leave it."** Life, Krishna is saying, is not determined by the existence or non-existence of a physical body. It was never the body that gave us life. We, rather, gave life to the body. The soul is ever-existent, and that soul is what we ourselves are: manifestations of Eternal Spirit.

Even after we have shed the physical body, it is not as though we had no body. This body is only an outer shell encasing our astral body, which in turn is only an energy-condensation enclosing our ideational, or causal body. None of these bodies supplies man with his life and consciousness: Rather, it is he who animates them.

(2:12) Nor are we here in this world for the first time. I, you, these royal ones whose (possible) death you lament: None of these has not lived here before, nor shall any of them ever cease to be.

(2:13) As the ego keeps the thread of self-awareness unbroken through infancy, childhood, youth, and old age, so also the embodied soul (which gave consciousness to the ego) maintains its awareness uninterruptedly, not only through the stages of earth life, but through the appearance of successive bodies.

(2:14) O Son of Kunti, sensations such as heat and cold, pleasure and pain are generated through the senses in (their) contact with the world. They are ideas only: transitory, each with its beginning and end. O Descendent of Bharata, bear with them patiently.

The way of wisdom is to be non-identified with anything outside the Self.

(2:15) O Flower among Men, one who is calm and even-minded, never ruffled during pain and pleasure: he alone gains consciousness of his eternal existence.

(2:16) That which is unreal does not exist. That which is real cannot cease to exist. Those who possess wisdom know the final nature of reality: of what is, and what is not.

(2:17) He alone, the Unchangeable Spirit, pervades all, and is imperishable. Nothing can destroy His eternal reality.

(2:18) That indwelling Self is ever changeless, imperishable, and without limitation. Only these fleshly garments can be destroyed. Therefore, O Offspring of Bharata, accept your duty (in this body), and fight!

(2:19) One who considers his true and eternal Self to be the slayer (of anything), and who believes that he himself, in essence, can be slain, does not know the truth. The true Self can neither slay nor be slain.

(2:20) This Self is not born, nor does it perish. Self-existent, it continues its existence forever. It is birthless, eternal, changeless, and ever the same. The Self is not slain when the body dies.

(2:21) How can one who knows the true Self to be imperishable, everlasting, unborn, and unchanging imagine that this Self can cause destruction to another Self? O Partha (Arjuna), who is slaying whom?

(2:22) Just as a person removes a worn-out garment and dons a new one, so the soul living in a physical body (removes and) discards it when it becomes outworn, and replaces it with a new one.

(2:23) Weapons cannot cut the soul; fire cannot burn it; water cannot drown it; wind cannot wither it away!

(2:24) The soul is never touched; it is immutable, all-pervading, calm, unshakable; its existence is eternal.

(2:25) The soul cannot even be pondered by the reasoning mind. It (the Self) is unmanifested and formless. Realize this truth, and abstain from lamentation.

(2:26,27) Even, however, if you prefer to think of the Self as perishable, why grieve? What is born must die. Whatever dies must be born again. Why lament that which cannot be avoided?

(2:28) (The periods) before birth and after death are veiled from your gaze. You are conscious only of that which is visible to your senses. Why lament a thing you can't see?

(2:29) Some (people) behold the soul in amazement. Others describe (the experience of it) as marvelous. Still others, hearing it, listen, and proclaim it wonderful. The rest, even if they hear all about it, comprehend it not at all.

This last stanza describes some of the ways by which the soul can be known: as an amazing, cosmic, and wondrous light; as cosmic wisdom; and, finally, as Cosmic Sound: the vibration of AUM.

There are false lights—projections of the subconscious mind. These have a certain vagueness to them, and are hazy and indistinct. The soul-light is "amazing" in its power to transform the consciousness of the meditating devotee.

There is false wisdom, usually associated with mere intellectual knowledge. Paramhansa Yogananda remembered times during his youth when he would wonder, unnecessarily, "Who was this person or that one in other lives? Who, for example, was Jesus Christ, Krishna, Shakespeare?" If you visit a castle, wouldn't it be wiser (he asked us rhetorically), instead of roaming about the garden and wondering what everything is, to befriend the lord of the castle and let him show you around? He will explain everything to you, and give it its proportional importance.

The sound of AUM will be described later: what it is, what it sounds like, and the important role it plays in deep meditation.

(2:30) O Bharata (Arjuna), there is one Self dwelling in all. That Self is inviolable. Grieve not, therefore, for anything (that occurs) outwardly in the manifested world.

(2:31,32) Even when viewed personally, from a standpoint of one's *dharmic* duty, there is no occasion for (either) grief or hesitation. Nothing is more propitious than for a *Kshatriya*, whose duty is to fight for righteousness, to battle for what is right and true. Blessed and fortunate are you, if you must give even your life for such a cause. Such a death will open to you the gates of heaven.

A slain warrior who has fought fearlessly in a good cause goes to heaven as a result of having held to an ideal higher than material existence. His willingness, in a righteous cause, to sacrifice his lower reality for a higher one entitles him to enjoy the beautiful astral regions after death.

(2:33,34) But if you refuse this opportunity for righteous combat, in rejection of your duty, you will incur sin. Other people (far from honoring you) will heap your name with ignominy. To a man of self-respect, dishonor is, verily, worse than death.

(2:35,36) Other warriors will assume that you have avoided fighting out of fear. Those who have thought

highly of you heretofore will come to regard you slightingly. Your foes will speak your name with contempt, and will ridicule your prowess. Could anything (for a warrior) be more painful?

(2:37,38) If you are killed in battle, you will attain heaven. If you win this war, you will obtain earthly glory. Arise therefore, O Son of Kunti (Arjuna). Determine to fight! Be even-minded in the face of pleasure or pain, gain or loss, victory or defeat. In this way, you will incur no sin.

(2:39) I have thus explained to you the ultimate wisdom of *Shankhya*. Now hear the wisdom of Yoga, equipped with which, O Partha, you will break the shackles of karma.

This last passage appears variously translated in different texts. In fact, however, the version given by Paramhansa Yogananda is clearly the most accurate. The word, "wisdom," which appears in the original, is conjoined with "*Shankhya*," and does not mean Gyana Yoga as some have it (spelling Gyana according to the pedantic, but unphonetic, tradition, as "Jnana"—a version my Guru deplored in personal conversations with me). Other translations refer to Karma Yoga, which doesn't even appear in the original text. What the Gita does speak of is that which "will loosen the bonds of karma." I have rendered the English translation more poetically by writing, "break the shackles of karma." The meaning is, of course, the same.

Paramhansa Yogananda discussed the three main philosophies of India: *Shankhya*, *Yoga*, and *Vedanta*.

He explained that the wisdom taught in Shankhya underscores the need to escape from *maya*, or delusion. Yoga tells the sincere seeker how to make good his escape. And Vedanta (literally, "Summation," or "End," of the Vedas) describes the nature of Brahman.

Classical Indian scholarship describes these three "philosophies" as different and even incompatible with one another. Yogananda explained that all of them are rooted in the same basic truth: Sanaatan Dharma. They simply emphasize the three basic aspects of the spiritual search: briefly, the *why*, the *how*, and the *what* of it. All three aspects are needed. One needs to know why it is necessary to seek truth, how best to go about it, and what one may expect (stated with as much intellectual clarity as possible, though emphasizing that direct experience alone bestows true understanding).

The Bhagavad Gita teaches all three "systems." In fact, as Yogananda explained, these are not "philosophies." *Philosophy* literally means "love of wisdom"—in the ancient Greek: *philos* (love) and *sophia* (wisdom). He explained that Western thinkers deserve the label, "philosophers," but that the great rishis and yogis of India have never been so much philosophers as "seers," who in every age have never been satisfied merely to theorize about truth, but have seen and experienced it directly, themselves. No Immanuel Kant, Arthur Schopenhauer, or Friedrich Nietzsche could demonstrate a fraction of the control of life, objectively as well as subjectively, that has been demonstrated from the most ancient times down to the present by the great "yogi-Christs" of India.

CHAPTER ELEVEN

KRISHNA'S CONSOLATION

CHAPTER 2 OF THE BHAGAVAD GITA BEGINS with Arjuna's deep distress at the thought of having to make war on his own kinsmen. Most of the succeeding stanzas quote Krishna's timeless words of consolation, wisdom, and encouragement.

Thus it sometimes happens that the devotee, disappointed with his spiritual progress to date, grows discouraged. He may think, "I gave up tangible pleasures for intangible joys. Now I am left with nothing!" Essentially, this despondency is rooted in a longing for spiritual freedom. Arjuna did not say—like a hoary but undevotional ascetic in a delightful story Paramhansa Yogananda liked to tell—"Goodbye God and all your crazy crowd!" He did not look back with longing on the false "delights" of the senses. He was discouraged, rather, because his hopes of spiritual experience had not yet been fulfilled. Torn between two worlds, but believing in the upward path, he sat back in his "chariot" and cried, "I can do no more!"

Krishna, who represents the Divine Presence within—that is to say, the soul—comforts the devotee inwardly and thrills him with loving reassurance.

Spiritual growth is rarely sudden, unless an individual is already blessed from birth with exceptionally good karma. The Lord does not necessarily speak with human lips, through vision, though He manifests himself in physical form through the human guru. Even the guru, however, teaches primarily through the disciple's own intuitive perception.

Even Arjuna's tears of despondency are wholesome, spiritually, for they also express an unfulfilled longing for divine truth, and rivet the mind on higher aspiration and his unquenched longing for the indescribable joy of divine communion.

From thinking rationally, the devotee passes to complete surrender to the unreasoning but clear-sighted perception of intuition. This is a necessary attitude for further spiritual advancement.

It must be understood that even such encouragement from silent intuition is a sign of much spiritual work in former incarnations. It may seem cruel on God's part not to respond instantly to human doubts, fears, and hesitations, but think how many lives the ego has wandered away from God, spurning every hint of His love, and resolved instead to seek fulfillment once again in the world of the senses. Arjuna no longer feels attracted to the world. Rather, he has reached that stage where the world no longer appeals to him, but still he hesitates to spurn it altogether. That God, at this stage, would offer strong hope and consolation of insights and intuitions to be attained, in time, is already an indication of considerable inner progress.

Does Arjuna's pity for his enemy-"kinfolk" indicate that he desires again the pleasures he has renounced? Because the Gita is written as a guide for everyone who seeks God, it must be allowed that this nostalgia might be Arjuna's problem, too, though the text doesn't indicate that it necessarily is. His despondency could be due only to his lack, so far, of spiritual fulfillment. In any case, the Lord says to him, "They are your foes. Don't be 'soft' on them, for their true intent is to destroy you." Pity for past pleasures can bridge once more the gap one has created between himself and them. It is a great mistake on the spiritual path to toy even idly with thoughts of what one has left behind. Renunciation of the world in thought as well as in deed is essential.

Watch the heart for any ripple of attraction there. You may feel safe from worldly desires, but if in your heart you find the least tremor of excitement, even on hearing about the pleasures of the senses, or on listening to stories about them—to "dirty stories," for example— shun them like the infection they really are. People may scoff, saying, "It's just in the mind." Exactly so! The mind itself is the battlefield. There is no other.

Sense delights seem pleasurable only by an act of the imagination. A mother, for example, might be able during a food shortage to convince herself that by feeding her children she was also sustaining herself. In time, however, even that self-denying act would no longer be possible for her. Such vicarious identification is comparable to imagining that one is sustaining his happiness through the senses. The true Self can be sustained only by spiritual states of consciousness, such as divine love, calmness, and bliss.

Sense pleasures are not even experienced on the surface of the body, as they seem to be. The nerves transmit sensations from them—visual and musical beauty, fragrance, taste, and touch—to the brain. Whether they are greeted with pleasure or distaste depends entirely on one's mental conditioning. The human mind, unlike the minds of lower animals, can train itself to like anything. The saying, "There's no accounting for tastes," is essentially mistaken, for the "accounting" depends on repeated mental association. Even sensations that for most people are unpleasant can be pleasing to some—if, for example, they grew up in environments where those sensations were common.

The bliss of the soul, experienced especially in deep meditation, is Self-born. That is why the sage Patanjali writes of enlightenment as a process of *smriti*, or memory. The instant that soul bliss, or love, is felt, it is recognized. It doesn't have to be learned, and the taste for it doesn't need to be acquired. Again, when the Cosmic Sound, AUM, is truly heard, one knows with intuitive certainty that he could hear it through eternity and never grow tired of it. The most beautiful music, by contrast, grows tiresome, even irritating, after a time.

"Heaven," referred to in Stanzas 32 and 37, means more here than the astral heavens where noble warriors go after death. The Bhagavad Gita is a scripture. As in the teachings of Jesus Christ, most of whose references to heaven meant the state of oneness with God, so what

Krishna means more deeply here is the limitless sphere of divine consciousness. For the devotee, the laurel of victory is soul-freedom in infinite bliss.

Unlike ordinary church preaching, or the compromise with the highest ideals that is offered by mere pundits, the Bhagavad Gita is very firm concerning the high truths it teaches! Rarely heard in Christian churches is the admonishment of Jesus: "Love God with all your heart, soul, mind, and strength." And when his statement is quoted, "Be ye therefore perfect even as God is perfect," its meaning is diluted either by telling people, "Be good," or else, "Be good because God, in His perfection, expects goodness of us." Hindu teachers at satsangs in India rarely admonish their listeners to live up to the highest truths expressed in the Gita. "Give Me thy heart; adore Me" becomes translated as, "Love Me also." Sukdeva's statement, "All time is wasted that is not spent seeking God," is conveniently forgotten, as people are reminded that wealth and normal human pleasures are sanctioned by the scriptures. Yes, they are—if one is satisfied with only good karma, and with continually rising and falling on the wheel of reincarnation! Krishna's higher teaching, however, is uncompromising.

At the same time it must be added that the Gita is for everyone—as are also the comparable teachings of Jesus Christ. As Krishna says later in the Gita, "Even a little practice of this religion will free one from dire fears and colossal sufferings." (2:40)

Stanza 10, which was not quoted above but was contained by implication in the over-all summary, states that Krishna, before exhorting Arjuna to do battle, spoke "as if smiling." This phrase, Yogananda said, is important, because it indicates that God is no stern judge of human behavior, but is "on our side." He *wants* us to advance spiritually, and forever forgives us if we err. The words, "as if smiling," indicate that Arjuna had already advanced far on the path to win such an indication of God's love. As Krishna remains inactive during the war, and participates only to guide Arjuna's chariot, so he often seems remote to the devotee, and even indifferent to the most earnest efforts to attain Him. Krishna's "smile," however, is ever there for those who seek him earnestly. It is not easily won, but loving reassurance is given from time to time, in one form or another. The devotee feels God's loving support in his heart. In time, he is conscious of that inward smile. It is with this smile that Krishna gives his discourse in the Bhagavad Gita. It is with sweetest love that God exhorts the devotee to seek Him unconditionally, as the only source of fulfillment there is.

The devotee, meanwhile, should not await, as if anxiously, God's smile of reassurance but should proceed even-mindedly toward his goal by performing ever calmly his karmically assigned duties. To be "even-minded and cheerful" under all circumstances is the first duty of the yogi. This obviously does not mean being cheerful about other people's suffering! One must respect, and even empathize with, their pains— as Krishna did. As regards one's own pains, however, the aspiring yogi must firmly banish all thought of ego-identification with both pleasure and pain. Pain may in fact be "happening," but he must not think of it as his own. The more he can resist the oppositional states of Nature— *maya's* dualities (*dwaita*)—the more he will find that he can remain inwardly calm under all circumstances. In that calmness, moreover, apart from not suffering when others howl with pain, he will find himself not suffering personally, even when he must endure the same pain as they. He will be at that calm center from which appropriate movement can be made instantly, in any direction.

A (to me) astonishing feature of my Guru's life was how he would instantly reflect the appropriate response to any circumstance. I have to say that, in the three and a half years I lived with him, I never saw him give exactly the same glance or reaction twice.

A good practice for the devotee is deliberately to submit himself to extreme opposites: heat and cold, pleasure and pain, etc. He should be careful not to test his powers too far beyond their proven ability so far. To do so would be fanaticism. Indeed, it might prove counter-productive: One could stand too long under a cold shower, and find himself hardly feeling warm again for months! One could even endanger his health. Along with the counsel to be even-minded and cheerful is an equally important one: Use common sense.

For even-mindedness, an important practice is to give up likes and dislikes. My Guru used to say, "What comes of itself, let it come." Again, deliberately eliminating those peaks and troughs of feeling can be a useful practice. Eat a food you don't really like (provided the food isn't bad for you!), or give a food, or perhaps some other pleasure, to someone else that you might particularly enjoy for yourself.

Remember, the opposites of duality are inseparable from one another. The farther forward a child's playground swing goes, the farther back it must go also. Excessive sense-pleasure produces a "hangover" of many kinds—perhaps a headache (in the case of too much drink), a stomach ache (in the case of too much eating), a depressed mood (in the case of too much hilarity), a sense of loneliness (after being too much with people).

Happiness lies in being centered calmly in one's self, even when that "self" is written with a lower-case "s." One who is inwardly calm is able to see things as they are. He might be described as the only sane person, when all around him are insane!

Important to an attitude of being "even-minded and cheerful" is to confront a thought Krishna raises in Chapter 2 of the Bhagavad Gita: the natural fear of death and dying. All must die, sooner or later. Life itself is a preparation for death's "final exam." It would be helpful to face this event matter-of-factly, not morbidly. When bathing your body, for example, tell yourself, "This arm I am washing will someday be ashes, or else dust. It isn't me, myself!" At night before going to bed, make a mental bonfire of all your possessions, your desires, your attachments. Cast them one by one into the flames, then watch as they crackle merrily and disappear. *Nothing* belongs to you—not even your own ego! Firmly holding this attitude is the way to inner freedom. *Enjoy yourself* as you watch everything disappear in those mental flames. Nothing—not even death—can touch you as you really are, inside.

Meanwhile, meet your responsibilities conscientiously in the world the next day, with an attitude of inner detachment. Give everything to God, and try always to please Him. Don't wait anxiously for His smile of approval, but live in the thought that you have it already, for the freer you feel in yourself, the happier you will be.

Live in the Self: Be centered in it as your abiding reality. Everything else is simply a dance around the "maypole" of that inner Self. Don't be caught up by anything. Whatever you do, be free inside. Inner freedom may be described as the highest of all moral virtues.

The most important practice on the spiritual path is whatever will help to free you from the sense of ego-involvement. You cannot refrain from acting, as Krishna makes clear later on. Even the refusal to act is a kind of activity. People sometimes give the false counsel, "If you see someone lying helpless in a ditch, do nothing to help him, for if you do so you'll incur karma." What absurd advice! First of all, by helping others you'll get *good* karma, which will offset to some extent any bad karma you've incurred in the past. Secondly, in this case, by not acting you are already creating karma—bad karma! The decision not to act is like restraining a horse by the reins: It takes an effort of will, and therefore implies an act of some kind.

What is the ego? Imagine the moon reflected in many vessels of water. Each vessel contains the same reflection, yet seems, in each of them, to be individual. When we look up at the sky, however, we see that the reflections are all of the same, one moon. At the same time, they may also differ from one another: for example, if the water in one vessel is agitated, or if it contains floating debris, or is colored differently. The soul of every human being reflects the same bliss of Spirit, but because that bliss is reflected in the individual ego, its appearance and character may seem greatly altered. If a mind is restless, its natural bliss will be distorted; if greatly distorted, it may even appear as suffering and pain. To the degree, also, that one's feelings contain the "debris" of desires and attachments, the actual bliss reflected by the ego will be distorted—though the distortion is only in the reflection. If one's awareness is colored, moreover, as water's surface may be—by prejudices, likes and dislikes, and mistaken notions—these hues, too, will affect the clarity of one's underlying soul-bliss, which otherwise would shine clearly in one's consciousness. Indeed, spiritual progress consists not in actually *achieving* anything, but in simply removing the distortions obscuring the nature of reality. All those distortions are contained in the confused reflections we produce of the true bliss of our own being. In the end, when we offer up our little reflection to the moon itself, we find in that transcendent bliss that even our old and seemingly discarded ego remains always with us—as a deathless memory.

One may ask, Why cannot the ego, after death, merge back into the oneness of Spirit? The truth is, we have other bodies to transcend. Imagine a corked bottle of sea water floating on the ocean. If the bottle breaks, then naturally the water inside it commingles with the water around it and becomes indistinguishable from the rest of the sea water. If, however, that bottle is contained in another corked bottle, and that second one is placed within a third bottle, the breaking of the outer bottle will not free the water in the innermost bottle.

The physical body is like that outer bottle. Inside it is what might be called the original model of that body—the astral body of light and energy. As long as the astral body is "polluted" with material desires, it must create another physical body to encase it once again.

Of course, no image is perfect. In literal fact, the outer bottle would be in closest contact with the sea, the water of which would be touching it on all sides. In spiritual "fact," however, body-consciousness is farthest removed from contact with the Supreme Spirit, and to live consciously in the astral body brings one closer to that ultimate contact.

Even in the astral body of energy, however, there remains a final casing: the causal body, made of ideas.

The physical body is made of blood, flesh, and bones. It consists, science tells us, of sixteen elements. Paramhansa Yogananda, comparing the astral and causal bodies to the physical, said that the astral body contains nineteen elements, which consist of various energies: the five senses, the power within those senses, and mind, intellect, ego, and feeling (*mon, buddhi, ahankara, chitta*). It is interesting to find the ego itself mentioned as an "element" of the astral body. The causal body, finally, consists of thirty-five "elements," which are a composite of the sixteen physical and nineteen astral "elements."

The word "element" appears, interestingly, in classical tradition in both East and West. It applies to the *stages,* not to the chemical elements, of physical manifestation: ether, air, fire, water, and earth. Interestingly also, these stages are identified with the five spinal chakras, and therefore with the five Pandava brothers.

When matter is first manifested, there is space, which Yogananda said is itself a distinct vibration, and which may be identified with ether. The next manifestation into matter consists of huge galactic gasses, the nebulae. These gradually condense as balls of fiery matter; next, as "water," or liquids (flowing lava, for example, which is matter in a liquid state); and finally as "earth," or solid matter. As the yogi raises his consciousness through the five spinal chakras, he gains a certain power over the elemental stages of manifestation: the ability to make himself as immovable as a rock, and extremely heavy. He can walk on water, then on fire. He can levitate. He can expand his consciousness outward into space.

All reality can be visualized, ultimately, as an infinite ocean: the infinity of Spirit. Waves appear on that ocean, manifesting individual forms. Every ego is represented by one of those waves. The goal of *sadhana* (spiritual practice) is to withdraw one's wave of manifestation back into the ocean, that it become, literally, infinite.

Yogananda used this example to explain what I have said about the ego's return and reabsorption in the infinite Spirit. He offered, as an example, a man named John, who has been manifested for aeons in many-shaped waves on the ocean of Spirit. Always it has been Spirit manifested in that form. It has seemed separate, however. When John's wave of individuality merges back into the ocean, it is no longer that wave, but realizes itself as God who became John for many incarnations until, at last, it understood that its separateness was an illusion. When it becomes God again, however, "John," the individual, doesn't cease to exist. The *memory* of who he was through all those incarnations is retained. Because of that memory, the ego itself continues to exist in Infinite Consciousness, and can be re-manifested whenever the Infinite so decrees.

Thus, Krishna, who was considered, even while he lived on Earth, to be God himself (thus he is symbolized in the Gita), was not only the infinite God taking on that little form of manifestation, but also *the same individual memory* of the ego who manifested in countless human forms, until achieving final liberation. Tradition holds that Krishna was an incarnation of Vishnu. Vishnu himself, however, is only an aspect of Infinite Consciousness. Indeed, Vishnu is an aspect of one of the triune vibrations of AUM—of which, however, more later.

It is interesting to contemplate the fact that ocean waves are not fixed realities. Anything floating on a wave will rise and sink as the wave passes on. The wave is real only as a kind of vibration. Even the ego is only a vibration on the surface, so to speak, of infinity.

God sent man to earth to be entertained by the cosmic movie. Alas, attachment and desires darkened human consciousness. Immersed in the seeming reality of the movie, man forgot that it was all nothing but a ray of light in the projection booth, passing through artificial images imprinted on a strip of celluloid. If man could live in this world with perfect non-attachment, he would again become aware that this is all a show: only shadows and light. The only reality is that changeless light which produced those fleeting images, and the bliss within that light.

An important point in the consolation Krishna gives to Arjuna is that his is not a teaching that one should be heartless. Human love is a part of divine love. It only becomes a mistake when it fixes in attachment on one, or on a few, particular forms. Our loved ones must be separated from us in death—whether by their death or by our own. Therefore we should always, with discrimination, keep in mind that all human beings, and everything, come from the same one God, Who alone should receive our first love.

Thus we come to Stanza 40, and the beginning of Krishna's teachings on the subject of yoga.

CHAPTER TWELVE

THE NATURE OF RIGHT ACTION

Y OGA IS INSEPARABLE FROM ACTION, FOR IT provides the "how to" of the spiritual path. It is not, however, action with a beginning and an end, like worldly deeds. It contains no unfinished act, like worldly actions, the consequences of which can be diverted by what Yogananda called "the thwarting cross-currents of ego." Every ego-inspired act, moreover, inspires a reaction, but to yoga practice there is no such dualistic reaction, for it is directed toward the termination of karmic activity. This is the teaching of the next stanza:

(2:40) In this path (of yoga action) there is no danger of "unfinished business," nor are there latent within it the opposite, canceling effects of duality. Even a little practice of this religion will free one from dire fears and colossal sufferings (which are inherent in the unceasing cycles of death and rebirth).

It is important to realize that in yoga practice as well, of course, as in any sincere search for God (the one Self, beyond all duality), there is no wasted effort, and no karmic rebound. There is, in other words, no "catch" to seeking God. With any other effort, no matter how glorious the consequences, it is always legitimate to ask, "What's wrong with it?" Only with the divine search is the answer a resounding, "Nothing's wrong!" Even to fail in this quest brings only good karma.

Think of other fulfillments in life. *Fame?* One famous man said, "I enjoyed fame at first, but it wasn't long before it turned to ashes. Now, it means nothing to me."

Money? Howard Hughes, the wealthiest man in the world at the time he lived, was asked if he'd found happiness. Hughes responded in bitter tones, "No, I can't say I've found happiness."

Human love? What a compromise is the most beautiful love story with infinite, divine love, which the soul experiences at the end of its search for God!

Power? Joseph Stalin, the all-powerful dictator of Russia's Soviet Union, was virtually mad toward the end of his life, fearing that everyone around him wanted to encompass his destruction.

Knowledge? Look at the dry faces, the furrowed brows, the bent shoulders of people who have pursued intellectual knowledge all their lives. Hear the brittleness in their voices!

No, nothing on earth brings lasting fulfillment. And even if a few people seem to have found fulfillment for a time, none would say that what they've attained is the summum bonum of life. In only one field does perfect unanimity exist: in the search for God, and especially in those who have found Him. In every religion, in every country, in every people, those who have found God are in complete agreement: *This* is the goal of all human striving. Without exception, those who have found Him have willingly accepted any persecution—even painful death—to bring this realization to their fellowman. God, they *know*, is the *only* worthwhile goal in life.

Yet, how often those who seek Him are ridiculed—and worse than ridiculed!

Later on in the Gita, Krishna answers beautifully, in words full of hope, the question put to him by Arjuna: "What happens to those who fail?" Already in the present stanza Krishna is saying, "No effort on the path to God is ever wasted." This is not to say that there cannot be wrong practices in the service of God. When people practice yoga (or other forms of religion) with wrong or self-serving motives—whether to develop spiritual powers, or to obtain control over others—they must pay the karmic price, for they have devoted their energies to dualistic ends, and must accept the consequences of pitting their own energies against the energies of others. When there is pure longing for truth and God, however, this stanza of the Gita offers a shining reassurance for everyone.

To desire salvation sincerely, even once, is to enter upon the path to eventual freedom. For all desires must be fulfilled. Even so, this one desire, once entrenched in the heart, cannot but lead eventually to liberation.

Thus, this passage contains one of the most deeply inspired and inspiring passages in all scripture.

(2:41) In this yoga there is only that one direction (with no polar opposite). The reasonings of the undecided mind, caught up as it is in duality, are endlessly variegated and ramified.

Krishna is not only saying that the path to God is undeviatingly straight, but also that one should follow only that path in life! For there are many detours from the search for God in religion, also—not to speak of the supreme "detour" of delusion itself. Religious spokesmen hold out pallid explanations for "perfection," saying that all God really expects of man is that he be good. Heaven is usually offered as bait: a place where people spend eternity in a beautiful, idyllic environment of great natural beauty, surrounded by "angels." To the sincere spiritual aspirant, little could seem more hellish than to be stuck for all eternity in an ego, even if the body in which one lives is forever healthy, supple, youthful, and full of energy.

Few people can think in terms longer than a thousand years—the millennium which Christians have, in fact, held up to them as the promise of supernal perfection. Now that we know, through the science of astronomy, that all the stars seen in the sky constitute only the outskirts of a single galaxy, and that there are at least a hundred billion galaxies in the physical universe, that figure, *one thousand*, seems paltry indeed! Even so, how many people are able to visualize even a million years. A billion? A *hundred* billion? It is inconceivable. Yet divine consciousness is eternal. It is also "center everywhere, circumference nowhere," and therefore omnipresent—meaning that it is as consciously present in the largest star as in the smallest "mud ball" of a planet in the most distant galaxy—indeed, as in the smallest pebble in your own yard—and, in fact, in just one atom of the countless number of them which comprise a speck of dust on that pebble.

It is amazing to contemplate how far divine truths have been distorted by so-called religious leaders and spokesmen—priests, imams, rabbis, pundits, and the numerous dignified holders of religious titles—all over the world. Indeed, only Hinduism (and I say this as one who was, himself, raised in orthodox Christianity) formally teaches *moksha*, or liberation from very ego itself, in union with the omnipresent, divine consciousness. Jesus Christ taught it. Few however, if any, of his self-declared followers believe that when he spoke of heaven he was referring to that same state of *moksha*: complete liberation. When Christian preachers in church on Sundays speak of the parable of the grain of mustard seed, how many of them understand the comparison Jesus Christ drew between heaven and that little seed: a comparison which has no perceptible relationship to the astral heavens they speak about? The heaven Jesus described as a mustard seed grows from minuscule proportions to the size of a great tree, on whose branches "the birds of the air come and lodge." In the next verse, Matthew 13:33, he compared the "kingdom of heaven" to the leaven used in making bread, which swells the dough that was first formed. Growth—expansion: He was speaking of expansion into omnipresence. Because most religious teachers offer a compromise of lower spiritual truths, they betray their own religion.

Paramhansa Yogananda used to say, "Jesus Christ was crucified once, but his teachings have been crucified every day, throughout Christendom, since that time." At first the dilution may have been deliberate, with a view to maintaining control over the "flock." Now, the churchmen themselves have forgotten—if, indeed, they ever knew—that the perfection preached by Jesus was not *human* perfection (veritably a contradiction in terms!). What he said was, "Be ye therefore perfect, *even as your Father in heaven* is perfect."

Judaism seems more preoccupied with following the law of Moses than with the soul's eternal salvation, or with finding bliss in God-communion. Do Jews even believe that it is possible to reach heaven after death? Many of them consider, along with the materialistic scientists, that such questions cannot be answered rationally and therefore should not even be addressed. Suffice it, they say, to live a good, God-pleasing life here on earth.

Buddhists have gone the same route. Because Buddha refrained from speaking of God, but rather tried to impress on people's minds their need to make a personal effort to purify themselves, his followers soon fell into the fallacy of atheism. True, God doesn't really have a human form: He is pure, absolute Bliss—infinite, eternal, and ever-conscious, as Shankaracharya later claimed. Shankara wanted to persuade people that the forms in which they had clothed God were purely for their own devotional upliftment: They were not literal realities. The *nirvana* of official Buddhism, according to an official document published some years ago in Thailand, is that the bliss of which Shankara spoke lasts only a moment, and is replaced immediately by eternal nothingness. Could anyone sincerely strive to attain *nothingness*?! Surely, when the moment arrives for the choice finally to be faced—whether to embrace a complete void, or to await a later "opportunity"—the ego will pull back in fear, electing rather to be a "bodhisattwa" indefinitely, out of "pure compassion" for mankind. Compassion, maybe, but it seems natural to prefer this compassion to becoming *nothing*!

Self-preservation is the deepest instinct of life. It cannot be, and indeed is not, founded on a delusion, for if it were, how could delusion itself arise out of total non-awareness? The very idea defies all logic.

What about Islam? How can any pious Moslem believe that his soul will go to heaven for killing an "unbeliever"? And what is that "heaven"? Has it ever been described in terms resembling the absolute liberation in omnipresence that is *moksha*?

If only Hinduism declares this highest spiritual truth, surely it is because only Hinduism has not been confined in the "straitjacket" of a religious organization! It has grown naturally, rather, and has not been suffocated in the musty air of official decrees regarding what is, and what is not, the highest truth.

Yogananda was quite caustic on the subject of religious rituals for priestly profit. The Gita, he said, warns against the desire even for an astral heaven as the reward for living a holy life on earth. One who desires any "heaven" short of oneness with God—the one supreme Source of Absolute Bliss—is in delusion. The Bhagavad Gita teaches the very highest truths, but how many Hindus, even, get this message? Most of them hope also to reach some limited plane such as *Swarga*, or *Vaikuntha*—images, all, of a "paradise" pleasing to the ego.

Many people believe the Gita teaches only Karma Yoga—how to be good, do good, and serve one's fellowman. No uplifting action, of course, is bad, but it must be strictly understood that what Krishna teaches in these passages of the Gita is a truth beyond duality—a truth to which there is no opposite, no possibility of a future fall, and no limitation in ego-consciousness of any kind, but absolute freedom in the Infinite Self. Even samadhi must be sought in a spirit of utter rejection of lesser identification with body, ego, family, and earthly or astral satisfactions. Indeed, to the true yogi the astral heavens themselves are a lesser ideal, and something rather to be shunned than sought.

Finally, as my Guru wrote, "A chronic wanderer in the path of theology seldom tastes even a sip of the pure, divine water of truth. He craves only newly flavored, ideational concoctions! This desire for untried novelties merely leads one into a desert tract of intellectual doubts." The God-thirsty seeker, Yogananda concludes, busies himself with imbibing the nectar of absolute, infinite bliss.

(2:42) O Partha (Arjuna), fixity in the state of samadhi cannot be theirs who cling to personal power and sense-pleasures. Those whose discrimination is blunted by the specious promises of teachers who,

ignorant themselves, promise heaven as man's highest reward, imagine nothing higher to exist.

(2:43) Vedic rituals (and other outward practices) lead not to oneness with God, nor do promises (or the hope) of superior pleasures in the astral world. All these lead, rather, to repeated earthly rebirths.

(2:44) Those who, incapable of discriminating between right and wrong, seek personal power and superior sense-pleasures (whether on earth or in the astral world after death) by the practice of Vedic rituals, deepen their ego-attachment. They cannot achieve the inner equilibrium that comes through meditation, and miss also the (one) true goal of life: union with God.

Even those who follow superficial religious practices may make great sacrifices in their quest for ultimate fulfillment, whether earthly or astral. Alas, they miss the only true goal there is: union with God. Not even the best of karma can bring one to God, for it comes from actions performed with ego-consciousness, with its attachment to the results of action. Those results, because of that attachment, must return to their source. Good deeds alone cannot win spiritual freedom, for as long as the ego is involved in doing them—as long, in other words, as one thinks, "It was I who did it"—there is bondage. More important even than good deeds are the *motives* behind them.

The *results* of everything one does should be given to God. The doing itself should be given to God. Indeed, in the last analysis it is He alone who does everything. This is not a counsel to passivity. One should do his best always, but at the same time he should hold the thought—which alone leads to Self-realization—that a Higher Power lives in him, works through him, and enjoys everything through him. As Yogananda said, "Pray in this way: 'I will reason, I will will, I will act, but guide Thou my reason, will, and activity to the right path in everything.'"

Attachment and desires are like radio static: they prevent the clear reception of the programs one is trying to hear. The mind should be free of such static, which keeps it constantly restless.

Reincarnation for any reason other than, as a free soul, to return here to help others is a cause for deep regret. Think of the virtually lost years in a person's life: infancy, childhood, adolescence, youth—much of which time is usually wasted in merely preparing himself for one more struggle to achieve success, to learn a few lessons (how *very* few, usually!), before one retires, sinks to physical, then perhaps mental, incompetence, and then dies. Spiritual karma does impel one upward, but environment also exerts a strong influence. Will one's karma be strongly spiritual enough, under every circumstance, to keep one arrow-straight on the path to God? One cannot be wholly sure. Detours may take one temporarily off the path! What person in his right mind, once he knows that the goal of life is the realization of God, would want to risk a renewal of ignorance in yet another body before good karma reawakens him to the understanding that what he *really* wants in life is God alone? Unless a person is already highly advanced spiritually, the likelihood of getting caught to such an extent that extrication becomes difficult, even if possible, is simply too great. Think of weeping mothers (life after life!), scolding wives, domineering husbands, wayward children, and outraged neighbors—all of them conspiring to hold one to the wheel of rebirth! Wise is he who, when the chance comes to seek God, seizes it with both his hands.

(2:45) The Vedas teach that the universe is a mixture of three basic qualities, or *gunas*. Your duty, Arjuna, is to free yourself from all three, as well as from the dualities of Nature. The way to this achievement is to remain ever calm in the Self, free from any thought of either acceptance or possession.

Between the opposites of duality there is a middle state, which either divides or unites them. Every ocean wave has a crest, a base, and a middle part. That middle part divides, as we said, but it also unites. Large waves produce towering crests: Such are the egotists of this world, boasting of their prowess, striving to out-do all others, and combatting one another in fierce competition.

During a great storm, the ocean surface is greatly agitated and knows no peace. The waves not only rise high: They crash against one another as if each one wanted to beat down the waves around it. In life, too, large egos know little peace. The farther they try to distance their egos from the calm ocean depths, by emphasizing their individuality, their likes and dislikes, their ambitions, and their zeal for victory, the more restless and agitated they become in their hearts.

Even the tallest wave, however, has its base in the vast ocean. Every human being, similarly, is fundamentally part of God, and is therefore, in essence, divine. God dwells in each ego, though many egos try to avoid any reminder of His inner presence by affirming their own importance. Thus, the part closest to the ocean is covered over and unseen, as people's egos tower high and they send energy out eagerly through the senses in their search for pleasure, excitement, power, and dominion over others.

The part closest to the ocean represents *sattwa guna*—that quality which most clearly suggests the ocean's calm depths. For any protrusion to exist on the ocean, however, there must always be those three portions of the wave: the lowest part, which is closest to the ocean; the middle part, which rises in eagerness for self-definition; and the highest part, or crest, which acts as though it wanted to affirm its independence from the ocean altogether. In the humblest saint there cannot but still exist all three parts to his wave of manifestation, for everything in manifestation is a composite of the three gunas, or qualities: *sattwa*, *rajas*, and *tamas*.

Tamas, or *tamoguna*, is that part of the wave of manifestation which projects farthest from its basic reality, and which most obscures the very existence of that reality. In this sense, spiritually darkened souls, blinded by egotism, possess what they think of as an entirely separate reality of their own.

Rajas, or *rajoguna*, represents the main portion of the wave: the central part, which gives substance to the wave and supports the towering arrogance suggested by the crest. The farther a person projects his consciousness away from his source in God, preening his ego and inflating it, as if like a balloon, the farther he divorces himself from his true source of power. Egotists usually produce a great deal of "sound and fury," but in their very pride they cut themselves off from their inner strength, narrowing it down to a little crest—which often becomes a mere whitecap—and thereby grows weak. We all have heard the saying, "Pride goes before a fall." As a wave loses supportive power as it projects too far from its base, it crashes. Tamoguna is dullness and inertia: a consequence of the spent force of ego.

This image is not perfect; no image can be. There are also, for example, egos that are not so much projected outward from the ocean bosom by pride as simply too dull to perceive any reality deeper than the ego. Their waves, therefore, may be sluggish rather than over-exuberant. Such might be the case, for example, on the ocean surface after an oil spill. Nevertheless, the reality of their vast source is least apparent at the top of the wave, and most obvious at its base.

The strength of a wave to rise comes from its central portion: from the agitation produced by the wind, and from the inner, upward push of the water. Rajoguna is active, restless, ambitious, "pushy." It is that which, thrusting itself upward toward ego-affirmation, ends in the dwindling power of a wave crest falling, or the rounded but still greatest separation from its source. In all cases, the crest of a wave represents tamoguna.

Sattwa guna is, as we've seen, that part of the wave which provides its base—not that power which surges upward, but rather that one which hugs the ocean, knows whence it derives its power, and, if the wave is only a low swell, seems hardly separate from the ocean at all. Saintly people may be described as little waves, or even ripples. They are ever conscious of being close to God. Even they, however, to the extent that they retain individual awareness, manifest all the three gunas, even though their principal manifestation is sattwa guna. That part of their nature which is farthest from God represents their insignificant measure of tamoguna. For even saints must manifest tamoguna to some extent; if they didn't, they would not be able to be manifested at all. They may do so, for instance, when they sleep, or when they rest idly. The degree of "tamas" they manifest might even be considered *sattwic* in some people, for all creation expresses the directional relativity of closest, farther, and farthest from the Source.

Rajoguna is the middle ground. Thus, also the duality of Nature is implied in the universal blend of the three gunas.

Arjuna was urged to rise above identification with the three gunas, and therefore also with the oppositional states of duality. Krishna told him to separate himself from outward identity by attaining absolute inner calmness. Inner detachment involves laying to rest the urge of the ego to keep on defining itself as a separate, individual reality.

Ego-consciousness is the inner urge to push the wave of one's individuality ever upward, hoping finally to tower above other waves. Again, no image can be perfect. In the case of the ocean, it is the wind, primarily,

which raises waves on the ocean surface. In the case of
the ego it is the "wind" of delusion, which in a sense
sweeps over the world, confusing people as to the
essential nature of reality. The power of delusion, however, comes primarily from within each person, not
from outside him. It is *inner* delusion which causes him
to err in his *response* to outer circumstances.

The primary need on the path to wisdom is to overcome
the ego's urgency to declare outwardly, and affirm
inwardly, its own, separate individuality. Later on in the
Gita Krishna proposes important ways by which this urge
can be diminished, then overcome. All of these ways, he
suggests here also, require that one seek his answers
primarily within himself. Scripture itself is no substitute
for self-effort.

**(2:46) To the knower of Brahman (the Supreme
Spirit) the Vedas are of no more use than a well when
the land all around one is in flood.**

There is a story from the life of St. Francis of Assisi, in
Italy. An old, nearly blind beggarwoman asked him for
alms. She couldn't see that he was dressed as poorly as
she, and was not likely to have anything to give her. It
distressed him, however, that he had nothing to give her.
And then he realized that he still had one thing in his
possession: his well-thumbed copy of the Holy Bible.
This he gave to her, in the hope that she might be able
to sell it for a few coins.

He then prayed almost apologetically, "Lord, in helping
this poor old woman I have even given away Your word!"

A voice within him replied, "Francis, I have planted my word in your heart. You have no need for that merely printed copy of it."

Whether it be the Vedas, the Gita, the Bible, or any other great scripture, the important thing is that God's truth be written on the pages of one's own heart. For of course Krishna is speaking here not only of the Vedas, but of true scripture generally. His reference to the Vedas, however, provides an opportunity for writing about them specifically without breaking the flow in the commentary, by including the thoughts Yogananda expressed about them.

The Vedas are unique among the world's scriptures in that they were composed in a high age when there was no division, such as exists today, between religion and daily existence. The people then had no need for separate places or times of worship. All life to them was, in a sense, worship, and every act an offering to God. As people's understanding declined in a descending age, it became necessary to write down in words the truths people had been able to memorize effortlessly. At that time an explanation for the gunas, for the duality inherent in all things, and for how everything came into existence became necessary.

In the descending age it was seen to be necessary also to offer people religious practices that would help them satisfy their increasingly worldly and ego-affirming needs: rituals that would enable them to gain what they wanted in terms of power, mates, children, and success. Although people's consciousness was diminishing in clarity, there was still a spiritual bias in everything they did. Rituals were therefore created that would enable human beings to work in cooperation with the *devas*, or astral beings of higher (angelic) nature, as well as with lower sorts to accomplish their ends.

Today, mankind has all but forgotten those higher, or at any rate subtler, entities, which otherwise would help man in the production of food, of good weather, of energies for success, and of countless benefits from which more aware people, living in tune with Nature, seek help as a matter of course. People scoff at nature spirits such as fairies, but, as Swami Sri Yukteswar is quoted in *Autobiography of a Yogi* as saying, they actually exist. Man's indifference to them has been causing those energies gradually to withdraw from our planet. This is a natural consequence of the fact of those beings finding themselves ignored. Scientists have actually said that there is less energy in today's food than there was a century ago. People who try to boost their production by chemical means don't understand that life depends on the life force, and not on that which is lifeless.

The astral entities, in past ages, were objects of worship. An attitude of awe is unnecessary; it is quite enough to give them appreciation—even love, as one ought indeed to love all God's creatures as His outward manifestations. To worship them, however—as began happening during the declining ages as human understanding grew weaker—is to enter, bit by bit, into the merchant consciousness that says, "I'll give you what you want provided you give me something in return."

Thus, the nature spirits, not themselves without ego, enjoy the special, worshipful attention they get from people who look to them for particular favors.

Krishna, during the time when he taught the Bhagavad Gita to Arjuna, needed to address also this defect in popular consciousness. Buddha, who lived possibly some two centuries later, warned people even more strongly against dependence on the Vedas and on their rituals as alternatives to self-purification.

Krishna is saying in this stanza, essentially, not to propitiate the lesser "gods" of natural forces, whose attitude is still "*quid pro quo*" in the sense of wanting some sort of ego-payment for favors rendered. The Lord is no merchant! Those who sincerely want Him ask for nothing in return, but pray selflessly only for His love.

What Krishna is saying, then, is, "Seek the direct experience of God. Don't be satisfied with anything less."

As Jesus Christ said also, "Seek ye first the kingdom of God, and His righteousness, and all these other things shall be added unto you."

It is the true seeker whom Sri Krishna addresses in this passage, as indeed in most of this great scripture. Those who seek lesser favors from God are asking for a teaspoon of soil when they might have the whole kingdom.

The problem in people's minds, of course, is that they think to *possess*. What Krishna is asking of them is that they *become*. The ego alone can own things—at least in imagination! The soul becomes one with God and, in that oneness, "possesses" the whole universe.

A great woman saint in India was once asked to visit another country. "Why should I go there?" she replied. "I am there already!"

(2:47) Action (in this realm of vibration) is a duty, but let not your ego crave the fruits of action. Be not attached either to action or to inaction.

Be like a divine lark, which enjoys singing without trying to impress or to gain anything from anyone. Those who act with ego-motivation become caught in the web of *maya*. The universe was brought into existence through the power of Cosmic Vibration, the great sound of AUM. So long as one lives in the realm of manifestation, and is not merged in Spirit, he cannot avoid acting in some way. The important thing is to act rightly.

To attain God-consciousness it is necessary to release all attachment to the thought of "I" and "mine." The infinite consciousness appears finite in the ego, as in the atom. That is merely an appearance, however. The atom cannot help whirling in its own minuscule reality, but the ego, being conscious, can aspire to be released from all vibratory manifestation. As Patanjali wrote, "*Yogas chitta vritti nirodha*: Yoga is the neutralization of the (whirling) eddies of feeling." The spiritual duty of every ego is to stop the movement it generates by achieving release from such "whirling" thoughts as, "Everything I do is for my own personal benefit!" Bondage to delusion consists of nothing but the constant reference of everything one does (and thinks, and enjoys, and suffers) back to one's own self. Not only action, but all one's enjoyments in this world—indeed, one's sufferings also—are tainted by the simple thought: "I am the doer. I am the enjoyer, and I am the sufferer"—and then the outraged demand: "But *why* am *I* the sufferer?"

The solution is not to refrain from acting. Some people—many hermits, for example—think to develop spiritually by refraining from all action. That idea is a delusion. As long as one must breathe, think, and move, he cannot rightly claim to be inactive. The yogi who sits breathless and motionless in samadhi is a different case. To go beyond action you must merge your consciousness in the Cosmic Sound of AUM, allowing it to act through you and around you until you merge in that infinite vibration, and then pass beyond vibration itself into the calm consciousness of the Supreme Spirit. As long, however, as you are conscious of having a body, you will only be deceiving yourself if you try to achieve the actionless state by not acting. All you will become, in time, is lazy and dull-minded!

To reach God, one must first learn to act without selfish motive: for God, not for personal reward. Indeed, it is necessary to be intensely active for God, if one would develop that intense awareness which alone lifts one to superconsciousness. Lazy people will not find God!

In everything you do, however, feel that God is acting through you. Wash your body, feed it, give it rest—do everything that is needful to maintain the body in good health and filled with energy—but always feel, "It is God I am serving through this physical instrument." The very enjoyment of good food, of beautiful scenery, of the good things of life can be offered up to God. Share those enjoyments with Him, rather than depriving yourself of them. What needs to be released are the thoughts, "I am doing, I am enjoying," and even the thought, "It is I who am suffering."

Even in meditation, it is important not to meditate with desire for the results. To eliminate the strain and tension of *trying* to concentrate, release also the thought, "I am meditating." Think, rather, "The Cosmic Vibration is reaffirming, through me, its own reality. Cosmic love, through me, is yearning for God's love. Cosmic joy, through me, is rejoicing in our Infinite Beloved."

(2:48) O Dhananjaya (Arjuna), immerse yourself in the thought of yoga (union with God), inwardly non-attached and even-minded in both success and failure. Perfect evenness of mind and feeling is itself the definition of yoga.

The only way to achieve the perfection described here is by meditation. Affirmations of calmness in the midst of stress often have the contrary effect of *creating more* tension! In any case, calmness can be affirmed effectively only with inner calmness. Such calmness can hardly be established without also stilling the thoughts in meditation.

(2:49) Action performed with desire for the fruits is greatly inferior to action guided by wisdom. Therefore, O Dhananjaya, seek in everything to be guided by wisdom. Misery attends actions performed for their fruits.

(2:50) One who lives united to cosmic wisdom passes beyond the effects of both virtue and vice even while he lives in this body. Therefore devote yourself, through wisdom, to achieving the oneness of yoga. Such alone is right action.

(2:51) Those who have mastered their thoughts escape the confines of the mind and become engrossed in cosmic wisdom. They (realizing the illusory nature of ego) become freed from the chains of rebirth, and attain that state which transcends all suffering.

Sorrow was not a deliberate part of God's plan. Inherent in the plan was that actions performed in contradiction to it would cause pain. This was an impersonal necessity, for if the heat of a stove, for instance, did not burn us when we touched it, we would have no protection against possible damage to the body. Our pain is also our protection, and not a sign that God *wants* us to suffer.

Legend has it that when God first manifested the universe He made it perfect. Men and women, realizing the need for living in perfection, sat in meditation and soon merged back into Brahman.

One or more similar attempts were made, all of them with the same result. God then decided, "I must impose delusion on people. They must struggle, advance by trial and error, and discover that kind of action, and that attitude toward it, which will lead them to bliss and freedom." Thus it is that we find ourselves in this "pickle." Scriptures such as the Bhagavad Gita are intended to lead man out of *maya's* "labyrinthine ways" into the free "air" of communion with the Infinite Source of all Bliss.

(2:52) When your perception pierces the dark mists of delusion, you will be indifferent to everything you have heard about this world and the next.

You will, in other words, be firmly established in the perception of truth.

(2:53) When your discrimination is no longer tossed about by opinions, but abides unshaken in soul-bliss, then you will attain final union with God.
(2:54) Arjuna said: "O Keshava (Krishna), what are the signs of one who has attained calm wisdom and is established in union with God? How does he speak, sit, walk?"

The question Arjuna asks is a natural one for those who are not yet enlightened to ask: How does the man of God behave? Can his saintliness be discerned from his way of speaking, of sitting, of walking? Are there other ways (Arjuna implies) in which such a person differs from ordinary people?

Krishna's answer, as we shall see, refers to the *cause* of saintly behavior, rather than to its effects. A divine person is not essentially different from anyone else. It is his inner *consciousness* which creates whatever dissimilarities there are.

The yogi (since Krishna doesn't answer this question directly, though it may well be of interest to many

people) reveals a joyful magnetism in the very tone of
his voice. In my Guru's case, whether he scolded or
encouraged, lectured (sometimes in thundering tones)
to a crowd or spoke quietly with a small group, there
was always vibrant in his tone of voice a quality of calm
bliss and wisdom.

The yogi sits straight, as my Guru always did, allowing the energy to move freely in the spine. When he
walks, he walks calmly, not restlessly or with jerky
movements. His walk reveals his consciousness of being
centered in the spine.

**(2:55) O Partha (Arjuna), one who has put away all
desires, being wholly contented in the Self, may be
considered settled in wisdom.**

His very movements and gestures, in other words,
reveal his inner state of consciousness. His voice vibrates
with calm wisdom. His posture is calm, not restless, and
demonstrates perfect contentment. His walk is relaxed
and serene.

One day Yogananda, as a young man teaching the principles of yoga in America, was late for a lecture he had to
give and set off at a run to make the appointment as soon
as possible. Someone cautioned him, "Don't be nervous!"

"One can run nervously," the Master replied, "or one
can run calmly, but not to run when the need arises is
to be lazy!"

**(2:56) He whose consciousness is unshaken by
affliction and is not excited by good fortune; who no**

longer hungers for earthly affection and is without fear and anger: such a man deserves to be considered a *muni* of steady discrimination.

Muni means one who has dissolved his ego-consciousness in God. He has withdrawn his consciousness from the distorted testimony of the senses.

Fear is born of the thought of failure, if one is attached to success. Anger is born of frustrated desire. The muni is beyond all such ego-centered emotions.

(2:57) He who, under all circumstances, is without attachment, and neither elated by goodness nor depressed by evil, is a man of established wisdom.

As the swan glides over water without its body being touched by it, so the man of wisdom glides through the waters of life unaffected by them.

Paramhansa Yogananda often used the analogy of the movies, pointing out how they create an illusion of reality by simply mixing shadows and light—and, more recently, by the addition of colors—all of which are only projections of the one light shining out of the projector. An enlightened sage is unaffected inwardly by the "movie" of life. This doesn't mean he is heartless or indifferent. His impersonality derives from not desiring anything for himself. Otherwise, because his perception of everything and everyone is *from within*, he feels keen sympathy for all, and, *for their sake*, rejoices in their good and grieves with them in their sorrow. He also grieves for their evil, and for what it will do *to them*.

His only desire—if, out of compassion, he still has any
desire—is to help others to know God.

**(2:58) When the yogi, like a tortoise withdrawing its
head and limbs into its shell, is able to withdraw his
energy from the objects of sense-perception, he
becomes established in wisdom.**

Control of what Yogananda used to call the "sense
telephones" is essential for deep meditation. Sense
control by withdrawal of the energy is the true meaning
of *pranayama*: "*yama* (control) of the prana (energy)."
Pranayama is a condition, not a technique. The practice
of *pranayama* is to achieve energy control.

This stanza offers one proof out of many that the
Bhagavad Gita, while embracing all paths to God,
places special emphasis on Raja Yoga in that it teaches
how to achieve the goal, union with God, and doesn't
merely say, "Seek God." Prana is often equated with the
breath, and *pranayama*, with breathing exercises. In
fact, there is an intimate connection between the breath
and the flow of energy in the body. Paramhansa
Yogananda often said, "Breathlessness is deathlessness." Yogic breathing exercises have the purpose of
enabling the practitioner to rise above the body's
normal need for breath.

Breathlessness is not *kumbhaka* in the sense of *forcibly*
retaining the breath. Rather, true kumbhaka comes
when the body no longer requires air for its maintenance. The purpose of respiration is to expel carbon
dioxide from the lungs, and to take in oxygen. In

pranayama exercises, the breath is used to produce a state of equilibrium in the body, in which state the physical activity of breathing is no longer required to maintain it in a condition of equilibrium.

When one rises above the need to breathe, the heart pump also slows down, then stops altogether.

There is a subtle connection, through the medulla oblongata, between the breath and the heartbeat. When breathing becomes unnecessary, the heartbeat, as just indicated, slows down and then stops. Between these two phenomena—the breath and heartbeat, on the one hand—and sensory awareness, on the other, there is a close connection.

The energy in the senses, as in the whole body, relaxes and withdraws—as happens, indeed, to a lesser degree, in sleep. A sleeper may be called—he may even be shaken—before he is even aware of being wanted. This diminished involvement with objective reality occurs because, during sleep, the energy is partially withdrawn from the body and from the "sense-telephones"—even as the tortoise withdraws its head and limbs into its shell.

It is only when the "sense telephones" have been "switched off" that the mind can wholly absorb itself in the inner world in meditation. The energy in the motor nerves, too, must be withdrawn, as happens naturally as the senses are being stilled.

The center of the body's energy is in the spine. In deep meditation, that energy must be relaxed from the surface of the body, as we saw earlier, and withdrawn up the spine through the chakras to the brain. The normal outward flow of energy, as it works to sustain the body, must be reversed to flow upward.

It may be helpful at this point to pause briefly and consider the relation between breath and the flow of energy in the spine. First, where the spine is concerned, come the two superficial nerves known as the *iḍa* and *pingala*, which are located, respectively, on the left and right sides of the spine. Fish eaters will be familiar with the two nerves that run the full length on either side of the spine of a fish. The energy flowing in these superficial nerves is connected with the reactive process of the emotions, which, in turn, is connected with the breath. The upward flow of energy in the astral spine, through what is called the *iḍa naḍi* (nerve channel), in the astral body, is the cause of inhalation. A downward flow through the *pingala naḍi* is the subtle cause of exhalation. It is this flow of energy in the astral spine that results in the physical breath. Otherwise, there would be no physical compulsion to breathe; one wouldn't know what to do about the body's need to expel carbon dioxide and bring in revivifying oxygen.

Causing the inhalation, then, is the upward energy-flow. This upward flow in the superficial spine is reminiscent of the deeper flow upward, in deep meditation, toward spiritual enlightenment. The upward flow through *iḍa*, therefore, accompanies any positive emotional reaction. Thus, with a positive reaction of any kind—joyful, hopeful, triumphant—to some outward stimulus, the energy flows automatically upward in the spine, causing the lungs to inhale.

When, by contrast, one's reaction is negative—pained, sorrowful, despairing—the energy automatically flows downward through *pingala*, and exhalation ensues. Thus, when, for whatever reason, one reacts with emotional delight to any stimulus—physically, emotionally, or mentally—he automatically inhales. And when, on the contrary, one reacts negatively, he exhales. That is why, when we feel emotionally pleased, we automatically inhale deeply, and when we feel disappointed, we automatically sigh.

Obviously, the breathing process is not invariably accompanied by positive and negative emotional reactions. It would be ridiculous to smile and frown alternately every time one inhaled and exhaled! The consciousness rests ordinarily in one or more of the spinal chakras. Worldly people—those, that is to say, whose interest is primarily in sense-enjoyments, and particularly in the thought of sensual pleasure—have their consciousness centered in one or more of the three lower chakras—especially in the two lowest ones. Spiritually minded persons, on the other hand—especially those with devotional natures—feel their consciousness centered in the *anahata chakra*, or heart center.

Even when one is centered in the *anahata*, one must be careful, if he is a spiritual aspirant. He must try to keep his energy flowing upward from the heart to the spiritual eye. Unless he is careful, his energy—suddenly attracted by some wakened desire (however unexpected)—may unexpectedly rush downward again from the heart into the lower chakras. The energy must be continually drawn upward by the magnetism emanating from the Kutastha, where the spiritual eye is seen, lest it descend inadvertently in response to some worldly stimulus.

In the *Srimad Bhagavatam*, a scripture which also was written by Beda Byasa (the author of the *Mahabharata* and the Bhagavad Gita), the counsel is given to visualize the heart as a lotus, the petals of which must be turned up toward the brain.

The best point on which to keep focused is in the spiritual eye at the point between the eyebrows. The center of the ego is the *agya chakra* in the medulla oblongata; hence, the advice is also given to center one's mind there (its natural position), and from that point to *gaze forward*, so to speak, at the spiritual eye.

Life begins its involvement with the objective world with the baby's first cry, or, rather, with the first quick breath required to make that first cry. This first breath starts the reactive process, and therefore begins the baby's involvement in the objective world. This moment is crucial to the baby's earthly existence. The moment of its first cry, therefore, is the point from which the horoscope for the baby should be computed.

At death, by contrast, there is what is known as the "death rattle": the final exhalation which occurs as energy enters the *pingala naḍi*, and the ego's energy flows inward more deeply, and back to the medulla. Thus it prepares for its departure from the body, exiting through the same "doorway" by which it first entered when the sperm and ovum united to create the body.

The spiritually advanced yogi's energy enters the deep spine on exhalation, and flows up through the *sushumna* to the spiritual eye in the forehead. The Kutastha, where the spiritual eye appears, is the positive pole, of which the medulla oblongata is the negative. Yogis, and saints in other religions who are able to exit the body through the spiritual eye, need not pass through what the ancient Greeks, as we said earlier, called the "waters of Lethe." In other words, yogis do not sink back temporarily, as ordinary human egos do, into subconscious rest, but soar out into superconsciousness.

The yogi learns to withdraw his attention from the reactive process: first of all by calming the feelings in the heart, which initiate the reactive process. One then detaches his feelings from the ups and downs of reactive energy in the spine: from the subjective influence of success and failure, fulfillment and disappointment, attraction and repulsion, love and hatred, pleasure and pain, joy and sorrow, triumph and despair. It is helpful, when trying to develop emotional detachment, to concentrate one's energy in the spine, and there to equalize the upward and downward flows of energy, which produce emotional reactions and are inextricably united to those reactions as long as the heart's feelings remain restless.

Finally, the yogi withdraws his energy into the deep spine, the *sushumna*. With this withdrawal he awakens Kundalini, which, being magnetized to flow upward, now begins its slow ascent through the deep spine toward enlightenment.

Beginning yogis should try to become conscious of the connection between their reactive emotions, both positive and negative, and the corresponding upward and downward flow of energy in the *iḍa* and *pingala naḍis*. This practice of centeredness in the spine will minimize their preoccupation with whatever occurs outwardly in their lives, and with what has already occurred in the past. The practice will focus their attention on the simple movement of energy in the spine. Thus, where most people's first thought is, "How *wonderful!*" or, "How *dreadful!*" the yogi, even if he is a beginner in yoga practices, finds it relatively easy to cease from defining outer occurrences as either good or bad.

If, for example, one is sitting in a dentist's chair having work done that most people might find quite painful, he should concentrate at the Kutastha—or, if he is conscious of feeling any emotional reaction, concentrate on the energy-flow in the spine. First, calm the heart's feelings. Then, breathe in the spine with deep, slow inhalation and exhalation—silently, so as not to disturb the poor dentist!—bringing the energy upward and downward, and seeing that flow as the *cause* of any emotional reactions one might feel.

Again, when anything or anyone threatens you in any way—not only physically, but by speaking angrily or, perhaps, insulting or accusing you—center yourself in the spine. At that center you will become confident that nothing can touch you. As Yogananda said, "You must be able to stand unshaken amidst the crash of breaking worlds!" The above practice will help to ready you for facing any circumstance in life.

(2:59) The man who (merely) abstains from sense enjoyments may forget them for a time, but the taste for them will linger. That person, however, who beholds the Supreme Spirit loses the taste for anything but the Infinite.

An example Paramhansa Yogananda often used was a person who is accustomed to stale cheese and has acquired a liking for it. If he is given good, fresh cheese to taste, however, he automatically abandons the liking he had for stale cheese.

(2:60) O Son of Kunti (the power of dispassion), Arjuna, even the wise man, devoted to self-control, may sometimes be swept away by the turbulent senses.

No devotee should underestimate the formidable power of subconscious tendencies. Their tentacles are farther reaching than anything the conscious mind can perceive or even imagine.

Paramhansa Yogananda warned that as long as ego-consciousness persists, one should not consider himself safe from delusion. "Remember, you will not be safe until you reach *nirbikalpa samadhi.*" Even in the lower samadhi stage known as *sabikalpa*, the ego must return from its infinitely expanded consciousness to outward awareness. One who reaches *sabikalpa samadhi*, therefore, can still fall. My Guru told me of more than one case in which this had happened. "Sadhu, beware!" the great master Sri Ramakrishna once warned a disciple, who subsequently did fall from the spiritual path.

The thing to watch out for is the slightest flicker of excitement in the heart, in the contemplation of any aspect of delusion. That little stir of energy should be seen as the first warning signal. The slightest stirring in the heart should be a sign to the aspiring yogi to withdraw immediately from even the thought of delusion.

Maya is very subtle. Never try to "tough it out." You cannot by any means be sure you'll win—if only because the very discrimination with which you think to do battle is already infected by the disease of *maya*.

(2:61) He who, having subjugated his senses, has become united with Me remains engrossed in the infinite Self, knowing it as the Supremely Relishable. Only mastery of the senses can bestow the steadfastness of true wisdom.

There are two requirements, above all, for the attainment of wisdom. One, to withdraw the mind not only from sense objects, but from the senses themselves; and, two, to remain merged in the consciousness of God as the most desirable of all goals.

Yogis who seek only to control their bodies and physical senses, and those also who seek only the abstraction of divine union without proper physical and mental discipline, can never achieve true fixity of purpose. Uprooting the weeds of ego-gratification, on the one hand, to their last tendril, and, on the other, becoming lovingly absorbed in the Infinite: Both of these are essential.

Many yogis seek ego-gratification not only through sensory pleasures, but in the development of spiritual powers. Many others (again) seek the ego-gratifying abstraction of intellectual wisdom. The true yogi seeks only to unite his soul with the Divine Beloved.

(2:62,63) Dwelling mentally on sense objects breeds attachment to them. From attachment arises craving.

From craving (when frustrated) springs anger. Anger produces delusion. Delusion causes forgetfulness (of the Self). Loss of memory (as to what one is, in truth) causes decay of the power of discrimination. From loss of discrimination ensues the annihilation of all right understanding.

Every step in this descent has a single linchpin: the ego. To rise again toward wisdom, the deluded ego must reach the point where it realizes that what it has understood of life so far has brought it nothing but pain. Its first question, then, must be, "Do I *like* suffering?" (No, obviously!) Next it should ask, "What increases suffering, and what, on the other hand, lessens it?" The answer is that suffering diminishes when there is a decrease of self-interest. The discernment of this truth leads to the first faint stirrings of recollection that a reality exists that is more than the ego and the body. The fog of delusion begins to lift from the mind, and one no longer strikes out at the world in anger for not giving him what he wants. From acceptance of what *is* comes a gradual decrease of worldly attachment. From lessened attachment comes lessening interest in the objects of the senses, and an increase of longing for true wisdom—a longing which awakens devotion in the heart, love of truth, and intense aspiration to know true and everlasting bliss.

(2:64) The man of perfect self-control is able to act in this world unaffected by it. Inwardly free from attraction and repulsion, he has attained unshakable inner calmness.

That state, as we have seen from what Yogananda said above, comes only when one's consciousness has passed beyond conditioned (*sabikalpa*) to unconditioned (*nirbikalpa*) samadhi, when one's consciousness has become so established in oneness with God that there is no possibility of a return to outwardness and the limitations of the ego.

(2:65) With the attainment of soul bliss, every vestige of sorrow disappears. Bliss gives perfect discrimination, and soon establishes one's consciousness firmly (in the Self).

(2:66) Those with unsettled consciousness have no discrimination. Those who are unmeditative cannot know peace. And for those who lack peace, how is happiness possible?

(2:67) As a boat moving on water may be swept off its course by a gale, so discrimination may be swept from its path by the vagaries of sensory influence.

The words to a favorite chant of Paramhansa Yogananda's go as follows:

I have made Thee polestar of my life.
Though my sea is dark and my stars are gone,
Still I see the path through Thy mercy.

The spiritual seeker may, on occasion, find himself swept off his upward course by outward temptations, not only sensory pleasures but a desire for less tangible temptations offered to the individual by *maya* to feed his ego-consciousness: name, fame, power, self-importance, and a host of other ego-boosting delusions. Instead of agitating himself with guilt feelings and self-accusation (which can only increase his susceptibility to delusion), he should return calmly to his pre-established course.

Mistakes on the path are always possible. The devotee should acknowledge them (at least to himself) sincerely and openly, and then simply forsake them without making the further mistake of becoming upset with himself. He should keep his mind focused steadfastly on the polestar of his true goal: union with God. Since the ego is a delusion, anything that tempts it to affirm its own reality as separate is a delusion also. And so too, indeed, is any distress one may feel with oneself for having succumbed to delusion.

When a rock is dropped into a pond, waves appear. Similarly, when anything occurs in one's life to cause an emotional reaction, waves of feeling appear. As those waves created by the rock flow outward to the bank, then return, they only gradually subside to calmness again. Even so, one's reactions to anything outward may flow back and forth, compounding the mistake made by reacting in the first place.

One should make it a practice, indeed, to separate himself in his mind from identification with anything—even an identity of thought—and to return to the affirmation, "God alone is the Doer." By thus dissociating oneself from any error the ego commits, the tendency to err will gradually subside, the gale will cease to blow, and the mind will become calmly centered and focused on its divine goal once again.

Otherwise, what can happen when one errs spiritually is that, by ego-identification with the error, one may wander for further incarnations, straying into other dead ends, and struggling all the while to find his way back to the true course on which he once embarked.

(2:68) Therefore, O Mighty-armed (Arjuna), withdraw your sense-faculties (the power to see, hear, etc.) from the senses themselves, and from sense-objects. Thus will your wisdom become firmly established.
(2:69) That which is night for the unenlightened is day for the yogi. And that which is day for ordinary people is night for the yogi-seer (who perceives the inner reality).

This passage contains more than one meaning. Superficially it recommends meditating at night, when the minds of worldly people are stilled in sleep, when the sounds they make during daily activity no longer fill the air, and when the yogi finds it easier to achieve inner calmness. Thus, the time when worldly people bestir themselves once again is when the yogi may find it more convenient to get his few hours of sleep.

On a deeper level, what seems real to the worldly person, living as he does in the conscious mind, is seen to be unreal at a superconscious level. The eager activity of the worldly person holds no interest for the man of wisdom. Even when the wise person, in order to sustain his existence, engages in outward activity and is thus, in a sense, in the world, he is not *of* it, for the world no longer defines his reality.

(2:70) Contentment is his who, like the ocean, calmly absorbs into himself all the rivers of desire. One (on the contrary) whose desires trickle outward (as if from a pond) is soon drained (of energy).

Generous desires—for example, to bring joy to others—do not drain your reservoir of peace, but add to it by the joy they awaken.

Whenever you feel pleasure, let it remind you of soul-bliss, inwardly. Whenever you see beauty, take into yourself the joy you feel in it. Let every worldly happiness remind you of the much greater happiness of the Self.

Some yogis recommend complete indifference to the world. What a dry outlook! Far better is it, my Guru taught, to enjoy *with God* the beauties and the pure delights of this world, by focusing on the inner joy you feel during experiences that uplift the heart's feelings. Raise those feelings toward God, rather than suppressing them with dry, intellectually "inspired" apathy. In this way, too, one can absorb into himself, instead of leaking outward, whatever joys and pleasures the world gives him.

(2:71) That person knows peace who, relinquishing all (energy-draining) desires, and fully satisfied with his state of desirelessness, no longer sees himself as a separate, individual ego.

The ego lies at the root of all delusions. Producing the plant of material desire, it is like a noxious weed, choking and killing the more wholesome plants of devotion, self-control, kindness, and other uplifting soul-qualities.

When one is fully satisfied in the Self, desireless and free from every attachment, one no longer sees himself as a separate wave on the ocean of Spirit, but realizes his true Self to be infinite, and one with the ocean.

(2:72) O Partha (Arjuna), this state is known as _Brahmisthiti_: absolute oneness with the Infinite. Anyone who achieves this state will never again fall into delusion. Even at the moment of death, if one concentrates whole-heartedly on this state, he attains perfect, eternal Bliss.

Dr. M. W. Lewis, Paramhansa Yogananda's first Kriya Yoga disciple in America, once asked the Master, "Can you resolve this dilemma for me? Is liberation a state one achieves only for this Day of Brahma? Will we, when Brahman manifests itself again in creation, be obliged to emerge from that oneness once more and go through the whole, long struggle again?"

"Never fear!" the Master replied. "Once the soul has achieved final freedom in Spirit, it is free forever."

Such is the aim of the Bhagavad Gita: to help sincere seekers to find the way to perfect union with Satchidananda: ever-existing, ever-conscious, ever-new Bliss.

Thus ends the second chapter, called "Shankhya Yoga," of the Upanishad of the holy Bhagavad Gita, in the dialogue between Sri Krishna and Arjuna discussing yoga and the science of God-realization.

CHAPTER THIRTEEN

WHY FIGHT?

(3:1) Arjuna said: "O Janardana (Krishna, the Divine Liberator), if (as it seems) You consider understanding superior to action, why, O Keshava, have You been urging me to this terrible action?

(3:2) "This apparent contradiction confuses me. Please tell me clearly: Which path will help me toward the highest good?"

ARJUNA IS SPEAKING ON BEHALF OF "SADHU Everyman," and playing the part of "Devil's Advocate." Calling Krishna his guru and "Divine Liberator," he says, "O Janardana, I am torn between the two duties You've given me. On the one hand, You tell me to become absorbed in the stillness of Spirit. On the other hand, You say I must fight against my natural foes—my evil tendencies—both for my own good and for the benefit of others. Why can't I simply rest, calmly and joyfully in the Supreme Self—as you've also enjoined?"

Unfortunately, what is "natural" for the ego is far from natural for the Self, or soul. Spiritual progress is achieved not by the tense effort demanded for material success, but rather by a process of *upward relaxation.* Spiritual progress may be compared to a rising helium balloon. The balloon's ascent is natural, and can be prevented only by ropes, or by heavy ballast. Devotion and divine aspiration lift the consciousness toward its source in God. Worldly desires and attachments, and the habit of directing one's energy-flow outward, are the ropes and ballast that resist the upwardness of soul inspiration. Effort on the spiritual path may be compared to cutting the ropes which hold the balloon, and pushing ballast out of the basket underneath.

It seems contradictory to say that effort should be required at all, since the idea is to attain effortlessness! In fact, however, the divine state can be attained only by serious application, which is a kind of effort. Interestingly however, that effort also *implies relaxation* upward with the energy-flow in the spine, which rises by a natural buoyancy toward the brain, and—were it not for worldly samskars (ballast)—would take one ever deeper into meditation. Because worldly achievements generally require stressful effort, many people, when they take up the practice of meditation, try "hard" also to reach inner calmness. In fact, the key to right meditation is relaxation—physically, emotionally, and mentally. The energy is drawn up the spine in response to another kind of "gravity": the upward pull of Spirit, which one feels first in the heart, and then at the Kutastha between the eyebrows, the seat of the spiritual eye. This is the pull of divine love. Its upward pull requires effort on the devotee's part only in the beginning, to release it from the downward pull, or "ballast," of material desires.

Thus, the symbolism of Kurukshetra as a war is to "fight" and conquer one's own evil tendencies. The "war" fought, however, is primarily to rechannel upward the energy in the spine which, so far, has activated those downward-pulling tendencies. The upward flow of energy *releases* it from whatever tendencies, in the worldly person, have been pulling it downward. All the effort one invests spiritually should be *in the direction* of effortlessness—"When efforts end in ease," as Paramhansa Yogananda expressed it.

Sometimes it takes a very great effort of will to resist some particular habit or temptation and throw it out of the mind altogether. A certain man (a true story) wanted for once and for all to overcome his tendency toward alcoholism. One day, finding himself on the point of succumbing once again to that old, evil habit, he suddenly became so enraged with himself that he removed from the cabinet all his bottles of whiskey, rum, etc., where he'd been keeping them, carried them out of doors, and hurled them furiously onto the ground. Every bottle was broken, and with their shattering, every attachment to drinking vanished from his consciousness forever. The vitreous devastation was only an outward expression of his inner, and very firm, emotional renunciation.

Usually, such renunciation is accompanied by deep inner calmness, but in this man's case, evidently, emotional revulsion was needed first, to break his deep-seated habit.

A thorn, the Indian scriptures suggest, can be used to extricate another one, after which both thorns may be discarded. Emotional rejection enabled this man to uproot the deeply imbedded "thorn" of alcoholism. After his emotional "purging," both the emotion and the habit were discarded. The point, in this case, is that emotion worked, and was just what the man needed to free himself forever of his habit.

That emotional act too, however, though it demanded both physical and mental effort, may be compared to simply heaving the ballast out of the basket under the balloon so that the balloon can rise of its own buoyancy. Sometimes, as was stated in *The Imitation of Christ* (a great Christian work which my Guru recommended), one must "do violence" to his lower nature in the name of ultimate ease. Such "violence" does not create an increase of tension, for it releases desire and attachment instead of suppressing them.

It should be added that the balloon may, after long disuse, have lost some of its buoyant gas. The spiritual aspirant must "pump" his balloon of aspiration again and again with fervent devotion and ever-deeper meditation. He must repeatedly return the compass needle of his attention to the polestar of ultimate divine attainment. Admittedly, to do so requires effort, especially in the beginning. His efforts will be increasingly successful, however, the more he feels that what he is doing is a *relaxation upward* into the higher Self, rather than a process of driving his thoughts higher by grim will power. The expression, "When efforts end in ease," should be held aloft in the mind constantly like

a banner by every meditator. It is the "monkey standard" which Arjuna held high to symbolize his control
over mental restlessness.

The need is not so much to develop love for God as to
receive His love: to *recognize* love and joy as supremely
relishable, and as, therefore, the only thing in life worth
having. Divine bliss is the most fulfilling of all possible
attainments, and therefore the only "thing" worthwhile to
desire. Devotion is simply a *response* to God's call in the
soul. High truths cannot be learned: they can only be
remembered in the Self. As the ancient sage Patanjali
stated, divine enlightenment is attained by a process of
smriti: divine recollection. When God is experienced, the
soul recognizes what it has always known, on deeper-than-
conscious levels of consciousness: its own, eternal reality.

The spiritual path is full of apparent contradictions.
Yogananda told the story of a master who said to a
disciple, "You should eat, and you should not eat." The
disciple quite naturally objected, "Master, what you've
said seems to me self-contradictory."

"The contradiction," replied the Master, "is in your
understanding; my advice is sound. You should feed
your body healthfully to keep it alive and well, but you
must resist the thought, born of ego, 'I am eating.' Tell
yourself, rather, 'God is eating through me.'"

Thus, too, must a person act in this world: not with ego-
motivation, but as a God-given duty, and with the feeling
that He alone, indeed, is the Doer, through His instrument.

**(3:3) The Cosmic Lord said, "O Sinless One, at the
beginning of creation, I established two means by**

which man could achieve salvation. The first was by wisdom; the other was by right action."

True wisdom means one thing only: the perception of Brahman, and oneness with Him. Those who are blessed with this perception have no need for action at all. Yogananda told a story of Draupadi, to whom Krishna once addressed the question, "Why don't you practice the yoga meditation techniques?"

"I would love to, Lord," she replied, "but how can I? I can't take my mind away from You long enough to do them."

"Hearing those words," the Master concluded, "Krishna only smiled."

The path to yoga through wisdom actually begins with the vision of God. As one saint put it, "I used to think that when I achieved *nirbikalpa samadhi* my spiritual work would be finished. Instead, I discovered that, with *nirbikalpa*, it had only begun!"

Once one has realized oneness with God, and understood that in everything one does God alone performs his every action, from then on, not the ego, he must still recall, and release into the Infinite, all the actions he performed in ego-consciousness through countless past lives. The sum total of those lives may be many millions: incarnations spent, let us say, as a pirate, a farmer, a stock broker, a housewife, a warrior, a king, a beggar.

The task of releasing the ego-motivation behind billions of past deeds may seem overwhelming— comparable to turning each molecule in a bar of metal in a north-south direction to create a bar magnet. As we saw pages ago, considering that example and relating it to the magnetizing of the spine for spiritual unfoldment, two elements in the task of inward release are infinitely more important than turning each molecule individually north and south, or than releasing, one by one into the infinite, all the deeds one ever committed in past lives.

Paramhansa Yogananda said that the deeply meditating yogi, during even one meditation, can release the deeds performed in delusion of an entire lifetime. The yogi sweeps the light of superconsciousness, so to speak, over the entire panorama of that incarnation, beholding God as the One who acted in all of them—even his misdeeds. Thus, the yogi doesn't have to view each deed. Rather, he sees the sweep of energy as it moved throughout that incarnation. God it is, in reality, who acts even when the parts He plays are those of villains. Satan himself is—when the whole tale is told—an instrument of God. As my Guru put it, "The villain is needed in a play, to make you love the hero." And villainy in one's own past is needed, over many incarnations, to bring one to the point where he realizes that doing harm to others never succeeded in bringing him happiness; nor was there any real fulfillment for him until he'd learned to offer up his ego into a more expanded peace and harmony.

The *jivan mukta* ("freed while living"), having been released forever from ego-consciousness, must recall all those lives when he lived in ego-consciousness, and must see himself as never having been anything but an individual manifestation of the Lord Himself. This path of wisdom leads to the highest state, *kaivalya moksha*, complete liberation.

I once asked my Guru, "How long does one remain a *jivan mukta* before he achieves full liberation?"

"In that state," he replied, "you don't care. Indeed, there is no 'you' *to* care! You may use your need to clear your karma of the past as an excuse to come back and help others, or you may say, simply, 'I am free,' and *be* free in God forever."

At this point a brother disciple of mine, as I mentioned in *Conversations with Yogananda*, said, "But if I myself said, 'I'm free,' I wouldn't *be* free, would I?"

"Oh, yes," the Guru replied. "But the thing is, you answered your own question! You said, 'I wouldn't be.'" He then told the story, also quoted earlier, about the man who tried to rid himself of a demon by chanting a Vedic incantation over a handful of powder and then casting it on the demon. The demon mocked him, saying, "Before you could even say your incantation, I myself got into the powder." Yogananda then explained, "The very mind with which you would affirm freedom is already infected with the disease of delusion. That is why you must first reach that high state of consciousness. Only then can your affirmation of freedom be effective."

At that stage, it is no longer the "I" that says, "I am free." Of the saints described in *Autobiography of a Yogi*, very few had attained full liberation. I spent several days with one such *param mukta* (so my Guru described him, though he had not included him in his autobiography). I said to this saint, "With all that you have attained, why have you so few disciples?"

"God has done what He wants to do with this body," was his simple reply. In that state, there is no

"I" to care one way or another about anything. The goal has been reached.

Intellectuals may consider it their nature to incline toward the path of wisdom. It takes more than intellect, however, to enter even the lower samadhi state of *sabikalpa*. As my Guru stated in the chapter "Experience in Cosmic consciousness," in *Autobiography of a Yogi*, "The experience can never be given through one's mere intellectual willingness or open-mindedness. Only adequate enlargement by yoga practice and devotional *bhakti* can prepare the mind to absorb the liberating shock of omnipresence."

Yogananda's great mystical poem, "Samadhi," which will be quoted in full later on in this book during the discussion of Arjuna's divine vision, omitted in later editions, by an inexplicable editorial emendation, a number of important lines. Among the omitted lines was the following:

> By deeper, longer, thirsty, guru-given meditation
> Comes this celestial *samadhi*.

Salvation comes—as, indeed, does every manifestation of creation—through an instrument of God, and not directly from Spirit. In this case, the divine instrument is the guru.

Thus, for practical needs, Krishna tells the devotee to follow the path of yoga. As he declares later on in the Gita, "Arjuna, be thou a yogi."

Meditative activity, and not just any set of religiously motivated actions, is implicit in what Krishna says here. As the apple blossom already contains the apple, and is inseparable from that final product, so yoga practice is inseparable from its ultimate fruit: union with the Infinite.

It must be strictly understood that the term *yoga* is not limited to specific meditative practices, taught initially thousands of years ago in India by great *rishis*, or sages. Spiritual seekers in any religion, if they pray and meditate sincerely, may rightly be termed yogis. A certain great Roman Catholic mystic in Italy was approached by a friend of mine who, during his traditional "confession," told the mystic he practiced Kriya Yoga.

"Hush!" the mystic replied. "It is better not to let anyone (other priests, especially) know! However," he added, "you are doing the right thing!"

The eightfold (more literally, the "eight-limbed," or *ashtanga*) path of yoga outlined by the ancient sage Patanjali was not describing one particular path to God. All who seek to unite their souls with God must follow that same path: *yama* and *niyama* (right action); *asana* (firmness of posture, and keeping the spine straight so as to enable the energy to flow freely through it); *pranayama* (control over the energy of the body); *pratyahara* (interiorization of the mind); *dharana* (one-pointed concentration); *dhyana* (absorption in deep meditation); and samadhi (oneness). Samadhi, as we saw earlier, is both conditioned and unconditioned: conditioned (limited), first, in *sabikalpa*, for the subtle bonds of ego-consciousness still remain to be wholly severed; and *nirbikalpa*, unconditioned by limitation of any kind.

One who attains *nirbikalpa samadhi* has reached the highest state there is. He has only to rid himself of memories of past incarnations of ego-identification.

Otherwise, he is like Christ, Krishna, and Buddha. From oneness with God it is impossible to rise any higher. Religionists often claim for their own founders a state above that of any other saint or master. No such state exists. As Yogananda once put it, "When you become one with God, you *are* God." Indeed, there is no "you" to be anything else!

Thus, when Krishna told Arjuna to be a yogi, he didn't mean necessarily to be a *Hindu* yogi. All those in every religion who sincerely seek God walk the same path, ultimately speaking, for their devotion turns them inward to experience Him. It cannot be otherwise.

The benefit of the "path" of yoga, as it was taught classically, and specifically the path of Kriya Yoga, is that its scientific techniques accomplish more directly what the most earnest devotion can only accomplish indirectly.

Yogananda once met a sincere Bhakti Yogi (a follower of the path of devotion), and, seeing his sincerity, urged him to accept initiation into Kriya Yoga. The man demurred, saying that he had been following the path of Bhakti Yoga sincerely for twenty years, and was loyal to that way—"Although," he admitted, "I have yet to experience God."

Yogananda explained to him, "You have been in a room for twenty years, trying to get out through the walls, the ceiling, the floor, but no one has shown you where the door is. Kriya Yoga will take you by the 'door' of the spine. I am not trying to change your allegiance. I am only saying, 'Here is the door: Open it, and walk through into the "free air" of divine attainment.' Finally he accepted my suggestion. Within a very short time he attained the experience of God which he had been seeking for so many years."

It must be understood that the Bhagavad Gita is for everyone, and not only for those who can meditate deeply. It is, indeed, for even the most worldly of human beings. It points the way for everyone to find the fulfillment of happiness, then joy, then perfect bliss that all men seek—most of them, alas, blindly, groping in darkness with no sense of direction. The Gita says, *"This is the way you are all seeking! Nothing sought in any other direction will ever give you what you yourself so ardently desire! Blindly though it be, and in ignorance of what life is all about, what you seek is the mystery of your own being!"*

Thus, this chapter on Karma Yoga, the Path of Spiritual Action, deals with *all* action, and with the way to direct action toward the realization of God.

The important point to remember is that the goal of Karma Yoga is not to *please* God: it is, in a true sense, to *please* one's Self: That is to say, it is to find bliss in one's own, divine Self! This is also the message of every true scripture: Do that which will bring you, not pleasure, and not even mere human happiness, but *bliss*! To emphasize the ego and its narrow self-interests is the pathway to hell. To de-emphasize it by expanding one's sympathies and awareness is the pathway to heaven. Ultimately, the true heaven which all seek is Satchidananda: ever-existing, ever-conscious, ever-new Bliss.

Thus, that action is spiritual which minimizes one's emphasis on the ego and on everything that feeds

ego-consciousness: desires, attachments, and every
warrior in the whole army of the Kauravas.

**(3:4) Actionlessness cannot be attained by mere in-
action. One who forsakes work (in the name of divine
aloofness from activity) cannot reach perfection.**

It is to set an example for their disciples that fully
liberated masters, who return to this world as *avatars*
(incarnations of God), engage themselves in various spiritually uplifting activities. Sometimes, indeed, they even
participate in world-emancipating tasks, such as Krishna
assumed in killing the demonic Kangsa. Avatars live as
willing participants in the divine drama of creation. Their
lives are also intended, however, to serve as examples to
devotees by showing them that it is important for everyone to be actively engaged in self-liberation, each one
according to his own complex network of karma. My
Guru explained that a liberated master, whatever his role
on earth, never loses his inner awareness of freedom.

**(3:5) No one can remain actionless for even a moment;
all are compelled (by Nature), whether willingly or
unwillingly, to be active, driven by the gunas (the three
qualities) of Nature.**
**(3:6) The person who restrains his organs of action,
but in whose mind rotate the thoughts of sense objects,
is (rightly) regarded as a hypocrite, and is self-deluded.**

Imagine utter motionlessness: no wind; no passing
clouds; no ocean waves; no rising or setting sun and

moon; no changing of the seasons; no growing things; no decay; no breath of life; no thoughts; no whirling atoms; and, because no movement exists, therefore no space—and, finally, since no movement, therefore also no time.

What utter folly in so-called philosophers, sophisticated thinkers, and aspiring truth seekers to imagine that the actionless state of Supreme Spirit is attainable by merely not acting! Can they cease from breathing by merely not breathing? Can they refrain from thinking by merely not thinking? Can they achieve silence by merely not speaking? One wonders how any aspirant to wisdom can conceive such absurdities!

All creation exists in a vibratory state. The very atoms are constantly in movement. *Prakriti* (Nature) *forces* man to be active. Anyone who tries to be inactive becomes merely lazy. Anyone who pretends to be disinvolved in the world around him is being merely hypocritical.

In order to achieve the actionless state it is utterly necessary to act *consciously*—not merely driven by Nature, but deliberately and intelligently, like a surfer going *with* the waves of circumstance.

(3:7) That man, however, succeeds supremely, O Arjuna, who disciplines his senses by an effort of mind, remains inwardly non-attached, and engages his organs of activity in God-reminding activities.

What (let us first consider) are "God-reminding activities"? They include every deed and thought which lifts the

mind toward superconsciousness. Mere piety expressed
prayerfully in church, temple, or synagogue; mere "holy"
sentiments displayed to impress others (or even uttered
fervently to "impress" God)—in short, any show of
religiosity is acceptable only according to the depth of
inner sincerity involved. The wish to impress indicates a
desire for results, rather than true sincerity of feeling.

Krishna's expression, ". . . disciplining his senses by
an effort of mind" suggests the importance of not adopt-
ing merely outward means of self-discipline: standing or
sitting, for example, with one hand upraised until it
withers from disuse; standing, but never sitting nor lying
down, as a mode of penance; lying on a bed of thorns:
these, plus long fasts, sleep-deprivation, and other means
of sense starvation designed for learning self-control, but
without a corresponding attempt at intelligent discrimination, are not what Krishna is recommending here.
Similar austerities in other religions include such
practices as self-flagellation, self-starvation, and many
practices similar to ones used in India. To list them all
would be futile, inasmuch as all of them are intended to
subdue the senses without the proper use of the will. For
inner freedom, the will must give its active *consent* to
inward release: It is useless to beat the body in an effort
to *force* it into submission.

Sense-control is never a question of bullying the senses.
What must be done is *withdraw* the energy from them.
The will acts directly upon the flow of energy. Yogananda
stated, "The greater the will, the greater the flow of
energy." The *direction* of that flow can be inward as well
as outward—upward as well as downward.

Therefore also Krishna speaks of *inner* non-attachment. Depriving oneself of material things may, and often does, feed the hidden fires of attachment! No activity engaged in merely to impress others (or even God) will, in the end, bear divine fruit. Spiritual progress is achieved above all by desiring it intensely, and not by inflicting violent discipline on the body.

With a willing attitude, with joy and devotion, it is possible to find God. Without the whole-hearted assent of one's will and of one's whole consciousness, that noblest of all ends—the pure consciousness of Bliss itself—cannot be achieved.

(3:8) Perform those actions which your duty dictates, for action is better than inaction. Without action, indeed, even the act of maintaining life in the body would not be possible.

The duty of every man is that which is particularly his own, ordained for him by the karmic bonds he himself has forged, and must untie to release himself from attachment to the ego. Only thus can his consciousness soar in infinity. One's dutiful actions are not necessarily the activities for which he has special skill. The spiritual duty of a person with a talent for acting, for example, may not be to become an actor. He may be very good at pretending to be someone else, yet have an active need to be wholly sincere as to who he himself is. He may have the magnetism to win plaudits from his audiences as an actor, yet may in the process bind himself more firmly to pride by his very success. This is not to say that acting is universally a dangerous career, karmically speaking. It may help some people to become less identified, and therefore less limited by, their own personalities. Acting may help some people, also, to realize more deeply that life itself is a play, in which nothing, in the last analysis, is real.

The complexity of karmic patterns in human life makes virtually every honest activity a dharmic duty for *someone*. The menial task of street sweeping may, for most people, be simply a paying job and a social necessity, but for some people it may be a karmic duty—if, for example, the sweeper lived in a past incarnation in idle squalor. The exalted job of president of a large corporation might be merely a burden for some people, and a cause of further karmic involvement, owing (perhaps) to a lurking desire for self-importance. For someone, however, who treats that position as an opportunity to serve others, and to promote a good cause, it can be a step toward liberation from ego.

How is one to know his karmic duty? Few people, it must be admitted, are even close to recognizing the abyss which separates the ego from Cosmic consciousness. With innumerable karmic battles remaining to be fought before their mental "troops" can make any significant advancement into enemy territory, it may be best simply to tackle whatever challenge lies closest to hand. Again, it is often best to undertake first those battles which one can be more confident of winning.

For example, suppose someone is unable, at present, to conquer his sex drive. In that case, to try to overcome it may only weaken his will all the more, for each time he fails will become, for him, a reaffirmation of his weakness. Far better would it be, then, in his case, to undertake an easier challenge which, once overcome, would strengthen his will power and prepare him gradually for the much greater challenge still awaiting him.

For one who is fortunate enough to have a true (God-realized) guru, the sage advice given by him is precious beyond any chest of diamonds and rubies. Obedience to his slightest word will be your raft over the roiling seas of delusion.

(3:9) Actions performed for selfish gain are karmically binding. Therefore, O Son of Kunti (that is to say, of dispassion), perform your duty without attachment in a spirit of religious self-offering.

The religious rite of *yagya* (my Guru preferred this transliteration over the scholarly version: *yajna*) symbolically offers the ego-self into the sacrificial fire for purification. One who aspires to liberation should do everything in a spirit of self-offering to God. God's power itself, then, is symbolized by the fire of yagya. Visualize yourself every night, before going to sleep, offering every thought and feeling that is centered in the ego (self-congratulation, for example, self-abasement, and any self-justification), along with every desire and attachment, into the blazing fire of God's love.

CHAPTER FOURTEEN

DIRECTIONAL DEVELOPMENT

IN THIS AGE OF DEMOCRACY IT IS EASY FOR PEOPLE—
especially for those who lack refinement—to think,
"I'm as good as anyone else." All growth is directional, however. Values themselves, though relative, are
directionally so: They are *from* one level *to* another level.
There is good, better, and best; or bad, worse, and worst.
Behavior that is acceptable in a little child may be suspect,
or even unacceptable, in an adult. If the child points a toy
gun at someone and cries, "Bang! Bang!" people may
smile at his behavior, knowing that there is no animus
behind it. If an adult does the same thing, however,
people might not feel so easy about his behavior.

We have seen that there is realistic justification for the
caste system—not for the way society has hardened it,
but for the simple fact that there is obviously, in human
nature, some kind of upward evolution. There are boors
and there are saints. Society is a mixture of all types.
One of the inducements people have for seeking God is
the very fact that they are exposed to so many different

135

levels of human refinement, some of them more inspiring than others, and many of them, rather, stern warnings of the consequences of wrong action. Some may inspire one to rise spiritually. Others may "inspire" one in a very different way, and cause him to recoil from delusion itself as from a venomous snake.

Life evolves upward from levels lower even than apparent animation. The wriggling worm—relatively high on the scale of consciousness—may become next a moth, then a bird, a mammal, and, after a long upward journey, a human being. Only after a very long time, and many further incarnations, does the human ego, which needs first to become focused on its humanity, evolve upward to the point where it craves liberation from the limitations of ego-consciousness, and from its imprisonment in a little body.

People who expand their selfish impulses by sharing generously with others go after death to an astral heaven. There, only a few of them are spiritually aware enough to advance further. Surrounded by "their kind of people," they feel no incentive to meditate or to try in other ways to evolve higher than the level they've so far achieved, which is vastly more enjoyable than the material plane. They get to live in the company of angels, or devas. They are, however, more in the position of the recipients of blessings than of generating blessings to others, themselves.

Animals evolve more rapidly if they mix closely with human beings. This is the benefit to them of being pets. *Shudra* types of human beings, similarly, can evolve more quickly if they are able to serve in the homes of higher types of human beings: *Vaishyas*, perhaps especially, to whose outlook on life they themselves may be better attuned.

Vaishyas, following the same rationale, might do well to mix specially with—or at least to seek the custom of—*Kshatriya* types. And Kshatriyas will gain the most from mixing with those of Brahmin temperament.

When higher types mix with those of lower consciousness, in a spirit of sharing with them out of a wish to uplift them, they themselves gain spiritually. Otherwise, to mix with lower types may be to their personal disadvantage, for it may pull them downward. They must keep a guard especially on their affections, which must be impersonal.

Women, whose role in society is more particularly that of preserving social values, may marry above their natural caste, but ought not to marry beneath it. It must be recalled, here, that "above" and "beneath" have nothing to do with people's families at birth, but only with individual types of human beings.

Thus, it is by no means demeaning to serve those who can help to uplift one. A person of Brahmin temperament who longs to know God may have the greatest good fortune of meeting, and being accepted by, a God-realized guru. In the Indian scriptures it is said that even brief contact with a saint can be a great blessing. "One moment," the saying goes, "in the company of a saint can be your raft over the ocean of delusion."

Again and again we find emphasized in the scriptures the importance of *satsanga*: of good (and especially spiritual) company. Most people, surely, can look back over their lives and recall some one, two, or even several people who were influential in their own mental or spiritual development. The boast of modern man, firm in his blind conviction that he's "as good as anyone else," extends that democratic outlook to religion also and to the belief that even relative goodness will earn one an eternal place in a beautiful astral heaven. "Why, we're *all* saints!" cries the Protestant Christian when someone proposes to him that sainthood is an ideal to which everyone should aspire. To be confined forever in a little ego, however, would surely be a confinement in hell, not freedom in heaven!

Man's understanding of the universe has grown enormously in recent centuries. Geocentricity was replaced relatively recently, owing to the discoveries of Galileo and others, by the belief that the sun was the center of everything. Only late in the nineteenth century was it discovered that our sun is only one star in a vast star system. More recently still, in 1918, was it discovered that this system, our "Milky Way," is only one galaxy among others. Now it is known that we live in a universe consisting of at least a hundred *billion* galaxies.

Our view of human development, also, needs to be expanded. Matter, it is now known to be a scientific fact, is only a vibration of energy. There are, according to India's ancient wisdom, many kinds of energy, emanating from the astral level of cosmic manifestation. We have discussed some of these energies already: conscious, egoic entities that produce and sustain life on this planet. Some of these entities are more highly evolved than others, and deserve the appellation devas, or shining angels. Others are nature spirits—fairies and the like. Still others are lower spirits: demons and devils.

Low types of humanity attract low astral spirits. High types attract the guidance and inspiration of devas, or angels, who can help them if they are open to receiving assistance from above.

A friend of the author's was, in his youth, an alpinist who in that capacity made several first ascensions. On one such climb he found, just when he was almost at the peak, that the mountain curved outward. It was impossible to climb any higher, and equally impossible to climb down again. He was faced with only two reasonable choices: to remain on the ledge and starve to death, or to take a suicidal leap off the precipice.

Both choices, he decided, were unacceptable. Though reason shouted against the third choice, he proceeded to climb higher. When the mountain began to curve outward, he fell back onto the ledge again. "I might as well die trying," he determined, "as die by starvation!" He tried again, therefore, and yet again. Each time, at the same point, he fell back onto the ledge again.

On perhaps the twenty-fifth try, as he was just at the point of inevitable return, a force suddenly pushed him against the mountain, holding him there until he reached the top. From there the descent on the other side was easy. How can that miracle be explained? Surely it can only be attributed to angelic intervention.

Very few human beings are ready for the highest spiritual blessing: the help of a true guru. That all human beings need any help they can get, however, is surely very evident to anyone but the most arrant egotist. The fact is that man, having reached that high ledge on the evolutional climb up the mountainside of consciousness where he finds himself the proud possessor of an ego, wants to enjoy it for a time. Alas, he doesn't realize how very long, probably, he has been enjoying it! A woman friend of mine was scolding her two-year-old son, "Come on, now, you're not a baby any longer." He replied, "But I *like* being a baby!" Such also are most human egos: They *like* themselves as they are! They *like* being unique and separate from all others, made a fuss over and coddled (when they can be). The climb isn't over for them, however, until they can expand their self-awareness, eventually, to embrace infinity. Meanwhile, the "advantage" of greater awareness, especially of the egoic self, comes with a disadvantage, also: a greatly increased susceptibility to suffering.

The other "selves" whose help he may scorn to accept are, in fact, closely related to his own self. In infinity they are all expressions of the *same* one Self! Man's task in the great scheme of things is to learn that he is only a small manifestation of Infinite Consciousness. The work before him, to achieve infinity, is colossal! With any wisdom at all he can hardly fail to see that he needs all the help he can get.

By helping others he helps himself, for he expands his sympathies. By helping those below him on the mountainside, he reinforces his appreciation for his own more advanced position. By accepting help from those above him, he finds it easier to climb. Without help from above he may think, smugly, "Why climb any further? I'm satisfied, now that I'm finally on this plateau, and can enjoy the more expansive view from up here." And so, then: shall he starve to spiritual death there, bereft of nourishment from ever-subtler joy? Many people, smugly centered in their egos, are simply settling in for the long wait for death. Life needs to be continuous progress. It cannot remain stationary.

There are devas—angels—to whom we can appeal, or with whose energies we can work in cooperation. As with other human beings, we gain much more if we *give* to them than if we try to snatch from them for our gain. Even in the ashrams of great gurus, those disciples receive the most spiritually who, by their appreciation, *give* energy and don't try to *draw* God's blessings self-centeredly to themselves.

When Buddha spoke against the *karmakand* of the Vedic rituals (when offered for self-gratification and egoic gain), he did so in an age when people generally had lost the sensitivity to appreciate anything higher than themselves and their own needs. The age we now live in is an upward-moving age (*not Kali Yuga*, as people in general still believe). Paramhansa Yogananda taught for people in this new age of ascending *Dwapara Yuga*. It is time again, he saw, to urge people to try to relate once more to higher entities and energies.

Mankind, in its materialism, has cut itself off from those subtle energies. People thinking to succeed by their efforts alone have died prematurely of heart problems and other ailments. Our very planet seems to be losing some of its vital force. I mentioned earlier that the food we eat today has scientifically been found to contain a significantly smaller quantity of nutrients than it did a scant hundred years ago.

It is time we included subtler beings in our reckoning. They are there, willing to help us. What wins their help is not flattery (if they truly are *higher* than ourselves: devas, or shining angels). Rather, what they respond to are such qualities as courage, selflessness, generosity, and—above all—love.

In our love for other people, it is best always to give them impersonal love: to see God in all, and not to look to others for personal gain. Love should be expressed as a concern for their well-being; its impersonality should be without self-interest. The same is true for man's attitude toward the gods, or astral deities: It should be self-giving. They should be loved as messengers of God, and certainly not flattered, ego to ego. Above all, we should love God in them.

The Vedas were first revealed to mankind in a higher age than our own. They contain an understanding of the power also of the devas. As a way of encouraging mankind to look to subtler energies for help, rather than depending solely on one's own strength and ingenuity, mantras were also given in the Vedas for purely personal gain: wealth, power, an increase of family, etc. The thought was that, to seek such things (which most people would seek anyway) from sources higher than anything material would direct gratitude toward those sources, causing people to depend more on higher help than on ego-generated power.

All things exist in a state of vibration. That is how the Supreme, ever-unmoving Spirit brought about the appearance of a reality separate from itself. As the blades of a propeller, in their rapid movement, give the appearance of a solid circular disk, so Cosmic Vibration, in its infinite number of intensely rapid vibrations, gives the appearance of substance, variety, even of solidity. Thus we have, for example, the rocks, which to our senses appear very solid but which are now known to be only vibrations of energy, and which, even as material substance, are composed largely of space.

The ancient *rishis*, or seers, understood how certain vibrations could bring harmony with levels of consciousness that would lift man, also, to higher levels of awareness. Those rites and ceremonies are effective, when recited correctly and especially with understanding. To imagine, however, that they excuse man from the need to make any personal effort to improve himself is why Buddha, in the descending age of *Kali Yuga*, denounced them.

Krishna in the next stanzas of the Bhagavad Gita, and speaking in the name of an understanding that had come down from a higher age, seems to be recommending the very thing which Buddha denounced. All the great masters speak, however, from the same state of perfect realization. When they give different emphases in their teachings, it is because they must address the special needs of their audiences. Krishna also said, in fact, what Buddha taught: Men *themselves* must strive for self-liberation; otherwise, the grace of God, the help of a true guru, and the blessings of higher beings will never be attracted.

Do not imagine, then, that you will gain very much spiritually by simply paying a *pujari* (priest) to perform some

Vedic fire ceremony for you with the correctly intoned mantras. The blessings derived from that path, which is known as *karmakand*, can be real (depending also, of course, on the power of the priest), but they will still keep you a wanderer in the delusive paths of duality and karma.

A final question comes up in this regard: to whom should one's prayers and chants be directed? For those whose goal is union with God, why should they chant to lesser deities—Ganesha, Indra, etc.? There are sentiments involved, of course, which should be respected. Images of Ganesha, the god of good fortune with his elephant head, are to be seen in virtually every Hindu home. Uplifting sentiments of all kinds should be not only respected, but encouraged. Man could not really live a life of any inspiration without images of some kind to inspire him, by reminding him of higher truths. Even Moslems, as Guru Nanak pointed out, bow in the direction of the sacred stone at Mecca. Without images, people's devotion becomes dry.

Ganesha is a sweet image. He has been "frozen," so to speak, into an abiding reality by the devotion of millions of worshipers for centuries. Certainly a Hindu should feel "safe," philosophically, in praying to him!

On the other hand, one's highest worship should always be directed toward the Infinite Lord. Therefore it may be said that, as the devotee is taught to see God in everyone, so he should see God in every lesser god, and chant only to those forms, using only those names, which remind him of the Infinite.

For even the recognized gods only represent the posts they hold, not their individual names. In an ancient

Hindu legend Krishna says to Uddhava, "See that beetle on the ground? It was once Indra." Indra, obviously fallen far from the august position that particular entity once held, was now a name, or title, held by another entity. The fall of anyone who engrosses himself again in *maya*—which can happen at any time prior to one's attainment of the very highest state, called *nirbikalpa samadhi*—is fear-inspiring. It will be a subject of discussion later on in the Gita.

The angels are not higher, as some Christians imagine, than the God-realized masters who live on the earth. The angels, too, are working for their own salvation. They too can fall, if their interests turn toward personal gratification. Satan is said, notoriously, to be a fallen angel, although that story belongs more in the realm of allegory than of literal history.

(3:10) Prajapati (God in the aspect of Creator) brought mankind into manifestation, and in so doing gave man the potential for self-offering into a higher (than human) awareness (through yagya). Along with this gift He enjoined mankind, "Whatever you desire, seek it by offering energy back to the source of all energy. Let this sacrifice (yagya) be your milch cow of fulfillment."

(3:11) (Prajapati continued:) "With this offering, commune with the devas (shining angels), that they may commune also with you. Through such mutual communion you will arrive at the highest good."

(3:12) (Prajapati concluded:) "By communion with the devas you will receive from them the (earthly) fulfillments you desire. He who enjoys the gifts of the

gods without returning due offering (of energy) to them is, verily, a thief."

For meditating yogis seeking oneness with God, there are subtler meanings to be drawn from these passages. For the energy in the body should be offered continually back—for "fine tuning," so to speak, to its source. The negative pole of that source, in the body, is the medulla oblongata; the positive pole is the seat of superconsciousness (in the frontal lobe of the brain, centered between the two eyebrows). The true yagya is Kriya Yoga, as we shall see later on. Kriya Yoga leads one up the path of the spine, enabling him to unite his little self—the ego—with the Infinite Self: God.

Raising the Kundalini power is the ultimate "fire rite," leading to a complete withdrawal of energy from the body and an offering of that energy into the Infinite. Kundalini begins this ritual by withdrawing energy from the body-sustaining energy in the chakras. Finally, the yogi offers himself for perfect purification in the blazing light of God.

(3:13) Spiritually minded people, offering up the food they eat to its source in divine energy (the devas), incur no sin. Those, however, who make no such offering (eating only for taste and pleasure) are verily feeding on sin.

Matter, as modern science has learned, is a vibration of energy. The more conscious man can become of the energy in his body, the easier it is for him to rise spiritually. When he moves his body, he should try to feel that it is *energy* which gives strength to his muscles and thereby allows them to move. When he inhales, he should feel that with the air he breathes he is taking in energy. In everything he does, he should try to be conscious of energy as his next step upward in awareness, on his way to divine union.

Next, he should feel that the energy which enables him to move and breathe is not his own, personally. Sin (delusion) begins with the gleeful thought, "All this is mine!" It is easier to imagine matter as something that can be possessed. It is more difficult to think of air or, more subtly, energy as one's very own. When energy can be offered up (to the devas, or to God) it is easier to raise one's consciousness also.

The food one eats is energy also. Its gross substance can stimulate gross pleasure, also, in the thought, "I, myself, am eating, enjoying, and delighting in all these pleasurable tastes." It is not "unlawful," spiritually, to enjoy one's food, but it is better to let that pleasure be a reminder of the changeless joy of the soul. Thus it helps, while eating, to let the pleasure one gets from food nourish the joy in the heart, by concentrating in the heart whatever delight one feels from the taste.

To "pig out," as the present-day expression is in America, is to feed not only the body but the ego. What makes doing so a sin is that it affirms the error of looking upon the body as one's own particular reality.

"Sin," here, means simply the error of ego-affirmation. It is one more bar, so to speak, in the prison cell of ego-consciousness.

(3:14) Creatures require nourishment from food; food must be nourished by rain; rain is sustained in its turn by fire (by heat from the sun, which causes bodies of water to evaporate), and heat is produced by the vibration of AUM.

The Bhagavad Gita here is suggesting, subtly, the elemental stages of divine manifestation, which are in truth our entire sustenance: earth, water, fire—these visible stages issue from the vibratory power of the cosmos: AUM. Vibration is action, which is to say, *karma.*

(3:15) Know this divine vibratory activity to have been produced by Brahma, the cosmic creative force. Yagya, or sacrificial self-offering, brings the great cycle of cosmic manifestation back (at last) to itself.

AUM, the Cosmic Vibration, has three aspects, each of which produces a distinct sound: Brahma, the creative vibration, with the highest sound; Vishnu, the preserving vibration, with a medium-pitched sound; and Shiva, the destroying or all-dissolving vibration, with a low-pitched, rumbling sound. This so-called Trinity is not comparable to the Christian Trinity of Father, Son, and Holy Ghost, as many scholars have claimed. That Christian Trinity is expressed, rather, in the Sanskrit threefold *"AUM-Tat-Sat,"* three words that indicate the basic aspects of God: *Sat* being the eternal Truth from which issues all creation; AUM, the Cosmic Vibration, from which proceeds cosmic manifestation; and *Tat,* the reflection, at the heart of all vibration, of the motionless Spirit, forever untouched by vibration.

AUM is properly written with three letters. The first letter signifies Brahma; the second one, Vishnu; and the third (properly pronounced as a slightly long-drawn hum), Shiva. The threefold AUM is for that reason chanted on three tonal levels: high, medium, and low. AUM, in English, is generally written "OM," because that vowel in English is not pure, but consists of two (and even more!) vowels: in America at least, a short *a* (as in "uh") and the universal *u*, which should be pronounced *oo*. In other languages—Italian, for example—there is no clear way of transliterating AUM. People in Italy pronounce the *A* long (or open), not short as it should be. AUM, properly, should be pronounced, "Uh-oo-mmm." *Tat* and *Sat* also are pronounced with short *a*'s, like the *a* in "about."

All things are manifestations of the Cosmic Vibration. The meditating yogi first hears the sound of AUM in his right ear. As he deepens his experience of it, he comes to hear it in his whole body as the entire body vibrates with that sound. Thus, feeling AUM throughout the body, he loses identification with self-consciousness as being centered in the medulla, and gradually expands with the AUM sound until he is identified with it in all creation. This stage is known as AUM samadhi.

His next perception is of *Kutastha Chaitanya*, or *Tat*, the Christ consciousness behind the vibrations of his body—and the center of the very vibration of the body, reflecting the motionless Spirit beyond creation. Gradually his consciousness expands with the Christ consciousness, or *Tat*, until he perceives it as infinite. It is after reaching that stage, my Guru explained to me, that one may be called a master. Thus, in the Sanskrit expression, "*Tat twam asi*," meaning, "Thou art that," the word "*Tat*" has a deeper meaning than most people realize. What it really means is, "Thou art '*that*': the Infinite Consciousness."

Beyond Christ consciousness, in the eternally watchful state, resides the Supreme Spirit, *Sat*.

(3:16) Whoever resists this great rotating cycle, living in sin and preferring the (ego-centered) enjoyment of the senses, lives in vain.

Krishna has been speaking of the great cycle of outward cosmic manifestation and inward return. Man's ego, similarly, is created by the soul's particularization in, and identification with, a bodily form. Its return to oneness with Spirit is accomplished by yagya (self-offering) to God, the aim of which is for the ego to become absorbed again in absolute oneness.

Elsewhere in the Gita, Krishna pleads with Arjuna (who represents "everyman" as devotee) to escape the ever-rotating wheel of birth and rebirth. Here he speaks, by contrast, of the eternal cosmic plan, in which all souls need to participate consciously. He has recommended yagya: offering up of the little self into union with the cosmic Self. Thus, he says that when one clings to littleness, out of attachment to the separate, individual ego, one lives in vain! One may describe such a life as scarcely different from that of a grub. The ego-defined "great" deeds of mankind amount to nothing at all, relative to the universal reality. Their only merit lies in whatever they accomplish for man himself, by refining his consciousness.

CHAPTER FIFTEEN

FREEDOM THROUGH ACTION

(3:17) For him whose only love is the Self, who delights in the Self and is content to rest in the Self, no duty remains.

(3:18) Such a person has nothing to gain by performing action in this world, nor anything to lose by not performing it. He is dependent on no one and nothing (outside the Self).

EGO WAS DEFINED BY PARAMHANSA YOGANANDA AS "the soul identified with the body." That identification drives one to action in the false belief that this world is real. These stanzas are not meant to imply that enlightened souls cease from acting. God Himself (the Divine Playwright), after all, wrote, staged, directed, and acts all the parts in His great drama of the universe. The purpose of the drama is to lead everyone gradually to the denouement of realizing that it was all simply a show, in which all acted, but were never really involved. He is satisfied if they want to become reabsorbed in Him after the curtain closes and oneness with Him has been achieved. He needs "workers in the field," however, and is therefore pleased also with those who want to stay on here out of a "desireless desire" to help Him with the production of the play.

The important thing is not to act with ego-motivation. Our separateness from God is an illusion. Every thought we think, every deed we perform, every desire we harbor is only a reflection of His infinite consciousness. The human playwright writes all the parts in his drama. His play may need a villain; if not, it will certainly need characters who are antithetic to others. Without dramatic tension there can be no drama, and the work won't hold the audience's interest. Indeed, if the playwright is good at his *métier*, he actually *enjoys* writing also the parts of villains, for it takes skill to show the inherent logic of evil (from its own point of view)! At the heart of everything that happens anywhere, there is a hidden secret: divine joy, without which the universe could not have been manifested. People who are attached to their bodies cry out in anguish, "But there can't be joy in suffering!" What stories they tell later, however! Almost proudly they speak of those very times when they suffered the most in their own lives!

Everything is, to varying degrees of manifestation, bliss itself! The very capacity to suffer is an indication of the more refined capacity to experience bliss. Suffering comes primarily from the thought, "Things ought not to be like this." Inherent in suffering itself, in other words, is the thought of how things *ought* to be, and (so the soul whispers to them) *can* be, eventually.

**(3:19) Therefore be conscientious during the perform-
ance of all actions, whether physical or spiritual, to act
without attachment. By activity without self-interest,
one attains the Supreme.**

Physical actions are performed by engaging the life
force on a material level of reality. Spiritual actions are
performed by *withdrawing* the life force from the
physical body. To act spiritually in this world means to
be conscious of the indwelling Self, and to radiate that
inner consciousness outward to others, and to the world.
Attachment is the pathway to bondage: Non-attachment
is the key to liberation. I once asked my Guru, who had
in past incarnations, he told us, performed roles of
major importance in the world, whether a master always
retained the high state of *nirbikalpa samadhi* when he
was sent to do an active work in the world. His answer
was significant: "One never loses the inner consciousness of being free."

**(3:20) By the path of right action alone, (Raja) Janaka
and others like him (karma yogis) attained perfection.
To offer guidance to others, you, too, should be active.**

King Janaka was, in fact, already an enlightened yogi
and a liberated soul from previous lives. His mission was
worldly, but it was to set an example of right action for
unenlightened souls: to do one's duty conscientiously,
but without attachment.

Lahiri Mahasaya often quoted the great rishi
Ashtavakra's teaching: "If you want to achieve freedom

from reincarnation, abhor sense pleasures as you would sugar-coated poison, and be as devotedly attached to acts of forgiveness, pity, contentment, and love of truth and God as to drinking nectar!"

The highest sattwic attitude, of course, is to be impersonal: to forgive, pity, feel contentment, and love truth and God—all these, impersonally, without referring anything back to your own ego. In forgiveness, for example, never think, "I am doing the forgiving," for in that thought, pride can enter the mind. Direct the flow of all your energy and attention outward, toward the person you are forgiving.

(3:21) Whatever the superior being does, lesser beings imitate. His behavior sets the standard for right living in the world.

The arrangement of this scripture into separate stanzas makes it possible from time to time to interrupt its flow with extraneous ideas. In this stanza we find not only a reason offered to spiritual people for living by high principles, but an answer to the common reproach worldly people often address to them: "If you are so concerned with doing a good thing, why don't you do more for the upliftment of mankind?"

This very common criticism is a rationale that often dissuades idealistic people from the spiritual search. "Why don't you do more for others?" It is astonishing how many ways there are of "doing good" in this world without really accomplishing anything worthwhile at all! Think of the "war chests" of political parties: money accumulated by people who believe this person or that will "change everything" for the better. Is any lasting good ever accomplished? That question hardly needs to be answered! "*Plus ça change*," say the French, "*plus c'est la même chose*: The more things change, the more they remain unchanged."

Think of the ardor with which people campaign to get others to behave "as they ought to." People who shout slogans angrily, mounting huge parades, spending vast amounts of money to persuade everyone to stop fighting. Will anger keep anyone at peace? Will merely "banning the bomb" bring a stop to war? Even if people had nothing but pitchforks, so long as their emotions could be aroused to anger they would continue to fight. And people who are eager to fight will certainly seek the best ways of winning they can find.

As an example of almost ridiculous folly—at least, it would be ridiculous if it hadn't also caused so much suffering—think of modern communism: Russia and China, between them, have slaughtered an estimated one hundred million of their own people with a view to imposing on them a philosophy supposed to promote "the greatest good for the greatest number."

What needs changing is not *social systems*, but human consciousness. The best way to change society, surely, would be to create little societies that can inspire others to make the recommended changes, individually, in themselves, rather than forcing everyone to march in lock-step togetherness toward some general "good" that often ends in disaster. If an example works, others may be inspired by it, and may *want* to change. Without the *desire* to change, no one will ever do better at anything.

The first responsibility the universe places on every person's shoulders is this: "Change yourself." One moon, it has been pointed out, gives more light than all the stars. One transformed human being has a more beneficial impact on others than a thousand people campaigning for "improvements" which, when the shouting is over, often leave everything no more changed than when a deck of cards is reshuffled.

Even a brief overview of history shows persuasively that in only one field of endeavor has there been consistency. The one and only impact on society with long-lasting, beneficial effect has been in the field of religion. There have, of course, been wars and persecutions in the name of God. These can and must be blamed on human nature, not on teachings that tell them to love God and to be at peace with one another. Imperfect human beings, eager for battle, will use the name of God—as a slogan, not as an expression of devotion, and, therefore, in vain. God never endorses such "religious" beliefs. People all too easily, however, infect one another with their own imperfections. The true saviors of humanity have ever brought to this world the one and only influence that has succeeded in permanently improving anything.

All great teachers have stated that man's first duty is to improve himself, not to inflict his own opinions about self-improvement on others. They have also said, however, that true improvement is really possible only in a higher, unitive consciousness. Most of them (with the exception, that is, of Buddha, who—as we have shown elsewhere—was by no means in disagreement with them) have added that permanent upliftment is possible only with the assistance and inspiration of God. One way to improve oneself is to *offer* to others (without imposing on them) whatever genuine inspiration one has found. To share that inspiration with others is the best "good work" one can do, provided one does it in a spirit of inner freedom. If one seeks God alone, without doing anything else for humanity, he will in any case (like the full moon against a field of much dimmer stars) have done greater wonders for the whole human race than any politician, after winning his campaign for election!

A sage who, after a lifetime—the task, indeed, requires many lifetimes—arrives at the direct perception of God and achieves the state of oneness with Him, need not make a move to help anyone. Even without doing so, his life will be a supernal blessing on the world. One who acts in the world, however, as an example of divine love, forgiveness, peace, and divine joy will be imitated by countless others. His impact on society as a whole will be incalculably great. Every spiritual seeker must understand that there is nothing greater that he can accomplish for others than that very thing he is already doing.

When such a seeker attains final liberation—so my Guru told me—seven generations of his family in both directions are freed also. Such is the immediate glory harvested from his attainment. What, then, of the disciples? "Oh, they come first!" was my Guru's answer to that question. The freedom of one's family members is not final liberation; rather, it is something like what happens when a person becomes an emperor, and his close relatives rise higher in society.

Those are greatest among human beings who help to bring masses to God. In this way only can a master's greatness be acclaimed. It is outstanding (among other masters) only for the good he does on earth. Otherwise, every *jivan mukta*, having achieved *nirbikalpa samadhi*, is as great as the greatest *siddha*, or perfected being. He may have past karma to work out; even so, he is one with God, and there are no gradations of oneness.

There is another distinction between one perfected master and another. One who is an "ascended master," having attained that state in the present lifetime, has the spiritual power to free only a few others. A *jivan mukta* who returns to earth to continue working out his past karma, and from that level also to guide his disciples, also has limited divine power, compared to one who is fully liberated, to uplift the human race.

One, on the other hand, who achieves full liberation, yet preserves the "desireless desire" unselfishly to bring understanding to the world, and is therefore born again in perfect freedom comes back with limitless spiritual power. Such a person is an avatar. Only one who achieved final liberation in a former life deserves that appellation. An avatar is a universal savior—like Krishna, Buddha, Jesus Christ. Thousands—indeed millions (at least in theory, though there are never millions at any one time who actually seek God)—can be carried to God by such a one, as a powerful railway locomotive is capable of pulling a very long train behind it.

(3:22) O Son of Pritha (Arjuna), no further duty compels Me. There is no state left for Me to attain, and nothing in the three worlds (material, astral, and causal) for Me to gain, yet still I work on for the upliftment of others. There, where all such good work is done, am I.

This passage contains two meanings: overt, and covert. Overtly Krishna is saying, "Free though I am, I still work in this body for the benefit of others." More esoterically, he is saying, "I, the infinite Spirit, am at the heart of all spiritually uplifting work, everywhere." The point is that, in any truly good work, God already *is* that work. The devotee who serves God sincerely with loving devotion need never be anxious that God might possibly be displeased with him.

(3:23) O Partha (Arjuna), if I were to cease acting in creation for even a moment, man, too, would imitate My inactivity.

How can any unenlightened person know whether God is active or not? Krishna is saying that he, the Divine, living as an avatar in a human body, is deliberately setting an example for how man ought to live. Many spiritual teachers counsel their followers to consider, rather, the actionless state of the Supreme Spirit, and, if they want to attain that state, to remain inactive, themselves. Such is not Krishna's teaching in the Bhagavad Gita. Because this important aspect of his teaching has been qualified by those who insist that all activity is a delusion, the question may remain in some people's minds: Which is right—action, or inaction? Is what Krishna says merely an opinion? Or has it, perhaps, been misinterpreted? Is he talking to a more worldly state of consciousness—offering a compromise, in other words, that people will accept more readily?

One answer is to go to those tamasic places where activity is at a minimum: opium dens, for example, and bars where people go only to get drunk. The torpid effect of such inactivity can be deadening; it may turn even the energetic in a short while into human turtles. This important subject will be addressed again, more than once. Here it may be emphasized that Krishna was speaking not to worldly people, but to Arjuna, whom he himself called "Prince of devotees."

The point here is that one need not actually *behold* God engaged in activity. How His avatars behave should be man's best teacher, and although the teaching varies in certain ways according to the needs of the times, all of them have taught the same basic truths, and all have been, in one way or another, active, simply in order to set mankind an example. The examples of the energy they devote to helping people are what inspire their followers to express more energy in their own lives.

(3:24) **If I were to cease being active in cosmic creation, the universe itself would cease to exist. Confusion would result, and mankind would be brought to ruin.**

There are two kinds of *Pralaya*, or cosmic dissolution: partial, and complete. Complete dissolution, of which Krishna speaks only glancingly here (his main topic, now, being the need for right action, leading to release from karmic involvement), means the total withdrawal of all vibrational manifestation, at the end of a "Day of Brahma" (the aeons-long period of cosmic manifestation), which is followed by an equally long "Night of Brahma."

Krishna is speaking here of partial dissolution, in discussing the need for God's presence in man's life and of the ruin that would result without divine inspiration. Partial dissolution is a diminished manifestation of God's conscious manifestation, with waxing chaos and the gradual ruin of mankind. The first sentence of this stanza touches only lightly on total dissolution, as if to remind us that, without God, nothing worthwhile could be achieved. The second sentence, in its reference to partial dissolution, makes it clear that, more than anything else, mankind *needs* God.

God's partial withdrawal from outward manifestation signifies a weakening of that magnetic power which draws people upward towards enlightenment. Were there no such upward draw, human nature itself would have little or nothing to lift it. Mankind *needs* divine grace, without which he might never turn to goodness— unless, indeed, temporarily, under the influence of suffering.

These few stanzas remind the devotee not to depend on human power and intelligence alone. Ego-inspired activity, though seemingly justified by common sense, is doomed to disappointment at the end of every attempt and leads, in time, to disaster.

Yogananda explained in his Gita commentaries that in an ocean there sometimes appear areas of relative calmness, where the surface may even, for a time, appear as smooth as glass. Normally on the ocean's surface there is agitation, and, sometimes, great agitation.

Similarly, there are places on earth where sattwa guna (the elevating quality) is predominant; others, where rajoguna (the activating quality) is pronounced; and still others where tamoguna (the darkening quality) reigns supreme. Where sattwa guna is withdrawn or obscured, mankind sinks into ruin.

There are ages, called *yugas*, during which people are relatively enlightened; others when they are primarily active in promoting their own interests; and still others when spiritual darkness prevails, during which periods warfare, hatred, and violence are the norm.

There are also whole galaxies that manifest predominantly one of the three gunas, or qualities. This is a fascinating subject, and will be given the deeper treatment it deserves later on.

(3:25) O Descendent of Bharata (Arjuna), as foolish people act out of attachment to ego in hope of rewards, so should the wise also act (even if wisdom has lifted them out of any personal need to be active), with dispassion and non-attachment, in glad service to others as their guides (on the path to enlightenment).

(3:26) Never should the wise condemn the ignorant

for the ego-motivation they manifest. Instead, being themselves enlightened, they should seek only to inspire others in the direction of *preferring* to perform right, dutiful action.

The condemnation so often encountered in religious works does quite as much harm as good. The way to help people out of their ignorance is to inspire them with a longing for understanding. To scold them for their ignorance would be like scolding a blind man for his inability to see. Judgmental attitudes endanger also the persons who harbor them, for though the judgment may seem to proceed from wisdom, it is invariably tinged with an ego-inspired sense of superiority, which drags the "preacher" himself down into greater delusion.

One's thoughts are colored by whatever clothes he wears. If he wears the gray even of gentle criticism, his own thoughts also may take on a gray hue. If he wears the black of severe condemnation, his thoughts will themselves become darkened. And if he wears the cheerful colors of kindness, acceptance, and forgiveness, he will not only inspire others to be like him, but will also enhance those colors in himself.

(3:27) The universal impulse toward activity springs from the three gunas, or qualities of Nature. Man, however, deluded by egoism, thinks, "I am the doer."

The ego in man tells him, "This is my body." Yet the cells of his body change over the years again and again. "Which body," it may then be asked, "is the person, himself?"

Ego tells him, "These are my thoughts." Yet thoughts come to him unbidden, from who knows what source? Paramhansa Yogananda wrote, "Thoughts are universally and not individually rooted." The person with a darkened consciousness can, with right effort and right influence, develop a light consciousness. Which mindset, then, is truly his own? The characteristics we *manifest* only seem to be ours. The quality of those characteristics depends on the level of our own energy and consciousness in the spine.

To drive a dark mood out of the mind, for example, try this simple method: Focus your energy and attention strongly at the point between the eyebrows. The magnetism you generate there will lift you out of the fogs of gloom to a higher atmosphere, where peace, joy, and complete acceptance reign.

Again, if sex temptation assails you, bring the energy up from the lower chakras (especially from the *swadisthana*, or sacral) to the heart by breathing deeply a few times. Then sit still, as has been suggested above, and focus deeply on the Kutastha between the eyebrows.

(3:28) O Arjuna, he who understands how the gunas work in human nature, and who knows therefore that (even) what the senses perceive depends on their indwelling *power* of perception, withdraws his mind and removes his attachment to things at the very source of his perception.

When a person sees (let us say) something ugly, he might close his eyes and simply refuse to see it. On the other hand, he might withdraw mentally from the perception of it, and then deliberately project joy and a oneness of beauty onto everything around him. Thus, the ugliness will not affect him, for he will see it as a manifestation of Eternal Bliss, which, in the last analysis, underlies all things. He may even—as the great artist Leonardo da Vinci did when he beheld ugliness—gaze at it in a new way and see it as an aspect of the Divine Beauty.

I am not saying that one should be indifferent to ugliness, squalor, and evil when he encounters it. He should not allow anything, however, to disturb his inner peace. Even if he sees wrong in the world, and accepts it as a manifestation of *maya*, he can remain inwardly undisturbed by it, and can work impersonally to improve matters in this world. The practical point here is that if one is himself affected by squalor or evil, he will be far less able to improve anything than he will if he is able to remain inwardly attuned to the flow of God's joy.

Withdrawal of the power behind the senses enables one to influence for good whatever he perceives in the world, and to act always in a state of inner freedom.

(3:29) The man of perfect wisdom should not bewilder the ignorant with his higher perception of the nature of reality. (He should bear in mind that,) deluded as they are by the gunas, they have no choice but to act under that influence.

Again it should be emphasized that one can help others more by inspiring them than by scolding them. Sometimes, it is true, when people are too obtusely arrogant they may require a good shaking. Thus, even wise masters will sometimes declaim against delusions, if people have become too entrenched in them. Krishna advises persons of higher perception, however, never to let themselves be negatively affected by other people's ignorance.

(3:30) Offer to Me your every deed. Devoid of egotism and desire, inwardly centered in the soul, (ever) calm and free from worries, be dutifully engaged in the battle of life.

(3:31) True devotees, focused on practicing My precepts and (the true teachings of) others, achieve freedom from all karma.

(3:32) Those, however, who scoff at this teaching of Mine and refuse to practice it, deluded (by ego) as to the nature of wisdom, know such persons, in their rejection (due to ignorance), to be courting doom.

(3:33) Even the wise act according to the dictates of their own nature. All living beings obey the dictates of Nature. Of what avail would be mere suppression?

Krishna offered to the world, through the Bhagavad Gita, not only the highest truths, expressed comprehensively and at great length, but a teaching of supreme common sense. This thirty-third stanza is a beautiful example of the reasonableness of his teaching. The Lord says to Arjuna, "Work with things as they are." History—indeed, perhaps the history of religion, especially—is full of people trying to convince others to be something other than what they are. Wars have been fought, persecutions inflicted, and revolutions stirred up in the name of making people think and become what others think they ought to be. Krishna, in this passage, says, very reasonably, "Work with what is, not with what you think it ought to be."

All human suffering is due to the simple thought that things ought to be other than they are. Even great physical pain can be transcended, after accepting it as it is. Try this practice: First, calmly recognize its existence. Second, center yourself at the *heart* of that pain. Finally, simply release it! You will find that complete acceptance of it empowers you to do that relinquishing.

Don't let others tell you what you ought, in their eyes, to be. On the other hand, never dismiss their advice arrogantly. Try at the same time, rather, to be always true to your own nature. You will never change yourself by suppression. Real change comes only by transcendence. If there is some quality in yourself that you don't like, try to raise your awareness to a higher level. If you find that you simply can't ignore that pain, however, then try to get to the heart of it. When mentally you arrive at its very center, offer the pain up to God. If you practice this suggestion with a strong effort of will, you may find that you can become, in an instant, a very different person.

(3:34) Attraction and repulsion (regarding) sense objects belong to the natural ebb and flow of duality. Beware of them both equally, for they are man's greatest enemies!

Attraction and repulsion are extreme forms of likes and dislikes. To like anything excessively is, virtually by definition, just as great an error as to dislike its opposite. The realization of God depends on neutralizing all one's reactions, on leveling out their peaks and their valleys, and seeing the one, changeless Spirit at the heart of everything.

The secret is not to cease from enjoying anything: That "solution" leads only to apathy, and, in consequence, to a deadening of awareness. The secret, rather, is to take every enjoyment into the heart: to feel its *cause* as lying there, in your reactions; and then to draw that energy consciously upward in the spine, from the heart to the brain.

Ordinary likes and dislikes are not, as such, man's enemies. Rather, they are like troublesome neighbors. Extreme forms of these emotions, however—strong attraction, and violent repulsion—can plunge a person into violent storms of emotion that toss him helplessly about on great waves of delusion. Never let yourself become infatuated (infatuation is extreme attraction) with anything or anyone. Never let yourself hate anything or anyone. Develop an attitude, rather, of accepting this dream as it is, even if it becomes a nightmare! Your only hope is to escape to a higher level of consciousness.

Some people do have ugly traits. Don't waste energy in reacting to them, neither by dislike nor by abhorrence. Don't welcome them into your "galaxy" of interests. Move through life like a swan, rather, off of whose back the rain flows lightly, never touching its body.

Protect your heart's feelings from the excitement of all extreme reactions. Surround those feelings by emanating peace and good will. Relax in the heart. Relax also *outward* from the heart, to the shoulders. Then direct your the heart's energy upward through the spine to the brain. When there are people around you shouting angrily, for instance—and especially when they shout personally at you—relax inwardly; be centered in the Self; smile in your heart, and remind yourself, "I love God alone!"

(3:35) To do one's own duty, even unsuccessfully, is better than to do someone else's duty successfully. It is better to die while trying to accomplish one's own duty than to settle for another's duty (though safer and easier), which course is filled with danger and uncertainty.

The supreme duty of every man is, of course, to realize the one Self: God. One's own path to that realization, however, may be quite different from those of others, and from any that others urge upon him. If one hasn't a true guru to tell him what is his own best direction, he should follow that inner prompting which tells him, "This is my course to true freedom." Freedom from further involvement in *maya* is the highest criterion of virtue. People may mistakenly say, "But I feel more *joy* going in the direction of sense-satisfaction." Since they haven't yet experienced divine joy, they may easily be tricked by the mere excitement of sense pleasure. Others say, equally erroneously, "But when I see this woman, or that man, I feel overwhelming *love*. Surely that feeling *must* be right!" The result, as they proceed along the twisting thoroughfare between birth and death, often takes such enthusiasts very far from their first emotions of infatuation! Inner freedom is therefore the safest moral guideline. Ask yourself inwardly, "Will I feel *freedom* in this contemplated enjoyment? Will I feel *freedom* in this desired love?"

The next question, of course, is, "What will I feel free *from*?" Freedom from the pinch of desire is not freedom: It is merely momentary relief! One's feeling of freedom must be calm and inwardly expansive.

Even so, as Yogananda once exclaimed, "People are so skillful in their ignorance!" It is hardly safe for ordinary people to trust their own judgment too far. The supreme need for every sincere seeker is the guidance of a true guru.

For those who have no such blessing, and who have, perhaps, no deep hunger for God, how shall they recognize their highest duty? The only guideline that may serve them is to ask themselves, "Will it take me toward greater inner freedom, and a sense of having done what was *right* for me?"

(3:36) Arjuna said: O (Krishna), by what is one impelled, even against his will, to do wrong, as if (he were being) forced to do so?

Every man, surely, has experienced times when temptation of various sorts seems to be forcing him against his will to act in ways he knows he ought not to. Arjuna's question is universally understandable.

(3:37) Krishna replied: It is desire; it is anger, both of which are impelled by rajoguna. Know these to be mankind's greatest enemies.

The soul is drawn out of itself by attachment to the body, and by resultant ego-consciousness—by the sense of having a separate individuality. The consciousness of separateness gives rise to feelings of incompleteness. Thus, the gunas, which caused the soul to feel that sense of separation in the first place, become more active as rajoguna.

Fundamentally, it is the activating impulse which drives people to seek self-completion by doing and acquiring things outwardly. Desires come as a result, and because desires, once activated, can become infinite in number, no one is ever able to satisfy them all no matter how wealthy he is. The result of frustrated desire is anger. Thus it is that desire and anger travel the path of life together. Desire (the eagerness for fulfillment) is never perfectly confident, and is always accompanied to some extent, therefore, by the grim thought, "And if I don't get it . . . ?" Rising to the surface of consciousness, with this thought, is always the potential for anger.

These twins are mankind's "enemies" because they rob him of his peace of mind. Desiring things, he thinks, "I won't be completely happy until I have them." Following quickly in the wake of that thought is the agitated fear of possible frustration, anger, and the loss (rather than the gain) of happiness.

(3:38) As fire is obscured by smoke; as a mirror is covered by dust; as an embryo is enveloped by the womb, so is human understanding obscured by the three qualities.

The reference here is to the three gunas. Sattwa guna (illustrated by the first example) is easily blown away by a light puff of the "breeze" of meditation, even as the smoke concealing a fire is easily dispersed.

A dust-covered mirror may need a little "elbow grease" to clean it, but with that rubbing it can reflect things clearly once more. Rajoguna, therefore, expressed in the right way and with energy comparable to the power of the delusion, can be transformed without too much difficulty, that it reflect the pure image of Spirit.

The embryo, however, cannot emerge from its womb until its full time is completed. Even so, with the person in whom tamoguna is uppermost, no amount of teaching, and no self-effort will serve any purpose. Time must simply pass for nature to take its course, bringing that person gradually to the point where, after repeated disappointments and the dim glimmering of hope for greater understanding, the inner person finally emerges, born with the full dignity of refined humanity.

(3:39) O Son of Kunti (Arjuna)! the constant enemy of the wise are his unquenchable flames of inner desire.

(3:40) The senses, mind, and intellect are declared to be their stronghold. Desire, through these (three), deludes the embodied soul and eclipses its wisdom.

(3:41) Therefore, O Best of the Bharata Dynasty! begin by disciplining the senses (withdrawing your energy from them into the spine), then destroy desire (by casting it from your heart). Desire is the sinful destroyer of wisdom and of Self-realization.

(3:42) The senses are declared to be superior to the body (since they convey perception); the mind is superior to the senses (both inner and outer, since it is the perceiver); the discriminating intellect is superior to the mind (since it *understands* what it perceives); and the Self is superior to the discriminating intellect (since it *is* both perception and understanding).

(3:43) O Mighty-armed (Arjuna)! thus cognizing the (indwelling divine) Self as superior to intellectual understanding, discipline your lower self (the ego) by dwelling in the true Self, and (thereby) overcome the foe who, wearing the armor of desire, is ever difficult to conquer.

Thus ends the third chapter, called "Karma Yoga," of the Upanishad of the holy Bhagavad Gita, in the dialogue between Sri Krishna and Arjuna discussing yoga and the science of Self-realization.

CHAPTER SIXTEEN

THE SUPREME SCIENCE OF KNOWING GOD

(4:1,2) **The exalted Lord said to Arjuna: I gave this imperishable Yoga to Vivasvat (the sun-god); Vivasvat passed on the knowledge to Manu (the Hindu law-giver); Manu taught it to Ikshvaku (founder of the solar dynasty of the Kshatriyas). Thus, handed down in orderly succession, the Rajarishis (royal rishis, or sages) knew it. With the long passage of time, however, O Scorcher of Foes (Arjuna), this knowledge of Yoga has become greatly diminished on Earth.**

T HESE PASSAGES REFER TO THE GRADUAL LOSS of knowledge during a long cycle of descent in earthly time. When the Earth, gradually descending from a higher age of relative enlightenment, entered (in 700 B.C., according to Swami Sri Yukteswar's computation) the dark age of *Kali Yuga*, the majority of mankind lost most of its former power, mental clarity, and understanding. The golden age of wisdom (*Satya Yuga*), which was a time of divine brilliance in human understanding, gradually diminished to an age of discrimination (*Treta Yuga*); from there to an age of energy (*Dwapara Yuga*); and from that it descended to the lowest age, *Kali*, when the understanding of most men was centered in the thought of matter as real and substantial.

That cycle, in our own time, and since that time when the Bhagavad Gita was written, has begun its upward swing again. It was in the year 500 A.D. that the earth entered an ascending Kali Yuga. In 1700, it entered ascending Dwapara Yuga. For the past three hundred years, man has been coming increasingly to understand that matter is really a vibration of energy. Electricity was rediscovered in the early nineteenth century, and now, in the twenty-first century, humanity is becoming dependent once again on a view of reality that sees energy as fundamental to all its functioning.

When *Dwapara* descended to Kali Yuga, the science of yoga, the essence of which is based on an understanding of the subtle energies in the body, was lost. General understanding of this science degenerated to a definition of yoga as *Hatha Yoga*: mere physical positions and breathing exercises. Hatha Yoga in fact developed out of the third "limb," or stage, of Patanjali's exposition on the stages of enlightenment, which people mistakenly call his "*Ashtanga Yoga* system." It is not a "system," for what he did in fact was systematize the universal stages through which the spiritual seeker, whatever his religion, must pass. Those stages entail a gradual withdrawal of energy and attention from the outer body to the spine; raising the energy in the spine; and the gradual absorption of one's energy and consciousness in the love and bliss of God until the absorption becomes total.

The third of these stages is *asana*, or perfect stillness of body, with an erect position and a straight spine. Patanjali, to reiterate what we've said, was describing the *stages* of withdrawal and absorption, and not specific yoga practices. The Hatha Yoga system was based on his third stage, and was intended to help yoga practitioners to achieve calmness of body and mind, physical and mental relaxation, and centering the energy in the spine.

That highest yoga was revived again by Lahiri Mahasaya of Varanasi, who received it from the great avatar Babaji in the Himalayas, giving it the name, Kriya Yoga. The Himalayan masters had perceived that it was time, in this re-ascending yuga, to resurrect the formerly held, deeper perception of man's inner nature. Paramhansa Yogananda, an outstanding exemplar of this teaching, was sent to the West to carry this ancient science to all mankind. After Swami Vivekananda, who may be described as having "broken the ice," Yogananda may be described as having taught people how to swim.

Dharma, during Satya Yuga, has been described as four-legged; during *Treta*, as having three legs; during *Dwapara*, as having two; and during *Kali*, as functioning on only one leg. During Kali Yuga, in other words, dharma is still able to stand, but only precariously. Man can enjoy (though with less energy, and therefore only relatively) his pleasures of the moment, but he cannot connect them to their inevitable consequences: for example, a depletion of energy and premature old age from sexual overindulgence; a serious, permanent loss of mental clarity from overindulgence in alcoholic drink; a steady increase of selfishness and self-indulgence (these being, simply, diseases of the ego) and an excessive attachment to wealth. During Kali Yuga, it is difficult for man to perceive that every state of consciousness already contains its opposite: that, in happiness, suffering is already present; and that (fortunately) suffering already contains at its center the seeds of joy.

Thus, in these two stanzas we see hope also in the opposite reality: there exist also, in the gradual loss described by Krishna, the seeds of future renewal and gain.

(4:3) Today I have taught you, My devotee and friend, that ancient science of Yoga, the secret to the highest blessings for mankind.

It is a thought wondrous to contemplate: As the devotee advances spiritually, he is accepted by the Lord Himself not only as a devotee, but as a friend. The relationship with God as Friend is in some ways the sweetest. For even the thought of God as Mother, which many consider the sweetest of all relationships, carries a hint of human presumption that God *must* take care of us, and pardon all our sins. As Yogananda taught people to pray, "Mother, naughty or good I am Thy child: Thou *must* release me!" When one is advanced enough, however, to think of God as Friend, there steals into the heart that sweet confidence by

which one feels, "But *of course* You love me! I am
Yours; You are mine. How could either of us ever turn
away from the other? We are one!"

The very science of yoga should be taught and
practiced with love, and not as an invitation to ego-
boosting power. Love and devotion help the seeker to
grasp the true essence of Yoga, which unlocks the inner
door to the highest blessings that can be known.

**(4:4) Arjuna said: Vivasvat lived in far-off antiquity.
You, however, were born recently. How am I to take
this statement that it was You who first taught this
sacred Yoga to mankind?**

Arjuna invited Krishna—for the sake of all devotees—
to announce his former incarnations on Earth: many
times, for human salvation.

Did Krishna really teach the yoga science from Earth's
earliest beginnings? How long has man been plowing
earthly fields, raising cities, worshiping in lofty tem-
ples—all the time seeking the key to happiness, which
only a few in every age are able to find as Perfect Bliss?

Mahavatar Babaji announced to his disciple Lahiri
Mahasaya that he himself was Krishna in a former earth
incarnation. My Guru told me that Lahiri Mahasaya
was Raja Janaka, of *Ramayana* fame. Paramhansa
Yogananda said that he himself was Arjuna, to whom
Krishna, in that life, delivered this most famous of all
discourses, the Bhagavad Gita.

I myself have come to feel, in years of editing
Yogananda's writings, that our entire line of gurus—

Babaji, Lahiri Mahasaya, Swami Sri Yukteswar, and Paramhansa Yogananda—have come back again and again for countless aeons—and perhaps even from the beginning of human history—as saviors of mankind. No doubt there are other lines of great masters also who, in their compassion for humanity in its suffering and confusion, have returned again and again to this planet.

I once asked my Guru, "Have I been your disciple for thousands of years?" He replied, "It has been a long time. That's all I'll say."

"Does it always take such a long time?" I asked (I wanted to be reassured that I wasn't the only laggard!).

"Yes," was his reply. "Desires for name, fame, and so on take them away again and again."

How long has mankind inhabited this planet? Not the few thousand years claimed by modern tradition. My Guru once stated that the time span of human history covers over fifty million years!

(4:5) The Blessed Lord said, Many have been My births, and many also yours. I remember all of Mine, though you remember yours not.

Had Arjuna actually forgotten his former incarnations? I doubt it! In the Bhagavad Gita he plays the role of earnest seeker. It is clear to me, however, that he was already a free soul. It is said that even during his lifetime with Krishna, they had been together long before, and had been, respectively, the ancient sages Nara and Narayan.

A story was told about Nara: One day *Maya* (Satan) tried to tempt him by materializing a supernally beautiful woman. As she stood alluringly before him, he gazed calmly at her, then materialized another hundred women, each one as beautiful as the first. What could Satan do? He had to give up!

(4:6) Though I (a fully liberated soul) am the Lord of all creation, and am in My true Self—and abiding (ever) in My Cosmic Nature—forever unborn, yet I, by My *yoga-maya*, assume (from time to time) an outward form.

(4:7,8) O Bharata (Arjuna)! whenever virtue (dharma) declines, and vice (*adharma*) is in the ascendant, I incarnate Myself on earth (as an avatar). Appearing from age to age in visible form, I come to destroy evil and to re-establish virtue.

There is a belief in India that the word avatar applies only to certain souls. Rama and Krishna are believed to have been avatars of Vishnu. According to legend, Kalki avatar is supposed to be Vishnu's next incarnation. I explained earlier that avatar really has a much broader meaning. It might help here to review these teachings of Sanaatan Dharma (the eternal religion).

Vishnu, to begin with, is not literally a person, but is that aspect of AUM which acts as Preserver. No master can be an avatar of Vishnu except insofar as he manifests God in the aspect of the Preserver of dharma.

My Guru once replied to me in response to a doubt I had voiced. "When you are one with God," he said, "you *are* God." There is no higher state than oneness with God.

Some religious believers insist that this saint or that one never incarnated on earth before, or that he or she was always perfect even if he (or she) did live on earth before. These are pious myths, and have no foundation in truth. It is true that even a master may sometimes make the statement, "I have not lived before." His words must be understood correctly.

Krishna states here that he was never born, but then he goes on to say that he has appeared repeatedly on Earth. It is similarly legitimate for anyone who has transcended ego-consciousness to claim he has never been born before, for he sees clearly that it was only God, always, who appeared, through him.

Christians claim that Jesus Christ is the only Son of God. Yogananda said, "Jesus could legitimately say that, because he had attained oneness with the Christ consciousness, which is the only reflection of the Spirit beyond creation and is therefore omnipresent in creation. Any soul that realizes its oneness with that Christ consciousness (the Kutastha Chaitanya) may rightfully be considered, in the same way, one with the only Son of God. He cannot, however, be less the Son of God than Jesus Christ was."

Hindus, similarly, think of Krishna as a *special* manifestation of God. Yogananda explained that it is simply not the divine way to create one special manifestation of Himself and label it as unique, whether as "God" Himself or as "the Son of God."

Think of the vastness of the universe! A hundred billion galaxies, each with an equivalent number of stars, and many of those stars, at least, supporting populated planets. (Hindu tradition states, and Yogananda fully endorsed, that the universe is *filled with living*, conscious beings. So-called UFOs, he told us, are simply matters of fact.)

Then think of this little mud ball, our Earth: It is not 4,000 years old, as Christian church tradition once averred, but very, *very* old. Think of the human race also as very old—possibly millions of years old. And think of God, then, as having *one* special son, or as becoming one special manifestation of Himself, or even as becoming a limited succession of manifestations. God is *Infinite* Consciousness. Only Kali Yuga consciousness could have visualized Him as uniquely possessing a human form—as people believed the Earth was the center of everything, and still believed as late as the end of the nineteenth century that our sun was the center.

Once every soul encased in an ego realizes itself as the Infinite Self, and not that little "sliver of glass" which seemed so individual in its reflection of the infinite light, it *becomes* the Infinite—indeed, one with God Himself. There is no difference, *in essence*, between Krishna, Jesus Christ, Buddha, or any other great master. There is no difference—again, *in essence*—between them and Everyman, once Everyman realizes himself as the one God who, for a time, thought himself encased in a human ego. *All is God.* In God, all comparisons and relativities cease. The soul of Everyman was never born; nor did it ever die. In Vedantic truth there was always only one reality, one Spirit: the Supreme Lord.

Thus, any soul that has achieved complete liberation, not only from present ego but also from the memory of all past egoic involvement, *becomes* that Supreme Spirit. Most souls, after many incarnations of struggling to reach that state, are satisfied to remain in blissful oneness with God for eternity. A few only, out of compassion for mankind, preserve that single little "desireless desire" which brings them back to earth as avatars for the salvation of many. No avatar, however, in ultimate Reality, can be greater than any other.

What would be the sense in God's creating a perfect being as an example to ordinary human beings, who are struggling to attain perfection? It would be like saying, "You yourselves (poor fools!) can never be perfect, but do try, anyway!" No avatar was ever *created* perfect. All of them were once like us, imperfect human beings who were finally washed clean in the realization of their own divinity. Orthodox religionists call this concept impious, but no master ever came to earth to show people how great *he* was. All of them came to show us *our own divine potential*. Jesus Christ is quoted, in the Book of Revelation, as saying, "Him that overcometh will I make a pillar in the temple of my God, and he shall go no more out. . . . To him that overcometh will I grant to sit with me in my throne, *even as I also overcame*, and am set down with my Father in his throne." (Rev. 3:12,21; italics added)

In this world of relativities, however, greatness is gauged in other ways. Thus, it is humanly acceptable to consider one master greater than another, or than many others, not by the standard of his *inner* greatness (his oneness with the Infinite, which is the same for all), but by the outer standard of the good he has done in the world.

My own Guru had a worldwide mission. In worldly terms, he was a very great master. I met another master, however, who (as my Guru himself told me) had achieved full liberation. This master had very few disciples, and was virtually unknown in the world. I asked this master why he didn't do more for mankind. He replied with beautiful simplicity, "I have done what God wanted done through this body." From a world-renowned master to one who was known by very few: the world would say the one was a world wonder, and the other a non-entity. In God's eyes, however—the one Unbribable Judge, whose only standard is truth itself—both men were not only completely equal, but were *one*! Indeed, they shouldn't even be considered human beings! They were the ever-blissful Brahman Himself.

These stanzas of the Gita are often translated personally in another way also, to mean that God destroys *evil-doers*. God never destroys anyone! The only thing He destroys—the only thing He *can* destroy, since He cannot destroy Himself—is evil itself, but never the evil-doer.

(4:9) He, O Arjuna! who by intuition comprehends the truth of My divine manifestations and selfless deeds in this vibratory universe, will never again, after he leaves his body (at death), need to incarnate in outward (egoic) form. (Soaring in freedom,) He will attain Me.

The terms, "ego," and "freedom," stand in mutual contradistinction to one another. Ego is endlessly constricting to the soul, for it insists on identifying itself merely with petty expressions of its infinite potential.

The delusive freedom to "do as one likes" is endlessly self-demeaning, for it keeps one identified with his little body, whereas one's own nature calls out in longing, "Let me soar high above the conflicting ripples of likes and dislikes. Let me rise in the endless skies of the joy of my own Being!"

To know the ways of God is to identify with those ways, rejoicing in them as *our* ways.

(4:10) Purified by ascetic wisdom, released from attachment, fear, and anger, and completely absorbed in Me, many have attained (oneness with) Me.

"Many have attained Me." Truth seekers must understand that finding God is not like the supreme effort required, say, to climb Mount Everest, the accomplishment of which is more arduous (if not life-threatening) at the end than at the beginning. Finding God is the simplest, most obvious, and most supremely natural thing to do in the world! At the end, one doesn't find himself straining with desperate, heroic zeal to merge in Him. Rather, one *relaxes*, supremely, into perfect Bliss. Strain, tension, ardor, heroic zeal: these end forever for the soul. What is left is Satchidananda: ever-existing, ever-conscious, ever-*new* Bliss.

(4:11) O Partha (Arjuna)! In whatever way I am approached, in that way do I respond. All men, by whatever path, come to Me.

(4:12) Those who work to fulfill their earthly desires worship the gods (which are ideals in various forms;

they are not idols!), aware that success of this kind can be reached with relative ease.

Lower aims are achieved more quickly and easily than supreme devotion to God. To build a house, one consults an architect and a builder (lower gods, in a sense); one doesn't confine himself to his meditation room and offer up prayers to God for a house! If one thinks to achieve perfect happiness in an ideal home, however, he will eventually be disillusioned. Boredom will set in, termites will invade and destroy the building. Or else, neighbors will be alienated out of envy. *Nothing* works for long in this world. When disillusionment ensues, people turn away to seek their fulfillment elsewhere. This is a round-about way to God, but it, too, reaches toward Him at least, inasmuch as repeated disappointments do, eventually, turn one to Him.

Thus, even though material fulfillment, sought in material ways or in ego-inspired appeals to some lower "god," can bring relatively speedy results, those results are like cement walls built with too much sand and too little bonding cement: they soon crumble to nothing.

(4:13) An admixture of the three gunas (the essential qualities) with the diverse karmas of individuals produces the four castes. Though I am active in creation through these influences, know that I (in My Self) am ever actionless and unchanging.

We have already discussed the gunas (qualities) and the caste system. The additional teaching, here, is the great truth that action itself is an illusion. God "acts, but doesn't act," for everything is a dream. A dreamer may do many things—swim, climb mountains, go to war— yet, on waking, he sees that his body never stirred from his bed.

As Paramhansa Yogananda explained (this point, too, was touched on earlier), the motionless consciousness of Absolute Spirit is *reflected* at the heart of every atom. At the heart of all movement, there is rest.

(4:14) Though acting, I am without attachment; nor do I desire any particular outcome from activity. He, similarly, who is one with Me, and identified with My nature, is unfettered by (the slightest) desire for the fruits of action.

(4:15) Understanding this (the nature of right action), the wise since earliest times have acted dutifully. Be like them (acting without desire for the fruits of action).

(4:16) What, indeed, are action and inaction? Even the wise (can become) confused on this point. I will explain the distinction, (armed with which knowledge) you will be freed from all evil.

The "wise," here, are those who have not yet attained the highest state of *nirbikalpa samadhi*. Actions performed with full divine awareness will always be dutiful. With the wisdom achieved even in *sabikalpa samadhi*, however, from which one is still obliged to return to outward awareness, the ego can still hold the thought, "I am the doer." In this simple thought lie the seeds of all evil, dormant, but waiting.

(4:17) The nature of action is difficult to know. To understand it, know the difference between right action, wrong action, and inaction.

One can act with great energy, working himself to exhaustion, and yet accomplish nothing: for example, by pushing strenuously on both sides of a door. Right action, spiritually speaking, is action with that attitude which leads to soul-freedom. That attitude includes non-attachment to the fruits of action, and acting with the consciousness that God is acting through one. Action that is inspired by His consciousness and energy, with the results given to Him without any ego-involvement, is right action.

Right action is not necessarily that which other people consider right because it pleases *them*. It can be *relatively* right, however, if it is self-improving (either physically, emotionally, or mentally): for example, wholesome physical exercise; efforts to develop concentration and will power; to acquire clarity of thought; to develop calm upliftment and expansion of feeling. All these are right action, for they help to "prepare the troops" for the great "war of Kurukshetra."

Wrong action is anything that nourishes the ego, whether by contracting it in selfishness or by inflating it with pride. Clearly, in the relativity of things, there can be a mixture of right and wrong action. Developing one's physical strength, for example, can help (as Yogananda put it) to prepare the body and make it fit for God-realization. If, however, the mind has not been prepared also by right understanding, one may become proud of his physical strength. In this case, right action can be diminished in its good effects, or even nullified, by wrong action.

Most activity in this world consists, in one way or another, of a mixture. Therefore, spiritual development, which ought to be simple, usually becomes complex and difficult. An invading army may make great inroads into enemy territory on one or more fronts, but may find itself beaten back on other fronts. Getting all of one's forces aligned in the war against evil requires consummate generalship.

Inaction, as we have seen already, is impossible. It can *seem* inactive, however, like that example of two equal forces pushing on both sides of a door without ever moving it. Thus, one may exercise physically and strengthen the muscles, but eat wrongly and thus, in other ways, weaken his body. As with right action, true inaction is possible in God alone, in the perfect relaxation of rest in ecstasy.

The secret, essentially, is quite simple: Since the goal of spiritual evolution is to sublimate the ego by self-expansion to Cosmic consciousness, that which assists one in the direction of ego-sublimation is right action. And anything that affirms the ego or that blocks any effort to sublimate it is wrong action. And that which saps, or which otherwise dulls any effort at ego-sublimation, is inaction.

(4:18) He is a yogi of true discernment who sees inaction in action, and action in inaction. He is wise among human beings, for he has attained the goal of (all) action (and is free).

(4:19) He who never acts with the motivation of personal desire, whose (ego-binding) karma has been burned up in the fire of wisdom: such a one (alone) may be considered wise.

(4:20) The wise, having relinquished attachment to the fruits of action, (being) ever contented and free (in the Self), do not (really) act even if they appear to be intensely busy.

(4:21) Even in doing physical labor (as opposed to meditative work) one incurs no (karmic limitation) who has renounced all sense of possession, who is without personal desires, and whose feelings (chitta) are under control of the inner Self.

Performing good actions even with a wrong motive, my Guru used to say, is better than performing no action at all. Everything in this world being relative, all action must be adjudged good or evil according to the *direction* it takes one. What is good for one person might be bad for another.

Were a Mahatma Gandhi or a Jesus Christ to awaken one morning with the resolution, "I'm tired of serving humanity. From now on I want to work hard and become a millionaire!" wouldn't everyone, including the grossest materialist, exclaim, "That man has fallen!"? But were a lazy lout, on the other hand, to rouse himself one morning from his bed of inactivity and express the same resolution, wouldn't everybody—even saints—say that his intentions were right and good? It is all a question of where one comes from, and where one is going.

Digging a ditch—mere physical labor, in other words—can be either good, bad, or self-stultifying depending on one's attitude while he works. Two people can be working side by side at the same job, yet one of them may be motivated by ego-inspired fears or desires, and the other may have no other motivation than to please God. The one acts in ego-bondage; the other, in spiritual freedom.

(4:22) He is free from karmic involvement who is contented with whatever comes to him uninvited; who is even-minded and untouched by duality; who is without envy, jealousy, and animosity; and who (finally) views success and failure with equanimity.

Though we have dealt with this subject before, it might be well to consider once again, briefly, its opposite case: one who allows himself to be upset by the unexpected; who is always jumping with joy or bowed down with disappointment; who is full of envy, jealousy, and hatred; and one, finally, who rejoices gleefully in success and is emotionally devastated by failure. Are such people ever blessed with peace of mind? For one who has no inner peace, as Krishna stated earlier, how is happiness possible? What passes in worldly minds for happiness is usually nothing but emotional excitement, or (sometimes) a temporary release from some cause for agitation or suffering. Excitement leads to fear, doubt, and uncertainty. Temporary release from excitement leads, not to contentment, but to eventual boredom and apathy.

It is interesting to notice how automatically people reveal, by their gestures, the way the energy is flowing in their bodies. See, when they are excited, how they jump up and down. It is because of the upward movement in the *iḍa naḍi* in the spine. And see also how little children, who are the least inclined to control their outward displays of emotion, may indicate a downward movement of energy in the spine, through *pingala naḍi,* by flinging their arms downward, stooping, repeatedly stamping their feet, and exhaling repeatedly with loud cries—even rolling on the ground and pounding their fists: all such downward gestures indicating the downward direction of their energy.

Contentment itself is a virtue, and not merely a consequence. It should be practiced consciously. One should tell himself, "I need nothing! I need no one. In my Self I am free!"

(4:23) All the effects of karma (action) are nullified (in oneself), and one achieves liberation, when ego-attachment ceases, when one becomes centered in wisdom, and when all one's actions are offered up (in sacrifice) to the Infinite.

(4:24) For such a person, (both) the act of self-offering and the offering itself are, equally, aspects of the one Spirit. The fire (of wisdom) and the person making the offering are both Spirit. In this realization, the yogi, freed from ego-identification, goes straight to Brahman (Spirit).

Any karma (action) performed has consequences—no less so in the case of a liberated master than of the worldly person. The difference is that, since the actions of a master are not performed with ego-identification, the effects of that action are not bound to ego, and flow out freely into the world, bringing only beneficial results. Their objective rewards are reaped by those who are in tune with them and accept them lovingly.

It is important for people, when they perform any religious ritual, to understand the hidden purpose of ritual itself. If it is truly religious in nature, it serves the symbolic purpose of offering the ego up into a higher reality. Even a simple bow is a gesture of self-offering. The ego, which is physically centered in the medulla oblongata (at the base of the brain), becomes relaxed at that point when one bows, and is offered forward. (At least, such is the intention.) Properly, that offering should be made to the spiritual eye in the forehead (the positive pole of the medulla). People generally, however, consider their bows as outward gestures: to something, or to someone, before them. *Arati* (a ceremony of waving light before an altar) is a symbolic offering of one's own light and energy up to God. *Puja* is performed by offering all the five senses, signifying ego-consciousness, up to God's representation on the altar. Yagya offers *ghee* (purified butter) and rice into the sacrificial fire—again, to symbolize various aspects of self-offering.

The Christian Eucharist, too, represents a commemoration of the Last Supper, and the worshiper's gratitude for what Jesus Christ brought to mankind. This ceremony is traditionally followed by receiving bread and wine, symbolic of the blessings brought to mankind by Jesus.

Hindu ritual is followed by the offering of *prasad*, to indicate—again, symbolically—the receiving of God's grace. Arati, too, is ended by the light being taken around to everyone, that all may receive God's light symbolically into themselves.

The entire spiritual path consists of offering up the ego to God for purification, and of receiving His grace (*kripa*) in return. Only thus can one eventually attain oneness with Him.

Religious rituals should be performed with both interiorized *consciousness* and devotion—not absent-mindedly, with mumbled words and vague gestures. The more whole-heartedly one can immerse himself in the *feeling* as well as the *meaning* of the ritual he performs, the more he will absorb divine inspiration into himself, until his very life becomes a ritual of self-offering, or yagya, to God.

The subsequent stanzas of the Bhagavad Gita all concern themselves with the various types of rituals that are performed by different spiritual aspirants.

(4:25) Some yogis there are who make sacrifices to the devas (deities); others see sacrifice (yagya) as an offering of the self into the cosmic fire of Spirit.

Most people find it difficult to love God as an abstraction. He is pure consciousness, but they find it easier to endow Him with a form that represents whatever divine aspect or quality most attracts them. God is beyond all forms, and is supremely impersonal. At the same time, God has also taken on every form in the universe. He is impersonal in that He wants nothing for Himself, but in each of us He has become personal by encasing His consciousness in our forms. He loves us individually, on our own level of understanding. Thus, He suffers in (and for) those who suffer. Yet in Himself He is ever in Bliss. He rejoices in our earthly joys, yet in Himself is not identified with them. The case is similar to a mother and her children. When they weep, she feels their pain. At the same time, however, she feels no pain in her own self.

Many people imagine that true sympathy for others means to suffer *with* them. True sympathy should, however, be *useful*. If someone were drowning, would it help him to jump into the water and drown with him? Obviously not! One can be of far more *use* to him by standing on dry land and throwing him a rope. Alternatively, if one wants to help him more closely, he'd better be sure of being a strong enough swimmer, himself. Truly to help someone who is suffering means to give him the kind of comfort he can accept: joy, above all, and kindness, calm understanding (from a higher point of wisdom than his own confusion and pain)— but, again, to express these feelings outwardly only if the sufferer is ready to receive them.

God is impersonal. With mankind, however, He is also very personal—closer to us than our very thoughts. The reason He doesn't respond every time we call Him is, as my Guru put it, "He knows most people only want to argue with Him!"

Thus, to visualize perfect love, for example, in a form which the human mind can comprehend may mean to worship "Him" as the Divine Mother, or as one's Ideal Beloved, or as one's Perfect Friend. Whatever quality most attracts the heart's devotion can be mentally clothed in a form that, for the individual worshiper, epitomizes or expresses that quality.

The deeper one goes in devotion, especially after receiving some answer in his heart from God, the more whatever form he has visualized fades into formlessness, as the state of consciousness behind what one has been visualizing is gradually perceived to be the Reality above form.

Paramhansa Yogananda gave further advice on this subject: "Whenever God comes to you in form—as, let us say, the Divine Mother—try to see in those eyes, not a human personality, but the consciousness of infinity."

The fact that Krishna in this stanza refers to yogis, and not to ordinary devotees, suggests that he is speaking of the various forms in which sincere seekers worship the Supreme Lord. He would not describe yogis, whose goal is union with God, as worshiping astral gods, to whom ordinary people appeal primarily for ego-gratifying boons.

There is also a deeper meaning in this passage. In yoga practice, the meditator offers his Kundalini up to the "*devas*," or "powers," residing in the chakras, that all his energy may flow up the spine toward unity with God in the *sahasrara* (thousand-rayed "Lotus") at the top of the head.

(4:26) Other spiritual seekers offer their inner power of hearing and of their other senses into the fire of

self-control. Still others offer whatever they hear or experience through the senses into the fire of higher understanding.

More is involved, it must be said, in offering the ego into the fire of Cosmic consciousness than the mere *thought* of doing so—even as more is involved in "conquering" a mountain than simply leaping to the top. This stanza and several more that follow cover this subject in a variety of ways. Each one is a means of offering up the ego into superconscious expansion.

(4:27) Others, by discrimination, offer up their sense activities, and the energy within those activities, in the fires of self-control. (They ask themselves, "Who is seeing? Who is hearing? Whose energy is activating me to experience these sensations?")

This method of offering ego-consciousness up to cosmic expansion comes down to the question, finally, "Who am I?" First one asks, "Who is this that is eating?" "Who walks, when my body walks?" "Who, really, is breathing?" "Who thinks?" "Who is reacting with positive or negative feelings?" "Who is asking these questions?"

And finally, again, "Who am I?"

This is the approach of Gyana Yoga (the path of discrimination), but it is one that everyone should include in his sadhana (spiritual practice). Watch yourself eating, walking, breathing, conversing, thinking. Stand mentally aside from your own body and mind. Become the silent observer of your own self. Gradually you will feel inwardly detached, and will accept that you are another reality entirely: the divine soul merely dreaming everything that happens outside of it.

(4:28) Some offer up their possessions as oblations; some, their actions; others concentrate on withdrawing their energy by yoga meditation (offering it up as an oblation); and still others, holding strictly to a vow of self-restraint, offer up all their thoughts to God, practice introspection, and seek wisdom through study of the scriptures.

(4:29) One practice of yoga offers the incoming breath (*prana*) into the outgoing breath (*apana*), and the apana into the prana, thereby, through *pranayama* (control of the energy), rendering the breath unnecessary.

The physical breath, as we saw earlier, accompanies the upward and downward flow of energy through the *ida* and *pingala nadis* in the spine. Indeed, it is this spinal flow of the energies known as prana and apana which prompts the lungs to inhale and exhale. Actually, prana also, more broadly speaking, means energy itself. Prana is *Paraprakriti* (as opposed to *Aparaprakriti*, Nature); it is immanent as opposed to overt Nature: the hidden reality behind the whole material universe.

The slow, careful, conscious circulation of energy around the spine constitutes the ancient science known (since the time of Lahiri Mahasaya in the nineteenth century) as Kriya Yoga. This circulation magnetizes the spine, and redirects the mental tendencies, called *samskaras*, toward the brain in a way interestingly reminiscent of the realigning of molecules in a north-south direction in a bar of steel. Similar to the bar magnet, the spine becomes magnetized in the sense that the energy, flowing ever more unidirectionally toward the brain, is drawn into the deep spine, the *sushumna*, where, with the awakening of the Kundalini, it rises through the chakras, lifting all one's energy and consciousness upward, toward God. Thus, the energy is brought to the spiritual eye, finally to become united with *sahasrara* (the "thousand-petaled" lotus) at the top of the head. That this yoga was taught not only in recent times (in the late eighteen hundreds) but anciently is evidenced by this stanza, and also by a later one, in Chapter 5 of the Gita (5:27,28), where Krishna describes the need for neutralizing the currents of prana and apana.

Sincere aspirants often wonder, "If Kriya Yoga is such an exalted science, why has it not been published in book form, so that all might learn it?" A reasonable question, certainly. The masters themselves, however, have said it should not be published precisely *because* it is a teaching that transcends reason itself. Right understanding of it depends on the unfolding intuition.

Kriya Yoga, in order to be wholly effective, must be received not only intellectually (in written or spoken form), but *vibrationally*, in the form of initiation. A magnet is created either by electrical realignment of the molecules, or by close proximity to another magnet. Attunement with a God-awakened guru influences the *samskaras* (comparable to the material molecules) to flow upward to the brain.

We are dealing here with a reality subtler, and much more difficult to master, than mere metallic molecules. Without an experienced guide, even mountain climbing can be fatal—though death, in this case, only ends a single incarnation. Spiritual mistakes can be costlier in terms of long-range suffering.

Guidance from the guru is not only helpful: It is essential. This does not mean that Kriya Yoga is dangerous. Far from it. But to take up Kriya Yoga signifies entering seriously onto the path to God. It is not a game, and should certainly be treated as a lifetime commitment. To treat it lightly is certainly, we should add, not the best of karma. Kriya Yoga initiation was formerly given only to *sannyasis* (renunciates) whose lives were already vowed to the divine search. This restriction was lifted by Babaji, when he gave this sacred initiation to Lahiri Mahasaya. The inward reason for his relaxing the ancient proscriptions was that the earth had already entered into a new age, Dwapara Yuga, when mankind was becoming more conscious of energy. Humanity as a whole was becoming more receptive to a teaching that focused on the body's energy. Nevertheless, any yoga initiation, and especially into the ancient science of Kriya Yoga, should be looked upon as a very sacred step in one's life.

Spiritual progress without the help of a true, or *Sat*, guru, cannot but be slow, haphazard, uncertain, and sometimes dangerous. The ancient tradition in India, where spirituality has been studied for thousands of years—not as a religion, but as a practical science ("practical" in the sense of results actually accomplished)—has always insisted that a true guru is the *sine qua non* for success on the spiritual path. Many spiritually ignorant people, even in India, insist that with literacy as widespread as it is now, and with books so easily available, spiritual teachings are accessible to virtually everyone and a guru is no longer needed. Truly, widespread literacy has had one unfortunate effect: the dissemination, not only of knowledge, but of ignorance!

True understanding comes not by intellectual reasoning, but by intuition. Inner, intuitive attunement with the consciousness of the guru is what most surely and directly brings spiritual awakening.

Has not everybody experienced, in the presence of certain people, a greater feeling of peace, harmony, and upliftment? If relatively ordinary people can affect one in this way, how much greater must be the effect of one who is, himself, spiritually enlightened!

In the Christian New Testament it is written, of Jesus Christ, "As many as received him, to them gave he power to become the sons of God." That is exactly what everyone needs: the *power* to rise! Such power cannot be self-generated. The ego, as we saw earlier, is already infected with the very disease (ignorance) it wants to banish from its consciousness. Only one who has himself escaped the clutches of ego-consciousness can, with his expanded consciousness, infuse into the disciple's awareness new insight, new understanding, and new *power* to rise spiritually.

Were such a sacred science as Kriya Yoga to be shouted from the housetops (as Ramanuja shouted the sacred mantra, "AUM *namo Narayana!*" from the roof of a temple) it would lack an essential ingredient of success. In all Indian tradition, initiation into the spiritual "mysteries" by a true guru is considered more important than the teachings themselves. Ramanuja's love and compassion for mankind notwithstanding, his guru had been right when he enjoined secrecy on him. Perhaps Ramanuja had the spiritual power thus to initiate so many, as Sri Chaitanya, centuries later, inspired thousands with *mahamantra (Haré Krishna, haré Krishna! Krishna, Krishna haré, haré! Haré Rama, haré Rama! Rama, Rama haré, haré!).* In Chaitanya's presence, indeed, thousands were inspired, as by no means all are who chant that mantra in the streets, exuberantly, in modern times. The tradition is that *mantra diksha*, or initiation into a mantra, should be spoken into the *right* ear, and conveyed, not only uttered, with spiritual power.

Kriya Yoga *diksha* is much subtler than *mantra diksha*. It involves not only that which can be spoken with the tongue or uttered mentally, but involves also an *awareness* in the spine, which must come from inside. This is why attunement with the guru is so essential, particularly with Kriya practice. One should invite the guru's consciousness to awaken one's own energy within the spine. This can be accomplished only by mental, intuitive attunement with the guru: by *receiving him*, as it says in the Bible, deeply into oneself.

How can one attune himself with the guru? One method is to gaze deeply into his eyes—a mere photograph will do—and, visualizing him at the point between the eyebrows, to call to him deeply, "Introduce me to

God!" Then listen, or feel, in the heart. The heart is the "radio station" in the body, where the divine presence is received, and where the guru's blessings and power are intuitively perceived.

Can this blessing be received from a distance? Can it be received after the guru has left the physical plane? The answer—as my Guru himself told me in specific terms—is that one needs at least one physical contact with him. That contact can be transmitted through a direct line of disciples of a true guru. If he is a world savior, like Yogananda, it is both right and fitting that those who come after him give initiation *in his name*. Thus, subsequent generations of disciples will always refer back to the supreme power of that savior (an avatar) for their ultimate blessing.

Students who have claimed discipleship to a great master, without having had at least one outer contact, show by their very auras that they have not received the same blessing in their lives as those who have honored this timeless principle.

What should one do, when he feels the guru's vibrational presence in his heart? He should release it from mental identification with the guru's physical form, and feel it radiating outward from his heart as love and bliss, until it fills the whole body. The disciple should then try to expand those blessings outward until he feels his consciousness infused by the guru. Thus, he should expand outward beyond the limited, physical identity of the ego.

The reason *mantra diksha* (initiation) is traditionally given in the right ear is partly because that is the positive side of the body. There is a special correlation, also, between the *inner* right ear and superconscious experience. Listening there helps to attune one with the highest mantra of all, AUM, the vibrational sound of the universe, or, "music of the spheres."

Listening to the sound of AUM in the right ear, one should try to extend that sound to the left ear—then, as I said earlier, to the whole body. As one *receives* AUM into his whole being, he *receives* also the guru's inner blessings and guidance. These things cannot be accomplished by tense striving, but only by deep, upward relaxation into the inner Self.

(4:30) Some, regulating the flow of energy in the body by correct diet, offer all their energies into the fire of that (upward) flow. All the above seekers understand the meaning of self-offering (yagya, or sacrifice), the inner fire which consumes all the seeds of karma.

The first part of this *sloka* is sometimes coupled with Stanza 29. Indeed, "correct diet" refers also to something deeper than mere food for the stomach. When the prana and apana are neutralized in breathlessness, the body is sustained by a higher, cosmic energy. What happens is that the body's energy is then connected directly to the medulla oblongata, by which connection energy flows directly from a higher source and sustains the body cells from within.

Paramhansa Yogananda developed a system which he called "energization exercises." These, when practiced faithfully, keep the body fit and sustained by that higher energy.

Correct diet, normally speaking, should consist of what is considered sattwic food. Such food is, to begin with, vegetarian, lightly cooked or raw, but not overcooked for overcooking destroys the life force in food. Fruits and nuts are excellent. It seems unnecessary to cover this subject here, as there are many good books on the subject, but an interesting story might be told here to show that Paramhansa Yogananda was no food fanatic. Indeed, he noted that health faddists are often unable to discuss with interest any subject except the physical body and its physical diet! He coined a word to express what he considered the ideal diet: propereatarianism!

One time Dr. Lewis, his first Kriya Yoga disciple in America, and still a young man in his late twenties, complained to him of mysterious aches and pains he was experiencing. He said, "I've been to a number of medical doctors, but none of them has helped me. What shall I do?"

The Master, after a momentary pause, answered, "The cells of your body have grown accustomed to eating meat. Now that you've adopted a vegetarian diet, they miss their former animal food! Eat a little bit of meat once a week, therefore. Avoid beef, veal, and pork, but feel free to eat a little lamb, chicken, or fish." Dr. Lewis followed this advice, and his problem disappeared.

(4:31) By eating the "blessed food" (prasad) left from any of these spiritual fire rituals, one attains to Brahman (the Infinite Spirit). Even the blessings of this world come not to one who gives nothing of himself. How, then, can one hope for happiness in a better world?

(4:32) The many ways of offering up the ego are declared in the Vedas (as if) through the "mouth of Brahma." Knowing their true purpose (which is an upward self-offering), you will be freed from all karmic bondage.

From whatever direction one approaches a mountain-top, as long as he continues moving upward he will reach the peak eventually. What is all-important is the *direction* of one's climb. In the spine, that direction is, of course, upward. The spine is central in the human body. Whatever else one does spiritually, he must also awaken and raise the spinal energy. This remains true even if one's path is devotional chanting, service to the poor, or in other ways helping to relieve human suffering. He may follow the path of mental discrimination, trying to distinguish between what is true and what is false in this world. If his energy, however, is not raised in the spine even by these indirect means, he can achieve no spiritual awakening. True religion—inner experience, that is to say, not mere belief—is not a question of pleasing some deity "up there." We ourselves must raise our awareness to the superconscious level, which for us, in the physical body, exists only "up there."

Thus, yoga, and particularly the science of Kriya Yoga, is supremely practical. This teaching is universal, since it addresses the central reality of what occurs anyway in the spiritual progress of every sincere aspirant, whatever his outward path or system of belief. Therefore it is that Krishna says, later on in the Gita, "Arjuna, be thou a yogi."

What is this "spinal highway," as Paramhansa Yogananda called it, which the yoga teachings describe? It begins with the Kundalini power, which lies as if sleeping at the base of the spine. This is (in one frame of reference) the opposite pole to the heart; in another, to the medulla oblongata and the spiritual eye, and (finally) to the top of the head (the *sahasrara*). At last, all one's energy must be united in the *sahasrara*.

The first chakra (center), at the bottom of the spine just above the Kundalini, is called the *muladhara*, which represents the earth "element." The opening of the central passageway (*sushumna*) in the spine is referred to in this verse as the "mouth of Brahma."

This important center is the start of the long upward journey. "Here," Krishna is saying, "is where it all begins."

Certain occult powers are attached to this chakra, as to each of the others. People who fear to meditate on the lower chakras, thinking that their connection with materialistic consciousness will be increased— sense-bound individuals live centered mostly in the lower three chakras—need to have a misconception clarified. When the energy flows *outward* from these centers to the physical body, it induces body-consciousness. When, however, it flows inward to the chakras and *upward*, it leads to spiritual awakening. Every chakra—even at this lowest point—brings heightened spiritual awareness when the energy in it is directed upward.

(4:33) The inner, spiritual fire ceremony of rising awareness is superior, O Scorcher of Foes (Arjuna), to

any outward act of self-offering. In this wisdom (alone) is all action (karma) consumed.

Outward spiritual acts, meant as self-offering, have two major disadvantages: First, they act only indirectly on the energy in the spine, and are therefore less effective in the only spiritual "work" that really counts: self-transformation, which also results in the highest good for other people. Secondly, they involve the mind outwardly, keep it restless, and cause one easily to forget such essentials on the spiritual path as devotion.

(4:34) Understand this (above all): By surrender (of self-will to the wise), by (sensitive inward and outward) questioning (of the wise), and by service (to the wise), those who have realized the truth will (be able to) convey their wisdom to you.

This stanza is meant especially to be applied to one's own Self-realized guru, for those seekers so fortunate as to have been led to one. The plural is used here, however, to indicate the need for devotees to honor all enlightened sages, generally. Surrender to the Infinite God in them, openness (whether by questioning or by deep, inward appreciation) to their uplifting influence, and support for that influence (through service to them) are important in helping the devotee to rise above the naturally narrow view of the ego.

Paramhansa Yogananda encouraged people to add to the prayers they offer regularly to God and guru (and, perhaps, to his line of gurus) these words of invocation: "saints of all religions."

(4:35) Having (fully) received that wisdom from a true guru, O Pandava (Arjuna)! you will never again fall into delusion, for you will behold all creation contained within your (expanded) Self, and then (behold it) in Me (beyond all creation).

First the fully enlightened being perceives the whole universe as waves, so to speak, dancing—rising and falling—on the surface of his oceanic consciousness. His next step, if he so wills it, is to withdraw his consciousness into what Yogananda called "the watchful state" of absolute, motionless Consciousness.

(4:36) Even the worst of sinners can, with the raft of wisdom, cross safely over the ocean of delusion.

Krishna offers this supreme encouragement to all humanity: No matter how steeped you are in bad habits, vice, self-degrading depravity, or evil, you are still a child of the one, infinite Lord who created masters and saints. Nothing less than divine bliss can define you forever!

Never, therefore, tell yourself, "I am evil!" Never say, "I have failed!" If you accept any failure as your reality, it will be so, at least for this lifetime. But if after every setback you say, rather, "I have not yet succeeded!" you can win—even in this incarnation!

Pray to God as the Divine Mother, all-forgiving and ever-accepting: "Mother, whether naughty or good, I am

Thy child! Thou *must* release me! Cleanse me of all sin."

"God doesn't mind your faults," Yogananda used to say. "He only minds your indifference!"

(4:37) O Arjuna, as fire burns wood to ashes, so does the fire of wisdom burn to ashes all one's karma.

Think of the long-abandoned Egyptian tombs. Darkness reigned in King Tut's tomb for thousands of years, yet once it was opened, light flooded in and the darkness of centuries was dispersed in an instant. The case is similar with every individual. No matter how deep his shadows of unknowing, the moment God's light enters his consciousness there is nothing but light!

Karma is of many kinds, since that word means action, only. Karma can be national, communal, family, individual: anything that proceeds from a coherent center of intention that can attract results back to that center. All action is karma. A national leader who does evil on his people's behalf will not have to bear the entire weight of that bad karma on his own "shoulders": The whole nation must accept responsibility. Good people in that country must bear it also, though their own karma may offset for themselves, and perhaps for a wider circle of people, any evil that must befall the nation as a karmic retribution.

When an airplane crashes, not everyone who dies in that event does so necessarily because it was his own karma to die. The group karma of the majority of passengers might outweigh an individual's neutral karma—if, for example, his karma to live was not strong enough. It does often happen, on the other hand, that when some great disaster strikes, certain persons, unaccountably at the time, are called away or otherwise prevented from being on the scene.

Group karma is highly complex. Everyone's first duty is to himself, to improve his own karma. Indeed, the more good one does by contributing toward a general upliftment of consciousness, the more greatly will the general karma be helped. One must begin, however, by uplifting his own consciousness.

For the individual, two kinds of karma need to be considered: *purushakara* and *prarabdha*. *Purushakara karma* is actions generated in this life under the influence, *not* of habit or desire, but of soul-guidance. *Prarabdha karma*, on the other hand, consists of present tendencies, and the results of past actions brought over from former lives.

Prarabdha karma is also of two kinds: those actions which, owing to present circumstances, are likely to bear fruit in this life; and those, known as *para-rabdha karma*, which are being held in abeyance until more favorable circumstances bring them to fruition.

A man may have the karma, for example, to be drowned at sea—or, for that matter, to be saved from drowning at sea. If he never even goes near a lake, however, and therefore is never in a position that makes drowning possible, that particular karma will have to await another life to be worked out.

Sometimes an unfortunate karma can be deferred, and even offset, by an opposite karma. An unavoidable temptation, for example, may be met by newly acquired inner strength that renders the temptation impotent. Karmic periods also pass, or are dissipated by offsetting actions. For example, a karmically "destined" failure may be deflected if one develops a new, more creative energy, or for that matter if one develops the wisdom to redefine the blow as a new *opportunity*, and not really failure at all!

A bad karma may loom above one like a dragon, ready to strike, but if one can find a way either of deflecting that blow or of protecting oneself (like using an umbrella when it rains), one may still receive the blow, yet avoid disaster. One may also, of course, do as Saint George of English legend did: slay the dragon. Certain it is that no threat of misfortune need ever be accepted with supine resignation! A powerful will can overcome, or can at least mitigate, virtually any misfortune that awaits one.

Bad karma can, for example, penetrate a weak aura, but it cannot penetrate a strong one, or the damage it inflicts will be minimized. If you have the karma to lose a leg, and your will is strong and you have deep devotion, you may receive only a scratch. Karmic consequences are inevitable, but how they are *received* depends on many circumstances, most of them arising in the individual.

Bad karma can also be offset by the creation of good karma. Good karma can be augmented by more good karma, directed toward the same end. Events that affect others need not affect one's self, or at least not in the same way: The secret, in this case, is to maintain an attitude of non-attachment, and not to react emotionally.

Indeed, emotional reaction can greatly augment any karmic effects. My Guru told a (probably mythical) story about a village in India in which three people died unaccountably of some disease. Concerned, the villagers repaired in a group to a solitary *sadhu* (holy man) who lived outside the village, and asked him to intercede. The sadhu meditated, and saw that the disease had been caused by a demon. He summoned the demon and told him, "This village is under my protection. Leave it alone." The demon promised to obey.

A week later, at least a hundred other people had died. It seemed a veritable epidemic. Again the villagers approached the sadhu and cried, "Your prayers have not helped us. There must be a terrible curse on our village!"

The sadhu summoned the demon again, and scolded him, saying, "I told you this village is under my protection. You promised to leave it alone, but now it appears you have broken your promise."

"No, I haven't, Holy One!" protested the demon. "It's true I killed the first three, but all the others have died out of fear."

The ultimate way to escape the results of all karma is to "evaporate" the causative ego, with its consciousness of identification with the little "cup" of the body. In deep meditation, that vapor of ego may rise and disappear altogether in the sky of infinite consciousness.

If the dragon strikes, and you are no longer there to be seized in its jaws; or if the rock falls from a precipice and you have removed yourself from the spot where it falls; or if the fickle multitudes acclaim you (and, inevitably, expose you to the dualistic opposite of public opprobrium, later on) and you are not there to respond: What happens? The same actions occur, but you will not be there to receive them.

The *jivan mukta* (one who is "freed while living"), having dissolved his ego-awareness in infinite consciousness, no longer develops any new, personal karma. Any deed he does from then on accrues to the benefit of others—who still, by the vortices of energy created by their own egos, benefit from the good deeds he performs for them. He himself, however, remains untouched even by good karma. His *prarabdha karma* must play itself out on his body, but he will no longer be affected by it.

When the *jivan mukta* has finally released into the free skies of Spirit the countless actions of all the incarnations that his ego lived in delusion, he becomes a *param mukta*: a supremely free soul.

(4:38) Verily, there is nothing in this world so sanctifying as wisdom. In due course of time every devotee who is successful in his practices will realize in his own Self the truth of this statement.

(4:39) The person of devotion who is engrossed in the infinite, having brought his senses under control, achieves wisdom, and gains that which he knows at once to be perfect peace.

Devotees who think there is a conflict between devotional love, yogic self-control, and true (as opposed to intellectual) wisdom, fail to realize that all these paths (devotion, yogic practicality, and calm discrimination) are aspects of the same truth, and result in the same realization.

The word for devotion in this sloka is *shraddha*, which usually translates as, "faith." The reference is to that kind of devotion which doesn't hold God at a distance by appealing to Him for divine favors, but which, like an arrow, flies straight to the bull's eye of His divine love as a natural inclination of the heart toward its true, intuitively perceived Source.

The highest goal, the true bull's eye of devotional focus, is not love, but bliss. Love itself is lovable, but it must have a pure motive, and that motive, or goal, is Satchidananda. It is good, surely, to seek God for His love, but the highest goal of all is ever-conscious, ever-existing, ever-new Bliss. Without this as one's goal, even love, if one seeks it as his highest goal, contains the danger of awakening the desire for *personal* love. True, perfect love is always impersonal, expansive, and ultimately infinite. It has no object save Bliss alone.

(4:40) The ignorant, the person who lacks devotion, the doubt-ridden: all these must perish. The man of vacillating temperament finds no happiness in this world or the next. For him, supreme bliss is impossible.

To be truly ignorant is to reject with a dull heart any offer of a way out of the mud flats of nescience. The truly ignorant, being dull-minded, ask no questions of life, and recognize no opportunity for improvement even if it offers them everything.

Worse than being ignorant is the inability to feel devotion. High aspiration eludes such a person. Aspiration of any kind, indeed, seems to him foolish and unnecessary. To what (he asks) is there to aspire? Why strive for anything? The less energy he expends, he knows, the less energy will life demand of him, the fewer challenges it will throw in his way, and the more, in consequence, he will be left alone. How can those not ultimately perish who, buffalo-like, insist on wallowing in the mud of a passive contentment? Stupidity, sloth, lack of any vital interest in anything: How can people who cling to such mental sluggishness expect the mechanism of their life not to run down very quickly? They refuse it even the proper maintenance.

The worst case, however, is that of the confirmed doubter. He has all the equipment he needs to rise to the heights, yet his compulsion is to keep listing all the shortcomings, the drawbacks, and the mischief by which others might try to undo him. He has the devotion, and the desire to rise to the heights, yet a cynical inner voice keeps whispering in his subconscious, "What will the end be—treachery? lack of appreciation? opposition? ingratitude?"

Paramhansa Yogananda once commented, "The doubter is the most miserable of mortals." He was referring, not to constructive questioning, but to the nagging tendency to oppose every constructive idea, to prejudge the idea for no real reason at all, and to be negatively prejudiced against everything wholesome or constructive. "It can't be right—therefore it isn't right! It can't work—therefore no matter what happens, it can't really work, not even if it seems to be doing so. People can't know what they're doing, therefore they *must* be wrong!"

To doubt a true teacher, especially if one is his disciple—owing to arrogance or simply to a habit of mental rejection—causes seething turmoil in the mind. One assumes dejectedly that whatever the guru says must automatically be wrong: not because one has checked it out, nor even because he *wants* to disbelieve a conclusion that is merely inconvenient for him, and not because he doubts the guru's motives. . . . The doubter deeply desires *something true* in life, and cannot accept what he finds. A strange twist of mind rejects, not out of disinterest, but rather out of *intense* interest. His doubt is born of almost a fear of finding himself deluded in the end, when he wanted so much to be sure.

Were he indifferent, his condition might be better at least in the sense that he'd then be able to direct his interest elsewhere. The tragedy, for him, is that he desires—his whole being yearns for—the very truths which subconscious habit impels him to reject. That habit proposes no acceptable alternative. It simply shakes its head and says, "No." The truths he wants—so that habit tells him—cannot possibly exist. The habit gives no reason. Darkly, instead, it poses the dire warning, "What if . . . ?

"What if all this should prove, in the end, to be chicanery? What if my guru's motives be not so generous as they seem, and all he really wants is somehow to squeeze others for his own benefit?" Such doubts quickly develop a life of their own, and create for

themselves an alternate universe: "What if— *everything!?*"
One's will power becomes paralyzed; hope withers
away, to become in time a dry twig. The sweetness of
friendship is soured by suspicion.

For all the above reasons it may be justly said indeed
that the doubter is "the most miserable of mortals."

Finally, the man of vacillating temperament can never
accomplish anything worthwhile. He will never commit
himself to anything. He has no loyalties. He drifts
through life as whims waft him, settling on no truth, and
forever uncertain of anything.

The determinedly ignorant person can only be left
alone to his own rhythms. Eventually he will come out
of his self-woven cocoon: when he has suffered enough,
and when, through suffering, he begins to *care* and, in
the caring, to make the first, faltering attempts to
develop his own latent abilities. *Then* he will emerge
from that cocoon.

The apathetic are at least aware that there are clouds
of unknowing to be blown away. They imagine that life
has nothing more to offer them. When their dreams of
passive contentment or resignation fade, they begin to
look around anxiously for viable answers.

It is the doubter, alas, who suffers the most. His thinking processes, despite his longing to be good and to do
right, become paralyzed. He yearns to find something on
which he can fix as his ideal, but then tells himself that,
for one reason or another, that ideal cannot exist. His
tragedy is that he yearns for bliss, but finds it denied him
by a compulsion in his own nature he can't understand.
How is he to overcome this self-damning tendency?

He must tell himself, "There is no road back. I have no choice but to go forward, even if it means only plodding heavily, one slow step at a time." He can expiate his karma by helping others to resolve their doubts. He can concentrate on his own yearning for truth, until the very yearning pulls him out of the dense fogs of doubt into the sunlight of a faith all the more certain because it has rejected gloomy speculation as a waste of time and energy. Helping others to resolve their doubts and uncertainties becomes, for him, a way of affirming his own solution-orientation. For him at last, supreme bliss becomes the only possible solution to every problem and difficulty in life!

(4:41) O Winner of (true) Wealth, Arjuna! one who has dissolved all his karmas in oneness with God, and has obliterated his every doubt by wisdom, becomes completely self-possessed. (Ego-free,) no further action can entangle him.

(4:42) Arise therefore, O Descendent of Bharata (Arjuna): Arise! Take shelter in (this greatest science of) yoga. Slash (to pieces) with the sword of wisdom the doubt you feel in your heart as to the nature of the Self (and of who you are, in reality).

Thus ends the fourth chapter, called "Gyana Yoga (Union Through Knowledge of the Divine)," of the Upanishad of the holy Bhagavad Gita, in the dialogue between Sri Krishna and Arjuna discussing yoga and the science of God-realization.

CHAPTER SEVENTEEN

FREEDOM THROUGH INNER RENUNCIATION

(5:1) Arjuna said: O Krishna, You speak of renouncing action, yet at the same time You recommend it. I would like to know for certain, which of these two is the better path?

(5:2) The Blessed Lord answered: (When rightly understood,) both action and non-action lead to salvation. Of the two, however, right action is better.

IN CHAPTER 3 OF THE BHAGAVAD GITA KRISHNA states unequivocally that, in this vibratory universe, it is not possible to refrain from acting. Here he states just as unequivocally that both action and non-action lead to salvation. Is he contradicting himself?

It must be understood that non-action has a different meaning, here, from inaction. The meditating hermit is still acting, even though he sits for long hours in silent meditation—in some cases, even for days or months at a time. The difference is that physical immobility need not indicate mental inaction, or inactivity of the subtle inner energies. The deeply meditating yogi is certainly

active, though in a very different way from most
people. His action is inward: He is directing energy
through the subtle nerves in the spine. He may, if he
is a *jivan mukta*, be expiating the karmas of past
incarnations: re-experiencing his past deeds in vision,
and offering them up on the altar of Spirit with the
realization that, even then, while he was living in ego-
consciousness, God alone dreamed his life and acted
through his ego-delusion.

The need to be outwardly busy disappears of itself
when one attains the state of *jivan mukta*, dissolving his
ego in cosmic consciousness. Even then, as Krishna has
already emphasized in the Gita, free souls who live in
this world often perform outward actions in order to set
an example of right living for others. They do so because
ordinary persons would find it all too easy, once
they take up *sannyas* (the monastic path), to become
mentally as well as physically inactive in the name of
complete renunciation.

My Guru said that many *sadhus* ("holy men," or persons dedicated to the spiritual life) go to the Himalayas
for a life of "meditation," but then, finding themselves
unable to meditate long hours at a time, spend the rest
of their time sleeping, eating, and gossiping. From
physical inactivity they become physically lazy. Having
nothing to engage their minds actively, they gradually
become mentally lazy also. Finally, having put their
minds to sleep by mental inactivity, they become spiritually lazy. What remains to recommend their so-called
"renunciate" way of life? Nothing! My Guru said,
"Many become bums!"

Many such sadhus, he continued, allow "householders" to feed them, which those people do willingly, having the means to do so and considering that service a means of accruing good karma. Meanwhile, some of those "holy men" actually look down on the people who feed them and consider them merely worldly, bound to the wheel of *samsara*.

It is sad that many renunciates in every religion, themselves "green" (in the sense of unripe) spiritually, tend to deprecate "householders," when the entire purpose of renunciation is to liberate ourself fully from ego-consciousness. To deprecate anyone is to affirm one's own ego. In fact, many sadhus, swamis, *brahmacharis*, hermits, and others, supposedly dedicated to living for God alone, allow their very life of spiritual dedication to feed their pride. The renunciate should strive above all to sublimate his ego in self-offering to the infinite.

The practice of entering a monastery and being disciplined by monastic "superiors" (an unfortunate appellation, indeed!) has its good points, but it also has its bad. Submission to a true guru is essential in one's search for God, for such a one knows the disciple's karmic needs and can guide him in what he must do, now, to escape the coils of past karma. The average monastery superior, however, has no such wisdom, and usually has the institution's needs as his priority, not the spiritual needs of the individual. Obedience to such a person, who is merely "the one in charge," can controvert the subordinate's real, but personal, spiritual needs, and may even ignore what he should do to rise spiritually toward God-consciousness.

The subordinate is commonly told, "The way to please God is to obey your superior." What, however, if the superior tells him to do something obviously wrong, or against the subordinate's conscience? The answer, for the subordinate, should be, Be careful! Obedience under such circumstances may be, or may be perceived to be, good for the community, but the consequences for the individual himself (these were my own Guru's words) is actually to *weaken* his will. The stock answer given in monasteries is, "If your superior is wrong in what he asks you to do, God will correct him." Indeed? I have never seen this bit of "monastic wisdom" justified in real life.

For many people, the monastic life is a wonderful way of serving and finding God. The old model, however, of absolute obedience to anyone and everyone in the name of eternal salvation is archaic—indeed, medieval. What is needed always, but especially in an age when people everywhere on Earth are becoming conscious that the true nature of matter is energy, is for one to live more freely in the Self—that is to say, in God. Those with some experience on the spiritual path may indeed be able to advise novices wisely; it would be ridiculous, indeed, in the name of affirming one's own free will, to ignore the voice of experience. Still, to be obliged to act merely to please someone who may, in fact, be not at all enlightened is to shift the burden of responsibility to where it cannot ever belong: onto someone else's shoulders.

Our responsibility before God is our own. As Krishna says in the Gita, It is better to fail doing *one's own* duty than to succeed doing the duty of another. Whatever may truly be one's own duty (and it is no easy task to discern what that duty is), one cannot accomplish it by simply handing that decision over to someone else.

Many monks and nuns in monasteries become pale images of their former selves: in a negative way, unfortunately, not in a positive, egoless way. Many hermits and others also, who justify non-activity by letting others feed them (while they "devote" their own lives to—well, to what? sleeping and gossiping?) become, in similar fashion, shadows of their former selves. One encounters few lion-like sadhus and swamis anywhere: heroes who have risen out of the ashes of fire-purified ego-consciousness to soar, like the legendary phoenix, in the skies of inner freedom.

It would be well to consider also a word that is too often used in a deprecatory sense: "householder." What *is* a householder? Many so-called householders have, to begin with, no houses to hold! They have no families (in the sense of children of their own), no wives or husbands, no great attachment to their possessions. It is assumed that the term means they are involved in the struggle to acquire and exult over possessions and power, to dominate over others, and to nourish their own egos with the rich food of worldly fame and admiration. None of these things add up to the word, "householder." True saints, moreover, may actually have the houses they live in in their own names. They certainly are not householders, for they, in themselves, have no sense that they possess anything.

The entire criterion must be raised to a higher level. The question is not what a person owns, or what he does. It is what he *is*, inwardly. Yogananda stated that to fulfill one's outward duties (as long as one still has duties to perform) is the higher path. It must be understood, however, that this is not intended as an excuse for running after worldly pleasures and "fulfillments"—which cease, in the long run, to be pleasures at all, and, instead of fulfillment, bring colossal disappointment!

Whatever one does should not be done for egoic pleasure, but only to please God. Man's duty in this world, once he develops even a little understanding of what life is really all about, is (as Krishna puts it) "to get away from My ocean of suffering and misery!" All else has one simply marking time and getting nowhere. Worldly success and failure, triumph and disappointment, joy and suffering—all these are mere waves that, occasionally, rise high on the ocean bosom of cosmic delusion, then sink back again, becoming equally deep troughs. There is no point to it at all! It is simply *maya*—God's *lila*, or play. One who lives without ego-attachment gets to enjoy the show for a time, if he so chooses, before sinking back into the "watchful state" of Satchidananda: perfect bliss. Otherwise, the free soul acts in this world only to help others: those still-seeking stumblers on the way, who aspire to eternal freedom as the one, eternal reality.

To try to achieve union with God by serving others, while maintaining control over one's self, is what Krishna recommends here above mere non-involvement in activity.

The true nature of specific duty poses a more difficult question than the general nature of right action—namely, without attachment to the results. It can be defined broadly, however, as that action which leads in the direction of calm, inner freedom. Indefinitely continued involvement in that duty may come in time to resemble the endless "forward movement" on a treadmill. The path of duty should never be a downhill slide to mental dullness. Always, whatever causes one's consciousness to rise is right activity.

That, finally, is why Krishna emphasizes activity over non-activity. Non-activity leads ineluctably to dullness—unless one is able to engage his energy positively in the performance of deep meditation.

(5:3) O Mighty-armed (Arjuna), only that person deserves consideration as a true renunciate who finds freedom from entanglement easy—having no likes or dislikes, and no attachment to duality.

(5:4) It is the ignorant, not the wise, who speak of the paths of wisdom (Shankhya) and Yoga as being different from one another. One who is truly established in either receives the benefits of both.

(5:5) The state attained through wisdom (Gyana Yoga, the path of discrimination known as Shankhya) is the same as that attained by action (the science of yoga). The two paths lead to one single realization.

(5:6) Renunciation, however, O Mighty-armed (Arjuna), is difficult to achieve without God-uniting activity (yoga). By the practice of yoga, the muni (whose mind is absorbed in God) soon attains the perfection of oneness with the Absolute.

(5:7) No taint (of karmic entanglement) remains for him who has been purified by right action and,

engaged in divine communion (yoga), has dissolved his ego (in infinity), has achieved victory over the senses, and has realized himself as one with the Self of all.

(5:8) He who, in the state of union with God, has cognized the truth fully understands: "I (myself) do nothing at all," though he sees, hears, touches, smells, tastes, moves about, sleeps, breathes, . . .

(5:9) . . . speaks, excretes, grasps (with his hands), opens or closes his eyes. Such a person knows at all times that (these) are but the senses engaging their (sense) objects.

(5:10) As the lotus leaf is untouched by water, so the yogi who acts without attachment, self-offered to the Divine, is not affected by sensory experience (whether gross or subtle).

The seeker must practice non-attachment to sensory experiences, for until he becomes firmly established in the Self he may find himself drawn out of it inadvertently by the fascination of new experiences. Milk, when poured on water, commingles with it. The milk must be churned to butter before it can float, undiluted, on the surface. By practicing inner centeredness, the yogi is said to "churn the butter" of his awareness by separating the "curds" of firm understanding from the watery "whey" of sensory dependency. He can then go anywhere, do anything, mix with anyone and remain inwardly unaffected by the illusory attractions of *maya*.

This stanza has a deeper meaning, which is why the common translations of "sensory experience" as "sin," or as the perfectly logical "karmic involvement"—both of which versions seem to encompass the full meaning—are in fact inadequate. Understood literally, and not figuratively to avoid what seems otherwise merely an unnecessary repetition, the expression here becomes a wonderful further explanation of the spiritual path.

When the life force is withdrawn from outward body awareness during deep meditation, the yogi beholds currents of energy trickling back through the flesh, like little rills of rainwater in a forest, to the great river of energy in the spine. When all of the body's currents are in this way withdrawn, they then pass successively into, and through, the three luminous *nadis* (channels) of life force in the astral spine: the *sushumna* (which is outermost), the *vajra*, and then the *chitra*. Passing through the *chitra*, the energy and consciousness enter the innermost channel, the *brahmanadi*, which constitutes the spine of the causal body. It was through the *brahmanadi* that Brahma, the Creative aspect of AUM, in His aspect of Creator of individual beings and their three bodies, descended into outward manifestation. It is through this final channel of *brahmanadi*, therefore, that the soul must once more ascend in order to become again one with the Spirit. As the yogi withdraws his energy up through this final channel, he is able fully to offer his separate, individual consciousness into Infinity.

During this process, he beholds wondrous astral phenomena. This stanza of the Gita is a warning not to be attached to such visions, either, lest they divert him from his goal of complete union. The opening of *brahmanadi* is at the top of the head. On reaching this point, the yogi becomes reunited with omnipresence, for the last sheath has been removed that closes him off from Infinity.

One who is tossed—let us say, in a rowboat—on ocean waves cannot see the broad surface of that vast body of water. When he rises above it, however—whether by standing on a cliff or by flying high in the air—he sees a vast panorama of waves. His attention is not necessarily drawn, then, to any one wave or small grouping of waves. The yogi, similarly, can behold the whole ocean impartially—or, again, he can withdraw into the ocean depths and, having no single specific point from which to gaze, but being rather one with all Spirit, finds that in the very act of seeing he both *is* that act, and that which is beheld. Knowing, knower, and known become one.

Meanwhile, remember something mentioned earlier in this book: If you go to visit a castle, and pass through beautiful grounds, you can take the time to view the grounds and wonder at all the plants, at the stream running through the property, and at the unusual trees and beautiful flowers, but that process may take you so long that you'll have to wait till another incarnation before you remember that you wanted to visit the castle! Far wiser is it to get to know the lord of the castle, first. He will show you around. Sharing its beauties with Him will be far more enjoyable for you, and you will fully understand everything, instead of merely marveling.

Powers, visions, and other phenomena can inspire, but if one allows himself to desire them, or to become attached to them, they can distract him from the path to Supreme Truth.

A disciple of the Master was experiencing his first Kundalini awakening, and was enjoying the feeling of it rising joyfully in the spine. Pleased with this phenomenon, he told the Master about it. The Guru, to prevent any foolishly premature satisfaction on the disciple's part, replied by exclaiming, "That's *nothing*!"

From the above passages it must be understood that "action" and "non-action" convey meanings far deeper to the yogi than anyone can imagine who is spiritually asleep. All those meanings were intended by Lord Krishna in these passages of his great discourse, the Bhagavad Gita.

A few disciples were lamenting that it takes *so long* to find God! To them the Guru said, "You have to live anyway! Why not live in the right way?"

In truth, it takes no time at all to find God, since time itself is a delusion. In fact, moreover, it takes less time in this delusive world than people devote, at the beginning of their souls' journey, to forgetting Him!

(5:11) For purification of the ego, yogis merely work *with* the body, mind, discrimination, and sense organs: (They are) never attached to them.

Yogis merely *use* the body; it never "uses" them. In other words, they never let any aspect of outward awareness exert the slightest compulsion on their will.

In the way a carpenter, when using a hammer to drive nails into a board, may say, "I am hammering the nail," when in fact he is only *using* the hammer and knows very well that he himself is not the hammer—even so, people use their bodies to work, their minds to observe consciously, their intellects to discriminate, and their sense organs to perceive objective reality. Identified with the body, they think, "I am doing whatever my body does." Identified with the mind, they think, "My awareness of what happens is defining the event itself." Identified with the intellect, they think, "I am thinking this thing through to its logical conclusion." Finally, identified with the sense organs, they think, "I see; I hear; I taste; I smell; I touch. By these means I define all that I experience in the world around me."

The yogi, by contrast, separates his self-awareness from what the body is doing, from what the mind observes, from what the intellect thinks, and from what the senses tell him in any situation to be the case. He knows that he, himself, is none of these, any more than the carpenter *is* his hammer or the nails he is driving into a board.

The distinction here is that, for the yogi (as opposed to the ordinary man), there is no thought of personal agency in anything he does. The yogi sees the body not as *his* body, but only as something he uses. He understands that his mind is not his own: It, too, is something he works through. He perceives the intellect as separate from his true, inner perception. And he cognizes the senses as cooperating *with* him, but independently from him.

As the carpenter uses his hammer to drive nails into a board, so the yogi uses his very ego. He knows it is not his self, except in the sense that he, the infinite Self, must keep that little unit of reality going.

The body enacts his wishes as though it were a hammer: He himself, in his expanded reality, is not that body. He uses it impersonally, as an implement to accomplish certain ends. He observes through his mind, but separates himself from the thought, "I am observing." When discriminating, he thinks only, "This is the intellect discriminating: It is not *I* who draw these conclusions." He perceives through the senses, but never tells himself, "I am perceiving," but rather is aware, "This perception is occurring." He removes, from all that he sees and does, any sense of personal identification.

The nerves are the main passages of life force in the body. They correspond to the subtler, more refined *nadis* of the astral body. Ordinarily, the nerve passages of the human body are "clogged" with toxins owing to wrong diet, and are impaired in their functioning by unnatural living. Because man seeks stimulation from outside himself, instead of drawing on his inner, spiritual resources, he vitiates the nerves, which grow tired and become diminishingly responsive to the very things people look to for stimulation. An outward flow of energy soon becomes habitual, resisting meditative efforts to relax by withdrawing into the Self. Yogis, therefore, advise purifying the nerves by proper diet, yoga *asanas* (postures), and the practice of yoga meditation techniques, among which Kriya Yoga is pre-eminent.

Asanas; mudras (*asanas* combined with special awareness of the flow of certain inner energies); *pranayamas* (breathing exercises that help to control the flow of energy); devotional chanting (for the very use of the voice in self-offering to God can assist an upward flow of energy); prayers (which, apart from appealing to God for an answer, help to focus one's own thoughts and feelings); using consciousness and energy to penetrate through the spinal chakras; concentration on the Infinite; and the deep self-offering of heartfelt devotion: all these help to purify the heart's feelings and the nervous system, making one fully receptive to divine inspiration.

(5:12) The God-united yogi, relinquishing attachment to the fruits of action, attains unshakable inner peace. That person, however, who does not direct his energies (upward) toward union with God is ruled by desire. Attached to the fruits of action, he lives in (perpetual) bondage.

The secret to divine freedom (this is a thought worthwhile to repeat again and again) is to renounce ego-motivation. A person has no choice but to act, whether outwardly or inwardly, with his thoughts and subtle energies. He must in any case, however, neutralize the *vrittis*, or eddies that draw the consequences of every act back to himself with the thought, "I did it; it is mine!"

(5:13) When once the embodied soul has controlled the senses, and, mentally releasing every attachment to activity, remains blissful (and secure) in the "city of nine gates" (the physical body), he (himself) no longer acts, nor does he impose action on others (or on his outer senses).

It is notable to how great an extent these slokas treat, not of the outer, but of the inner, "world," which is "populated" by the thoughts, attitudes, and qualities of the meditating yogi. The very symbolism of the *Mahabharata*, emphasized from the beginning of the Bhagavad Gita, relates to the inner man: to his "population" of millions of thoughts and tendencies.

This last stanza might easily be taken to mean that the yogi who is completely true to himself will never impose his will on other human beings. Certainly this is the outward, superficial meaning of this stanza. How we behave outwardly, however, is only a reflection of what we are in ourselves. The Gita is dealing primarily with inner causes. Its assumption is that outwardly sattwic activity *depends on* inner, sattwic attitudes. People who try to impose peaceful, harmonious behavior on the world without first changing themselves have grasped the wrong end of the fire brand they flourish!

Nevertheless, it is also true, and is a point never overlooked in the Bhagavad Gita, that *outward* right behavior helps to focus the mind *inwardly* on right attitudes.

The "city of nine gates" is, of course, a reference to the body with its two eyes, two nostrils, two ears, two organs of excretion, and mouth. The yogi who has renounced ego-consciousness dwells securely, at perpetual rest, within the "city" of his body. No enemy can attack him, for his energy (like the limbs of a tortoise) has been withdrawn into the Self. He is no longer the body, but has become like a certain yogi who, "saddled with" a nagging wife, told my Guru when he was a young boy, "She doesn't know it, but I've escaped her! The 'I' she thinks I am is no longer there to be nagged!"

(5:14) It is not God, the sovereign Self, who *creates* in mankind the consciousness of acting in this world. God neither *causes* people to act, nor entangles them in the (karmic) consequences of their actions. It is *maya,* the cosmic illusion, which acts through them.

This stanza might seem mere casuistry: God might be taken as trying to shift the blame elsewhere by saying, "*He* did it!" In fact, however, it can be a great aid to the spiritual aspirant to realize how much a puppet of delusion he is. God created the delusion, true. Yet God Himself remains unaffected by it, for in His Supreme Spirit He is beyond all vibration. The yogi must feel, at his center within, that he, too, is immovable and at peace. *Maya* (cosmic delusion) acts *through* him, but cannot define him.

There is another "angle" on this teaching, however, which seems to contradict what has been taught above. Yogananda used to say, "It is better, if you do commit an error—whether a slight mistake or a great sin—to tell yourself, 'God did it through me.'" He continued, "God likes that! For you will find it easier, by doing so, to release the feeling of guilt which makes people beat themselves, thinking, 'I did that! Oh, how *weak* I am! How wrong of me! How sinful!'"

My Guru used to say, "The greatest 'sin' is to call yourself a sinner." Instead, if you don't want to blame

God (which Yogananda insisted, however, is perfectly fine with God!), tell yourself, *"Maya* (cosmic delusion) committed this deed through me. I dissociate myself from everything connected with it. I am, in my true Self, untainted and ever free!"

"Of course," my Guru added, "you must then act in such a way as not to commit that error again!"

Every time you slip, rather than moaning, "I've failed! I'm a fallen soul!" tell yourself, "I haven't yet succeeded!" If you do this, your words, instead of being a negative affirmation, will be an affirmation of eventual success.

"The best time for sowing the seeds of success," Paramhansa Yogananda used to say, "is the season of failure!"

(5:15) The All-pervading is not concerned about people's sins or virtues. Wisdom (though it is the natural state of every man) is eclipsed by cosmic delusion. Mankind thus becomes bewildered (as to the difference between right and wrong).

Yogananda often said, "God is not worried about your mistakes. All He wants from you is your love, and that you love Him ever-more deeply." He also said, "God has everything—except one: He loves you, and wants your love in return."

God (it should go without saying) is not touched by human wrongs. What is sin? It is nothing but error! Because it springs from delusion, it does not really exist. The thought that God could be "angry" with anyone is itself an error—indeed, an absurd one! How could the ocean depths be affected by even the most violent storm at the surface?

Imagine a young man brought up in a city slum, drawn almost inadvertently into some local gang, then caught up in gang warfare during which he shoots someone to death. He is then shot and killed, himself. According to many traditional dogmas (falsely named "orthodox"), he will be damned to hell for eternity. Imagine, then, some few billions of years from the time of his death, some fellow inmate in that cosmic prison asking him, "What sin did *you* commit, to be down here with the rest of us?"

The young man scratches his chin awhile, then replies, "I don't really remember!"

Time and space are illusory. In God, neither of them exists. Billions of years are not essentially different from one second. To human beings, a thousand years may seem like "eternity." Christian tradition promises a "millennium" as if that time span meant something! Billions upon billions of years comprise not even the winking of the divine eye, in eternity!

The yogi should live mentally beyond time and space. How to do that? He can begin by, in a sense, transcending space, becoming deeply aware of being *right here*, wherever "here" is. As a diver at sea can plunge under the surface and find himself in a medium where all seems one and the same, so even a traveler who feels himself to be fully present, wherever he is at the time, thinks not of where he came from or of where he is going. In a sense, he is equally in both places, without being physically in either of them. The more, indeed, he becomes centered in himself, in his own depths, the more he feels that he is in contact with things and with people who may even be far away. The best way to understand other people, and even abstract projects and problems, is to be centered, first, within oneself, and then, from that center, to intuit realities with which he has no outward connection. With practice, success can come to him relatively easily.

The next stage is to try to live in the present moment. If one can do that—by living *behind* the moment, in the Eternal Now—he will comprehend more easily what happened in the past, what is likely to happen in the future, and how to condense into insights that require hardly a moment a labor that might, reasonably, take a person months or years.

Paramhansa Yogananda could commune instantly—for time in God is one—with people who lived thousands of years ago. Every person can achieve comparable feats, though he acts from a lower level of realization. Try it: Withdraw deeply to your own center; then think of someone who lived long ago, and focus your mind at *his* center. You will see that, from your center to his, there forms a connection—as if your two islands, seemingly separated by ocean water, were connected more deeply by the earth underneath. Everyone who is not you is simply your own deeper Self, manifested differently, in a different form, and even at different times.

A sense of the oneness of all life helps the meditating yogi to approach God inwardly without fear or tension: to relax completely in divine love. Whatever happens in your life, you are one with the great sea of Truth. No one, however viciously he may treat you, can take away your love for God, or God's love, in all eternity, for you. God, and God alone, is your true treasure.

The person living in delusion can banish his delusion, not by discrimination alone (his mind being already hypnotized by the seeming reality of the errors he wants to dismiss), but by offering it up to God. God then, out of infinite, divine compassion, will send to him an enlightened guru whose liberated consciousness will lift him out of the mire he is struggling to escape.

(5:16) In those, however, who have banished ignorance by wisdom, the true Self shines forth like an effulgent sun.

(5:17) Their thoughts immersed in That One, their souls united with it, their entire devotion and allegiance absorbed in it, their being purged of the poison of delusion by the antidote of wisdom—such (liberated) souls achieve the state of no return.

(5:18) Such souls view with equal gaze a pious priest, a cow, an elephant, a dog, and an outcast.

(5:19) Even on this (earthly) plane of existence the relativities (birth, death; pleasure, pain) are overcome by one who views all even-mindedly. Those who can do so are, verily, enthroned in the unblemished, never-distorted Spirit.

(5:20) Such sages, established in the one Supreme Being and unwavering of discrimination, are neither jubilant when they confront pleasant experiences, nor depressed when they confront painful ones.

(5:21) Feeling no attraction to the sensory world (whether subtle or gross), the yogi lives in the ever-new joy of his own being. United to Spirit, he attains perfection in Absolute Bliss.

(5:22) O Son of Kunti (Arjuna)! because sense pleasures spring from outside the Self, they all have a beginning and an end, and bring only misery. No one of any understanding would seek happiness through them.

(5:23) He is truly a yogi who, while living on earth, and up to the last moment of his earth life, can master every impulse of desire and antipathy. He (alone among mortals) is a happy human being.

(5:24) Only one who possesses inner bliss, who is firmly centered in the inner Self, and is illumined by the inner Light (dependent on nothing outside the Self for his understanding) attains complete liberation (both while living and after death).

(5:25) His doubts (and hesitations) removed, his karmas all obliterated, his senses subdued, his delight only in the good of all, he (the sage) attains emancipation in Spirit.

(5:26) Renunciates who are without desire or anger, controlled in mind, and Self-realized are inwardly free whether living in this world or merged in the Infinite.

(5:27,28) The muni (one for whom liberation is the sole purpose of life) controls his senses, mind, and intellect, removing himself from contact with them by neutralizing the currents of prana and apana in the spine, which manifest (outwardly) as inhalation and exhalation in the nostrils. He fixes his gaze in the forehead, at a point midway between the two eyebrows

(thereby converting the dual current of physical vision into the single, omniscient spiritual eye). Such a one attains complete emancipation.

Yoga, as is well known, is not so much a philosophy as a science, which offers definite, practical techniques for raising man's consciousness inwardly through the spine, and uniting its myriad directional tendencies (*samskaras*) with one's own highest potential in the Self.

A fascinating aspect of this process is that one does not need to *reach out* for oneness with infinity: he has only to attain a level of perfect refinement in himself in order to attain that level of consciousness where separations cease to exist. It is—as Swami Sri Yukteswar explained in his book *The Holy Science*—a matter of removing the *koshas*, or "sheaths" which limit and enclose us in individuality. Freed not only from the ego, but from the last causal "vapor" of individual consciousness, there is nothing left to be attained. *We are that Infinite One, already!*

Eternally we have been with God, in God, and immersed in nothing but God. We have merely been enclosed—as if by thin veils at first, then by shawls, then by heavy curtains, and finally by the heavy, solid armor of egotism—and have taken, as our point of departure in everything that we are, do, see, and think, this little point of consciousness in infinite space: our little self.

These two vastly different perceptions of reality—on the one hand personal, confined, and even petty, and on the other hand impersonal, unlimited, and omnipresent—cannot be spanned intellectually. Yogananda described

divine attainment as "the liberating shock of omnipresence." Only by mental attunement with the consciousness
of an already-liberated guru can one make that leap across
the yawning abyss which separates the ego from Infinity.

The attunement one seeks should not be with the
guru's personality so much as with that level of his
consciousness which is beyond personality—one with
the Infinite.

To prepare the mind for so vast an expansion, however,
one cannot simply keep an open mind and "go along for
the ride." Only a spiritual hero can attempt the journey,
even *with* the help of the guru, who has made it already.
The courage required is not the "daredevil" type which
declares, while preening itself, "Just watch me: Of course
I can do it!" It is of a different type altogether—seeming
to require at first, perhaps, a very feminine kind of surrender which says, "I trust *you* to do it right." Instead,
however, there is nothing of either the feminine or the
masculine in this great leap of faith. The heroism required
is the courage implied in the words of a chant by
Yogananda (paraphrased here): "I will drown myself in
the Infinite to find my true Self to be infinite." True faith,
it must be understood, is very different from blind belief.

The artist who paints a line on an almost completed
work of art, knowing that the line will either make or
hopelessly mar his work, must *know* what he is doing.
His knowledge must be intuitive, not intellectual. This
kind of work isn't something that could be done by a
committee. Though the artist *knows*, his only way of
showing his knowledge is by *doing* it. That is the meaning of faith: a sure intuition, and an inner, complete

certainty which no amount of reasoning could either support or demolish.

What these two stanzas of the Gita teach is the importance of self-preparation for that supreme act of faith. This is where yoga enters the picture.

To concentrate one's gaze at the point midway between the eyebrows is not so strange a practice as it may seem at first. Whenever one is inspired by a new insight or idea, he lifts his gaze upward as if instinctively. The seat of superconsciousness is in the forehead. (That of the subconscious is at the back of the head.) The frontal lobe of the brain, which is located just behind the forehead, is the advanced portion, added by human evolution to the brain itself. The foreheads of lower animals slant sharply back—indicating the absence of a frontal lobe.

Yogis in ancient times discovered that the part of the frontal lobe that needs to be particularly stimulated is the portion just behind the point midway between the eyebrows.

We saw earlier in these pages that the physical act of breathing is intimately associated with—and is, indeed, *caused* by—the energy rising and descending in the spine through the *iḍa* and *pingala naḍis*, or nerve channels. *Iḍa* begins on the left side; *pingala*, on the right. Breathing in the astral body takes place in these two *naḍis*. The breath in the astral body is in the spine, and is composed of energy, not of inhalation and exhalation by the lungs. The ascending energy is called prana; the descending, apana. One yoga technique (I once observed my Guru practicing it) involves alternately closing the right and left nostrils to allow air to pass only through the left, then the right, stimulating the prana and apana in the spine. Stimulating that flow of energy by deliberately breathing in one nostril at a time is, however, an indirect technique. To control those currents with the attention focused on the outward activity of closing and opening the nostrils directs one's attention more to the breathing aspect of the exercise than to the energy-flow in the spine.

Kriya Yoga is the science that was particularly recommended by my own Guru and by his line of gurus. Kriya Yoga was first given in modern times by the great Himalayan master known simply as Babaji ("Revered Father"). According to my understanding, Babaji is himself an incarnation of the great Indian master of ancient times, Narayana, who, more recently, was Lord Krishna himself.

Babaji told his disciple Lahiri Mahasaya, whom he initiated into Kriya Yoga in 1860, that Kriya is the supreme ancient science of yoga, and that he himself in a previous body had given it to the world. This science may be called God's greatest gift to humanity for the soul's salvation.

Kriya Yoga helps one (as we discussed earlier in this book) to equalize the incoming and outgoing breaths, and to absorb one's energy in the spine, where one feels the currents as a cool (rising) and a slightly warm (descending) current.

There is another simple technique, helpful to practice as a preliminary exercise: With mental detachment, watch the breath flowing naturally in the nostrils. A mantra should be uttered with the breathing process: "*Hong*" as the breath flows in (allowing the flow to occur naturally); and "*Sau*" as it flows out. Gradually transfer your focus of attention from the feeling of breath in the nostrils to the point, higher up the nose, where it enters the head. This, of course, is also the point midway between the eyebrows.

My Guru told me also to practice, after some time, feeling the energy flowing up and down the spine with the incoming and outgoing breaths—not to control the flow, but to feel it as the subtle *cause* of the physical breath. This technique is not Kriya Yoga, but my Guru sometimes referred to it as the "baby Kriya."

(5:29) He finds peace who knows Me as the Enjoyer of all offerings (yagyas) and austerities, as the Infinite Lord of creation, and as the Dearest Friend of all.

Man usually thinks of himself as enjoying personally whatever blessings he receives from spiritual practices. It is, in fact, God's bliss enjoying itself! We love with *His* love. We enjoy with *His* joy.

Thus ends the fifth chapter, called "Freedom Through Inner Renunciation," of the Upanishad of the holy Bhagavad Gita, in the dialogue between Sri Krishna and Arjuna discussing yoga and the science of God-realization.

CHAPTER EIGHTEEN

THE TRUE YOGA

(6:1) The Blessed Lord said: The true renunciate and the true yogi are those who perform dutiful actions without desire for their fruits, not those who, making no self-offering, act with ego-motivation, nor those who (in the name of renunciation) abstain from action.

MUCH OF WHAT KRISHNA SAYS HERE HE HAS said before. Here, however, his message is broader. He is re-emphasizing that the essence of the spiritual life is ego-transcendence, whether one lives in the world, in a monastery, or solitarily in a cave. Krishna has already stated that action, whether outward or inward, is essential for the aspirant. One who has transcended the need for outward activity can do so only in a state of physical breathlessness, for in that state alone can one work dynamically with the subtle inner energies. Until that point, whether he is a *sannyasi* (renunciate) or is obliged to live an ordinary life among worldly people, his essential need is for some kind of ego-freeing activity. The fact that a person lives an ordinary life and has a normal job may make ego-renunciation more difficult, but it does not make it less obligatory. Both sannyasi (renunciate) and *"samsari"* must achieve the same results, with or without formal renunciation. The spiritual path is not a matter of "scoring points" in the game of pleasing God! The inner need of every human being, if he would unite himself with the Infinite, is the same.

Let us consider the differences between being a yogi-renunciate and a yogi-*samsari* (one who must contribute to the outward play of *maya*). It should be said at the outset that a *"samsari"* need not play his part with ego-attachment. It is indeed pleasing to God, and a great help to spiritual advancement, for one to participate in the divine play without egoic attachment, instead of scorning to involve oneself in it. This world was, after all, made by God. He Himself finds joy in His handiwork; otherwise, wouldn't He have learned long ago not to create universes at all?! An expansive spirit is a natural part of the creative process, and is therefore intrinsic to the "ever-newness" of divine bliss. The key word for participation in *"samsara,"* then, is to "play one's part" with conscious non-identification with the ego.

The scriptures say that God created the universe "in order that He might enjoy Himself through many." Certainly the Lord does *not* enjoy the fact that His creatures suffer! His enjoyment, then, must come (outwardly) from seeing every story come to a happy ending at last, as His human creatures one by one attain final release from all ego-limitation in infinite bliss. He wants us to merge back, eventually, into His ocean of

Satchidananda. Those few in every age who attain that goal, however, and who want also to continue helping the struggling mortals (among whom they once were counted), are certainly pleasing to Him in a very special way. The philosophical question, "Which is greater?" doesn't arise, since all are equally great in God. Certainly, however, His manifested creatures must be grateful for the fact that a few liberated souls, feeling this commitment, actually come back to help them.

It is supremely ironic that these few souls, even outstandingly among mankind, so often attract the fiercest persecution during their earthly service to mankind! Inwardly they are untouched by the way others treat them, for they are above the ego, but how pitiable it is that so many human beings should, in this way, "bite the hand that feeds them"! The tragedy is not theirs who receive persecution, but mankind's, that man should again and again be offered divine love, yet should spurn it so contemptuously in preference to its own ego-degradation. All this is a part of the divine "plot," with its myriad sub-plots, "red herrings," and intricate distractions from the one, true theme.

The essential difference between the joyful actor in the play of *samsara* and the hermit who disdains to participate in the play at all is superficial. Both types of *sadhakas* (truth seekers) offer themselves up to God, to let Him do with them as He wills.

The path of marriage, job, and involvement with family has certain obvious disadvantages which make spiritual progress more of a challenge, outwardly. A nagging wife or domineering husband, obstreperous children, demanding relatives who think blood ties entitle them to meddle in a person's life (whether out of family attachment, or out of concern for their own reputations): All of these can create powerful obstructions on the spiritual path.

Sadashiva, a great sadhu in southern India, lived as a young man with his parents, meditating in his room and earnestly studying the scriptures. One day he emerged from his room to find a commotion in the home.

"What is happening?" he inquired.

"We are preparing," his parents told him, "for the arrival of your intended bride."

Sadashiva, on returning to his room, reflected: "If my bride's merely *prospective* arrival can create such a disturbance, what effect on my daily routine will her *actual* arrival have?" Quietly, that very night, he slipped out the back door and left the neighborhood, never to return.

Considering the danger of ego-involvement for anyone who accepts the role of wife or husband, parent, dutiful member of a close or extended family, and his need to support himself and others by taking a job or by creating and selling for profit: all these factors certainly help to explain why anyone whose heart is filled with divine fervor would want to live "away from it all"—in woods or cave, or even in a populous ashram or monastery, where at least there are other dedicated souls.

Paramhansa Yogananda said, "Those who marry as a necessity will have to be born again, that they may learn to live for God's love alone." At the same time, it must be said that many of my Guru's own most advanced disciples either were or had been married. The important thing for everyone is to reach that point, whether late or soon in life, where he wants only God. My Guru told me that one disciple of his, an old woman in her eighties, had been an atheist all her life. On meeting him, however, she was converted to the spiritual life. So intensely did she seek God thereafter that, as he said to me, "She found freedom in this life."

The desire for a companion has deep roots in human nature. It takes many incarnations to understand that the "companion" one seeks has always been God Himself. The Lord is our supreme Friend, our only eternally faithful Lover, our ever-forgiving Mother, our firm but forever-accepting Father. He is, as my Guru put it, "the Nearest of the near, the Dearest of the dear: He is closer to you than your very thoughts."

Marriage and family is, for some people, the best way of realizing to its depth the eternal need of the soul: its deeper-than-conscious longing for God alone. Those, however, who have understood to their depths that the only thing they want already is God, are wise to dedicate themselves to a life lived for Him alone.

One problem with giving this counsel is the fact that so many people seek the path of renunciation not because of wholehearted devotion to God, but because of a wish to live an easy life of minimal responsibility. It is to such people above all that Krishna addressed those words, "those who (in the name of renunciation) abstain from action."

Those who follow the renunciate path find it easier to direct all their energies to God. That very path, however, imposes also the broader responsibility of helping others spiritually: One should not live for himself alone. A temptation sannyasis face is to center their attention too narrowly on their own spiritual search, forgetting the needs of others. In that selfishness they strengthen, instead of weakening, the hold exerted upon them by the ego.

One who would live entirely for God must be sure in his own heart, first of all, that in so doing he is not merely shirking responsibility. The unfortunate truth is that few so-called "renunciates" embrace their calling with an entirely pure motive.

The other side of this story is that one embraces a spiritual calling not because he is already pure and perfect, but so that he may become so. Thus, whichever path you yourself embrace, let it be one in which you feel able to direct your energies more and more one-pointedly *in the right way*, toward liberation in God.

(6:2) Understand, O Pandava (Arjuna), that what the scriptures call *sannyasa* (renunciation) is the same thing as yoga. Indeed, without renunciation of selfish motive (*sankalpa*) one cannot be a (true) yogi.

(6:3) The muni, aspiring to the (spiritual) heights through (scientific) yoga action (karma), on achieving his goal finds perfect, vibrationless peace.

(6:4) He who has overcome attachment not only to sense objects but to (sensory) activity, and who has achieved freedom from all ego-motivated planning, is said (by the wise) to have attained *yogarudha*: the firm union of soul and Spirit.

Paramhansa Yogananda described at this point some of what that "scientific yoga" action, or karma, entails. It may help the aspirant here to understand something important: What is involved in spiritual awakening concerns far more than making a clear philosophical resolution.

The word "karma" in stanza three signifies the practice of specific yoga *pranayamas*—exercises, that is to say, for gaining control of the inner energy, withdrawing it from the body, and centering it in the spine and its subtle chakras, which—with the inclusion of the medulla oblongata at the base of the brain, and also of the brain (the *sahasrara*, or "thousand-rayed lotus")—number seven in all.

The medullary center has two rays of energy, described in the Book of Revelation of the Bible as "a sharp two-edged sword." (Rev. 1:16) These twin currents, positive and negative, supply the two hands, the two feet, the two lungs, the dual-branched nervous system, the two eyes, two ears, the two sides of the tongue, and the two hemispheres of the brain. The brain stores the energy entering the body through the medulla oblongata. The energy then enters the spine, passes down it, and flows out into the nervous system. The dual currents in the medulla pass down the spine through the chakras to nourish the body. The energy flows outward through the chakras in various directions: From the *bishuddha*, or cervical center, it flows out in sixteen rays; from the *anahata*, the heart, or dorsal, center, it flows out in twelve rays; from the *manipura*, or navel (the lumbar) center, its rays number ten; from the *swadisthana*, or sacral center, six; and from the *muladhara*, or coccyx center, four.

In the initial state, the yogi's meditative "job" is to withdraw his energy from the physical body into the spinal centers. At this point he sees, through the spiritual eye, his astral body with its subtle chakras. Beholding the astral body, he offers his ego—the central "element" of the astral body—up to its ideational origin of separate individuality in the causal or ideational body. Thence, reaffirming soul-consciousness wholly at last, he offers that separate identity up to Infinity to be dissolved in cosmic consciousness.

Already at the causal level the soul cognizes all cosmic manifestation as a dream of God's. To attain *yogarudha*, firm or complete union with Infinite Spirit, he must waken completely from the cosmic dream and realize himself as the one Self beyond all space, time, size, and any other limiting conditions: behind manifested existence itself.

(6:5) Let man uplift himself by his own effort, and let him not debase himself. Indeed, one's self is his own greatest friend—or (if he so chooses) his own greatest enemy.

Useless is the human tendency to blame others for one's own misfortunes. Indeed, there *are* no misfortunes. "Conditions are always neutral," Yogananda said. "They only appear good or bad, joyful or sad, fortunate or unfortunate owing to the positive or negative attitudes [and expectations] of the mind." The yogi must learn to gaze even-mindedly upon whatever happens to

him. When, however, the ego chooses to refer back again
and again to itself everything that can possibly affect it,
it "debases" itself by becoming involved in downward-
and outward-flowing energy through the chakras, then
through the senses, to the surrounding world.

When others treat you unkindly, unfairly, or even
cruelly, make it a definite point never to react with
emotion. Never strike back; never complain; never
resist either defensively or aggressively, out of ego-
consciousness. Sometimes a wrong must be countered
with a right, but even when duty calls you to such
action, try always—as Krishna counseled Arjuna—to
conduct yourself in such a way as to ensure that your
own attitude is ever impersonal.

**(6:6) For him whose (lower, egoic) self has been
conquered by the (higher, soul) Self, that Self is the
friend of his (lower) self. The true Self, however, is
not friendly to the false self, and is (in many ways)
its enemy.**

People are often stunned by the severity with which
great sages—who are ever the true friends of everyone's
higher Self—may sometimes treat them. A saint accepts
worldly people more or less as they are, without
concerning himself particularly over their foibles and
defects. If, however, they show a glimmering of desire to
know God, he may sometimes treat them with unexpected severity. If, moreover, they place themselves under
him as disciples, he may seem (to worldly eyes, or even
to the unprepared disciple!) to behave toward them

quite harshly. His "job" is not to pamper their egos. It is to cauterize forever their egoic "shortfalls," and make them pure vessels that can receive into themselves the supernal blessings of divine love and bliss.

(6:7) The tranquil sage who has conquered the (lower, egoic) self abides ever in the Supreme Self. He views with equanimity all the dualities: cold and heat, pleasure and pain, praise and blame.

(6:8) That yogi who is blissfully absorbed in the wisdom of the Self is known as being unshakably united to Spirit. Unchangeable, the controller of his senses, he views with equal mind a clod of earth, a stone, and a bar of gold.

(6:9) He is a supreme yogi who gazes equally upon patrons, friends, enemies, strangers, peacemakers, those who cause trouble, relatives, the virtuous, and the ungodly.

These last two stanzas do not mean that the yogi isn't capable of recognizing the differences between one material object and another, or between a good human being and an evil one. As my Guru once put it, "He is not *dumb*!" The difference between the wise yogi and the ordinarily ignorant human being is that the yogi accepts with equanimity whatever *is*. To him, all things, and all creatures, are simply plays of divine light and shadow on the screen of duality. He reacts appropriately to all, both virtuous and ungodly, but in his heart he sees both as aspects of the eternal drama of God.

(6:10) Free from the hopes (engendered by) desire, and untouched by any craving for possession, the (waves of feeling in his) heart controlled (by yoga concentration), the yogi, retiring alone to a quiet place, should try to unite his little self with the Supreme Self.

It is important to understand that Krishna, who has repeatedly stressed the importance of right action over non-action, also recommends to Arjuna here the apparent "non-action" of meditation. Obviously, he is saying that meditation, too, is a kind of "right" action. An important saying in the Indian scriptures is: "When a duty conflicts with a higher duty, it ceases to be a duty." That rarely accomplished yogi who is able to sit in deep meditation during all the hours when he is not performing necessary bodily functions—eating, sleeping, taking a little exercise, etc.—is fulfilling that "higher duty" which precludes the necessity for engaging in any other activity. For most aspiring yogis, however, although they might well find unbroken solitude a mistake (leading to greater restlessness, then laziness and gradual inertia—as opposed to what Krishna calls non-action), it would nevertheless be a great aid to them in their sadhana (spiritual practice) if they could spend some time—a week or two, or even longer—every year, and at least one day a week, in seclusion. Meditating for long hours, reading books that are spiritually uplifting, taking long walks "with God," doing a little mental work such as writing in a spiritual diary: All these activities can provide a spiritually strengthening balance to constant outward activity.

During one's periods of seclusion, one should maintain complete silence, and not speak outwardly to anyone. He should make it a practice, instead, to talk mentally with God, or to carry on a mental dialogue with his guru (if he is blessed to have one). His guru will convey more understanding to him in this way than he could teach, outwardly. (It is, indeed, fairly normal for true gurus to be *maunis*, never speaking outwardly. Their method of teaching is in any case more by thought transference than by outward speech.)

It should be understood, finally, that true solitude begins when the energy is withdrawn into the spine, stilling the senses, and when the mind contains not a ripple of restless thought. One who can enter this state has no need for outward solitude.

(6:11) The yogi should have a firm, clean seat, neither too high nor too low. He should cover his seat with *kusha* grass first, then (cover that with) a deer or tiger skin, and then (place upon that) a (wool and/or silk) cloth.

A foundation mat of interwoven kusha grass is a way provided by Nature for protecting the meditating yogi from dampness in the earth. There is no other reason nor any special, mystic meaning for using kusha grass. Its use is only its dampness-dispelling properties. Since this grass, though it grows abundantly in India, is not available everywhere, its non-availability need be no excuse (as a few bigots have actually insisted!) for not practicing yoga in other countries!

To begin with, even sitting on a firm, flat surface in *Padmasana*, *Siddhasana*, or some other yoga *asana*, while helpful for young yogis in keeping their bodies steady and for calming their nerves, is not essential for older devotees. Many Westerners, especially, find that sitting cross-legged forces them to concentrate more on their aching knees than on the spine and in the spiritual eye! For such persons, and for those everywhere who are so completely accustomed to sitting on chairs that any other position would constitute an unnecessary penance, Paramhansa Yogananda recommended that one simply sit on a straight-backed, armless chair, with the back upright (not touching the back of the chair), and the hands placed palms upward on the legs at the junction of the abdomen. The chin should be parallel to the ground, and the shoulder blades drawn slightly together (to hold the spine straight by "corrugating" the back). The chest should be held high, not sunken: there should be no forward stoop. The stomach and abdomen should be relaxed, not held in, and should therefore protrude slightly forward.

This position of the spine and chest is what is meant in the Gita by "Arjuna's bow," which (as we saw) Arjuna allowed to slip. What that means was that he slumped forward. The bow didn't literally "slip from his grasp," as Chapter 1 of the Gita symbolically suggests. The position indeed suggests a bow, with the front of the body resembling the arch of the bow, and the spine resembling the string.

More is given on the meditative position in the next stanzas. In this stanza Krishna says to cover the mat of kusha grass with the skin of a deer or a tiger. Traditionally, these animals should have died a natural death, though if one wants such a skin he must more or less take what he can get these days. (My own Guru's deer skin clearly displayed a bullet hole.) Animal skins are not easily come by, and serve a purpose for which other coverings—woolen blankets, or silk cloths—can be substituted. Deer skins are said to be helpful in achieving peace of mind. Tiger skins are said to generate will power, and are generally recommended only for those who practice sexual self-control, in the thought that the energy generated will conflict with that of people who don't practice abstinence, and will therefore cause tension between the upward-pulling energy in the spine and its downward-moving tendencies.

All this is, however, quite arcane. The physical effect of these skins is negligible compared with their more mundane purpose: to insulate subtle energies in the body from other, downward-pulling earth energies.

Perfectly adequate for general purposes, and for most people (so Paramhansa Yogananda said), are the energy-insulating properties of wool and/or silk. If you sit on the floor, place a woolen blanket beneath you. If you sit on a chair, place the woolen blanket in such a way that it comes under the feet, over the seat, and over the back of the chair. You may, if you like, cover the wool with a silk cloth.

It is important that your seat be firm (not wobbly), and clean. Preferably, no one but you should ever sit there. Some of the benefits of solitude can be achieved by setting aside a room in your home for nothing but meditation. By allowing no other activity to take place in that room, you will gradually build up vibrations there that will tangibly help you to achieve inner silence. You will, indeed, feel those vibrations the moment you enter the room.

If you cannot set aside a separate room for meditation, it will be possible to create some of the same effect by screening off a portion of some other room—perhaps your bedroom.

One reason for having one's seat (suitably insulated) on the ground when you meditate is to protect your body, in case you should slip suddenly into a deep meditative state, in which case your body might fall over and injure itself. The best position for this purpose, and one which presses on certain nerves that, Yogananda used to say, will help to steady the body, is *Padmasana* (the lotus pose).

A firm seat need not mean a hard one! Hardness will not only soon become uncomfortable, but will cause the legs to go numb. Ease and relaxation are primary considerations.

Yogananda mentioned also, in passing, another, symbolic reason for the above advice Krishna gave. The earth-grown grass, the animal skin, and the silken cloth symbolize the lower three chakras, above which the yogi's energy should rise. The grass represents the earth element, which is the vibration of the lowest (*muladhara*) *chakra*. The animal skin (a coating for blood and flesh) represents the water element, which is the vibration of the next chakra up, the sacral or *swadisthana*. The silk cloth (which people sometimes use to generate static electricity) represents the fire element: the vibration of the third chakra up, the *manipura* or lumbar (navel) center. Since the purpose of all these coverings for the seat is to insulate the body from downward-pulling energies, it may be more than symbolically that they represent the lower three chakras.

(6:12) Seated firmly there, with one-pointed concentration of the mind, and neither roaming mentally nor reacting to sense stimuli, let him seek self-purification by yoga practice (using the techniques prescribed by his guru).
(6:13) Holding the spine, neck, and head firmly erect and motionless, let the yogi focus his gaze at the starting point of the nose (*nasikagram*) between the two eyebrows; and let him not gaze elsewhere, but keep his gaze calmly one-pointed.

This stanza completes the Gita's instructions on the right posture for meditation, including the position of the eyes. Translators have often taken this stanza to mean, "Focus at the tip of the nose." *Nasikagram* (the Sanskrit word), however, means not only "front" (which has been taken to mean the *tip*), but also "*origin.*" As Swami Sri Yukteswar stated, "origin" is the right meaning. There is nothing spiritual to be gained by concentrating on the tip of the nose! Krishna is clearly referring to the point from which the nose protrudes from the face, where the air enters the head: the universally recognized seat of the spiritual eye, the Kutastha, which, as Krishna has already indicated, lies at the point midway between the two eyebrows.

Why *gaze* at this point? The direction of one's gaze is an indication of one's state of consciousness. It also helps to *induce* the state of consciousness one desires. A downward gaze is associated with the subconscious, and tends to induce subconsciousness. Gazing straight ahead is not only associated with wakefulness, but helps one to be "awake and ready" if he feels himself growing sleepy. And an upward gaze is associated with superconsciousness. It is natural for a person who feels inspired by some thought, or if he is entertaining hopes for the future, to gaze upward almost by instinct.

There is more involved in the ideal meditative position of the eyes. First it may be pointed out that saints in every religious tradition have been seen, and are so depicted by artists, as gazing upward. Popular thought imagines them beholding visions "in the clouds," but in fact the gaze in ecstasy is drawn upward. For saints, this position is not a practice but a natural *consequence* of being in a superconscious state.

For the meditating yogi, a good practice is to gaze upward—not with crossed eyes, but with the gaze slightly focused on a point in the near distance—as if looking at one's thumb, held outward and slightly high, at arm's length.

It is best (but more difficult because of visual distractions) to meditate with open eyes, the gaze (as we've seen) slightly inward, and the lower eyelids slightly raised. Thus, closed eyes are naturally associated with sleep; wide open eyes, with wakefulness; and slightly raised, finally, with the lower lids in a "half open and half closed" position, is associated with superconsciousness.

Interestingly, the eyes of worldly people whose consciousness is heavy with the descending flow of their energy, tend to show more white under the irises. The eyes of yogis generally show none, or little, of that white area. This, too, is a result of the upward "lift" on the lower lids accompanying a raised consciousness.

(6:14) Serene and fearless, steadfast in his vow of *brahmacharya* (sexual control), his mind controlled, and his attention centered in Me, the seated yogi should meditate on Me as the ultimate goal (of all striving).

A natural question arises (here as well as elsewhere in this scripture) in the minds of true seekers: Is absolute sexual self-control essential on the spiritual path? If so (many think), it means that most people, unless they escape worldly society altogether and live far away from it as hermits, are doomed to a path that, aside from all the other problems it incurs, is not only difficult but impossible.

The great Himalayan master Babaji, however, who initiated Lahiri Mahasaya (a married man with children) into Kriya Yoga, instructed his disciple to give Kriya Yoga initiation to all (to people who were living and working in the world, as well as to sannyasis) who "humbly cried for help." Those, in other words, who are unable to practice complete sexual abstinence are not debarred from the yoga path.

That complete abstinence is an aid on the path is well established in yoga tradition and in many religions.

Therefore it must be added that, the more perfect the abstinence, the easier it is to rise spiritually. That much said, however, it must be stressed simply that being married should never be taken by any sincere seeker as license for sexual overindulgence. True seekers should all make a sincere effort to be temperate. There are, on the other hand, degrees of *brahmacharya*: once a month, for example; or—the example set by Yogananda's parents—once a year. Daily indulgence, or even more frequent indulgence, is a clear indication that one is too worldly, and is not really serious in his spiritual search. It is impossible to run in two directions at once. The results of overindulgence are mental vitiation, weakened health, and premature old age.

(6:15) The self-governed yogi, his mind fully controlled, attains the peace of supreme nirvana (the state of individual extinction) in union with My spirit.

Nirvana, the explicit ideal of Buddhism, has been mistakenly identified with an utter extinction of consciousness. Such could never be the case, since the only reality in existence *is* consciousness, everything in the universe being a manifestation of consciousness. Even the atoms are conscious to a degree; otherwise, they could not exist. Paramhansa Yogananda went so far as to declare that every atom "is dowered with individuality."

Nirvana is the extinction of individuality, which is, in fact, the goal of every true spiritual path. Individuality is an aspect of *maya*, which makes all the waves on the ocean of Spirit appear separate and real. Yet—remaining with this metaphor—they are made of water, and only appear real as the surface moves with passing vibrations, which are caused by the wind and by the Earth's movement. The waves, as such, have no individual existence. The same must be said for thoughts and tendencies, which merely appear for a time in the mind but have their roots in infinity, and do not define the ego. An analogy would be a piece of flotsam on the ocean, which rises and sinks with the passing waves without moving relative to stationary objects such as the shore, or a ship at anchor. Flotsam works as an image because, being a different substance from water, it is visible. Actually, of course, there is only one "substance": consciousness.

The ego really is more like an invisible drop of ocean water, enclosed, like the message of a shipwrecked mariner, in a floating bottle of appearances. The bottle might be thought of, in this context, as being made of ice, placed on a plate of ice, and the plate resting on an iceberg. That foundation (the physical, astral, and causal bodies) must be melted before the drop itself, also frozen, can merge into the ocean. This image is labored, its logic forced by the analogy of a wave, but the point of this exercise is that the drop of water (the individual soul) doesn't cease to exist: It merges, on liberation, into the ocean of consciousness. Having nothing further to contain and confine it in the limited space implied by individuality, it *becomes* the vast ocean of consciousness itself.

(6:16) O Arjuna! Yoga is not for him who eats too much or who fasts too much, who sleeps too much or who sleeps too little.

(6:17) One who is temperate in eating, recreation, working, sleeping, and wakefulness attains yoga, which destroys all suffering.

Nowhere in the Gita does Krishna more clearly teach moderation than in these two stanzas. Moderation was taught also by Buddha, and by many other great world teachers. If the teachings of Jesus Christ seem more extreme ("Take no heed for tomorrow"; "take no money with you in your purse. . . .") it was because he taught at a time when people were too much bound by rules, and too intolerant of views different from their own. They needed a stern teaching. Jesus also counseled compassion, however, as he showed, for example, in the story of the woman taken in adultery.

It is an interesting fact that the sterner approach to religion has been taken in India, where Krishna taught moderation, and that the more lenient approach—often bordering on outright materialism—has been taken in the so-called Christian countries of the West. It is ironic that, in this basic respect at least, Christians have been truer to the teachings of Krishna, whereas Hindus have been truer to the teachings of Jesus Christ!

Be that as it may, moderation has also been a basic teaching of all great masters. As Yogananda said, "It is better not to go to extremes in self-discipline until you have achieved at least some realization." If a brittle twig is bent forcibly, it will snap.

Nevertheless, the moderation counseled here by Krishna is hardly the materialists' idea of this concept. For worldly people, a few minutes of meditation every day may seem already to be bordering on fanaticism! Buddha, on the other hand, who taught moderation, sat determinedly under the Bodhi tree and didn't move from it until he'd solved the mystery of life. "Let this body dissolve, but until life's mystery I solve I never, never from this spot will move." He sat there for forty days and nights, until at last enlightenment came. The average person could only comment, "So *that's* moderation?!" Moderation means doing everything you can to advance spiritually, without pushing yourself too far.

Krishna's mention of recreation is interesting and helpful. Too many spiritual seekers think that frivolity of any kind is harmful. The English saying, "All work and no play makes Jack a dull boy," is significant in this context. Many monasteries, with their strict daily routine and firmly imposed rules, all intended to make monks and nuns holy, often have just the opposite effect. The inmates, under obligation to follow a routine too monotonously regular, tend to become dull-minded. With too many rules, moreover, they tend to become excessively rigid, and lose any hint of the spontaneous creativity that is so essential for spirits seeking self-expansion.

One imagines a bishop, abbot, or some other high churchman trying to justify some light pleasantry by commenting, after suppressing a light titter, "A little harmless merriment is not forbidden, I believe?" Without a wholesome balance of sufficient recreation, one may come to resemble a stuffed frog, looking self-important, though unable to say anything of interest to anyone!

In India there is less self-consciousness in that respect, but the human tendency of religious figures everywhere to take themselves too seriously, and never to laugh except drily, is (one suspects) a worldwide phenomenon.

(6:18) When the chitta (feeling) is completely calmed and centered in the Self, the yogi, freed from every attachment and desire, attains the state known as union with God.

Entanglement with delusion begins not so much with the ego itself as with the reactions of *feeling* in the heart to the fluctuations of *maya*. Even a master needs to retain enough ego-consciousness to recognize that certain duties in his world, though God-ordained, are his own. He is not identified with his ego, but rather works through it, somewhat in the way a trumpeter blows his horn. What really traps people in delusion is the thought, "I *like* this!"—or, "I *dislike* that!" Even liberated masters need enough ego-consciousness to hold the atoms of their bodies together. In the illustration of the waves and the ocean, the master is the low, sattwic wave, the very crest of which is still close to the bosom of the ocean.

Therefore it was that Patanjali gave his definition of yoga as, "*Yogas chitta vritti nirodha*: Yoga is the neutralization of the eddies (whirlpools, great and small) of feeling."

(6:19) A candle flame burns steadily, protected from the wind. Even so is the consciousness of that yogi who has subdued his chitta (feelings).

The moon's reflection on a lake is distorted by ripples in the water. Such are the ripples of feeling, which often grow to great waves of agitation. They distort the clarity of human perception. To calm the mind, that it may reflect the truth as it is, one must calm the waves of reaction in the heart. Only when the flame of concentration can burn steadily, and one accepts calmly whatever *is* rather than trying to view it differently and *wishing* it were different, can one achieve complete truthfulness. One must learn to remain unmoved by either good fortune or adversity. Only then is the deep perception of Infinity possible.

Yogananda often spoke of the "sense telephones"—the sensations carried to the mind by the senses of sight, hearing, smell, taste, and touch. These, he said, can be "switched off" during meditation, when the breath and the heartbeat are stilled, and the energy becomes withdrawn into the spine from the body's surface. Krishna is not speaking here, however, of the meditative state only, but of the yogi in normal daily activity also, who can keep his feelings unruffled by the emotionally reactive process of human feeling.

It is important to understand how central the emotions are to any involvement in delusion. Only consider an example we saw earlier: the uncensorable reactions of a little child to any unexpected occurrence. The child jumps up and down with delight, or stoops over and stamps his feet with displeasure. His emotional waves prevent him from seeing anything clearly. To tell a child, "All this will be over, by evening" would be useless! His entire "reality" is in his own reaction of the moment.

To him, things will never be different. Emotional moments are like scenes captured with the click of a camera lens. Although that image will last as long as the film or the print endures, the scene itself may change completely in a single moment.

The wave crest has no permanence. The person rising and plunging in a rowboat on an agitated sea cannot get a clear glimpse of anything stationary on the land nearby. Even so, people caught in the storm of delusion can comprehend no fixed truth, and are in fact too restless to think about it for two seconds together.

Even this recognized fact has been distorted by delusion! Scientists believe that, in order to judge the facts clearly in any experiment, they must rigidly exclude feeling as foreign to "scientific" objectivity. The truth is that without *true* feeling—which is to say, intuition—any insight gained will be sterile and lifeless. Gyana Yogis, similarly, imagine that by eliminating feeling (which, again, means intuition) from their understanding of truth, they will develop clear understanding. They deprive themselves, however, of real *insight*, for intuitive feeling is essential to true understanding. It must be calm, however, centered, and upwardly directed toward superconsciousness— located physically, as we have seen, in the frontal lobe of the brain in the region behind the forehead, midway between the eyebrows.

The intellect can see, analyze, and explain: Only the addition of the heart's feeling, however, can bestow *understanding*.

Indeed, it may be questioned whether, without feeling, consciousness can even exist.

(6:20) The state of complete inner tranquility, (which is) attained by yoga meditation, wherein the little self (the ego) perceives itself as the Self, enjoys itself as the Self;—

(6:21) that state in which bliss, transcendent above the senses and accepted as such by intuitive intelligence, can never be expunged;—

(6:22) the state which, once attained, is considered the treasure beyond all other treasures: In that state (alone) does the yogi become immune to grief even (in the face of) the greatest tragedy.

Paramhansa Yogananda has been quoted already as saying, "You must be able to stand unshaken amidst the crash of breaking worlds." In these stanzas Krishna explains the state of consciousness in which so firm a stance becomes finally possible.

(6:23) That state is known by the name of yoga, the condition untouched by any pain. The practice of yoga, therefore, should be followed resolutely, with undaunted heart.

Stanzas 20–22 describe the progress from conditioned (*sabikalpa*, or *sampragyata*) samadhi to unconditioned (*nirbikalpa*, or *asampragyata*) samadhi: the state of ultimate union with God, referred to here in Stanza 23 as "the condition untouched by any pain." In the first state, *sabikalpa samadhi*, ego-consciousness is still present, though dormant. Thus, the intuitive intelligence (which combines feeling with discrimination) is still active; the

calmly to discipline this fractious colt, the mind! It will gradually come under control, and will behave as he wants it to.

(6:26) Each time the fickle, wavering mind wanders from its course, let him withdraw it and redirect it toward (the task of) controlling it.

(6:27) The yogi who has completely calmed his mind, whose passions (rajoguna) are at rest, and who is freed from every impurity: such a one, truly, attains oneness with the Spirit, and supreme blessedness.

(6:28) The yogi, freed from imperfection, ceaselessly engaged in (activities that lead to) divine union, easily attains the state of blissful union with Spirit.

(6:29) United to the Supreme Self by the practice of yoga, he beholds his Self in all beings, and all beings in that one Self.

(6:30) He who beholds Me everywhere, and who beholds everything in Me, never loses sight of Me; nor do I lose sight of him.

My Guru very often quoted this last stanza. His tone of voice and his expression, as he did so, were blissful. He was reminding us that God is ever near. What seems to hold the Lord at a distance is only our indifference. If we will do the work needed to calm our thoughts and feelings (above all), we will find Him there, waiting for us. People who wail miserably over His continued silence, and His seeming heedlessness of them in their suffering, need only apply the principles that they already know from daily life.

Do they want worldly success? They know—or learn soon enough—that it won't be dropped into their laps: They must work for it. Do they want human love? They know it won't come to them if they simply sit at home, languishing. Do they want rubies, diamonds, gold? These things are not found lying about on the ground: They must be mined by someone with great effort, and paid for by others at great cost.

How is it that people think God *owes* them an answer for their brief, restless, and usually shallow prayers? *Anguished* prayers? Sometimes—but the anguish passes, and they soon forget Him again as they go off in pursuit of some new will-o'-the-wisp. God sees all this and says, "I will wait." He wants to be sure of our love, for He has been seeking it, with hardly ever a glance in His direction from man, for millennia!

(6:31) That yogi rests forever centered in Me, whatever his way of outward living, who sees Me at the heart of all beings.

An exercise worth practicing, whenever one looks at another human being, is to think, "My higher Self is also in him. In him, too, our one Self is struggling through his ego to find its true nature: complete, perfect bliss through all human experiences; true love in a human companion; true, divine recognition in human fame; true, divine power in fancied power over others; true, inner wealth in property and a swelling bank account." All mankind longs for basically the same fulfillment. Try, then, to see God everywhere, and never exclude Him mentally from anything you behold or experience. In this way it will be easier for you to approach Him, who is everywhere, and to whom all souls are equally dear, and equally His own.

(6:32) O Arjuna, the best yogi is he who feels the needs of others, their sorrows, their joys, as though they were his own.

(6:33) Arjuna said, O Madhusudana (Krishna), owing to my restlessness I've achieved no lasting results in the attempts You've taught me to steady the mind.

(6:34) Verily (Arjuna continued) the mind is restless, tumultuous, powerfully stubborn! O Krishna, I consider it to be as difficult as to master the wind!

Consider how, in *Autobiography of a Yogi*, Paramhansa Yogananda, as a disciple in his guru's ashram, said one day of his meditative efforts, (My disobedient thoughts) "scattered like birds before the hunter." That was the very day his guru gave him his first experience in cosmic consciousness.

It is common to lament the slowness and difficulty of one's spiritual efforts. Heroic courage is needed to win in this most challenging, but also most important, of all struggles. Many devotees, after a little effort, flee the scene and return to the life they were living before. Incarnation after incarnation they try, fail, then return. Perhaps they return with renewed will to try again, but often they struggle with discouragement and disappointment. A common lament is, "But—it's so difficult!" Well, of course it is! Can the "pearl of great price" be won without great effort? Yet there simply *is no* alternative! Whoever puts his hand to the plow should finish the job, as Jesus Christ put it in Luke 9:62, "not looking back, or he won't be fit for the kingdom of God." Let him tell himself that, even in the effort to succeed, he is already among the "elect" of mankind. Few—indeed, *very* few—have acquired the good karma to know that finding God is the *only* goal of life.

The science of yoga is priceless in its importance for the spiritual seeker. It offers techniques that can aid the mind in its efforts to achieve calmness.

The second of these stanzas itself hints at the answer to Arjuna's problem. He says he considers the mind "as difficult to master as the wind." Wind is, indeed, the clue to the solution to his problem, as solutions are often implied already in the way the questions are phrased!

The solution, here, is the breath. "Breathlessness is deathlessness" is a common saying among yogis. In a recent stanza (6:19) we saw this image of the wind used already: "A candle flame burns steadily, protected from the wind." As the wind agitates a candle flame, so breathing agitates the mind. We see a reverse effect upon the breath: when the mind, and especially the feelings, become agitated, the breathing becomes restless. Any major shock causes the heart to beat faster and the breath to heave in and out with corresponding excitement.

The yoga science works backward from this automatic effect. People understand this truth naturally, at least to some extent. When someone suffers a shock, they commonly advise him, "Just sit down; breathe slowly and deeply for a few moments. Calm yourself. Now then, tell me what happened." Other people, wanting to help one another, naturally begin also by advising one to breathe slowly. Without realizing it, everyone knows more about the yoga science than he realizes!

People, again, automatically look upward when they feel elated. They sit straighter on receipt of good news. They place their hands automatically over the heart when their feelings are suddenly and deeply affected. They knit their eyebrows when they want to concentrate deeply. They try to breathe more slowly not only when they are agitated, but whenever they want to concentrate on anything deeply.

Breath is the mystic key proffered in the yoga science for controlling the mind.

(6:35) O Mighty-armed Arjuna, the mind is undoubtedly fickle and unruly, but it can be controlled by yoga practice, and by the exercise of mental dispassion.

(6:36) Here is My promise: Yoga, though difficult to attain for the ungoverned mind, can be reached through proper methods if one strives (earnestly) to achieve self-control.

Yoga practice (*yoga abhyasa*) implies working both outwardly and inwardly, making *repeated* efforts to return to one's calm center within. Dispassion (*vairagya*) means disengaging the mind (again, by repeated efforts) from all forms of sensory pleasure, subtle as well as gross. Avoid any stimulus that reminds you of worldly fulfillments, especially if you sense the danger that you might be distracted from soul-bliss.

(6:37) Arjuna said: O Krishna, what happens to one who is unsuccessful in yoga practice: who tries devotedly to meditate but finds himself unable to bring his mind under control?

(6:38) Doesn't he become like a riven cloud, scattered and dispersed: unable to find Brahman, and equally unable to return to the delusory world he has rejected?

(6:39) Please, O Krishna, release me permanently from these doubts! Who else but You can banish my uncertainty?

The discouraged devotee pleads with God as the Cosmic Physician to heal his self-doubts. For not every aspiring yogi achieves the divine goal in one lifetime. There are three ways of failing in yoga practice. One of them, alas, is fairly common: to return to the world, wanly hoping to find again somehow the fulfillment that was denied him before. Such failed seekers are, unfortunately, all-too common. They may wander for incarnations after such a fall, until the desire for God reawakens in their hearts. For although that desire may seem sometimes to disappear, once it has been wakened in the heart it can never die.

Another type of fall takes place, so to speak, on the battlefield. A person practices yoga zealously at first. After some time, however, he relaxes his efforts. Having been carried along at first by his initial zeal, a lack of perfect non-attachment in the heart may cause him to become discouraged and to lessen his efforts, thereby making him lose his focus on soul-bliss. When death comes, his mind, influenced by past worldly karma, looks back with reawakened interest upon the worldly pleasures he once enjoyed. Distracted, consequently, from his one-pointed longing for God, he falls short of union with Him. Self-doubts assail him: Does he *really* want God? Might it not satisfy him to attain something less challenging—a harmonious life, for example, in an astral heaven? Is he, perhaps, not fit to scale the heights? Is there, possibly, no hope for him to rise any higher?

In such a state of mind, the aspiring yogi would do best not to be too analytical. He should simply love God, and leave the decision as to his fate in the hands of the Divine. *Nishkam karma*—action without desire for the fruits of action—should be his motto all the way to, and beyond, the door of death.

The third type of failure is simply to have fallen short, so far, of perfection. Such a person may remain for a long time amid the beauties of an astral heaven— which, when he returns to earth, will remain with him subconsciously as a constant reminder that this world is not his true home. Or, he may return quickly to earth, filled with the zeal to continue his search for God. In his next life he may begin his spiritual efforts again at a young age, and never rest until the divine goal is attained.

Alternatively, he may fail to reach God but be liberated, at last, from earthly karma and continue his quest for perfection on the astral plane.

My Guru often used the example of planting the seed of a tree. It takes time for the seed to sprout. It takes more time for the shoot to protrude up out of the ground; then for the sapling to rise—slender at first, then gradually stronger and taller. The seed must be watered.

It must be protected from lower life-forms that may threaten it. When it becomes a sapling, it may need protection within a wire enclosure from larger animals. Once the tree has "grown up," even a deer may be able to strop its antlers on the bark without devastating the trunk. For this long process, however, patience is necessary. Don't keep digging up your plant of faith to see if it is growing. Act as you should, for the present, and leave the results in God's hands. Whether you succeed in finding Him in this life, or must wait until another, or even wait several more lifetimes: these things should not be your present concern. Only think how many incarnations you built up an opposite momentum. It takes time to break out into the vastness of eternity from the hard shell you have created over many lives. Be content to do your best, for now, and leave the results in God's hands.

The path to God is not like plodding wearily over a barren desert in hope of finding an oasis. Every step of the way becomes more beautiful: verdant, flowery, and infinitely varied. The longer one meditates with sincerity, the more his senses become refined. Colors become to him more beautiful; sounds, more thrilling; scents, more delightful. All life becomes, for him, increasingly wonderful. When he is able to penetrate behind the physical senses, the subtle, astral senses provide him with even keener delight. He must go beyond even astral experiences, but it is encouraging to know that those inner sights and sounds become far more wonderful; smells, more pleasurable; tastes entrancing. Yogananda wrote once that God can come to the devotee as a thousand delectable tastes all crushed into one. As for the sense of touch, sex desires make one seek pleasure in touching and being touched through the skin, but this touch is a pale substitute for the thrill of touching everything from within, through expanded consciousness.

On should live more wholeheartedly right now, enjoying his yoga practices, thinking of this moment, not of the future, but simply loving God in the present and offering oneself up to the Lord without any expectation of a reward. You should remind yourself, indeed, that there is no *you* to be rewarded!

The chief reason people get discouraged is their expectation of specific results. Learn to expect nothing. Is it not joy enough to be at least *seeking* Him, and not running ceaselessly toward mirage images that, as you know full well, will evaporate even as you approach them?

God is the *only* answer to man's quest for happiness! What more do you need, that you think may satisfy you before you once again start seeking Him?

(6:40) The Blessed Lord answered: O Arjuna, My son! One who performs right actions can *never* be destroyed. Whether in this world or the next, his fate will never be evil.

As we saw above (after 6:34), everybody knows he must work to achieve outward success. What seems so difficult on the spiritual path is that God is, in fact, so close, and yet so hard to find! Monetary riches are outside us, and need to be acquired. God is, as my Guru said, "the nearest of the near." Why, then, does He seem so far away?!

There is a story Yogananda loved to tell about the musk deer of the Himalayas. At a certain season of the year this deer secretes, in a pouch in its navel, the delightful fragrance of musk. The deer runs frantically about, trying to find the source of this wonderful perfume. Sometimes, in the desperation of its eagerness, it plunges from high crags to its death in the valleys below. The huntsman then finds it, cuts out the pouch, and sells it for a high price in the marketplace. "O musk deer!" a poet once wrote, "Why could you not understand that the fragrance you sought was ever with you—in your own self?"

This is the struggling yogi's greatest difficulty: His energy is already habituated to flowing outward through the senses. My Guru pointed out that any attempt to satisfy personal hunger by feeding someone else would result in starving one's own self. To seek fulfillment by feeding the senses is to feed something one is not. As my Guru said also, "You have to live anyway. Why not live in the right way?" The failed yogi, despite the deep and unavoidable disappointment he feels with himself, is much greater as a human being than the most successful materialist.

"So long as you continue to make the effort," Yogananda said finally, "God will never let you down. But if you tell yourself, 'I've failed,' it will be true—at least for this life—though your subconscious desire for God will bring you back to the spiritual path again and again until you succeed in finding Him. But why delay?

If you slip or even fall, tell yourself, 'I know what I really want, and I am going to keep on trying till I succeed!'"

Remember the popular saying, "If at first you don't succeed, try and try again." God is your own Father/Mother, as Krishna reminds us all by addressing Arjuna in this stanza as his son.

(6:41) A fallen (but sincere) yogi gains entry (after death) into the world of the virtuous. He (may) remain there for many years. Afterward, he is reborn on earth in a good and prosperous home.

The idea that one's birth is decided only biologically is largely a myth. One's genes do have something to do with the shape of the physical body, but even its shape and other characteristics are determined also by personal karma. It may be somewhat determined also by mass karma, which can dictate such matters as skin color, racial influences, and even the sex of the body. The mental and spiritual qualities of a spiritual person, however, attract him to families that will encourage the advancing yogi to continue in his spiritual search. Prosperity is also given him as a means of helping him to satisfy whatever lingering material desires he has.

The fallen yogi described here is one who, as yet imperfect in his spiritual quest, has slackened or even abandoned his spiritual efforts, temporarily. Otherwise, yogis who have been unsuccessful, but are still eager to continue their spiritual efforts, may return to earth relatively soon. Spiritual progress, except for those who have attained a high state of advancement, is not possible for them in the astral spheres. Life there, for the virtuous, is so beautiful and harmonious that one who is only a visitor from this earth plane of existence, having still some material karma to work out, feels little or no incentive to continue his spiritual practices. The very realm to which he is attracted will be inhabited only by those whose tastes and interests are similar to his own, or they may contain beloved family members, or may have such conditions as will help to fulfill some deeply held personal desire. Refined earthly desires—such as for beautiful music, "heavenly" scenery, a harmonious community of friends, or otherwise idyllic conditions— can be satisfied better in the astral world than on earth.

Thus, those yogis who attract a prolonged stay in the astral world—it may be even for hundreds of years—live there in consequence of their spiritual practices on earth, even if, here, they fell away from their practices. Those who practice even a little bit of meditation in this life— its natural focus being on developing the intuition—are attracted to heavenly astral regions and discover an increased power of enjoyment there.

Yogis, on the other hand, who leave their physical bodies at death with a deep desire for God, but who still retain a few lingering (perhaps only subconscious) material desires, will often reject the attraction of astral delights, viewing them as a detour on their upward journey. Such souls, aware that more incentives exist for continued progress in a physical body, may choose to be reborn relatively quickly on earth. (The time of their sojourn in the astral world will depend, among other factors, on such things as how intense their desire is to continue their spiritual progress, and on their compatibility with karmic conditions on this earth, or on some other planet, at the time.)

There are countless inhabited planets in the material universe. People are by no means limited to reincarnating on Earth. As mankind advances into higher yugas, or ages, those souls who reincarnated here in darker times may be attracted to less enlightened civilizations on other planets, where the level of advancement is more compatible with their own actual state of refinement.

The universe, considered by modern astronomy to be almost devoid of conditions for intelligent life, is actually teeming with it. Even the stars, Paramhansa Yogananda declared, are peopled with intelligent beings with highly refined bodies, whose "food" and "breath" is fiery light. Accounts of "UFOs" visiting this world are (many of them) perfectly true. Such visitations come from many planets, some of them friendly, others with primarily self-serving interest. In the last analysis, the entire universe is a vast, interconnected web of consciousness. Modern science declares it would be impossible for the inhabitants of planets that are situated many light years away from us to make such a long journey. Yogananda's answer to that declaration was that science is still in its infancy. It is definitely possible, he declared, to travel over vast reaches by other means than those imaginable so far in materialistic science.

Those yogis who, upon leaving this world, are "fed up" with it, but who still have some earthly karma to work out, may have a very long stay in the astral world before earthly karma pulls them back and obliges them to cope with it again.

(6:42) On the other hand, he may reincarnate on earth in a family of enlightened yogis. Such a birth, however, is difficult to attain in this world.

(6:43) (In his new family) he recovers the yogic discrimination he attained formerly, and sets himself with even greater zeal to achieve (final) spiritual liberation.

Krishna describes here what happens to the third kind of "fallen" yogi—fallen only in the sense that, at death, he has not fully expiated his conscious and subconscious ego-motivated desires.

Rebirth in the home of advanced yogis is difficult to attain, for few such people marry, and those who do so may prefer not to have children. My Guru related to me, in this connection, the story of Byasa (author of the Bhagavad Gita) and Sukdeva. Byasa was a realized soul. When his wife conceived Sukdeva, he taught the child, through the mother's subconscious, while the unborn infant was still in its mother's womb. The child, after birth, received the name, Sukdeva.

Sukdeva, when he reached the age of seven, set out from home to find a guru. His father, who was himself well fitted to play that role, followed after the little child with the plea that he remain in the family and pursue his spiritual practices there. The child looked back disdainfully.

"Keep away from me!" he said. "You have *maya*!" (As if telling his father he had an infectious disease!) What

Sukdeva disapproved of was the lingering thought in his father's mind that Sukdeva was his son.

Byasa then sent him to another great yogi who would be able to give him enlightenment. But that subject is not germane to the present discussion.

One's spiritual attainments in past lives are enduringly retained in the astral brain. Like seeds, they sprout when the conditions are right. What triggers a "right" condition may be almost anything. Sri Ramakrishna, the great master who lived in Bengal, India, in the nineteenth century, had his first spiritual awakening as a child on beholding a flock of cranes flying in graceful beauty against a gray sky.

(6:44) The power of former yoga practice is sufficient to impel, as it were, the reborn yogi on his upward path. Even one who seeks only a theoretical understanding of yoga is more highly advanced than one who is dedicated to outward scriptural (Vedic) rites.

Paramhansa Yogananda stated that the last few words of this stanza can be translated alternatively to mean, ". . . than someone who is dedicated to merely reciting the Vedic word of Brahman: the sacred AUM."

People of spiritual insight know that the main purpose of performing rituals, and even of chanting AUM, is symbolic. It can exert a kind of power that attracts certain beneficial results. It cannot possibly, however, produce freedom from karma, being itself a karmic act that involves the doer in a variety of subsequent reactions, none of which can extricate the ego from bondage to the limitations of individuality.

Infinitely more important than chanting AUM is it to *listen* to AUM in the right ear in meditation. Closing the tragi of the ears with the thumbs (the elbows resting lightly on a crosspiece of wood), AUM is chanted mentally at the point between the eyebrows while the mind concentrates on the sounds appearing (as has been stated) in the right ear. One should concentrate on only one sound at a time. The very concentration on that sound will attune one to subtler levels of sound, until one hears the Cosmic Vibration. This yoga technique should be learned personally in its various ramifications from a true teacher. It is an important part of the path taught by Paramhansa Yogananda.

(6:45) Diligently following his (chosen) path, and cleansing himself thereby of all sin (karmic debts), the yogi after many births attains perfection, and enters at last into the Supreme Beatitude.

Lahiri Mahasaya, who first reintroduced Kriya Yoga to the world in modern times, explained this passage also in an esoteric sense. When a man exhales and cannot inhale again, he dies. Later, when he is reborn in a new body, he inhales to make his first cry, and thus resumes living in this world. Similarly, when a meditating yogi goes breathless, the breath is forcibly drawn out of his body. This condition is a kind of "partial death," reminiscent of something Saint Paul said in the Bible, "I die daily." In this sense, when the yogi returns to outward consciousness and resumes breathing, his first act is to inhale again. Thus, during meditation in his present body he undergoes, in a very real sense, the process of death and rebirth.

In this way he can fulfill, even in one lifetime, the promise of Krishna that will hasten his evolution—a process which normally requires "many births"—and can complete the long work even in his present body.

There is a more superficial, but very helpful, practice that can be conjoined to the breathing process. The time to affirm, or embrace, a new state of consciousness is after a deep inhalation. The time to expel from the body any unwanted thought or habit is while deliberately exhaling—blowing that thought out of one's nature, so to speak. "Habits," Yogananda used to say, "can be changed in a day. They are simply the result of concentrated energy. Direct that energy in a new way, and the habit you want to overcome can be dispelled in an instant." The breath is the best medium, when accompanied by strong mental affirmation, for bringing into one's nature the thoughts and qualities one wants, and for ridding oneself of those which one wants to dismiss. In this case, too, each exhaling breath can be a little death (of the discarded quality, anyway), and each inhalation can be a little rebirth into some new quality one wants to adopt.

(6:46) The yogi is greater than those ascetics who (strive for spiritual perfection through) discipline of the body, greater even than those who follow the path of wisdom (Gyana Yoga) or of action (Karma Yoga). Become, O Arjuna, a yogi!

The goal of physical discipline is twofold: to bring the body under the control of one's will, and to rechannel the energy from the body so that the energy can serve a higher purpose. In Christian monasteries, self-flagellation (whipping one's back, even to the point where blood was drawn) used to be a common practice (it is no longer allowed). The idea behind it was to "punish" the body for its carnal desires, and thereby to discourage them from becoming too insistent in their efforts to sway the mind—as if the mind were ruled by the body, instead of the reverse!

As Yogananda, in challenge to the thought that the body *causes* nervousness, said: "Hold up a piece of paper in your hand. Will it shake on its own? Never! To shake it, you yourself must do the shaking." The mind is *influenced* by physical awareness, but its response, always, comes from the awareness itself. Carnal desires originate not in the body, even though they obviously are influenced by the body. The origin of temptation, however, is in the mind. Nothing inert can influence the mind without the mind's willing cooperation, whether consciously or subconsciously. Thus, the Roman Catholic Church was right to rule against self-flagellation. It is an indirect and fundamentally unsound spiritual practice.

In India the practice developed ages ago (Buddha encountered it in his own spiritual search) to discipline the body for other purposes: to cause the energy, by blocking its outward flow, to reverse that flow inward. We mentioned this practice in the commentary following Gita 3:7. Certain ascetics, for example, practice holding one arm continuously aloft until the muscles wither away, and the arm looks like skin and bone. It comes easily to "modern" people to ridicule such a practice: It *does* seem extreme—to the point of fanaticism. Yet, one wonders: could such practices have endured for thousands of years, had they not shown *some* benefits?

An American soldier after World War II was in India, and happened to come upon a sadhu seated with one shriveled arm raised high above his head.

"Hey, there!" called the soldier mockingly. "Are you praying to God to drop fruit in your hand?"

"Why don't you try it yourself?" was the smiling reply.

The American jokingly raised both arms to the sky. To his dismay, he found he couldn't take them down again.

"Please, sir," he cried. "Let me lower my arms!"

"Why don't you finish what you started?" replied the other.

"What do you mean?"

"Ask God to drop fruit into your hands," said the sadhu.

The American, feeling very foolish, called out, "Heavenly Father, please send me some fruit!"

Immediately, several fruits materialized in his hands. Later on, having lowered his arms and returned to his friends, he commented, "They were delicious!"

Physical self-discipline does "bear fruit" of a kind. Even self-flagellation cannot but have had some positive effect, for it to have been practiced for so many centuries. What Krishna is saying in this stanza, however, is that disciplining the body is an *indirect* and incomplete way of freeing one's mind from body-consciousness.

The same may be said of the other disciplines mentioned here: Gyana Yoga and Karma Yoga. (Karma Yoga, it should be mentioned, or inward Karma Yoga, is also used by Krishna in reference to the yoga of inner action—Kriya Yoga.)

For deep meditation, it is necessary to rise above body-consciousness by withdrawing the energy from the senses to the spine. Outward, physical practices may be described as an attempt to bludgeon the body into surrendering its hold on the energy. Gyana Yoga tries—again, indirectly, and for most people ineffectually—to separate the mind from the body by mental discipline: the exercise of calm dispassion. This practice is helpful too, and can be effective to some extent. It is indirect, however, insofar as it doesn't work on the energy itself, to withdraw it from the body.

We used the example in the commentary following Gita 2:58, of a visit to the dentist. One can separate his *concentration* from the pain in his tooth while the dentist works on it. One way of doing so is to think of something else—to concentrate, for example, on solving some problem in one's life. Another way is to divert the mind by calmly watching the breath (following the technique mentioned earlier). Still another way is to tell oneself, "I have lived for x number of years, and have had many happy hours and days. What, by comparison, are these few minutes of pain?" Thus broadening his time base, the pain he endures for those minutes will seem insignificant and, with sufficient exertion of will power, will be easy to endure.

Karma Yoga, also, is an indirect way of withdrawing the energy. By *nishkam karma*—renunciation of attachment to the fruits of action—one withdraws his energy from avid feeling toward anything outward, and mentally centers his consciousness in the Self. By meditating with the same attitude of offering the fruits of meditation up to God, one becomes less anxious, and achieves even to that extent a degree of inner peace.

None of these methods, however, nor any other among the countless religious methods in the world for uplifting the mind, is as effective as working directly on the energy itself. Once a person understands the true purpose of chanting to God; dancing in God; offering oblations (of ghee, rice, etc.) to God; of beating drums during worship (reminiscent of the sound emitted by the lowest, *muladhara chakra*); of playing the flute at religious ceremonies (reminiscent of the sound produced in meditation by the next higher center, the *swadisthana chakra*); of plucking harp strings in reminder of heavenly harp music (reminiscent of the sound produced by the lumbar, or *manipura chakra*); of ringing bells (reminiscent of the sound of the heart center, the *anahata chakra*)—once one understands the hidden reason for why these sounds actually inspire and uplift the mind, it is an inescapable conclusion that the mind is really uplifted by raising the energy in the spine, and that this effect can be produced even more effectively when one's concentration is directly applied to the energy itself.

Again, this is not to say that those outward practices are "mere superstition." Dr. Lewis, Yogananda's first Kriya Yoga disciple in America, was a "staid Bostonian"; he cringed when our Guru pounded an Indian drum during group chanting. "Learn to enjoy it!" said Yogananda. "It helps to loosen the karma in the spine." (He may have meant "the *samskaras*," a term with which Dr. Lewis was less familiar. Alternatively, the Guru may actually have said "karma," to pair his explanation with the disciple's understanding of Indian terms.) What he meant was, "The drum, beaten with a sensitive rhythm— and not with the heavy pounding of a 'bongo' drum or similar instrument, intended only to inflame the emotions—helps to release blockages in the lowest center so that the energy can flow upward in the spine."

(6:47) He who, full of faith and love, becomes fully absorbed in Me, I regard as best attuned to My path to perfection.

What is that path? It is the balanced, moderate path which has been explained thus far in the Bhagavad Gita.

Krishna emphasizes faith not as blind belief, but as the certainty born of complete intuitive understanding and acceptance. He emphasizes love because, without devotional love, the seeker cannot (as Swami Sri Yukteswar put it) set one foot before the other on the path to God.

Raja Yoga is not a *separate* path to God. Other forms of yoga, and other religious disciplines, may rightly be spoken of (as Yogananda did) as bypaths, or as subsidiary streams contributing to the mighty river of energy which flows up the spine to the brain.

Gyana Yoga, or discriminative understanding, is essential for separating one's energy-flow from outward involvement, and for keeping it moving upward, toward God. Bhakti Yoga, which is the exercise of intense devotion, is essential as a means of awakening and channeling all one's feelings upward. Otherwise, with *gyana* alone, one might be like the man living next door to a famous restaurant who never went into it for food, because he craved only "hot dogs" (sausages) and greasy fried potatoes.

Thus ends the sixth chapter, called "Dhyana Yoga (Union Through Meditation)," of the Upanishad of the holy Bhagavad Gita, in the dialogue between Sri Krishna and Arjuna discussing yoga and the science of God-realization.

CHAPTER NINETEEN

KNOWLEDGE AND WISDOM

(7:1) The Blessed Lord said: O Partha (Arjuna), hear how, by following the path of yoga and absorbing yourself in My consciousness, and taking shelter (wholly) in Me, you will realize Me wholly as I am (both in My infinite, unmoving Self, and, outwardly, with all My attributes and powers). (Knowing Me thus,) you will transcend every possibility of doubt.

PARAMHANSA YOGANANDA WAS GIVEN A WORD OF advice by Bhaduri Mahasaya when he was a boy. He related the episode in the chapter, "The Levitating Saint," from his *Autobiography of a Yogi:*

"'You go often into the silence, but have you developed *anubhava* [actual perception of God]?' [The master] was reminding me to love God more than meditation. 'Do not mistake the technique for the Goal.'"

In the above stanza, Krishna is implying the same truth as that contained in the well-known saying, "The flower falls off when the fruit appears." Yoga implies more than a set of practices: The word itself means *union,* which is the end of all spiritual practices and the state of perfect realization.

(7:2) I am about to unfold truth to you in its entirety, both as theory and as intuitively realized experience. (Armed with this understanding,) there will be nothing left for you to know in all the world.

An amazing aspect of omniscience is that its perception truly encompasses *everything*. It is "center everywhere, circumference nowhere"—the knowledge of everything *from within*, and at the same time from without—in other words, in both its theoretical and experiential reality. As Jesus Christ put it, "The very hairs on your head are all numbered." (Matt. 10:30)

The Bhagavad Gita, amazingly also, includes all three completely: the theory as to why one should seek God; the methods—those which are best, those which are indirect, and those which are least praiseworthy—for finding Him; and also the nature of the goal itself.

All these things Krishna now promises to reveal.

(7:3) Among thousands of men, scarcely one strives for spiritual perfection; and among those blessed ones who seek Me, scarcely one (out of many thousands) perceives Me as I am.

These words might seem to be sounding a discouraging note for the earnest seeker, who doesn't want to think his chances of success are all but non-existent! This passage should, however, be understood also in the larger context of the many planes of existence through which the soul must pass to reach absolute perfection. Few there are indeed who, from the earth's low valley, make it directly to the top of the mountain. Most souls climb by degrees. Once they rise above the ordinary astral heavens, spurning its comparatively "gaudy" delights, they ascend to higher regions—*Hiranyaloka*, for example, on which Yogananda's guru told him he had been born as a savior (see the chapter, "The Resurrection of Sri Yukteswar," in *Autobiography of a Yogi*).

We saw earlier that the path to God in no way resembles a barren desert, over which weary travelers trudge until at last they reach the oasis of God-vision. Most seekers—even those who are highly advanced—go from earth to higher regions for further enlightenment. The path is long, but at every step it is extremely rewarding. Even a few days spent in an uplifting environment among spiritual people, practicing regular meditation with them (or for that matter practicing it alone in one's home, if one is content to proceed without such outer encouragement), produce in the eyes a newly radiant happiness, virtually impossible to encounter among sensation-hungry *kayasthas* (body-bound human beings).

In this stanza, Krishna is not trying to discourage people, but only to stiffen their spines with a challenge not to dabble with one finger in shallow waters. The spiritual path is for heroes, not for cowards or weaklings. The common argument, "Why should I try to be different from everybody else?" deserves to be answered with another question: "Do you want to go on suffering, like 'everybody else'?"

That argument often continues: "I don't see all that much suffering around me. People smile when they meet others. They bear up bravely under hardship. Some of them do suffer, but I also see a lot of gladness, many happy homes, and much laughter and general contentment." What they really see, however, is people's *hope* for all these things, and the masks they wear. Many hide their gnawing emptiness by looking forward to a future when, so they affirm, everything will change for the better. It doesn't.

A survey was once conducted in America to find out if people were satisfied with their income. The survey covered people in most income brackets, from the relatively poor to the wealthy. A majority of the respondents replied that they *would* be happy, *if* they had ten percent more. That ten percent represents the carrot on a stick, which draws the donkey forward as it pulls a heavy load behind it. Delusion leads one onward in the expectation of, finally, achieving happiness and contentment. It is the soul's desire for bliss, really, forever prodding the ego to think it can somehow embrace infinity! No one is really either happy or contented. What passes among men for contentment is mostly numbness! People think, *"Tomorrow* I'll get (this, or that, or the other thing) that I want." How very few people exclaim in the final moments of death, "I got all that I ever wanted!"? Indeed, only those worldly people (*samsaris*) die more or less satisfied who settled in early youth for a pale compromise!

My Guru sometimes quoted the first (*Adhi*) Swami Shankara, "Childhood is busy with toys; youth is busy with sex; middle age is busy with earning money; old

age is busy with regrets, nostalgia, and illnesses: Nobody
is busy with God!" My Guru's comment was, "Well, he
was bitter, but such is indeed the human condition. How
many people try to find anything *real* in life?"

**(7:4) Earth, water, fire, air, ether, the perceiving
mind (*manas*), discernment (*buddhi*), and causative
self-awareness (*ahankara*): such are the Eightfold
divisions of My manifested nature (Prakriti).**

Krishna is speaking here in cosmic, not in limited
individual terms. In so doing he pushes outward the
very edge of what mankind in this age is capable of
understanding.

Again we should stress, as we have done before, that
"earth, water, fire," etc. are Spirit's *stages of manifestation into gross matter*. Tradition calls them elements, but
the "elements" as the term was used formerly were never
intended in chemical terms.

The elemental stages of Spirit's manifestation into
matter begin with "ether," or space, which Paramhansa
Yogananda declared to be a distinct vibration, separating the astral from the physical universe. Out of ether,
gaseous clouds (nebulae) emerge: the "air element." The
atoms of space, wandering without any apparent
aim, may be as far apart from one another as sixteen
miles. If two of them happen to collide, their gravity
increases, and one might say that their "purpose" also
increases, for it becomes increasingly likely, as more
atoms coalesce, that they will "amount to something,"
in time. Gradually that growing clump may increase

enough in size to exert the gravity to attract atoms from far away—ultimately from as far away as many millions of miles. Thus, as this mass increases, it becomes large enough eventually to become an incandescent star (the "fire element"). If such a mass is not large enough to achieve incandescence—or if, perhaps, a relatively small mass gets expelled from a star—it becomes a smaller, molten sphere: a planet. Thus is brought into manifestation the "water element." As molten matter cools, it becomes solid, whereupon it manifests the "earth element."

Nature (Prakriti) contains other "divisions": mind (*manas*), which perceives all; intuitive intelligence (*buddhi*), which comprehends all; and the ego principle (*ahankara*) on a cosmic scale, which is the one Self in all outward manifestation. Egoism, in this case, is still a principle, but not individualized as it becomes in man with his sharpened perception of himself as identified with a particular human body. As the ego is the soul identified with the body, so cosmic (causal) Self-awareness, as separate from Brahman, is that Self identified with the whole manifested universe as its body.

It is interesting that Krishna, in this stanza, does not give the fourth aspect of consciousness that is listed classically: chitta. Chitta is feeling. We perceive with the mind; define with the intellect; identify personally with the ego; and *feel* one way or another about things with the chitta. Most people identify their capacity for feeling with their emotions, and therefore with their reactive process, both subjective and objective. Yoga itself is defined as the neutralization of this feeling process—not as its cancellation, but as (so to speak) its subduing or pacification. Thus, one might expect Krishna to have not only listed, but *stressed*, this aspect of consciousness.

On the other hand, chitta is more than an *aspect*, merely, of consciousness: It *is* consciousness. In man, chitta is far more than the reactive feelings in the heart: It is the deep, intuitive feeling which defines the very consciousness of self. In divine consciousness, chitta becomes cosmic feeling: not of the ego, but of the divine Self: Absolute Bliss. Bliss is ever-existing, ever-conscious, and (as Yogananda added) ever-new. In the chapter of *Autobiography of a Yogi* titled, "An Experience in Cosmic consciousness," Yogananda stated of his first experience of that state, "I cognized the center of the empyrean as a point of intuitive perception in my heart."

In ordinary, unenlightened human beings, the ego is centered in the medulla oblongata. The yogi looks forward, as it were, from that point to the Kutastha, or "Christ center" between the two eyebrows. The more he concentrates on that point, the more his consciousness becomes identified with it—to the point where his center of self-awareness shifts from ego to superconsciousness. Most people, in whatever they do, radiate energy outward from the medulla oblongata at the back of the head—the seat of ego in the body. An enlightened master, by contrast, radiates energy outward from his transformed self-awareness, which is centered in the Kutastha at the point between the eyebrows. This still is the ego, which even the enlightened man needs in order to keep his body functioning. The divine Self, as differentiated from the enlightened ego, has its center in the heart.

As the yogi raises his own consciousness through the spine, his awakened Kundalini passes upward in reverse order from that of its descent. First it passes through, and awakens, the energy in *muladhara*, the coccyx (or "earth") center. Next, it awakens the energy in *swadisthana*, the sacral (or "water") center. Third, it enters and awakens the energy in *manipura*, the lumbar (or "fire") center. The fourth center it awakens is *anahata*, the dorsal or heart center ("air"); then *bishuddha*, the cervical ("ether") center. As each chakra is "awakened"—which is to say, as the energy in it is released to flow upward—a specific yogic power appears: an ability to become extremely heavy (the "earth element"); to walk on water (the "water element"); to walk on fiery coals and not be burned (the "fire element"); the ability to levitate or even fly (the "air element"); and finally, the ability to expand his consciousness beyond the confines of the body (the "ether element").

These powers are helpful in that they can assure the yogi that his attainments are not merely imaginary. They can also be dangerous, however, in posing a temptation to the ego. Saint Teresa of Avila, in Spain, was a Christian saint who used to levitate as she kneeled at prayer. So anxious was she not to draw attention to herself that she tried, ineffectively, to hold on to her seat in order to keep from rising in the air. Many are the stories of saints in both East and West that describe the phenomenon of levitation.

With the yogi's rise spiritually, yoga practice purifies his ego to the point where he perceives egoism as a general, impersonal principle, and not as limited to his own (human) ego. His perception, then, is with the cosmic mind (*manas*), and is no longer limited to his individual self. His intellect, too, becomes a universal, intuitive intelligence and understanding.

The Supreme Spirit, in manifesting the universe, set a portion of its consciousness vibrating to produce the great sound-vibration of AUM. This is God in His aspect of Divine Mother: *Para-Prakriti*, the pure aspect of the Cosmic Vibration. In its outward manifestations that aspect becomes, simply, Prakriti, or *Aparaprakriti*: the outer "show" that we see through the senses: trees, hills, people—the whole star system around us. People who try to "commune" with Nature in beautiful sunsets, colorful clouds, and soaring mountains cannot enter into true communion with the Divine, even though these things do (or at least ought to) remind one of God. True communion with Nature, however, can be done only inwardly, through communion with AUM.

The yogi, in deep, inner communion with AUM after raising his consciousness at least to the *bishuddha* (cervical), finds his awareness expanding—first to the whole body, then outward to encompass all space. This state is described also as AUM samadhi. Next, he perceives the Kutastha Chaitanya, or Christ consciousness, behind the AUM vibration in his body. Gradually he expands that consciousness to encompass Christ consciousness in all manifested existence.

I once asked my Guru, "What point must one have reached to be rightly considered a master?"

He replied, "One must have attained Christ consciousness."

Thus, this stanza of the Gita provides details regarding both Spirit's manifestation in matter, and its ascent back to Spirit, through the deep practice of yoga.

The sense-identified mind is centered outside the spiritual eye. Intuitive intelligence works from *inside* the spiritual eye. From this point a subtle connection takes the yogi's consciousness up to the many-rayed *sahasrara* (the "thousand-petaled lotus") at the top of the head. Union with this point produces Cosmic consciousness. Perfect inner union and Cosmic consciousness are one and the same thing. Time and space are illusory. To probe to its depths the single "atom" that is the ego is to understand, simultaneously, the mystery of the universe.

(7:5) Such is My lower nature (Aparaprakriti). Understand now, O Mighty-armed (Arjuna)! that My other and higher nature (Para-Prakriti) sustains the soul (jiva), which is individual consciousness, and sustains also the life-principle of the universe.

The jiva, or soul, is individualized consciousness: the infinite limited to, and identified with, a body. The beginning of its existence as an individual soul comes with the causal body. The soul's further encasement in an astral body is what causes it first to manifest ego-consciousness. Identification with that body of light is what causes one to think, "I am unique and different from other beings of light." Ego-consciousness becomes further bound to objective reality when it assumes a physical body, and all its energy is directed outward through the physical senses.

In the material world, man's awareness of outer Nature (Aparaprakriti) virtually defines his concept of reality. In the astral world, that outward direction of awareness is only partial. Though limited by ego-consciousness, he nevertheless senses the reality of the energy within him, which subtly links him to the objective realities around him. In the causal world, he knows that everything is made of idea-forms, or thoughts. Separate ego-consciousness ceases, for him, to exist, and he knows himself as the soul (jiva), a manifestation of Para-Prakriti: pure Nature. He is attuned to the Kutastha Chaitanya—the Christ con-sciousness underlying the universe. Blessed with this high state of realization, and virtually freed from every self-limitation, his consciousness is crowned with almost infinite power.

The universe, seen from without (through the senses), is composed of gross matter and—in the astral world—of unsheathed energy that can manifest beautiful heavens, but also terrifying hells where hatred, despair, and other violently negative emotions are no longer confined within and, to that extent suppressed by, thick walls of flesh.

The satanic force is not another, separate reality from the divine. It is simply the outwardly manifesting creative force (Aparaprakriti) which, once set into motion, is bent on continuing its momentum. Without that initial impetus, the universe could not have come into being.

This impetus toward continuing that outward thrust becomes, at whatever point one stands on the long climb back toward God, the force of evil. It is a conscious force, universal rather than any mere mental weakness. It is not personal any more than the Cosmic Vibration is personal, but we can attract that evil power to ourselves (as we can also, of course, divine assistance) by any draw we feel toward lower influences.

Good and evil, it should be understood, are relative terms. A saint who found himself drawn to self-gratifying actions that, in other people, would be perfectly normal would open himself to the outwardly flowing energy of Aparaprakriti. Others wouldn't see him to be operating under the satanic influence if he began wanting to boost his own sense of self-importance, to seek name and fame, to pursue (in ways that others might consider perfectly right and normal) a few of the pleasures to which most of humanity are addicted. Nevertheless, he would, through his growing attraction to it, be responding to the satanic force.

Satan is impersonal. He is willing, however, to draw man downward to any degree of degradation man's will can accept. There is no limit to how far the individual can fall, as there is no limit to how high he can rise.

The inward pull of Para-Prakriti (the mighty sound of AUM) is ever available to the soul. If one insists on looking outward for his satisfactions, however, he will succumb to the outward pull of Aparaprakriti, Satan, which is ever at the disposal also of those who, though they laugh at "temptations of the devil" and at "the devil's wiles," think it merely fun to get drunk, perfectly

normal to lose their temper and shout angrily on
occasion, and—so far from it seeming wrong as to be
virtually expected of them—to seek endless sexual enjoyment. To tell such people that they are acting under
satanic influence might well invite them to explode in
gales of mirth. Nevertheless, the downward slope, once
one starts on it, exerts at least this much appeal: it
appears easy. Those who walk, run, or slide eagerly
downhill would rather not think about the long, hard
climb back uphill again.

In the astral world, both angels (*devas*) and demons
(*asuras*) exist. They are attracted to their own kind
among human beings. Angels go where goodness is
predominant, and where they can inspire people with
heavenly thoughts. Demons, or devils, go where *maya*
(Aparaprakriti) holds sway: to bars where people drink
to get drunk, to the madness that reigns on the floor of
a commodities exchange, to the corridors of power and
corruption, to places of infamy, violence, and hatred. If
demons are able to, they go beyond merely *influencing*
people to greater negativity and to more harmful
emotions: Sometimes they succeed—for example,
through the weakened power of self-protection in a
person who is drunk—in entering a person's mind and
body, and even in committing crimes through him,
using his body—deeds of which he himself, later on, has
no recollection.

"Thoughts," Yogananda wrote in *Autobiography of
a Yogi*, "are universally and not individually rooted."
Inspirations are not *created*: They must be invited. Acts
of hatred and violence are a sign of man's openness to

demonic forces, and are not by any means initiated only by human beings themselves.

The great masters who come (rarely, alas) on earth do so in response not only to need, but to humanity's *consciousness* of that need. Once here, they try (within the strictures of divine law) to be of universal help. Paramhansa Yogananda, for instance, during his early years in Los Angeles, would sometimes walk up and down a street containing many bars and other places of iniquity. He said nothing, but clearly he was trying to influence any patrons of those places who were receptive to his spiritual vibrations to change their way of life.

Normally, alas, what causes man to change his ways is suffering. God doesn't *want* man to suffer. When one goes contrary, however, to the direction that leads to harmony, it is inevitable that he will experience disharmony.

Hell—contrary to some popular beliefs—is not a place of permanent confinement. The Biblical term, "everlasting hell," is simply a myth, and (probably) a misconception either in the reporting or in the translation. "The thing is," Yogananda said, "hell *seems* everlasting." Such, indeed, is the nature of sorrow and suffering: The sufferer thinks nothing will ever improve for him again. Every state of consciousness creates a *vritti*, or vortex, which seeks to draw into itself whatever comes within its orbit.

Don't be fooled into thinking that because a state of consciousness, or a way of behavior, is common or even seems universal, it is therefore normal and right. To be in "normal" health is to be well, physically. To be "normal" spiritually is to be out of delusion and fully aware of oneself as a child of God. Everything else is abnormal!

"Lord," prayed the Christian Saint Augustine, "Thou hast made us for Thyself, and our hearts are restless until they find their rest in Thee."

(7:6) Know that all beings, (both) the pure and the impure, are born of this twofold Prakriti. I (alone) beget and dissolve the (whole) universe.
(7:7) O Arjuna! There is nothing above Me, nor beyond Me. Through all things, as through the gemstones of a necklace, runs the thread of My all-unifying consciousness.

As the thread is what supports and unites all the beads, so God's consciousness supports, sustains, and unites everything in creation.

(7:8) O Son of Kunti (the quality of dispassion), I am the fluidity of waters; I am the light of the moon and the sun; I am pranaba (AUM) in the (teachings of the) Vedas; I am (the "silent" roar of cosmic) sound in the ether (the subtle vibrations of space); I am the manhood in man.

Throughout the Bhagavad Gita, there are hidden, as well as overt meanings. The "fluidity of waters" is a subtle reference to the vibratory motion of the "elements," which we've discussed above. The "moon and sun" refer to negative and positive polarities in the universe, and also in man's body. The pranaba (AUM) taught in the Vedas refers to the subtle inner sounds (which emanate from the chakras). The "sound in the ether" is audible, though not to ordinary ears; other traditions (notably the Greek) have described it as "the music of the spheres." The "manhood of man" refers to that special attribute possessed by mankind (among earth's creatures) which enables him to advance spiritually by free will.

(7:9) I am the wholesome fragrance of earth; I am the radiance of fire; I am the life of every creature; in holy ascetics, I am their austerity.

As in the previous stanza, the reference here is subtle as well as overt. Earth and fire are the "elements" of two of the lower chakras. It is divine vitality which vibrates in the "air," or *anahata* (the dorsal, or heart) chakra. Self-discipline emanates from the Kutastha center between the eyebrows, and (ultimately) from *sahasrara*, the "crown chakra" at the top of the head. A magnetic polarity (as we said earlier in this book) exists between the earth center (*muladhara*) and the dorsal (heart) or *anahata* center. By meditating on the heart center, with support from fiery self-control (the quality of the lumbar, or *manipura* center), it is easier to raise the energy in the spine above the lower chakras. From *anahata* it is easier, next, to draw the energy upward to the Kutastha between the eyebrows, and thence to the highest chakra, the *sahasrara*, and Cosmic consciousness.

(7:10) Know Me, O Son of Pritha (Arjuna) to be the seed of all creatures! I am intelligence in the discerning; in those who are glorious, I am their glory.
(7:11) Among the powerful, O Best of the Bharatas

(Arjuna)! I am power without personal ambition and attachment; I am that sexual desire (*kama*) in men which is in keeping with dharma (righteousness).

Because desire is such a strong factor in the lives of human beings, it should be pointed out, incidentally, that good (that is to say, dharmic) desires bring good results, but temporarily only. Desirelessness alone leads to liberation.

(7:12) Know that all manifestations of sattwa (the elevating), rajas (the activating), and tamas (the darkening quality) emanate from Me. They exist in Me, though I am not apparent in them.

Paramhansa Yogananda often illustrated his lectures by comparing "real life" to the fantasy world of motion pictures. In a movie, he said when discussing the above stanza, the same beam of light produces on the screen both good and evil people. They are only images of shadow and light. Although they seem real, they are in fact true only to sight and sound.

The "cosmic dream movie" is true not only to two human senses, but to all five of them! And yet, just as the light emanating from the projection booth in a movie house produces mere images of reality, so also does God's light produce mere appearances. The universe itself is only a projection of shadows and light. Everything is produced by God. More than merely showing a movie true to the five senses, he produces the script, directs the action, plays all the parts, composes and plays all the music, and even provides the audience!

A playwright knows that actors portraying both good and evil are necessary to his story. He is in all of them, in a sense, but they are not in him: in other words, they don't define him. If he approaches his work with proper skill, he does so impersonally and rarely expresses personal feelings of his own: his likes, dislikes, social outrage, or prejudices. He himself need not possess any of the qualities possessed by his characters to express their natures. Were those characters actually living, they might not understand him at all. Yet he must live all their lives—from a distance, as it were. He must enter even into the villain's consciousness, to give him verisimilitude. He must view everything the villain does from the villain's point of view. He may even enjoy the villain's twisted self-justifications, and must make them as believable and as seemingly reasonable as they would be to the villain himself. His *enjoyment* in writing that part is not sadism. He knows that the man's villainy will only make the conclusion of the story more beautiful. The tension he creates in delaying the action will bring the story to a more satisfying dénouement.

A disciple of Paramhansa Yogananda's once said to him, "I have such a deep longing for God! Why does it take so long for Him to come?"

"Ah," the Master replied with a blissful smile, "that's what makes it all the sweeter, when He does come!"

When the English novelist, Charles Dickens, was writing his famous tale, *The Old Curiosity Shop*, he realized at a certain point that it would be necessary to the integrity of his story for Little Nell, his main character, to die. It is said that when this understanding came to him he walked the streets of London for hours, weeping. Yet he had no artistic choice but to "kill" her. Otherwise, he would have been untrue to his own story line.

God, Yogananda said, also weeps for mankind: for man's follies and sufferings. He weeps for human wickedness, also, for though it produces grief for the recipients of wickedness, it produces even more grief, in time, for the wicked themselves. Yet the Lord lets His show go on. He created it without any sense of personal involvement. The drama of every individual's life must work its slow way, by however winding a road, to its eventual, *inevitable* conclusion: reabsorption in the bliss of Satchidananda.

God is conscious of every thought, every flicker of feeling in every single one of His creatures. Yet He stands apart from it all. Even in the story of the Bhagavad Gita, although Krishna served Arjuna as his charioteer, his condition for doing so was that he would take no part in the battle. Arjuna knew that the Lord's mere presence was enough. And in fact Krishna did intervene in a sense, when the need became crucial. The same is the case when a devotee lives for God and in the thought of Him. God never intervenes openly, yet some-how everything comes out all right in the end for the devotee—indeed, it comes out in the best possible way. As Krishna stated, "Arjuna, know this for a certainty: My devotee is *never* lost!"

The question is often asked, "Why, if God loves us, does He allow this 'show to go on'? Why the suf-ferings, the pains, the disappointments—the outright tragedies?"

Several answers may be given to this all-but-universal question. One is what Swami Sri Yukteswar is quoted as saying in *Autobiography of a Yogi*: "Leave a few questions to be answered by the Divine."

Another answer is that the little child cannot know why the father must leave home daily to work. He has yet to achieve the adult point of view.

Still another answer is one that has been quoted already in this book: "God created the universe in order that He might enjoy Himself through many." That "enjoyment" can seem very long delayed to the ego. No one who has ever found God, however, has ever said accusingly, "He didn't have to do it *that* way!" Everyone has said, rather, "Ah! It was well, well worth every seeming pain and difficulty!" The story of every life is thrilling, beautiful, and completely satisfying in its ending for every soul.

(7:13) Deluded by the three qualities (gunas) of Nature, mortal beings do not perceive Me—changeless and beyond all qualities.

Moviegoers in a theater sit forward on their seats—sometimes anxiously, sometimes in eager anticipation, their emotions deeply involved in the activity on the screen. Fearfully they may anticipate the worst. Delightedly they may expect the best. To them, it all seems very real.

Yogananda once was watching a movie of the life of the Christian saint Bernadette. He said, later, that he identified personally with many of the episodes in the saint's life. "And then," he said, "I looked up at the light coming from the projection booth. Everything on the screen, I was reminded by that light, was only a play of shadows and light." Few human beings, absorbed as they are in this "movie" of life, think to "look up" to the spiritual eye in meditation, and perceive God's One Consciousness producing and directing all the action.

(7:14) It is indeed difficult to waken from My cosmic hypnosis, instinct as it is with the three gunas (qualities) of *maya*. Only they who take shelter in Me can find freedom from the wonderful power of illusion.

There is a symbolic legend about Narada, an ancient Indian sage, and God in the form of Vishnu. Narada, after years of meditation, realized God in that form. When the Lord appeared to him as Vishnu, he asked if Narada would like to request from Him a boon.

"Yes, Lord," replied Narada. "Please help me to understand how people get caught up in Your *maya*. It all seems so simple to me, now that I'm out of it. How can people be so foolish?"

"Very well, My son," replied the Lord. "Come, let us go for a walk."

As they went, they came to a desert. The day was hot, and the sand made it much hotter. After some time, both of them felt the need for water to drink. And then, on the horizon, they saw a wisp of smoke rising, and giving evidence of a village.

"Narada," said Vishnu, "I am very thirsty. Would you go to that village and fetch me some water?"

"Certainly, Lord!" replied Narada.

He trudged over the hot sand until he reached the small village. At the first house he came too, he knocked on the door. It was answered by a beautiful maiden. Anciently familiar she seemed to him. In an instant he forgot everything else! Her parents, who were at home, welcomed him as their own. He and the maiden were married, and set up a home and business in another part of the village. Years passed. They had a son; then another one.

After twelve years, his wife gave birth to their third child. While this third one was still a baby, there came all of a sudden a flash flood from a swollen river high up in the hills. In little more than a moment the flood wiped out their home, their business—the whole village. Narada escaped with nothing but his little family and the clothes on their backs. They waded through the swirling water around them, as high as their knees. Narada held one child by each hand, and slung their baby child over one shoulder. His wife struggled along by his side.

Suddenly Narada stumbled slightly on a stone. As he tried hastily to regain his balance, the baby slipped off his shoulder into the water. Desperate to save it, he released his other two children's hands and reached out to rescue the baby. Alas, it was swept away before he could catch it. The older boys, lacking his strong grip, were swept away also. At that moment Narada's wife, her knees buckling with grief, fell also and was carried off in the flood. In just a few minutes Narada had lost everything he had worked so hard, over twelve years, to create. Despondent, his will failed him, and he collapsed, letting the water take him, too.

Long afterward, it seemed, he came back to consciousness. Looking around him, he saw on all sides what looked like a muddy expanse of water. "I must," he thought, "have been swept onto a little mound." Then, recalling his tragedy, he began softly to weep.

"Narada!" sounded a voice nearby. Why did it seem so familiar? He looked about him again, and realized that what he'd seen around him was not muddy water, but a vast expanse of desert sand.

"Narada!" came the voice again. He looked up. To his amazement, he saw Vishnu standing there.

"Narada, what happened?" inquired Vishnu. "Half an hour ago I sent you for a drink of water, and now I find you sleeping in the sand. What has happened?"

Such, indeed, is the power of *maya*! Time passes—incarnations? thousands—millions—billions of years: who knows? Time is an illusion. Once one awakens from it, it seems as though time hadn't passed at all!

(7:15) Evildoers (in whom tamas predominates), lowest of human beings, dull-witted and bereft of understanding by (the power of) *maya*, failing to take shelter in Me, partake of the nature of demons.

One meets such people in the world. They are not *rakshasas*—evil monsters with slavering jaws, avid to devour human beings. They are human beings themselves, though cruel, callous to other people's pain and suffering, absorbed in themselves, sex-hungry, bent on obtaining riches by any possible means (to such people, honesty means nothing), power-drunk, ruthless. Such people are not demons, lurking in wait for the unwary. They can be seen any day of the week, walking the streets of the cities. I remember my Guru seriously describing a well-known movie star who had come to him for an interview: "She is a devil," he said.

After death, souls are drawn to their respective levels in the astral world.

It must be strictly understood, however, that no one is evil *by nature*. All are children of God. What differentiates the demonic from the angelic is only the thickness of the veil which covers their understanding.

(7:16) Those who seek shelter in Me, O Arjuna, are of four types: those who are in distress; those who seek understanding; those who seek power (in this world or the next); and those who are (already) wise.

A saying among soldiers at war is, "There are no atheists in the foxholes." Most people who turn to God do so in times of affliction. (People ask why God permits suffering! What other incentive is there for most of them to seek help from Him?)

Bewildered by life's countless anomalies, some few (those who tire of shaking their fists in anger at God) turn to Him for understanding. "Why?" they ask repeatedly. When that question is asked sincerely, answers begin coming to them: through books; through well-read teachers; through teachers of varying degrees of understanding born of experience. Only when a person very sincerely wants to *know*, however, does God send him someone who, himself, *does* know: a true guru.

Often, on the pathway to wisdom, people get side-tracked by the desire for powers and phenomena. They go to spiritualistic séances. They go to "miracle workers." They spread word (especially in India) of every "saint" they meet whom they've seen perform wonders. Vicarious power over matter, or the desire to achieve power personally, may catch them for incarnations in a net of delusion.

Those, finally, who seek *perfection* in wisdom, spurning all other "attractions," offer themselves up wholly to God. Such devotees are, among all those who are virtuous, the most pleasing to God.

(7:17) Outstanding among the wise is he whose devotion is constant and one-pointed. I am, above all things, dear to that sage, and he, of all beings, is dearest to Me.

Is God, one may ask, really more fond of one person than another? How could He be? He is ever and supremely impersonal, having no individual self to be especially pleased with anyone! It is *through people's own love* for Him that His love is expressed. Those who love Him purely and entirely, however, are best able to *receive* his love, which He would shower unceasingly on all who are unhindered by doubts, uncertainties, or any karmic blocks. In an I-and-Thou relationship with God, He may respond quickly to even the slightest loving demand of His perfected devotees.

(7:18) All of the above (four kinds of virtuous) men are noble (for the direction of their consciousness is upward), but the sage who has established himself firmly in Me as the highest goal, him I look upon as indeed My own Self.

Is it wrong, in light of these words, to pray to God for His gifts? Not at all! Man has certain needs: It is always better to seek their fulfillment from God than by outward, ego-driven efforts alone. One who says, "God helps those who help themselves," and then busies himself with fulfilling his desires entirely by his own efforts, in forgetfulness of God, says to himself when success comes that it was by his own efforts alone that he achieved it. Thus, later on, he looks back gratefully upon his own ego as the achiever. This is hardly the way to liberation from ego-consciousness.

Best is it, then, to pray to God for *everything*, always adding, "Fulfill this prayer, Lord, only if it is in keeping with Your will."

Man can spare himself much pain in life if, even in praying to God, he practices *nishkam karma*: non-attachment to the fruits. Otherwise he may, by the power of his own mind (which increases vastly in power when it is united to God's consciousness), attract what he wants in life—only to find that what he got was, for him, disastrous.

Swami Sri Yukteswar enjoyed recounting the following fable to show the importance of seeking only God's will, not one's own.

A certain yogi, having developed the necessary psychic power, came upon a tree during his wanderings in the

Himalayas which he intuitively recognized as a *"kalyana kalpataru"*: a magic wishing tree. "How splendid!" he thought in delight. Sitting beneath the tree, he wished for a palace.

Instantly a beautiful palace materialized before him in the forest. He entered it, and found that it was perfectly in accordance with all his wishes. The edifice, however, was empty. "Let there be beautiful furnishings: sofas, carpets, wall hangings, paintings, artistic curtains." Lo! it all became so.

"This place is already wonderful beyond my wildest dreams!" he thought. "But it lacks people to enjoy it with me, and to rejoice with me in my good fortune. I wish these rooms to be filled with laughing, happy men and women." Suddenly—lo! it was so. People thronged the room he was in: the reception hall, the dining room, the staircases, the foyer.

He enjoyed all these delights for a time. Then he thought, "Let me go now from room to room, so as to see and take pleasure in *all* my new treasures!" He went by himself, exulting in his good fortune. After some time he came to a room on the ground floor in which there were no human beings. The window stood open. Because this miracle had come into being out in the forest, the surrounding woods were as Nature had made them. Suddenly he heard a tiger's roar outside the palace gates.

"Ah!" he thought in alarm. "I'm in this room all by myself. The window is wide open, and I'm on the ground floor! What if that tiger should leap in through the window and eat me?"

He forgot that he had produced all this under the magic spell of the wishing tree. Instantly a tiger appeared outside, leapt in through the window, and devoured him before he could cry for help.

The moral of this story is that if, especially by the practice of concentration, one has developed a strong mind, he will be sitting under the wishing tree of his own spinal energy. He should offer all his desires, his understanding, and his will up to God alone for fulfillment.

(7:19) After many incarnations, the sage realizes Me in My true nature. A person so illumined that he sees Me as all-pervading is rare (and hard) to find.

It is true, certainly, that the soul must pass through many incarnations before it attains God. For many people, even one lifetime scarcely suffices them for overcoming a single deep-seated bad habit. In this passage, however, Krishna is speaking of the *sage* who, after many incarnations, has reached perfection and has realized God. The meaning here is much deeper than what it appears to be superficially. For, consider: one who is a sage must be very close to realizing God. Otherwise, he would not be truly sage, or wise.

We saw earlier that every inhalation can, in effect, become a birth in a new incarnation. Some say that even the heartbeat can, in this sense, be turned to advantage, each beat becoming a new life. To bring about such an effect, one would have, however, to be unusually aware! The sage (certainly not the ordinary seeker!) can utilize his breath and heartbeat to pass through many births and deaths even while inhabiting a single body. Most people, of course, must literally die and be reborn many times to accomplish any significant inner change.

How to make such a teaching universally helpful? Sages, after all, don't really need to study scripture: Their wisdom is already inscribed in the "book" of their own consciousness. The point for everyone to bear in mind is that time is not an essential factor in self-upliftment. As my Guru said to me, "Habits can be changed in a day. They are only the result of mental concentration. If one has been concentrating one way, he can simply determine to concentrate in a new way." The yagya, or fire ceremony, prescribed in the Vedas, and mentioned often in these pages, is symbolic of the ego's voluntary self-offering to God in meditation. This ritual can be performed inwardly and constantly by the mind.

Every time the tendency arises to refer back to one's self such thoughts as, "*I* did it!" "Why was that done or said *to me*?" "I am too important to be treated that way!" he should mentally cast that thought into the fire of devotion, which he should keep ever burning in his heart. Consume in your mental fire everything in your nature that will not lift you toward God.

Most people take a long time to confront and change their shortcomings; they lack the incentive, or the will, to do so. They say, "I'll get around to it some day." A thought my Guru liked to express for our benefit was, "Eventually? Eventually? Why not *now*?!"

Another thought has been expressed in these pages: Concentrate first on those battles which you think you can win. If you are not strong enough yet to conquer some habit, or if other duties command so much of your time and energy that you simply cannot deal with it yet, then simply resist it mentally. Never admit to yourself that you haven't the power to overcome any defect. Every time your mind resists a bad habit, instead of embracing it gleefully, you build up more inner strength, which will enable you eventually to overcome.

Thus, the incarnations that others require to pull themselves out of the mud of delusion may take you only a relatively short time. Be a strategist: Await your opportunities calmly and dispassionately. Then, when it comes: *Strike!* Affirm your potential (as a sage, even though you are still wandering in back alleys of delusion), and it won't be long before you discover that you, too, "see" God in everything: that He is your only treasure, and your only reality.

To pass from that understanding to the realization described in this stanza is not a very long leap. If you don't make it in this incarnation, you may find yourself, ere long, living on higher planes where such sages are not so "hard to find." You may, indeed, become one of those sages, yourself, in time.

Paramhansa Yogananda added his own assertion to that of Lahiri Mahasaya, Sri Yukteswar, and other masters of the Kriya Yoga line that the practice of Kriya Yoga—the science taught by Krishna to Arjuna thousands of years ago—greatly accelerates the yogi's spiritual evolution. The Kriya Yogi can attain Cosmic consciousness, they said—according to the depth and intensity of his practice—in three, six, twelve, twenty-four, or forty-eight years. Yogananda added wryly

(I suspect he did so because few people in their lifetime will have a chance to practice for twice forty-eight years!) that if the Kriya Yogi doesn't make it in forty-eight years, he may as well expect to continue the practice in his next life!

(7:20) Those, however, who prefer (to follow) their own will (rejecting the path of inward communion with God), whose discrimination has been vitiated by this craving or by that, and who (perhaps) feel inclined toward cultish teachings, seek lesser gods.

Krishna utters a warning here to beware of ego-motivated self-will. One's discrimination can be carried away by desires, which cause one to endow almost any outward circumstance with the attractive halo of expectation: "It just *has* to be!" Thus, he may tell himself—indeed, he may insist to himself, and also to others—that this time he *knows* he is right: He *must* possess this thing, or affiliate with that person.

Anything one desires intensely becomes for him, in a sense, a god. This is the true meaning of "idol worship." An idol is not a statue or a painting that people use to remind them of some high ideal. Such people are, indeed, "ideal worshipers," not "idol worshipers." Idol worship means to harbor a desire for anything other than God.

Every man, unless he loves God alone, is in this sense an idol worshiper! To love something, or some person, because it reminds one of God is a virtue, not a fault. To get to the top floor of a building one must ascend by the other floors: No one can leap all the way to the top. To feel love for God as He really is, formless and impersonal, is almost impossible for human beings. Such love comes naturally, however, to those who first envision divine perfection in some human form. The important thing in such worship is always to keep in mind that the form one loves (even of a living person) serves one only as a window onto infinity.

Self-will, particularly where intense desire is concerned, is difficult to discern in oneself. One's discrimination can be snatched away in a moment by some sudden infatuation. The key to intelligent behavior in such situations is to watch the heart's feelings.

The poet Wordsworth wrote, "My heart leaps up when I behold a rainbow in the sky." He described exactly what happens when one is suddenly seized by any strong attraction. That rainbow soon vanishes, but the feeling remains. The objects of any sudden affection all vanish, but that "leap" in the heart continues its upward spurts for a time. We have seen that an upward flow of energy is desirable—indeed, essential for spiritual awakening. The flow must be *calm*, however. Upward leaps of feeling indicate outwardness of attention. Watch the heart: Do its feelings "leap up" at any sudden infatuation? If so, challenge them! Let not your discrimination be fooled by anything that uplifts the feelings in emotional excitement, instead of calmly, in uplifted devotion.

People, finally, who allow their feelings to become uplifted emotionally are often susceptible to sensation-mongering. They may pass from one "cultish" fancy to another—attending séances, going to miracle workers, flocking eagerly to listen to every new lecturer who arrives in town. All these activities are symptomatic of the disease of ignorance: the desire for outward stimulation, rather than for inward inspiration.

(7:21) Whatsoever form a person worships (a saint, a master, a deity—whether real or imaginary), it is I who (uplift his heart) and make his devotion steadfast and true.

(7:22) Absorbed in his devotion, intent on worshiping that form, he derives true, spiritual benefits, and has his desires (his prayers) fulfilled. The blessings he receives come from Me alone.

Even with the worship of lower gods, so long as it is offered sincerely and is not merely a prayer for selfish fulfillment—and even when the prayer *is* for selfish motives, but is offered up to a higher power rather than as ego to ego—it is God Himself who answers through those more limited channels. The important thing is not to concern oneself with theological niceties (how many religious pedants waste time and effort in that preoccupation!), but to offer one's energy *upward*, *past* the ego to a higher source.

Interestingly, even "man-made" deities like the symbolic images of Kali, Durga, Saraswati, Vishnu, Shiva, and Ganesha become what Yogananda called "blueprints in the ether." They have acquired a reality of their own, and can be communed with perhaps more easily in those forms than in some form that one has imagined only personally.

As Yogananda wrote of his own *Whispers from Eternity*, and of his *Cosmic Chants*, he "spiritualized them" by drawing, by deep repetition of them, a divine response. Any response from God that is generated superconsciously remains "in the ether," and can continue forever to convey special blessings. Such also is the power of pilgrimage, when devotees seek blessings where divine manifestations have taken place.

(7:23) Men of meager understanding, however, (in limiting their worship to the lesser gods) receive limited results. Devotees of the lower gods go to those gods. Devotees who worship Me (the Infinite One) come to Me.

Those who worship any form of God as a reminder of the Infinite One are not the ones described here as limited in their worship. Those, however, who worship lower forms with the attitude described above—ego to ego—with a view to gaining fulfillment for some personal desire, go to those regions where subtler egos still exist, albeit in exalted forms.

People sometimes ask, "Are not the angels higher than earthly masters?" A true master, it must be said, is *far* higher than any angel! He has merged his ego in God, whereas angels, though lofty compared to most human beings, still possess egos—pure, exalted, sattwic egos, but for all that limited by the consciousness of being separate from God.

There is the story of a saint in India who lived long ago. A deva, or angel, offered him the boon of transportation to heaven in his physical body. (Thus did ancient Indian tradition express the concept of leaving the body consciously at death.)

Legend tells us that this deva came to him one day in a heavenly chariot, long before his own destined time to die, to carry him off to heaven. "So great are your virtues," said the deva, "that you have been deemed worthy to receive this great blessing."

"Wait a moment!" said the saint. "I'd like to know first what advantages I will reap by going to this heaven of yours."

"Well," replied the angel, "that is a most unusual request. Most people are happy enough to get to heaven at all! Still, since you've asked me I must respond. In heaven you will enjoy a wonderful environment— beautiful, serene, harmonious. You will get to mix with the gods. What more could you possibly want?"

"Well," replied the saint, "in everything I've experienced in this world of *maya* I've always found some disadvantages. Even in beautiful surroundings, duality intrudes. Tell me, therefore, what disadvantages will I find in going to heaven?"

"I must say," exclaimed the deva, "your question is *most* unusual! Still, since you've asked me, I must answer you once more: You will get to stay in heaven only as long as the good karma lasts which took you there. You will not be able to progress further there, spiritually. Living with angelic beings and with good people will bring you great happiness, but once your karmic time comes to return to earth, your happiness, like forest leaves in autumn, will fade and lose its color, then drop to the ground. You will experience deep sadness, as you realize that you must leave that world. Until then, however, everything will be wonderful!"

"I very much appreciate your coming all this way," said the saint, "to offer me this gift. I can see that what you've offered me would be, for many people, a great blessing. I must say, however, that the disadvantages you've outlined seem to me so colossal that I cannot imagine any sane person accepting this 'blessing'! Were the situation you describe to last a thousand years, it would still end after that length of time. Please tell me, isn't there anywhere I can go that offers something permanent?"

"Yet once again," said the angel, "you've asked me a question I must answer. Yes, such a place exists. It is beyond our place of astral beauty—beyond the astral light itself. We ourselves have only heard about it. If you want to reach there, however, you will have to remain here on Earth and continue with your spiritual disciplines, for only thus will you be able to soar to that highest plane of manifested existence. For this reason it is said that even the gods would like to be reborn on Earth."

The saint declined the angel's invitation, and decided to remain on Earth, where he could continue his yoga practices. In the end, he attained the God of gods, and merged in oneness with the Infinite.

(7:24) Men who lack wisdom think of Me, the Unmanifest, as limited (when I appear) in bodily form. They comprehend not My higher nature: changeless, unutterable, supreme.

Devotees without wisdom think of the supreme Godhead Himself as limited in essence to His special manifestations. They may even worship God in one of those forms as the *only* God: as Krishna with his flute, for example, as Shiva with his trident, as Kali with Her four arms, or as Jehova or Allah (who have names, but no form). God is all of these, but is so much more besides that He cannot be either named or imagined in His true essence.

To worship the Unutterable by any name, however, and to visualize Him in any form, cannot be avoided if man is to worship God at all. What Krishna means in this sloka is not that it is erroneous to worship God with name and form, but only that it is wrong to try to *confine* God in that way. God is everything—and He is nothing—that is to say, no specific thing. He is both in and beyond everything, and, in truth, is not even the "things" He has manifested, since they are but dreams, and are "real" only as dreams are real.

(7:25) Hidden by My veil of *yoga-maya*, I am invisible to mankind. Humanity, therefore, bewildered (by appearances), sees not that I am (in essence) ever unborn, and ever deathless.

(7:26) O Arjuna, the past, present, and future of all beings is known to Me. Me, however, no man knows (so long as he knows himself as only human).

(7:27) O Descendent of Bharata, Scorcher of Foes (Arjuna)! Birth in a body subjects all beings to the power of delusion, with its dualities, which produce attraction and repulsion. (Such is the storm of *maya* on the surface of My ocean of consciousness.)

A baby's energy at birth is necessarily outward. A child continues that outward direction of energy as it learns gradually to relate to the world. People's bias, imposed upon them from birth, continues to be outward. They must learn to distinguish right behavior from wrong as they grow up, that they find which paths lead to true, long-lasting fulfillment, and which ones lead to disappointment, pain, and suffering. It is not easy to find God, and unfortunately the very movement of a person's energy from the time of his birth inclines him toward outwardness.

Even liberated masters may allow themselves to live for a time under the partial sway of *maya*. Thus, Lahiri Mahasaya—who had been anciently liberated—came back wearing the semblance of mortality. Though he sat long in meditation as a child, when he grew to manhood he took a job, married, and produced a family. He was well into maturity before he met his guru, Babaji, and received from him his enlightenment once more.

Swami Sri Yukteswar also married, had a daughter, and lived (to outward appearances) as a normal human being before he received enlightenment from his guru, Lahiri Mahasaya.

Paramhansa Yogananda, in his turn, accepted human limitation. During his boyhood he played the ardent seeker instead of showing himself—and perhaps even before perceiving himself—as he was: a great master from long before who received enlightenment anew from Swami Sri Yukteswar. Yogananda often said in public, "I killed Yogananda long ago. No one lives in this temple now but God."

I once asked him, "Does one who is born liberated come with the active consciousness of oneness with God?" I asked that question because it seemed to me that my Guru, and other masters, had played many human roles that would surely have been incompatible with being consciously in that high state of oneness.

"They never lose their consciousness of being inwardly free," he replied.

God's lila (play) is endlessly diverting. My Guru told us that the gopis in their lila with Lord Krishna as a boy in Brindaban were in fact reincarnated rishis. "Their role on Earth," he said, "was to enact the divine play of lover and beloved."

Krishna at that time was only a boy. He had come as a *mahavatar*—a *purna* or full manifestation of God, and was universally recognized as such. From the beginning of that life he manifested not only divine attributes, but divine perfection. The fabled love between him and the gopis was no ordinary human love. Indeed, all the gopis were married women. Their faithfulness to their husbands was never in doubt. The *rasalila*, their divine dance with Krishna in the forest during which each gopi saw him as her very own, was enacted in order to inspire human beings with longing for a perfect human love. The love which the gopis shared with Krishna *was* perfect. Unfortunately, human consciousness being what it is, their love in time became greatly misunderstood. "The legends that have grown up around the life of Krishna," my Guru told me, "are mostly allegorical. Don't take them all as literally true." As often happens, a few facts were built up into a large body of legend.

(7:28) Righteous men, however, their sins expiated, and no longer subject to the oppositions of duality, worship Me steadfastly.

It is noteworthy that already-free souls, even if they come to earth with a mission that necessitates a slight assumption of delusion, are always pious and high-minded.

The expression, "righteous men," need not indicate souls that are liberated, of course, even though Krishna describes their "sins as having been expiated." Those with good spiritual karma, also, are usually drawn back soon to the spiritual path, and are born with virtuous tendencies. Nevertheless, the uncertainties that accompany birth in a new body should give to everyone a powerful incentive to work hard at finding God *now*, assuming one's circumstances are supportive enough of that desire to make one want God. What man, indeed, can know what his own future holds?

(7:29) Those who, clinging to Me, seek release from (the debilities of) old age and from (the finality of) death become true knowers of Brahman (the Absolute), of *Adhyatma* (the Overself), and of all the secrets of karma.

The debilities of old age are notorious. They include increasing illness, physical and mental weakness, and possible senility. It is always sad to see someone who was once robust and full of energy decline to decrepitude both outwardly and inwardly. People often spend their life savings in their final years on medical care. Those who cling to God are the most likely to die with dignity.

The Overself watches over them in old age better than any human doctor could do. Inwardly—it is evident to those who know them intimately—they are unchanged and, indeed, remain spiritually robust—"ever the same," as the great woman saint Anandamayee Ma declared.

Those with any lingering doubts or questions as to the "whys" of life—the disparities of fortune; the seeming injustices of life; the endless intricacies of karma—find all their questions answered in Brahman: the great Overself of all beings.

(7:30) Those who perceive My presence within their physical (*Adhibhuta*), astral (*Adhidaiva*), and spiritual (causal, or *Adhiyagya*) bodies, their hearts united to Me, retain their perception even at the time of death.

Death is the "final exam" for which all of life is the preparation. To leave the body consciously is a blessing not accorded to many. Most people slip back into the after-death sleep. One's experiences prior to death may be painful, but death itself comes as a relief, and is without pain. Mainly, whatever pain people experience at death is mental: their fear of losing their bodies, to which they've grown not only accustomed, but attached—very often to the point of identifying with it *as* their actual self.

Death is an ordeal everyone must face: sometimes even masters, although for them the ordeal is brief. The sudden realization that everything one has known, all the people to whom one has related, all the work one has set into motion, the many people who are—for good or for ill—dependent on one, all the things one may have left undone, and above all the sum total of one's bad and/or virtuous deeds: All these must be faced, accepted as facts, relinquished into eternity, and turned to some kind of resolution for the future.

The consciousness one brings to death determines his future existence—whether in this world, in a higher world, or in eternity. The weight of error may cause one to recoil in rejection. That recoil itself may suffice to make him fall back into subconsciousness in hope of a healing. The struggles of life may have brought him to a point where he feels a need for rest. This is why many people, in old age, already begin to draw away from active involvement in outwardness. Senility itself, for them, may be a kind of escape. Those who have lived wasted lives may, after resting for some time, suffer "nightmares." Those who have lived evil lives may wake up in ghastly-seeming circumstances which cause them purgative anguish and even suffering. Those, on the other hand, who have lived virtuous lives may wake up in an astral heaven, and enjoy there for a time the fruits of their goodness. Memories of the past may linger, though less vividly than those who are left behind might expect. Sometimes, a person's departed relatives may come to him in dreams—to give him help, warning, or encouragement.

The thoughts with which one leaves his body have a great influence on his future state. Exaggerated remorse for one's mistakes is a negative affirmation that may attract to oneself unnecessary suffering. Far better than useless regret is an affirmation of positive intent to correct one's errors. "Sin" itself is only, and quite simply, error. As people lie dying, they should resolve to do better in future. To seek absolution from sin at the time of death may only cause one to focus on his sins. It may cause one to leave his body with a negative affirmation in his mind, as he recalls all the wrongs he has committed. Instead of "absolution," then, a better practice will be simply to offer one's heart in loving surrender to God, leaving to Him (once again we see here the teaching of Krishna's) the fruits of all one's actions.

Those who at death can fix their minds at the point between the eyebrows, and call deeply in their hearts to God, will go to Him. Any priest, therefore, or anyone dear to the person who is dying, will do well (instead of devoting time and effort to absolving him of sin) to place his forefinger on the person's forehead, at the point midway between the eyebrows, and, sending energy there, encourage him (or her) to focus the body's energy completely at that point.

The ego often struggles against death's final, firm decree. It may cling adamantly for a time to the spine and brain, like someone hanging onto a cliff by his fingers. Sometimes such persons actually return to their bodies, striving to reactivate them. For this reason cremation is safer than burial for the dead. It is better not to have a body to return to than to reawaken in it once it has been buried, and once one's actual departure has been accepted by others as a fact.

Realized saints, on the other hand, about whose bodily non-attachment there need be no concern, are not traditionally, and ought not to be, cremated. Their interred bodies emanate vibrations that may bring healing and blessings to many devout persons.

In the astral world, after a time of either rest or enjoyment, egos that have not finished their material karmas begin to feel a muffled longing for earthly gratification once more, one that cannot be fulfilled in the astral world. As they gather there, waiting to be reborn, couples on earth, uniting sexually, produce a light in the astral world generated by the union of their sperm and ovum cells. According to the quality of that light, disembodied souls are drawn to it. This attraction accounts for the affinity that often (though not always) exists between parents and children. There will certainly, in any case, be points of resemblance.

Those discerning human beings who, during their earthly sojourn, practice non-attachment, adherence to duty without egoic identification or desire, and above all love for God, go either straight to Him, or to some high astral heaven where they may be conscious enough to continue the great work of ego-transcendence and reabsorption in God.

Thus ends the seventh chapter, called "The Yoga of Knowledge and Discrimination," of the Upanishad of the holy Bhagavad Gita, in the dialogue between Sri Krishna and Arjuna discussing yoga and the science of God-realization.

CHAPTER TWENTY

THE OUTER AND THE INNER UNIVERSE

(8:1) Arjuna said: O Best of the Purushas (Krishna)! Please tell me, what is Brahman (Spirit)? What is Adhyatma (the Kutastha Chaitanya underlying all manifestations and individualized as the souls of all creatures)? What is Karma (action—cosmic and individual—born of AUM)? What is Adhibhuta (the consciousness immanent in physical creatures and the physical cosmos)? And what is Adhidaiva (the consciousness manifest in astral bodies and in the astral cosmos)?

(8:2) O Slayer of (the demon) Madhu (Krishna)! What is Adhiyagya (the Supreme Creative and Cognizing Spirit), and in what manner is Adhiyagya (the soul's self-offering) possible in this body? How, finally, at the time of death, are the self-disciplined to know You?

ARJUNA IS PERPLEXED BY THESE TERMS, WHICH Krishna used toward the end of Chapter 7. In these stanzas he asks for clarification.

(8:3) The Blessed Lord replied: Brahman is the Indestructible and Supreme Spirit. Adhyatma is Brahman's manifestation as the essential soul of all beings. Cosmic karma is AUM (the Cosmic Vibration), which causes the birth, sustenance, and dissolution of all creatures, and also the diversity of their natures.

Brahman (the Supreme Spirit), in order to manifest His cosmic dream, set a portion of His consciousness in vibration. Thus came into being the Cosmic Sound, AUM. This Cosmic Vibration is the primordial karma (action), out of which all individual karmas are manifested. Self-conscious (human) beings, in whatever forms they manifest on different planets, are all governed by the "rhythmic law" of individual karma.

A playwright is conscious of the characters he creates from both inside and outside of their minds—both subjectively and objectively, that is to say. At the same time, he observes them while remaining untouched, himself, by their personalities. Even so, *Brahman* has divided His functions—not Himself—into the watchful but never-affected Viewer (the Spirit Itself); the action in the play as a whole (Cosmic Vibration), which determines (but also, on a micro-cosmic scale, is determined by) the characters, each with his own individual destiny (karma) to work out. The third division of functions is the Kutastha Chaitanya, the reflected consciousness of vibrationless Spirit in every tremor of vibration in the universe. In a way similar to a chip of wood rising and sinking with every passing wave, though its horizontal position remains unchanged, the divine consciousness at the heart of each ripple of Cosmic Vibration remains a motionless reflection of the vibrationless Spirit.

Individual karmas, relative to the over-all activity at the ocean's surface, might be compared to the wake behind a motorboat or a ship: never affecting the over-all ocean level—any more than storm waves affect it—nor even effecting much change anywhere, except locally.

Adhyatma is the pristine reflection, the Kutastha Chaitanya, within creation itself of the vibrationless Spirit *beyond* creation. Its manifestation is both macro-cosmic and micro-cosmic: throughout space, and in each individual being. Karma, similarly, is both macro-cosmic and micro-cosmic: universal vibration, and the individual acts of every being—the results of which rebound, either to the egos themselves which set them in motion, or (more generally) to species as a whole which have not yet (by higher evolution) developed individual self-, or ego-consciousness.

Adhibhuta is the "macro" physical universe, and also its "micro," or individual expressions. Adhidaiva is the expression of the same "macro-" and "micro-"relationships on the astral plane.

Adhiyagya is the same inter-related truth applied to the causal plane. On the causal plane, self-consciousness has been offered up in the purifying fire of wisdom, and no longer exists—hence that word, yagya, or self-sacrifice. Individual consciousness, on a causal level, is hardly separate from Cosmic consciousness. Thus it is that souls living in the causal body have the power—as Swami Sri Yukteswar explained in the chapter, "The Resurrection of Sri Yukteswar," from *Autobiography of a Yogi*—to "bring universes into manifestation even as the Creator. Because all creation is made of the cosmic dream-texture, the soul thinly clothed in the causal has vast realizations of power."

Whether "universes," as Sri Yukteswar used the word, means "galaxies," or entirely new and different universes, I never heard my Guru explain. I did hear him use the term "island universes" in reference to what are now termed galaxies.

Images are symbolic of reality, and cannot be used entirely to replace them. Thus, to use the waves that are raised in the wake of a ship as an analogy for individual activity, or vibration, in its relation to the wave-vibrations of a whole ocean has this disadvantage: The ship is a foreign body agitating the surface. The micro-vibrations of individual waves, on the other hand, are activated in the water itself by the ego. Imagine, then, the waves of the ocean all being conscious. Individual waves, to the extent that they are not only conscious but also attached to their individuality, may of their own accord push themselves farther away from the ocean bosom and thereby create high crests, or they may choose to remain humbly close to the ocean bosom, as little ripples.

The simile may be extended: In a storm, many waves tower high in response to the wind's force, but a few waves, even in the midst of the storm, (owing to opposite forces) resist that tendency and remain small. So, when the influences surrounding them on earth plunge most egos into a veritable storm of delusion, causing them to feel anger, violence, and warlike fervor, a few egos resist that influence even if it surrounds them, and remain calm, loving toward everyone, and all-forgiving.

Thus, the AUM Vibration manifests on both a cosmic and a micro-cosmic, or individual level. The cosmic Adhibhuta manifests similarly: macro-cosmically (from outside) and micro-cosmically (from inside) every atom, and, again, in every ego. And the same holds true in the astral and causal universes.

When the waves of duality become stilled in the yogi's consciousness and he merges his one soul in the Cosmic Vibration of AUM, the dual opposites merge together and become the oneness of Spirit.

Adhi means "above, or original." *Adhi-atma* is written with a "*y*"— *Adhyatma*—because that is how it is pronounced. Adhyatma is the same, on the subtlest plane, as the other "*adhis.*"

An animal's life is determined more by macro- than by micro-karma: by the group karma, for example, of a species, a region, or even a planet. Mankind, though affected also by these group karmas, has also self-awareness, which enables him to act with some degree of free will. A tiger is ferocious by nature, not by choice. A Chihuahua is different from a Great Dane—again, not by its own choice, but by nature's. Free will, in man, depends not on egoic whims but on guidance from a level of superconsciousness. Egoic will, which we have called whimsical, is in fact imposed upon man by his past karma. It is whimsical only in the sense that, though an act may seem to be deliberate, in fact man is normally guided by his past actions, and by the tendencies he built up in consequence of them. Thus, his liking for (let us say) the color blue is not a matter of free will, but of past conditioning. His choice to become an engineer is, again, whimsical in the sense that, even if deliberate, it is not a choice of free will but of past conditioning. The will is free only if it is guided by superconscious inspiration, and even then that inspiration must be filtered down through the mind's prior conditioning: a poet, for example, will receive influence from the superconscious in the form of words, whereas a composer, receiving perhaps the same inspiration, will express it in melody, rhythm, and harmony.

(8:4) O Supreme among the Embodied (Arjuna)! Adhibhuta is the basis of physical existence; Adhidaiva is the basis of astral existence; and I (the Spirit manifested ideationally, both macro- and micro-cosmically) am Adhiyagya.

Paramhansa Yogananda stated that, as Adhibhuta, God's presence in the physical universe and in the physical body can only be inferred. As Adhidaiva, God's presence is *felt*. As Adhiyagya, His presence in the causal world is known intuitively.

(8:5) He who, at the hour of death, thinks of Me only enters unquestionably into My Being.

Krishna now answers Arjuna's final question (posed above): "How, finally, at the time of death, are the self-disciplined to know You?"

A person's final thoughts at death determine his after-death state. This does not mean that one can live any sort of life he pleases, then hastily summon up thoughts of God at his last moment of life and thereby, leaping over the hurdle of karma, fly to the arms of Infinity! Many people hope by such clever ploys to avoid the consequences of their mistakes.

There is a supposedly true story about a dacoit (brigand) in India who, having heard that anyone dying in Varanasi (Benares) will be automatically saved, decided that here was his "way out." Not wanting to pay the price for his many sins, on reaching old age he had both his legs cut off above the thighs, then settled down to die in that holy city, determined never to move again.

One day someone riding by on a horse showed such poor horsemanship that the "feat" raised gales of mockery in the ex-dacoit. "Why," he cried, "even without my legs I could ride better than that!"

He insisted that he be lifted onto the horse's back. As soon as he was firmly seated, the horse bolted. Varanasi is bounded on one side by the Varuna river, and on the other side by the Asi. When the horse got just beyond the Varuna, it threw its rider, breaking his neck and causing his death.

One's thoughts at death cannot but be influenced by the way one has lived. Even were one to chant, "Ram! Ram!" this is not to say that his thoughts would necessarily be immersed in God, to whom only his lips are chanting. Even if his mind is on God, his heart may be thinking, "What favors would I like to ask of Him?"

Krishna's meaning here is that if, at death, one's whole consciousness is immersed in unconditional love for God, without any thought of ego-fulfillment or reward, then and then only can he merge in the Infinite. The meaning of "unquestionably," is double: Krishna's words are unquestionably true, but, in the mind there must be no flicker of doubt, or questioning.

(8:6) O Son of Kunti (Arjuna)! the uppermost thought in a person's mind as he dies determines his next state of existence.

The whole of human life is, as we've already said, a preparation for the "final exam" of death. There flashes before the mind at death an overview of one's entire life. Things that may have seemed to him important when they occurred may be seen, during these last moments, as quite insignificant. And things that may have seemed to him trivial may now be realized as having had great significance for him. Things at that moment of dying are beheld as they really were—good, bad, or insignificant—rather than as they may have been cast at the time by mere opinion.

(8:7) Therefore, remember Me (throughout life), and fight the battle (of right action)! Surrender to Me your mind and understanding. In so doing, you will without a doubt come to Me.

The Bhagavad Gita, amazingly, never wastes a word. What does Krishna mean by telling Arjuna to surrender *both* mind and understanding to God? The average reader would lump these two words together and not give a thought to the fact that they have different meanings.

Mind is that aspect of consciousness which *receives* impressions. *Understanding* is that which defines those impressions and gives them meaning. One should, in other words, on seeing (for example) a sunset, enjoy it *with God*. He should offer up to God the joy he feels in that beauty, and discriminate inwardly that the joy he feels inside is, for him, the reality of that experience. Were it not for that inner ability, the sunset would hold no special meaning for him. Thus, both the experience and the discernment of its reality for him as being inward, not outward, is what Krishna means in saying, "Surrender to Me your mind and understanding."

In such surrender, finally, all doubts are dismissed. The mind no longer stands back hesitantly, like a boy pausing on a riverbank before daring to plunge into the water, and fearful of finding it too cold. He simply dives.

(8:8) That person attains the Supreme Effulgence, O Partha (Arjuna), who, his mind (by long practice) firmly fixed on Me, thinks of Me only.

With practice, this "firm fixity" is not a consequence of stern determination, but of total *relaxation into* the truth of one's being, as he has perceived it and knows it to be.

(8:9,10) The yogi, at the time of his death, attains that supremely effulgent state: provided that, with

deep love and with focused power through the practice of yoga, he succeeds in penetrating his conscious energy through the Kutastha between the eyebrows (the seat of the spiritual eye); and if he maintains his attention unwaveringly on that Being who, beyond all delusions of (gloom and) darkness, shines like the sun—whose form is subtler than the finest atom, who is the Ultimate Support of all (existence), and the great Ruler (of all), eternal and omniscient.

Here we find listed the three major qualifications by which a true yogi at death passes into, and merges with, the Divine Essence: divine devotion; yoga mastery (which comes through the practice of Kriya Yoga); and perfect concentration. Yogananda stated that the true yogi "always knows in advance the hour of his death."

These two stanzas refer twice to God as Light. The mention of a yoga technique is also specific in these stanzas, as will be seen with increased clarity in Stanzas 12 and 13. The inner light is "supremely effulgent"— brighter, it states later in the Gita, than a thousand suns. Yet the inner light is not hurtful to the eyes; it is only thrilling to the soul. The soul *knows it is itself* that light, as, when one hears AUM, one *knows he is, himself*, that Cosmic Vibration. As the AUM vibration plays upon the harp strings (so to speak) of one's very being, so also the light thrills one's consciousness with the awareness that it *is* Light. The "light of knowledge," and, "the light of understanding" are no mere figures of speech.

This radiance "as from a thousand suns" merges into multi-colored rays in an "ever-new display," issuing as if from a spherical fountain, its rays spraying outward from an endless number of points in space. The single, spiritual eye in the forehead bestows on the yogi a spherical vision, its luminosity ever changing, blissful, omnipresent.

This vibratory light, an aspect of AUM, carries the yogi beyond all of *maya*'s dualities. He realizes oneness with the transcendent Lord, "whose form is subtler than the finest atom, the Ultimate Support of all (existence), the great Ruler (of all), eternal and omniscient"—out of whom issue the causal, astral, and material universes.

The yogi who has attained complete control over his own consciousness beholds the divine consciousness everywhere, manifested in all the three universes. He perceives God in all His eight aspects: Light, Sound, Peace, Calmness, Power, Wisdom, Love, and (above all) Bliss. (Peace and Calmness differ from one another only in that Peace is the soothing cessation of all agitation of feeling, whereas Calmness is dynamic, and is the silent, essential core of creativity, impersonal love, and divine wisdom.)

Krishna, in speaking of the inner light in these two stanzas, and of concentration at the point between the eyebrows, is referring to the light that people universally can *behold* at that point. The spiritual eye is not a poetic or mystical image. Many people who know nothing of yoga have beheld it. It is a reflection, as we stated earlier, of the medulla oblongata (the *agya chakra*) at the base of the brain. It consists of a circle of golden light encasing a blue field, with a brilliant five-pointed star, silvery-white in color, in the center. The bodily eye is, in a sense, a reflection of the medulla also, with the white of the eye, the iris, and the pupil at its center.

This phenomenon, as we have stated, is universal. It is described in the Book of Revelation of the Bible: "And he that overcometh, and keepeth my works unto the end, to him will I give power over the nations. . . . And I will give him the morning star." (Rev. 2:26–28) The "star of the East" is also the star seen by the wise men who came to see the baby Jesus after his birth. They saw it "in the East"—not because they came *from* the East (it was said to "go before" them as they traveled westward), but because they saw it in what is known, in mystical tradition, as the "east" of the body: the forehead. To "open" this spiritual eye is to see through it and, after long practice, to be able to pass one's consciousness through it.

We have already discussed how the unenlightened person sinks into a peaceful state of deep slumber after death—a healing state after the turmoil, tests, and challenges, the sufferings and uncertainties of earthly life. After a healing period spent in this condition, he may (if his intuition is somewhat developed) awake to the beauties of a higher astral world (or to the temporary terrors of hell), in a body similar to the one he has left—made, however, of astral light. The attractions of his new life cause him to forget his physical existence for a time, though love always binds him to those who are close to him.

The great yogi, however, through his spherical spiritual eye, observes the entire phenomenon of death. Even one who is only somewhat spiritually evolved may see a beautiful light at death, and find himself temporarily uplifted into a higher state of consciousness. The yogi who has, during his lifetime, practiced withdrawing his energy and consciousness from the body is able to greet death as an old friend. Permanently released by conscious transition, he emerges from the body with great joy. If his yoga practices have taken him beyond the astral and causal bodies to God Himself, through the "energy-knots" (chakras) in the astral spine, and through their corresponding "idea-knots" in the causal body, he soars out into union with the vibrationless, transcendent Spirit.

(8:11) I will now relate to you briefly that truth, and the method for attaining it, which Vedic seers declare to be Immutable, and which sannyasis (renunciates) gain by dissolving their attachments through a life of self-discipline and transcendence of all passion.

Krishna assures Arjuna in this stanza that the divine goal can be attained by the practice of a specific method, which he proceeds to outline in the next two stanzas.

(8:12,13) That person reaches the highest goal who closes the gates (openings) of the body, sequesters the (receptive) mind in the heart center, channels all his life force to the brain, and engages steadfastly thereby in the practice of yoga: Such a one, established in AUM—the Holy Word of Brahman—is able to remember Me at the final moment of his emergence from the body.

For this purpose the Kriya Yogi learns, and practices daily, a technique known as *Jyoti Mudra*, the purpose of which is not only to see but to pass the life force and consciousness through the spiritual eye into infinity. The mind (*manas*, perceptive sense-consciousness) is withdrawn upward from the lowest three chakras in the spine (which are associated with outer consciousness), and is focused in the heart chakra (the second "stopping place" in the spine, after *manipura*—located opposite the navel—for the rising energy). In *Jyoti Mudra* the fingers are used lightly in such a way as to close the eyes, ears, nostrils, and mouth openings, and to direct their energy inward and upward, focusing it in the spiritual eye at the point between the eyebrows. The spiritual eye is the "inner gateway," which opens onto infinity.

Krishna has spoken several times already in the Gita of communing with AUM. Most translators imagine that this means chanting AUM with the voice. Indeed, that sound is, of all mantras, the highest, and helps to attune the mind to the Cosmic Sound. To chant that sound, however, is not the same thing as communing with it superconsciously. AUM is itself the true "name of God," whose name cannot really be uttered by human lips.

The true meaning of this passage, then, is not merely (as most people take it to be) that one should "utter the syllable AUM," but that he should commune with and finally merge into the mighty sound of the universe.

Experiencing the omnipresence of AUM, he becomes conscious of the Kutastha Chaitanya—the Christ consciousness underlying all creation—and unites his consciousness with that. From there the yogi's consciousness is absorbed into the Transcendental Absolute, beyond vibratory manifestation. This is what Yogananda described as "that watchful state": Infinite, or Boundless, Consciousness.

This state must be practiced during physical life itself. If, having done so, one can hold his consciousness firmly focused at the time of death in the manner prescribed, he will attain final freedom from all vestiges of ego-consciousness, and unite his soul with God.

(8:14) O Partha (Arjuna)! I am reached easily by that yogi of single heart (the heart's feeling focused and uplifted) who keeps Me in his consciousness daily, continuously, focused wholly on Me.

It often happens that people's religious and spiritual practices come to be repeated, after a time, "by rote." The positive results of Kriya Yoga practice—which are inner peace and joy—make it less likely that it will be practiced mechanically, but still, one must be careful to keep the heart's feelings uplifted devotionally, and should always bear in mind the goal (God) even as he travels the path (by yoga practices).

A good rule for the sincere seeker is this: Never go to bed at night before experiencing at least something of the divine presence within—peace, love, upliftment of consciousness, or joy.

(8:15) Those great souls who love Me, and (out of love for Me) merge in My spirit, achieve the highest success (the only kind worth striving for). They

need never return again to this ephemeral, grief-stricken world.

Many spiritual aspirants equate success with some achievement that falls short of total oneness with God. They are like mountain climbers who are satisfied with climbing a moderately high peak, when Everest (the highest of them all) is nearby—or else they are satisfied to rest on a plateau, and don't make the final push to reach the mountaintop.

Spiritual powers, worldly respect, people's devotion, ardent crowds of followers, success in one's outward accomplishments—these and countless other things often seduce even (relatively) good yogis to settle for less than total absorption in God. The underlying temptation comes from ego-attachment—not to pride, but rather to the simple thought, "I'm *me*! How can I give up everything I know and am for a truth I haven't experienced?"

One such "lower peak," widely approved by people on this earth, is the thought, "If only I could make this world into a perfect paradise!" The ego-attachment, here, is refined and sattwic, or spiritually elevating. One has, indeed, a duty to bless and help others to the degree that one is able, in order that they, too, climb toward the highest fulfillment. Nevertheless, this duty must be seen in relation to the highest blessing of all, God- (or Self-) realization. Less than that, the fruits of anything one does with ego-consciousness can never be higher than ego-consciousness itself, which is, alas! the source of all man's suffering!

This world is a school. The reason children go to school is to become educated—that is to say, in a spiritual sense of the word, to become perfect. The goal of every system of education is the training of children, not the improvement of the school itself (except, of course, with the higher aim of providing a better education). One creates good karma by whatever good work he does, but even good karma, as long as it remains "hitched to the post" of ego, returns one to earth again and again.

No one can make a paradise of this earth, for people themselves are imperfect. No one can ordain what people's desires shall be. Nor can anyone decree that they shall be desireless. The best way to improve matters objectively is to work with a few people, who themselves *desire* a better way of life, and then to hope that they, by their example, will inspire a few others who too are susceptible to being convinced, in the face of strong sensory evidence to the contrary, of the truth. Even so, how much can one person, one small group, or even one large group of people accomplish in this world? Relative to the vast size of this world, what man can do is very, very little!

Do whatever will purify and sublimate your ego-consciousness in self-expansion. Any work that remains after you leave this earth may be taken up by others, who have been inspired by your example. Beyond that, one should remember that one moon, as we said before, gives more light than all the stars. One Self-realized soul accomplishes more by his simple presence in this world than all the "stars" of busy (but mostly frustrated) world changers.

(8:16) Those living in every world, from the highest to the lowest, are subject to rebirth. (Only) on entering into My consciousness do they gain release (from karmic bondage).

CHAPTER TWENTY-ONE

FINAL LIBERATION

(8:17) They truly know "day" and "night" who comprehend the Day of Brahma, which endures for a thousand *mahayugas*, and the Night of Brahma, which endures for another thousand *mahayugas*.

(8:18) At the dawn of Brahma's Day, all creation, remanifested, emerges from its (night) state of unmanifestation: At the dusk of (approaching) Brahma's Night, all creation sinks back into its (previous) unmanifested state.

I ASKED MY GURU ONCE WHAT THESE ACTUAL TIME periods were, as they do not seem to correspond to the present age of the universe according to the claims of modern science. He replied, "Well, Krishna may have been only making the point that vast periods of time are involved. The Bible expresses itself symbolically also in saying that God created the world in six days."

In our discussion of Chapter 4 of the Gita, Stanzas 1 and 2, we went somewhat into a discussion of one *mahayuga*: that of 24,000 years. The reader is referred back to those pages. It may well be that there are greater cycles of time even than that one within the greatest *"mahayuga,"* a Day of Brahma. Certainly there is also our solar system's cycle entirely around the galactic center—a period of time that embraces hundreds of millions of years.

Here, Paramhansa Yogananda adds to that former discussion the interesting fact that the four yugas (Kali, Dwapara, Treta, and Satya, or *Krita*) correspond also to the four castes: Shudra, Vaishya, Kshatriya, and Brahmin. The number four has a natural resonance with the progressions of relativity in the Indian teachings. There are also the four ashrams or stages of life. Even the gunas were given four divisions by Yogananda, with rajas having a sub-category of sattwa-rajas. In the Dark Age, called Kali, the Shudra mentality is uppermost. In Dwapara Yuga (the age we now live in, of energy), Vaishya consciousness is predominant. During Treta Yuga, when mind power comes into its own, Kshatriya consciousness is predominant and leaders have a natural sense of honor and nobility. During Satya Yuga, the spiritual age, Brahmin consciousness is uppermost.

No progression, however, is wholly linear. As day follows night, and night follows day; as winter progresses to summer, then back to winter again; as the ocean waves and tides rise and fall; as the moon waxes, wanes, then waxes again: so also the yugas—long ages of time, some longer than others—advance and recede alternately. Even in the life of each man there is rising power, then a slow decline into old age and death, preparing him for yet another try (in a new body) at extricating himself from the hypnosis of *maya*.

(8:19) Again and again, O Son of Pritha (Arjuna)! the same people throng back to earth to be reborn. (The cycle of) reincarnation ends for them only temporarily with the descent of Brahma's Night. It resumes again with the dawn of Brahma's Day.

How long does the "show" go on? This stanza provides a spine-stiffening, if not utterly dismaying, answer to those who tell themselves, "Everything will work itself out, in time." A Day of Brahma lasts—judging from the evidence of modern science—some billions of years. Many self-aware egos, appearing at the dawn of Brahma's Day, are still wandering in delusion at the fall of Brahma's Night. One cannot but pursue the question further: How many Days of Brahma do most souls, in fact, wander in delusion?

The answer is not circumscribed by time. It might be countless Days of Brahma! Yet the cosmic destiny of every soul is final liberation in God. "Eventually?" we quoted Yogananda above as saying, "—eventually? Why not *NOW*?" When the soul finally escapes the great wheel of "destiny" (which is only a cycle of unceasing karmic return, until karma itself ceases to enchain), one realizes that the time elapsed was non-existent! Time is an illusion: In eternity, it is not even a second.

A worrying question arises: Is personal spiritual progress also not linear but cyclic, like everything else? What this stanza of the Bhagavad Gita suggests is that any rising wave of good karma should be seized with a firm grasp. Don't waste the opportunity! For even though time doesn't exist, it certainly seems very real to us as we labor under its yoke! "Seize the day!" is an expression: this Day of Brahma; this yuga of earth time; this season; this day, this very moment! Spiritual progress comes not with the passing of years, but with every moment of sincere effort. "The minutes," Yogananda said, "are more important than the years."

Live now in God! Now is the only time you will ever have, since tomorrow too will be only another "now" when it arrives. "Who cares what happens in five years?" was a question flung scornfully by a young woman at her questioner in a famous movie. Many people think, similarly, "Oh, some 'future time'! Who cares what happens then? Now is the only time I'm concerned with." Unfortunately for this blithe way of thinking, that "future time," when it arrives at last, will be very much "now"— even if it happens in a future body. It is very unwise—not to say foolish—ever to offend against karmic law.

Right action will give you good karma, which will bring you corresponding happiness. It will not, however, release you from the constant turning of the mill that grinds every delusion, in time, to powder. The goal of the Gita is not to show you the way merely to a better life— perhaps on Earth; perhaps in heaven. Rather, it is, as Yogananda quoted Krishna, to help you to "get away from My ocean of suffering and misery!"

One by one, and by no means in consequence of any mass societal or evolutionary step forward, every soul escapes from the wheel at last, into the arms of Cosmic Wisdom. Be such a one, yourself!

The astonishing thing is that this step is really quite easy to take! It seems difficult when we look around us, and see how many there are who fail to make it. If we will look into our own hearts, however, instead of judging ourselves by the criterion of others' values, we must see that the job is *not* so difficult as it seems. It all hinges on two or three very simple thoughts: First, Do you prefer happiness to suffering? Second, are you willing to do the work to find a happiness that won't, in time, change to suffering? Third (and most important), are you willing to offer into the fire of wisdom—which is the true perception of things as they are—that pathetically little, insignificant "I"? Are you, in continuation of this final question, willing to say, "Thou, Lord, art the Doer. Thine is the importance. Thine is the prominence before others. Thine also is the blame for every sin this little 'I' has committed, which I hereby cast into Thy flames to be purified in order that its reality be destroyed forever."

Now—as a physician might say to a little child after giving it an injection—was that so very difficult?

The path to God is easy! For one thing, the tests in life would come anyway, seemingly without any cosmic reason. For another, there is no alternative to it! And for a third, every step of the way is more rewarding, more joyful, and more completely satisfying!

(8:20) Beyond the unmanifested state (known as the Night of Brahma) there is the Absolute Unmanifested, forever immutable, which remains eternally untouched by the recurring cycles of creation.

People sometimes take hope when they learn about the Night of Brahma, thinking they may be able simply to wait long enough, and then, at the time of Pralaya or cosmic dissolution, they'll be able to merge back into God. Nothing, however, can happen without the conscious consent of the will. When everything merges back into Spirit again, becoming unmanifested, it retires only to a "way-side station." Final liberation is not attained so irresponsibly. The Cosmic Night, though described as having an equal length to that of Brahma's Day, is *not* the unmanifested state of Absolute Spirit. Instead, it is simply a state of quiescence: a temporary resting period during which all beings and all things remain in a condition not unlike that of seeds in wintertime, which lie dormant underground. The seeds, in the (partially) unmanifested state, are not material, but the ever-living, conscious nuclei of idea-forms.

(8:21) The (aforesaid) "Absolute Unmanifested, forever Immutable" is (what sages speak of as) the Supreme Spirit. Those (only) who attain it by self-effort gain eternal freedom from obligatory rebirth.
(8:22) Singlehearted devotion, O Arjuna! is what lifts one to that supremely unmanifested state. Only the ever-conscious, Omnipresent Spirit is the (ultimate) repository of all (things, and all) beings.

"On a little piece of thought," my Guru used to say, "rests the cosmic lot. Rub that thought away: The universe is wiped away." How strange it is to think that, surrounded by an ocean of consciousness, and being conscious *ourselves*, we can seem (though only in consciousness!) to be so separate. It is thought itself that separates us: the little notion that ours is an individual reality! Otherwise, whether passing through the Day or the Night of Brahma, we are ever (to ourselves, however, unconsciously) in Him. Our abode—both actual and deluded—lies in Him alone.

(8:23) I will now declare to you, O Best of the Bharatas (Arjuna)! the two paths open to departing souls: the one, the way of the yogi, which leads to (eternal) freedom; the other, the way to rebirth.

(8:24) Fire, light, daytime, the bright half of the lunar month, the six months of the northern course of the sun: pursuing this path at the time of death, the knowers of Brahman go to Brahman.

(8:25) Smoke, night-time, the dark half of the lunar month, the six months of the southern course of the sun: following this path at the time of death, one attains only the lunar light and so returns to earth.

(8:26) These two paths of exit (from the body) are eternal alternatives: the way of light leads to freedom; the way of darkness, to rebirth.

Stanzas 24 and 25 are among the most abstruse and esoteric in the whole Bhagavad Gita. Intellectual scholarship alone could never fathom them; indeed, translators deserve forgiveness if they simply skip over them, as some do, evidently in the hope that readers won't notice the omission. Only a great yogi could make any sense of them—or, indeed, could show that they have deep meaning.

Paramhansa Yogananda explained that the path of spiritual ascent is by awakening the Kundalini. "Fire" means *life energy*: the fire of yagya, symbolizing the divine energy into which one offers his ego for purification and for ultimate consumption.

"Light" stands for what Jesus Christ, in an equally esoteric passage in the New Testament of the Bible, described as "the light of the body": the spiritual eye, beheld in the forehead.

"Daytime" signifies that period of time when the yogi is divinely awake in superconsciousness. The "sun" of the spiritual eye shines upon him, bringing what is described in all mystical traditions as *enlightenment.*

The "bright half of the lunar month" marks the time of spiritual awakening. It is also the period of time the yogi spends in superconsciousness, as opposed to the hours (whether few or many) devoted to fulfilling his worldly duties. The moon is symbolic of the ego. In traditional works of Indian art, the moon is often depicted as a crescent-shape in the forehead of the enlightened yogi, signifying that his ego-consciousness has become enlightened, and is one with the divine Self.

The "six months of the northern course of the sun" denote, first, that half of the year when the sun rises higher in the sky. Second, they denote energy rising in the six spinal chakras, culminating in the Kutastha and the spiritual eye (this being the positive pole of the medulla oblongata at the top of the spine). "North," in mystical terminology, indicates the top of the body: the *sahasrara*, or "crown chakra." North, therefore, indicates the upward flow of energy in the spine toward that highest point.

Kundalini, to recapitulate, is the south pole of the body, located at the base of the spine, where the outward-flowing energy, from the spine to the nervous system, becomes "locked," so to speak, in its "southward" direction. Kundalini is said to be dormant: Kundalini awakening signifies that moment when the downward flow of energy relaxes its grip on outwardness and begins to make its return journey in the direction of its source in divine consciousness.

As there is no limit to how far the energy can flow upward in expansion of consciousness, since spiritual development "ends," as Paramhansa Yogananda put it, "in endlessness" (infinity), so also there is theoretically no limit to how far it can flow downward. Though the negative pole of energy in the body is said to lie dormant at the base of the spine, it represents the lower extremes of subconsciousness. Nothing in the universe is wholly unconscious: It cannot be. The "collective unconscious" of Carl Jung is, literally, an impossibility. *Everything in the universe* is to a degree conscious, since it is a product of divine consciousness. Thus, although Kundalini represents the dormant energy of man at the base of the spine, and therefore stands for his lower-than-conscious awareness, it is by no means stationary. Kundalini can move further downward toward greater nescience, like a mole burrowing ever deeper into the ground. Thus, human beings can sink ever deeper, toward relative (but never absolute) unconsciousness.

Kundalini can be awakened by yoga practices. If, however, those practices are not accompanied by a corresponding purification of the ego, they can raise more

energy to the medulla oblongata than the ego is prepared
to send forward to the spiritual eye (in the self-offering
known as inner yagya). This excessive energy then forms
a vortex around the thought of ego, creating an imbal-
ance in one's awareness, and the yogi cannot maintain
his heightened state, but falls back again toward the base
of the spine. Yogananda made it clear that the raising of
the Kundalini force must be accompanied by conscious
purification of the heart's feelings. The most important
part of its awakening depends, indeed, on kindness, generosity, truthfulness, and all the basic virtues, recognized
as such in every true religion.

On the other hand, every time one is unkind, ungener-
ous, untruthful, or behaves in any way contrary to those
virtues, his Kundalini continues its downward course
into ever dimmer awareness. Taking the upward course
of energy and consciousness, its direction is outward to
infinity, and therefore has no limits. Its potential
downward course toward the infinitesimal, is also without limits. More of this dismaying potential later on,
however. Let it, for now, be only something to ponder as
to the seriousness of its implications.

Yogis who follow the upward course raise the fiery
energy in the spine, and awaken, in passing, the chakras
in the spine. The greater the upward flow of energy, the
greater the light at the point between the eyebrows.
Indeed, the clear vision of that light reveals a differently
colored light in each chakra, which is seen in the spiritual eye: yellow for *muladhara*; white for *swadisthana*;
red for *manipura*; blue for *anahata*; smoke colored, with
little specks of light, for *bishuddha*; and in the spiritual

eye, as has already been described, a ring of gold surrounding a field of deep blue-violet, with a silvery-white five-pointed star at the center.

It is tempting to compare the colors of these six chakras, along with the seventh in the so-called crown chakra at the top of the head, with the colors of the rainbow. The rainbow is certainly *comparable* with the seven chakras, especially with their gradual change in hue from materialistic red to spiritual violet (red, orange, yellow, green, blue, indigo, and violet). This comparison must be written off, however, as more poetical than literal. The colors stated above by Paramhansa Yogananda are the actual chakra colors seen in the spiritual eye.

The upward "way of light" takes the yogi, as was described earlier, through the spiritual eye and through the progressively deeper channels in the astral spine—*sushumna, vajra, chitra*—then through the channel in the causal spine—the *brahmanadi*—into infinity.

The downward way is implied by the above.

"Smoke" implies ignorance, as smoke can hide a burning fire. Ignorance, like a dark cloud, obscures the light of wisdom and makes the correct perception of anything impossible.

Darkness implies complete obscuration of the light. Which of these two—the worldly mind asks—is the reality? Darkness seems to reign supreme until a light—whether of the sun or of a candle—is introduced into it. Even so, the man living in ignorance accepts that state not only as normal for him, but as, objectively, the universal state of things everywhere. Light is considered by worldly minds a foreign reality. In a similar display of ignorance, science has introduced what it calls The Second Law of Thermodynamics, according to which all warmth in the universe is being gradually lost—dissipated at first, and then dwindling to the temperature of absolute zero.

Such is mankind's perception of reality. As man doesn't see that everything begins with absolute consciousness, and not (as materialists believe) with "absolute" unconsciousness, so he doesn't see that energy, and not a total absence of energy, is the underlying reality even of matter. Thus, he sees darkness, not light, as the eternal reality; coldness, not a process of final equalization, as describing the final outcome of all "progressive" evolution.

"Smoke"—that cloud of ignorance which obscures human consciousness—is not the norm. "Night-time," too—the second condition of existence described in Stanza 25—is the time of spiritual sleep, in which the unenlightened human being drowses.

"The dark half of the lunar month" refers to the waning of the moon of ego-consciousness. Human beings—in contradistinction to the lower animals—are endowed with egoic awareness. This fact might be considered unfortunate (inasmuch as the challenge of the spiritual life is to transcend the ego), but in fact one has to become *aware* of a limitation before he can transcend it. During the "bright half of the lunar month" the ego becomes sufficiently self-aware, in time, to offer itself up completely into infinite freedom. During the "dark half of the lunar month," by contrast, the ego, though clinging to its individuality, loses that fine edge of awareness which distinguishes oneself from, but also identifies oneself with, all life. During this "waning moon" of ego, self-consciousness becomes obscured also, instinctive rather than distinct. The ego, if it chooses to move downward into ever-darker consciousness, can plunge so far as to find itself again in the body of a lower animal. (Of this, again, more later.)

The "six months of the southern course of the sun" are, at this point, obvious. They signify the downward course of energy and consciousness through the six chakras of the spine, back to its base again.

The reference in these stanzas is, specifically, to the course of man's consciousness at the time of death. Those commentators, however, who try to give the stanzas a literal interpretation are at a loss. The death of a great yogi has no relationship to the phases of the moon, nor to the time of year. The references in these stanzas are all metaphorical.

(8:27) No true yogi, understanding these two alternate paths, is ever deluded (into following the downward way). Therefore, O Arjuna! Keep yourself firmly at all times in a (state of) yoga.

(8:28) He who knows the (hidden secret of) these two paths goes beyond any merits (with its fruits of good karma) gained from study of the scriptures, or from the formal practice of yagyas, austerities, or gifts in charity. That yogi attains his (self's) Supreme Origin.

Religion is the path. True experience is spirituality: the attainment of the goal. Krishna is not deprecating religious acts. He is reminding Arjuna, however, that such acts have their end. Even (Krishna is saying) in the practice of spirituality, and of all the religious virtues, keep your heart and mind fixed on God alone.

Thus ends the eighth chapter, called "Union with the Absolute Spirit," of the Upanishad of the holy Bhagavad Gita, in the dialogue between Sri Krishna and Arjuna discussing yoga and the science of God-realization.

CHAPTER TWENTY-TWO

THE SOVEREIGN LORD OF ALL

(9:1) The Blessed Lord said: To you, who have conquered the carping spirit, I now reveal the sublime mystery (the immanent and transcendent nature of God). Armed with this (intuitive) wisdom, you shall escape all evil.

THE IMPULSE TO CARP AT EVERYTHING IS A KIND of illness of the mind. It prevents people from opening themselves to new ideas, and causes them to see themselves as presiding judges, in a sense, in the courtroom of life. In other words, it is a negative symptom of ego-consciousness.

The carping spirit inclines one to respond to every suggestion with the cautionary objection, "Yes, but. . . ." Seldom does it bring one to any firm conclusion, for even its conclusions are tentative. This is not the self-torturing condition of spiritual doubt, but it keeps one forever in a state of indecision: a condition endemic to the intellect, which, without the certainty of intuition, can never really *know* anything. The very proofs of

Euclidean geometry leave one at least *wishing* he could find a "catch" in them.

One who is tired of this habit in himself should live more in his heart, and try to develop there a calm, intuitive feeling about the rightness of things. Until he can do so, life will remain for him a rocky ride of perpetual uncertainty which causes him to challenge every statement, almost compulsively, with qualifications.

(9:2) (The way to this) realization is the highest of sciences, the (secret of) secrets, the essence of all dharma (right action). Through (yoga) methods, easy to perform, this way bestows the direct perception of truth.

(9:3) Men lacking faith (and even interest) in this dharma, (seeking their fulfillment elsewhere) do not attain Me, O Scorcher of Foes (Arjuna)! Again and again they take the path of *samsara* (delusion) and mortality.

Indifference is the greatest spiritual disease. One doesn't expect a turtle to ask, "Why do I need a shell into which I can withdraw?" At the first sign of danger, it simply retracts to comparative safety. Man, however, is above the mental level of merely instinctive responses. If, in suffering, he asks only, "Why me?" without probing more deeply into the reasons for his suffering and inquiring what he might do about it—if, in short, he behaves like a sparrow indifferent to (because it doesn't see) the swooping hawk—life will gobble him up before he knows what is happening.

Many people, when they are introduced to spiritual teachings, respond by saying, "Frankly, I'm not interested." Are they more interested, then, in dancing their lives away while the house in which they live collapses? Urged to take their own destiny more seriously by seeking truth, they respond, "But, it's difficult!" So—the question must be asked—is suffering *easier*?

How sad, that so very few people are willing to face the one reality that, if they but knew it, would mean everything to them. Their physical, emotional, mental, and spiritual security is at stake, yet they push away the thought that anything menaces them by seeking diversions, and think, "Oh, it will all take care of itself—someday." It never will "take care of itself"! They themselves must face a reality that will never leave them alone until they've solved its mystery.

The thing is, as Krishna says here, yoga practice is really much easier than any other path one might follow through the wilderness of life. For one thing, it is the only path that actually leads somewhere—indeed, that provides answers that are permanent, secure, and supremely fulfilling. For another thing, yoga and meditation really aren't difficult, but demand simply, as Krishna states in this great scripture, that one "slay" the foes which threaten his own happiness. All that one does is redirect the energy that he has devoted, under the influence of habit, to things that do not and never will give him what he wants. He must simply channel that energy away from conclusions that have brought him misery, and direct them into channels that will provide him with perfect happiness, joy, and—in the end—bliss.

So many things militate, however, against this simple, obvious, and in fact inevitable decision (inevitable in the end, that is): habit, for one (perhaps habit is even paramount); and the thought, caused by delusion: "I am this body, separate from all others. I need to make a place for myself, protected from the hostile forces surrounding me." The greatest thing which militates against the obvious, however, is simply hope. People hope to find happiness in specific things; material things, usually. When at last they fulfill a dream—and almost, though not quite, at the very moment of fulfillment— those dream-fulfillments turn to dust and are blown away on winds of changing circumstance.

Through the swirling mists of *maya* a face appears; the mists then close again, and the face vanishes. If ever through them it comes back again, it is somehow coarsened, changed, and painful to contemplate.

You never, in all eternity, have anyone but your own self. Must you not, then, love others? Certainly you must! Love them as they are, however: as extensions of yourself—not of the ego self, but of the true Self of all. No other reality exists! That one Self exists in all things. Images—swirling, haunting, dream-like—come and go, changeless forever yet forever changing. Until you know yourself in infinity, you will have to live alone with your dreams. The chasm between you and them, between you and everything in existence, yawns ever wide and defies you to cross it.

What people really want (though they see it not!) are not things, nor others to love, but ideas, fantasies, mere will-o'-the-wisps. Consciousness alone is real! Mankind dances with idea-waves on the sea of chitta (feeling), and sees not that all hopes are but wisps of imagination!

(9:4) I, the (eternally) Unmanifested, pervade the entire universe. All creatures abide in Me, though I abide not in them.

Krishna made a similar statement in 7:12: "They [the gunas] exist in me, though I am not apparent in them." Here, it is *creatures* themselves of which he speaks when he says: "I abide not in them." He (the Spirit), in other words, is beyond those abstractions—the qualities— which permeate mankind in a constantly varied mixture. He is also beyond mankind itself, with its ego-driven ideas, ambitions, and deeds. We ride on waves rising up out of the ocean of divine consciousness—never relaxing to mingle with the water around us, never letting our-selves become absorbed in it, and never allowing Him to penetrate into our hearts.

We imagine that we, like little icebergs, are substan-tially different from Him, and that He, similarly, is different in essence from us. Poor mankind! that it should suffer so needlessly. Water is water, whether frozen, liquid, or evaporated in the form of steam.

(9:5) Behold My divine mystery! All beings seem not to exist in Me, nor I in them: Yet I am their sole Creator and Preserver!

(9:6) Think of it thus: As air moves through space, but is not space, so do all creatures have their being in Me, but are not I.

(9:7) At the end of a cycle (*kalpa*), O Son of Kunti (Arjuna)! all beings return to the unmanifested state of My Cosmic Nature. At the beginning of the next

great cycle, I cast them forth again.

(9:8) By reawakening My own emanation, Prakriti, again and again, I repeatedly produce the vast host of creatures, all subject to Nature and to her finite laws.

(9:9) These activities do not bind Me, O Winner of Wealth (Arjuna)! for I, remaining aloof from them, am forever non-attached.

(9:10) O Son of Kunti (Arjuna), it is My impregnating essence alone that makes Mother Nature give birth to (both) the animate and inanimate. By My power alone (through Prakriti) do the (very) worlds revolve.

God as Nature is the Divine Mother. His "Son" is the reflected, vibrationless consciousness at the core of every vortex of atoms. He is Spirit's "uninvolved" presence in every life.

To attune ourselves with God, we too must try to view objectively not only what happens to us, but our very reactions, for all these are simply parts of the storm of *maya* raging around us. We must feel ourselves centered as much as possible at the core of that vortex, untouched by anything—even as Spirit, our essential self, is untouched.

(9:11) The ignorant, oblivious of My transcendent nature, though (I am) the Creator of all, are blind also to My presence within (themselves).

(9:12) Blind to all (valid) insights, vain in their aspirations, deeds, and thoughts, human beings (who were made for a nobler purpose) may partake of the nature of monsters and demons.

By "monsters," here, are intended human beings self-afflicted with "monstrous" natures: those of extreme cruelty, for example, or of distorted and unnatural appetites. Such people, after death (which releases their emotions from the enclosing physical walls of the body) become demons, their very forms displaying in grossest caricature the foulness of their own consciousness. Such human beings are at the darkest end of the spectrum of the three gunas, or qualities. They are veritable personifications of the darkening quality of tamas.

(9:13) **Great souls, however, expressing in their human nature the higher qualities of divinity, pay undeviating homage to Me, the Imperishable Source of all life.**
(9:14) **Constantly absorbed in Me, prostrating to Me with love, steadfastly resolute in their high aspiration, they worship Me with (unceasing) adoration.**
(9:15) **Lesser beings also, offering Me themselves with clear discrimination, discern Me first in the manifested many, and then as the One (behind the many).**

The two paths of devotion (*bhakti*) and discrimination (*gyana*), love and wisdom, become one when united in the Ultimate Vision. *Bhaktas* (those who proceed by the path of devotional *bhakti*) do not ask, and are not interested in, all the reasons for loving God. He is their own: What is there to ask? *Gyanis* (those who proceed by the path of *gyana*) must love also, otherwise (as Swami Sri Yukteswar stated) they will not be inspired to set even one foot before the other on the path to God. Their intellects, however, want satisfaction also. Nor is this a contradiction in human nature. *Bhaktas* need the discrimination to turn their feelings Godward. *Gyanis* need the devotion to *long deeply for God*, without which they would feel no inspiration to seek Him.

How can discrimination help one's devotion? In this way: Look at a leaf; then, instead of analyzing it minutely (as science and the intellect both incline to do), expand your consciousness of that leaf into a broader reality. Instead of thinking how to squeeze your understanding of the leaf into a definition—as if to place it in a catalogue—think of the many things that are marvelous about a leaf: the fact, for instance, that something so simple could be replicated by human beings in a thousand ways, yet never be more living than a sculpture in stone.

What impulse of life could produce a leaf? Could the form of that leaf be contained already in the seed? If so, how? Is there not some *idea*, hidden within the leaf, that springs forth at last to form that one leaf, among countless others?

What great impulse is there in life itself that produces such a little, fragile object, and yet to continue, in the face of endlessly falling leaves, to bring life back again and again to other leaves? What consciousness is there in the universe that could, perhaps from its beginnings, have visualized that leaf? Did it know, in those nebulous clouds of primordial time, what it would accomplish at each stage of evolution? Was love at the heart of the leaf's first conception? Does God love, and does He enjoy, the simple creation of that leaf?

And what about man himself? Whence come his thoughts? Is his thinking merely a response to subconscious, perhaps repressed, impulses of the body? Or does the fact that all men, in one way or another, have identical, or similar, thoughts mean that there is some cosmic "reservoir" generating the power to motivate them?

In these ways, by ever-expanding inquiry into the underlying cause and nature of things, discrimination can become, instead of a path of dry inquiry, a pathway also of love.

(9:16) I am the sacrificial ritual; I am the sacrifice itself; I am the oblations offered to the ancestors; I am the (medicinal) herb; I am the sacred mantras; I am the ghee (clarified butter, which is offered in ritual worship); (I am also) the fire (and) the very act of offering.

(9:17) Of this world I am the Father, Mother, Forefather, Preserver; I am He who sanctifies; I am the Object of all Knowledge; I am the Cosmic AUM; I am the lore of the three Vedas (*Rig, Yajur,* and *Sama*).*

(9:18) I am the Ultimate Goal, the Upholder, the Lord, the Witness, the Abode, the Refuge, the One Friend. I am the Origin, the Dissolution, the Foundation, the Cosmic Storehouse, and the Imperishable Seed.

(9:19) I bestow heat; I send or withhold rain. Immortality am I, and mortality as well. I am both Being and Non-being (*Sat* and *Asat*).

---

* The fourth Veda, *Atharva*, was added at a later time.

If one thinks of God as existent, He is existence. If an atheist thinks of Him as non-existent, He is non-existence itself! No thought can exist without His sustaining presence. It is He who fosters faith, and He also who nurtures doubts (in those who have them). Without Him, nothing can exist. People's very rejection of Him is sustained by His consciousness and energy.

"I'm too busy to seek God!" is an oft-heard objection to meditating and to performing other spiritual practices. "What if God," replied Yogananda when people made this remark to him, "were too busy to think of you? You'd cease in that instant to exist!" Yet I asked him once, "Can the soul ever be destroyed?" Very forcefully he replied, "Impossible! The soul is a part of God. How could God be destroyed?"

"Who made God?" is another question commonly asked. Yogananda's reply was, "You ask this question because you are living in the realm of causation. God, however, is the Supreme Cause. He is self-existent." To assume that a thing has been caused is, necessarily, to accept that it will, in time, be "uncaused"—which is to say, destroyed. God is neither living nor non-living: He simply *is*—without a cause, without a reason, beyond all inference or disproof, beyond either acceptance or rejection.

Wise are they who, contemplating Him, simply marvel in silence.

(9:20) Those who follow Vedic (or other) rituals, cleansing themselves by the *Sama* rites, or worshiping Me by prescribed yagyas, doing (all these) to win

heaven, succeed in going there, and (may) attain the realm of Indra (lord of the gods), where they enjoy the delights of heaven.

(9:21) After enjoying those lofty regions for a time, and when the merits they have acquired (that have brought them) there have been exhausted, they return to earth. By following the scriptural regulations in their desire for celestial rewards, they (endlessly) repeat the cycle of ascent and return.

Endlessly repeated last-minute reprieves, followed by a return in chains to the same old prison: What a choice destiny! Reading scripture, obeying its "commandments" to please God (but not to attain His bliss for oneself) is surely sattwic, or self-elevating, and is therefore not something to be criticized or condemned. And yet—how far short it leaves one of the fulfillment every soul so deeply craves!

(9:22) To those who meditate on Me as their very own, (their hearts) ever united to Me by incessant (inward) worship, I supply their deficiencies and make permanent their gains.

The merits acquired through worship of the lesser (astral) gods are temporary and limiting. The merits—that is to say, the good karma—one acquires by doing kind deeds, by being honest, by telling the truth, and so on, are also temporary, and self-limiting. Krishna taught in a country, and at a time, when religion and religious practices were wholly identified with the Vedas.

Hinduism itself was a name given only centuries later to the religion of India. The indigenous name, as we stated earlier, was Sanaatan Dharma: the "Eternal Religion." Krishna speaks throughout the Bhagavad Gita of beliefs and practices that people in other religions came to define as Hindu. The truths he taught, however, are timeless and universal. Sanaatan Dharma ought rightly to be understood as the spiritual way of the entire universe: that is to say, inward, not outward through the senses. Thus, people in every religion can benefit enormously from the teachings of the Gita, simply by substituting for expressions like "Vedic rituals" the scriptures and rituals of their own religions. Worship of the "gods" can be understood as special reverence for the angels.

To admit the existence of nothing higher than man himself is to condemn oneself to an almost pathetic pettiness. We must seek ever to grow in understanding and sympathy. Not to do so is to decline, which means to shrink inward in consciousness upon the ego. For there can be no stasis in life. Movement is an inevitable fact of manifested existence. Even stagnation is a kind of movement, implying as it does a kind of inward deterioration.

Without at least the concept of God, however, there can be no clear direction of movement. No wonder ancient societies, lacking that clear upward direction, made the "gods" themselves over into very human figures, with jealousies, rivalries, lusts, and prejudices. Without the concept of a Supreme Lord, to what "bull's eye in the target" could they point their arrow of discrimination?

Thus, the Indian scriptures speak of the lesser gods, and say that man should honor and even pray to them. Mankind in its relation to the gods might be compared to the lower animals in their relation to man. Animals that have a close association with human beings evolve more quickly, and are likely to be promoted sooner to the human level of evolution. People, similarly, who seek piously to associate with the gods evolve spiritually more rapidly than those who consider themselves sufficient unto themselves.

Such evolution is slow, however, and never certain, for it is rooted in ego-consciousness. Incremental progress of this sort is like the illustration of the magnet, and the effort to magnetize a bar of steel by turning every molecule, one at a time, in a north-south direction. By the time one had advanced only a short direction up the bar, the already-oriented molecules, possessing as yet no strong magnetism to hold them to that orientation, might easily become random again in their direction.

Again, incremental progress, working painstakingly to advance only by developing good karma, is like washing a shirt. An air bubble may raise one section of the shirt above water. If we try to submerge that part, the air bubble simply moves elsewhere and raises another section. Concentration, similarly, on the transformation of one bad karma into a good one, or of one weakness into its opposite virtue, might work if a few traits only required attention. Considering the fact, however—which the Bhagavad Gita makes clear—that our "mental citizens" are comparable, in number and variety, to the population of a large country, the task of transforming each one of them individually seems all but hopeless. One incarnation may not suffice to change even one deep-seated flaw.

Scriptural rules—prescriptive and proscriptive—are what Paramhansa Yogananda described as the "bullock cart" approach to perfection. Worshiping the gods, similarly (or giving reverence to the angels) is a "bullock cart" approach. In the realm of relativity, what goes up must eventually come down. Good karma, sought only as an astral "merit badge," can fall again as easily as the crest of a wave.

Thus, the highest teaching, which Krishna expounds here, is to love above all God, the Infinite Spirit: "to meditate on Him as one's very own." God alone can lift us out of the relativities of karmic merits and demerits into the absolute peace and freedom of Infinite Being.

(9:23) O Son of Kunti (Arjuna), even the devotees of other gods, if they sacrifice to them with faith, are worshiping Me alone, however improperly.

(9:24) For I alone am in truth the Enjoyer and Lord of all sacrifices. Those, however, (who worship Me in lesser aspects) perceive Me not in My true nature, and so they fall.

What constitutes "improper" worship, mentioned above in Stanza 23? Worship of any kind is an offering up of the ego. Most people indulge in self-worship: offering the self, so to speak, into the same little self, and thereby inflating it with arrogance. Those who offer themselves to others by showing them respect, are—again, in a sense—suppressing their egos, but theirs is no serious move toward overcoming the ego. Suppression, as Krishna has indicated already, is not possible. An ego held temporarily in abeyance is still ego, and can break out anew, like a disease, when outward circumstances permit.

Self-offering to the gods implies at least a raising of consciousness, for it is an offering of the qualities one possesses into a greater goodness and a purer aspiration. Why, then, is such worship "improper"? It is so only in the sense that the increase of goodness and aspiration in oneself is only a step into a higher ego-consciousness, not into absorption of the ego in infinity.

Even so, because it is a step upward in spiritual evolution—and although that rise must be continued to the top of the stairs, where the "bird of paradise," the soul, can take wing and soar in endlessness—attunement with higher beings, whether conceived of as gods or as angels, is acceptable by the Supreme Spirit insofar as the blessings they receive (from Him) will purify their understanding and help them to prepare for the "final assault."

The danger, however, expressed in Stanza 24, is that because the devotee thinks whatever blessings he receives through the gods come *from* them, rather than from God Himself, worshiping them ends in an exalted, but still limited, form, and thus becomes merely an extension of the ego, not an absorption of it. The reason they who worship the gods fall back again into delusion may be explained by an elastic band, which, though stretched to its limits, cannot but snap back in time to its original position, once the force that extended it is released.

In offering the ego up to God, there is no question of self-extension; there is no band to stretch out and snap back. The ego is *dissolved* in the Infinite Self, and thereby ceases completely to exist (except as a memory in omniscience).

Worship that needs to keep on being offered cannot be forever effective. In the end, it becomes habitual, and what is habitual no longer has the full force of will behind it. Worship of the Supreme Lord, by contrast, is not only reinforced by divine joy itself, but ceases in time to have an ego to do the worshiping: The ego merges into, and becomes, that which it contemplates.

(9:25) Those who worship the gods go to them; those who worship their ancestors go to the abode of ancestors; those who worship the nature spirits go to them; but those who are My devotees come to Me.

This famous sloka is a reminder to all to make God their primary object of worship throughout their lives, and especially, when they reach the doorway of death, to keep their consciousness focused on Him.

It is the heart's feelings that direct energy. One is drawn in wherever direction his feelings pull him.

Small-minded or materialistic persons find it difficult to understand abstractions. To them, consciousness itself seems possible only if there is a physical brain to produce it. To such persons, statements like these may easily be interpreted to mean—as some people actually believe—that the Supreme God, being Krishna, is (in keeping with the Krishna legends) blue-colored and playing a flute. To them, he has to be saying in the above passage that He, Krishna, is above other gods in some relative sense—higher, larger, more powerful, wiser, more effulgent. Effort has been devoted in these pages to clarify the truth that the Infinite is above all relativities. There is nothing sectarian in Krishna's teachings. Nevertheless, it may be helpful to state once and for all, in connection with a passage that bigots sometimes use to justify their sectarianism, that in Krishna's exalted view of Truth there is no spirit of competition.

(9:26) Whenever anyone, with a pure intention, offers Me (even) a leaf, a flower, a (piece of) fruit, or water (whether poured out or held up in a vessel), I accept his offering (as symbolic of his love).

Some people are foolish enough to think God is *satisfied* only with these offerings. They may even discuss what *kind* of leaf, flower, or fruit is most pleasing to Him. Many people in Bengal who worship God in the form of Divine Mother Kali hold the traditional belief that the red hibiscus (*jawba*) is in itself particularly pleasing to Her. Tradition insists that certain offerings are correct, and that others are incorrect. In reality, what God wants from us is our love. The things we offer to Him are only symbols of that love. If we offer them without devotional love, however, He will never accept them, however "correct" and traditionally sanctioned they are.

In this passage, Krishna is simply saying (as though to little children) "You must practice offering yourself, first, in little ways. If you cannot yet make the supreme offering of your ego-consciousness to Me, then practice the thought of making little gifts. Any slight offering, made with love, is a step in the right direction, and is *for that reason* acceptable to Me."

The first snow that falls on the ground in wintertime does not immediately whiten the earth. Gradually the snowflakes cool the ground until it is cold enough to accept them without melting them. Whiteness then becomes visible as if suddenly, everywhere.

Some people say, "I will wait until I'm old. *Then* I will give my life to God." Or they declare in all earnestness, "I will wait until I've fulfilled my worldly desires. *Then* I will dedicate myself to seeking Him." Foolish ones! How can they be certain that, in old age, they'll have the strength, the good health, and the mental clarity to do anything but sit, gazing into the middle distance and dreaming vaguely of what might have been? How do they imagine that their desires will *ever* end? What is it that keeps the ego going, life after life, era after era; yuga after yuga—Day of Brahma after Day of Brahma!? It is, simply and entirely, the power of desire—of wishful thinking!

Krishna is saying here, "Start wherever you are on the pathway to the Infinite. The smallest step you take will bring you closer, and will give you the understanding and also the ability to offer yourself ever more completely, until that final day comes when giving yourself will be like stepping joyfully into the arms of the Beloved."

(9:27) Whatever action you perform (with dispassion), O Arjuna! whether eating, or performing spiritual

rites, or making gifts in charity, or in austerities (self-discipline), dedicate that action in offering to Me.

(9:28) In this way, nothing you do will bind you to either good or evil karma. Firmly anchored in Me by self-renunciation, you will achieve freedom, and will come to Me.

(9:29) I am impartial to all. No one is (specially) hateful or dear to Me. Those, however, who give Me their hearts' love are in Me, as I am in them.

(9:30) Even an evildoer, if (in his heart) he rejects all else and worships Me alone, should be counted, because of that resolution, among the good.

(9:31) (Such a one) will soon become virtuous, and will achieve lasting peace. O Son of Kunti (Arjuna), know this for a certainty: My devotee is never lost!

(9:32) Taking shelter in Me, all can achieve Supreme Fulfillment—whether they be of sinful birth, or women (the preservers, traditionally, of family values and therefore of *samsara*), or Vaishyas, or lowly Shudras.

Stanza 32 intends no slur on anyone, but states only that social distinctions (sex, caste, race) have no meaning before God. Man, out of egotism, creates barriers. God simply ignores them.

(9:33) How easy it is, then, for (true) Brahmins, who know God, and for *Rajarishis* (true Kshatriyas, whose sole desire is to serve God in all) to attain Me. Ah! You who have come into this transient world, full of misery: worship Me alone!

(9:34) Keep your mind fixed on Me! Be My devotee!

In ceaseless worship, bow to Me in adoration! Thus, becoming one with Me and knowing Me as your highest goal, you shall (ever) be My very own!

Thus ends the ninth chapter, called "The Sovereign Lord of All," of the Upanishad of the holy Bhagavad Gita, in the dialogue between Sri Krishna and Arjuna discussing yoga and the science of God-realization.

CHAPTER TWENTY-THREE

FROM THE UNMANIFESTED TO THE MANIFEST

(10:1) The Blessed Lord said: O Mighty-armed (Arjuna), hear now My supreme utterance: Speaking for your highest good, I will say more to you, who have listened with joy.

(10:2) Neither the multitude of gods (angels) nor the great sages (in their human state) know Me in My Unmanifested state. I am their Source and Origin.

(10:3) Whoever realizes Me, however, unborn and without any beginning, as well as (even now) the Lord of Creation, has conquered delusion, and is sinless though he inhabit a human body.

IT MAY BE HELPFUL FOR PEOPLE TO REALIZE THAT even *jivan muktas*—indeed, even fully liberated masters—accept, in their human state, some human limitations. They may, for example, seem to suffer for others—and even, on occasion, for themselves. They express hopes, enthusiasms, and disappointments that they don't really feel at their own center. Though completely non-attached, they "play the game" of life.

I used often to observe, when my Guru expressed perfectly natural human feelings, that he always did so in a sattwic manner. His eyes, too, were fathomlessly calm. It was obvious to me that he was inwardly untouched. Yet to be acceptable to human beings, he accepted humanity for himself as part of the teachings he was sharing.

Once, for example, when a disciple tried to call his attention to the higher teachings during a discussion of world events, the Guru responded, "Well, but now we are speaking in human terms."

When, during his early years in America, an Indian disciple betrayed him, our Guru expressed great sorrow. Yet another disciple, who years later visited India, learned that the Master, while still a boy, had predicted this very betrayal. We might compare his later grief to someone seeing a movie for the second time. Wanting to enjoy the plot as it unfolds, he deliberately ignores his prior familiarity with it.

(10:4,5) Discrimination, wisdom, calm clarity, forgiveness, truthfulness, sense-control, inner peace, joy, sorrow, birth, death, fear, courage, harmlessness, equanimity, serenity, self-discipline, charity, fame, notoriety: these states, vastly diverse as they are, derive from My one Self: They are modifications of My one (essential) nature.

As, in dreams, the thoughts and emotions expressed are experienced as projections of the dreamer's consciousness, so in the cosmic dream all aspects of it are projections of the Divine Consciousness. The most significant difference between the divine dream and human dreams is that human dreams may (though they don't necessarily) reveal something about the person projecting them, whereas God's dream reveals nothing of His cosmic nature. God is beyond all qualifications. The potential manifestations of consciousness itself are infinite in number, and express no attachment or desire on the Creator's part.

(10:6) The seven great *rishis*, the Primeval Four, and the (fourteen) Manus are all modifications of My nature, born of My (projected) thought, and endowed with (creative) powers like Mine. From these (progenitors) come all the life forms on earth.

These "modifications" of God's nature, though meaningful to people who are steeped in the ancient lore, possess less significance for the modern mind. The important thing is that God, the Eternal Spirit, does not act directly in producing His cosmic dream, but creates "executives": channels of His consciousness, through whom He, in His overarching power and wisdom, manifests and unfolds all later developments.

(10:7) He who realizes the truth of My prolific manifestations, and the creative and dissolving power of My divine yoga, is unshakably united to Me.
(10:8) I am the Source of everything. From Me all creation emerges. Realizing this great truth, the wise, awe-stricken, adore Me.

As opposed to the details that produce the sum total of all knowledge, there is a flow to wisdom which of its own nature rejects a superfluity of detail, though complete wisdom knows them all. Its primary focus is on the direction of movement. What is awe-inspiring about Supreme Truth is not the sheer number of its manifestations—which are, indeed, beyond numbering—but its cascade of overwhelming bliss.

(10:9) Their thoughts engrossed in Me, their beings surrendered to Me, enlightening one another and conversing of Me, they are ever contented and filled with joy.

Ordinary human beings, accustomed to the pleasure of conversing together, of gossiping and retailing the latest news coupled with their opinions and reactions, imagine that in God all this fascinating variety will be lost. Krishna suggests, in this stanza, that such is far from the case. Not only is the bliss of Satchidananda "ever-new," as Yogananda declared, but those who know it find, even in conversing together of divine matters, a level of delight which worldly people never know. People's sheer need for variety indicates the barrenness of their hearts, which drives them to seek anxiously a few raindrops of diversity in hope of somehow slaking their thirst. When two people meet who know God, they may not converse much, but the flow of divine love and bliss between them is completely satisfying to them both.

(10:10) To those who are attached only to Me, and

who worship Me with love, I impart that discernment of wisdom by which they attain Me completely.

(10:11) Out of pure compassion (that is, out of the selfless gift of love with no admixture of compulsion), I, the Divine One who dwells in all, set alight in their (hearts) the blazing lamp of wisdom, which banishes their darkness of ignorance.

It is important for the spiritual aspirant to realize that he doesn't *earn* anything, by seeking God. Divine grace is still a gift of compassion, and may be withheld from those who follow the law exactly, but who—perhaps out of dryness of heart—fail to win His love. God may, on the other hand, reward with the highest wisdom those who, in their surrender of perfect devotion, only love Him.

Through the intervention of the *Satguru* alone do such blessings come.

(10:12) Arjuna said (in adoration): O Lord, Thou art the Supreme Spirit, the Supreme Shelter, the Supreme Purity, the One, Self-manifested Being, the Causeless, the Eternal, the Omnipresent!

(10:13) Thus do all the sages—the divine seer Narada, Asila, Devala, Byasa, and You Yourself, Krishna—declare.

Those who know God speak the same essential truths regarding Him.

Were an architect, a landscape designer, and a civil engineer to go to London from New Delhi, they would all return with the same basic descriptions of its size, variety, busyness, climate, etc. They might well in addition, however, add their own perceptions of the city in terms of their own special interests. The architect might not only speak of the buildings, but might place so much emphasis on them that his listeners would imagine London to consist of nothing but noteworthy buildings. The landscape designer, on the other hand, might devote so much time to describing the beauty of the parks that his listeners would envision London as consisting of only parks. And the civil engineer might elaborate on the roads of London to such an extent that automobile drivers, braving the monsoon-produced potholes of New Delhi, would think of London only as a city "blessed not to be cursed" by these public menaces. Yet all would have seen, and would be describing essentially, the same city.

The same may be said of those who know God. Their descriptions of Him are, in essence, one and the same. Yet each may also emphasize a particular aspect of His awe-inspiring magnificence. Those who hear these reports and think, "I have heard all this at first hand," may declare loudly to others, with partial authority: "This is what God is." God is so much more, however! Therefore Arjuna seeks the support of countless authorities to support his declaration of the divine wonders.

(10:14) (Arjuna continues:) O Keshava (Krishna)! I consider all that You have revealed to me as the eternal truth. Neither gods nor demons (can) know Your (multifarious) manifestations.

None of those who are ordinary, though permanent, residents of the astral world can know supernal truths that are higher than all the manifested spheres of existence. How much less so, then, can earth dwellers know in their merely human state! Masters are omniscient on whatever plane they live, but those earthfolk who hope for full enlightenment from mere angels, or who pay heed to any boastful promises by demonic beings, are destined for disappointment.

(10:15) **O Supreme Person (Arjuna continues), Origin of beings, Lord of all creatures, God of gods, Sustainer of the world! verily You alone are Self-Knowing.**

(10:16) **Please expound fully to me Your perfect powers by which, being omnipresent, You sustain the universe.**

(10:17) **O Supreme Yogi (Krishna), how shall I meditate on You, to know You as You are? In what forms and aspects can I most accurately think of You?**

(10:18) **O Janardana (Krishna), tell me at length of Your yoga powers and manifestations, for I never tire of listening to this nectar-like speech of Yours.**

(10:19) **The Blessed Lord said: O Best of Princes (Arjuna), I shall willingly relate to you something of My manifestations—but I'll relate only those which are outstanding, for of My variety there is no end.**

With this stanza there begins a long list of divine manifestations, the net effect of which is to convince the devotee that, whatever desires he harbors in his heart, their highest fulfillment lies in God who is the very essence of all fulfillment. The devotee is encouraged to look behind even his delusions to see how, in their most exaggerated form, God calls to him, "Wake up!"

"Among deceivers," he says, later, "I am gambling" (10:36). What other purpose could there be for Krishna to announce this "manifestation" to Arjuna? Gambling, a pastime which seizes and all too often ruins many people: What could be a more deceiving lure to improbable, but ever-possible, riches? God, even in the extremes of delusion, says to mankind, "Can't you see for yourselves how foolish it all is?"

Stanza 20 sets the scene: God is the Hidden Presence at the heart of *everything*.

(10:20) O Gudakesha (Conqueror of Sleep—Arjuna), I am the true Self dwelling in the heart of all creatures. I am the beginning, the continuation, and end of their existence.

In addressing Arjuna as the "Conqueror of Sleep," Krishna implies that the highest truths can only be known when one has fully wakened from the sleep of delusion. Krishna says here that the Lord, in his essential Self, is the sole Dreamer: that only in Him does anything exist. This is the answer to the challenge of those who say, "I have no time for God." To that all-too-common objection Paramhansa Yogananda often answered, "And what if God had no time for you? In Him alone do you have your existence."

(10:21) Among the *Adityas* (Vedic gods), I am Vishnu; among luminaries (in the sky), I am the sun; among the wind gods, I am Marichi (the most beneficial wind); among (nocturnal) luminaries, I am the moon.

In this passage, and in the subsequent ones in this section, Krishna is saying that, whatever man views as most special, God is that.

(10:22) Among the Vedas, I am *Sama* Veda (on account of its musical beauty); among the gods, I am Indra; of sense-perceptions I am Mind (the perceiver); in creatures, I am their intelligence.
(10:23) Among the Rudras (the intelligent life forces) I am Shankara (their empowering intelligence); among Yakshas and Rakshasas (astral abstractions of human desire) I am Kubera (the god of wealth); among Vasus (the vitalizing forces) I am Pavaka (Agni, the god of fire); among mountain peaks, I am Meru.

Meru, in classical tradition in India, symbolizes the highest spiritual attainment.

(10:24) Of priests, O Son of Pritha (Arjuna), know Me to be Brihaspati (guru of the gods); among generals, I am Skanda (Kartikeya, the god of war); among bodies of water, I am the ocean.
(10:25) Among great rishis, I am Bhrigu; among words, I am the syllable AUM; among yagyas (sacred rituals) I am *japa-yagya* (silent, superconscious chanting); among things unmoving, I am the Himalaya.

(10:26) Among trees, I am Ashvatta; among the divine seers, I am Narada; among the Ghandharvas (gods of music), I am Chitraratha; among perfected beings, I am Kapila (the exponent of Shankhya).

Later in the Bhagavad Gita Krishna describes the human body as the (true) Ashvatta tree, "with its roots above and its branches below": the spine, in other words, with the nervous system the "branches," and the many-rayed *sahasrara* (the roots) at the top of the head.

It need hardly be added that most of the names in this section of the Gita correspond to Hindu myths and legends, and have little correspondence to modern knowledge. Many of them are, of course, symbolic, and refer to spiritual teachings that are given more explicitly elsewhere in this scripture. In this portion of Chapter 10 they are offered more for information than for instruction or inspiration. The essential significance Krishna gives them is that whatever is brightest, best, strongest, most glorious, or most intelligent is the clearest manifestation of God—not so much in the sense that the highest wave is more His manifestation than the lowest, but in the sense, rather, that when tamas and restless rajas least obscure a divine quality, the result is like a thinning cloud-cover which veils the moon, and renders it more visible. The metaphor of a rising wave may indicate egoic tension, but God is especially evident wherever His effulgence shines forth most naturally in this world.

(10:27) Among horses, I am the nectar-born Ucchaisravas; among elephants, I am (Indra's white

elephant) Airavata; among men, I am a monarch.

"Horse," it may be mentioned in passing, symbolizes power: specifically, it refers to that power which carries energy, whether downward or upward. *Ucchais* means, "upward."

(10:28) Among weapons, I am the thunderbolt; among cows, I am Kamadhuk (the fulfiller of desires); in sexual desire, I am procreation; among serpents, I am Vasuki.

(10:29) Among the Naga serpents, I am Ananta (endless); among water beings, I am Varuna; among departed ancestors, I am Aryama; among those who maintain law and order, I am Yama.

(10:30) Among the Daityas, I am Prahlad; among measurers, I am Time; among animals, I am their king (the lion); among birds, I am Garuda ("lord of the skies"; in classical symbology, the vehicle of Vishnu).

(10:31) Among purifiers, I am the wind; among wielders of weapons, I am Rama; among aquatic creatures, I am Makara (vehicle of the ocean god); among rivers, I am Jahnavi (the Ganges, holiest of rivers).

(10:32) Among all manifestations, O Arjuna, I am their beginning, middle, and end; among the various branches of knowledge, I am the wisdom of the Self; among debates, I am the clearest reasoning.

(10:33) Among all letters, I am the first in the alphabet; among compounds, I am the connecter; in time, I am the immutable; in creation, I am the Omnipresent, and ever turn My face in all directions.

(10:34) I am all-dissolving Death; I am Birth; I am the origin of things yet to be; among feminine manifestations (the qualities of Prakriti, or Mother Nature), I am fame, success, the illuminating power of speech, memory, intuitive discrimination, firmness in loyalty, and patience.

(10:35) Among hymns, I am *Brihat-Saman*; among poetic meters, I am Gayatri; among months, I am Margashirsha (the auspicious winter month); among seasons, I am Kusumakara, the flower-bringer (spring).

(10:36) Among deceivers, I am gambling; of the glorious, I am glory; for those who strive to win, I am victory; among the good, I am Sattwa (the elevating quality).

(10:37) Among Vrishnis, I am Vasudeva (Krishna); among the Pandavas, I am (yourself) Dhananjaya (Arjuna); among the munis (saints), I am Byasa; among sages, I am Ushanas.

(10:38) I am the rod of discipline; I am the skill of the victorious; I am the silence of hidden things; among knowers, I am wisdom.

(10:39) Whatsoever constitutes the reproductive seed of all beings, that I am. There is nothing, O Arjuna, moving or unmoving, that exists apart from Me.

(10:40) O Scorcher of Foes (Arjuna), the manifestations of My divine attributes are without limit; this brief declaration of them merely hints at them.

(10:41) Whatever being is endowed with power, prosperity, or glory, know that endowment itself to be only a spark of My effulgence.

(10:42) What need have you, however, O Arjuna, for these manifold details? Know this only: I, the Unchanging and Everlasting, permeate and sustain the entire cosmos with but a fragment of My essential being.

Thus ends the tenth chapter, called "From the Unmanifested to the Manifested," of the Upanishad of the holy Bhagavad Gita, in the dialogue between Sri Krishna and Arjuna discussing yoga and the science of God-realization.

CHAPTER TWENTY-FOUR

THE DIVINE VISION

(11:1) Arjuna said: In Your compassion You have revealed to me the secret wisdom of the Self, and have thereby banished my delusion.

(11:2) O Lotus-eyed (Krishna)! You have spoken extensively of the beginning and end of all beings, and of Your eternal sovereignty.

(11:3) O Great One! You have declared Yourself to me; I accept as true everything You have said. And yet, O Purushottama! I long to behold You for myself, in Your infinite form.

(11:4) O Master, Lord of Yogis! If You deem me fit, reveal to me Your Infinite Self!

THE INDIAN SCRIPTURES CONTAIN OVER A THOUSAND names for God, each with a different nuance of meaning to suggest in human terms one aspect of the infinity of truth. Purushottama, in this third verse, is an appellation for God in His highest, unmanifested aspect.

(11:5) The Blessed Lord said: Behold, O Son of Pritha (Arjuna)! by hundreds and by thousands My divine forms: multicolored, multifarious!

(11:6) Behold the Adityas, the Vasus, the Rudras, the twin Aswins, the Maruts, and many wonders hitherto unknown!

(11:7) Here and now, O Gudakesha (Conqueror of Sleep, Arjuna)! behold unified in My Cosmic Body all the worlds, all that moves or is without movement, and all, besides, that you desire to behold.

(11:8) You cannot behold Me with mortal eyes, however. Now, therefore, I give you divine sight. Behold My supreme yoga power!

(11:9) (To Dhritarashtra) Sanjaya said: With these words Hari (Krishna), the exalted Lord of yoga, revealed to Arjuna his Supreme, Divine form.

(11:10,11) Arjuna saw the Supreme Deity, infinite in variety, omnidirectional in radiance, all-pervading— as if adorned on all sides with celestial robes, garlands, and ornaments; the divine weapons (celestial powers) upraised (as though ready for use); fragrant with exquisite essences, and with faces and eyes seemingly everywhere!

(11:12) Were a thousands suns to appear together in the sky, their brilliance could suggest only dimly the splendor of that exalted Being.

(11:13) There (in that vision) did Arjuna behold the vast universe with its endless divisions, all united as one, within the form of the God of gods.

(11:14) Then Dhananjaya (Arjuna), wonder-struck, the follicles on his arms raising their hairs in awe,

prayerfully joined his palms together and, bowing his
head to the Lord, exclaimed, marveling:
(11:15–31)
   Most wonderful Lord, adored of gods!
Within Thy cosmic form I behold
the vast universe of beings,
saints and sages divine
sequestered in remote caves,
their serpent nature (Kundalini),
formerly virulent, now tamed,
raised by love on the rod of awakening.
Lord Brahma, God of gods,
seated on the head of each sage,
his seat the shining lotus of a thousand rays!
   O Cosmic-bodied Lord of all worlds,
I behold Thee everywhere, and in everything!
Innumerable bodies, faces, eyes reveal Thy energy!
Inscrutable to me are Your origins,
Your reigns, Your endings.
O Blazing Effulgence! Overwhelming Light!
The glory of Thy name spreads everywhere—
to darkest corners of the universe!
   Diademed with stars,
wielding the mace of sovereign power,
Your discus of whirling vortices of light
dazzling, illuminating, thrilling all!
Immortal, Supreme Brahman,
Supreme resting-place of all created forms,
Guardian of eternal law: high wisdom's throne,
Thy Self-born luster shields Thy devotees from harm,
Protecting all beings,

and calling them to wakefulness in Thee.
   O Sovereign One, the beings of earth,
the astral gods—all, awe-stricken,
with folded palms offer Thee adoration;
with prostrations they enter Thy cosmic temple,
and offer Thee their love, their hearts' devotion:
their hymns rising to the starry dome of heaven,
they worship Thee, and Thee alone.
   The lights of heaven—blazing suns,
the "lamps" of consciousness—hermits, sages,
emperors of benign rule,
noble heralds of Thy peace,
the strong, the powerful, desire-filled, ambitious,
bow in wonder before Thy radiant throne,
or else fall before Thee, fear-filled,
vanquished, their petty lives consumed
in the cosmic fire.
   Thee I behold! Thy feet walk everywhere,
Thy countless limbs are active throughout space.
Thy mouths consuming, Thy eyes flashing,
Thy hair streaming out with energy across the sky,
O Thou, joyous, overpowering, all-obliterating Light!
I stand trembling before Thee, awe-filled!
Egos, karmas, desires, ambitions, victories—
all rush toward Thee for reabsorption in Thy bliss,
or else soon crumble into wasted dust.
So do the rushing rivers of innumerable lives
flow, impetuously, blindly, to Thy sea.
Moths, drawn to a flame, there perish:
So do human lives, drawn by ambition,
ever hopeful, but ever doomed to devastation,
the fog of passion obscuring from them the truth.

Who art Thou, Lord? What is Thy cosmic will?
What is Thy purpose?
To what end has all this been done?
(11:32–34) The Blessed Lord said:
I am *Kala*: I am Time.
Disguised as Endless Doom I come.
I seize; I obliterate.
Even were you not to fight,
these foes you gaze upon at Kurukshetra
would perish, Arjuna, slain by My mighty will.
Indeed, I slew them long ago:
You are but My instrument.
Your destiny is to carry out My will.
I need you not: It is you, Arjuna,
who have need of Me!
I know the past, present, and future of all men.
Make war for Me, if you would embrace
eternal life, and victory, and bliss!

(11:35) Sanjaya said: Thus hearing, Arjuna, with folded hands, trembling in awe, prostrated before Krishna and spoke these words:

(11:36) O Krishna, rightly does the world rejoice in Thy glory! The demons, terrified, in vain seek refuge from Thy wrath. And the multitudes of perfected beings bow in the surrender of true worship.

(11:37) Ah! how could they not pay Thee homage, Thou more-than-exalted Lord? Greater art Thou than Brahma, who created all! O Infinite Being, God of gods, Shelter of the universe—Thou the Imperishable, the Manifested and Unmanifested, the Ultimate Mystery!

(11:38) Thou art the First of Gods, the Primal Person,

the refuge of the world. Thou alone knowest all there is to be known. Thou art the Supreme Goal. By Thee is the universe pervaded, O Thou of infinite form!

(11:39) Thou art Vayu (the wind). Thou art Yama (the destroyer, and god of death). Thou art Agni (god of fire). Thou art Varuna (the sea god). Thou art Sasanka (the moon), and Prajapati (the grandsire of all). Hail, all hail to Thee a thousand times! Hail, and hail to Thee again, and yet again!

(11:40) Hail to Thee in front, behind, and everywhere. Boundless in power and immeasurable in might, Thou art in all, and therefore Thou *art* all!

(11:41) For whatever disrespect I may have shown Thee in jest, addressing Thee as "Friend," "Companion," "Krishna," "Yadava" (Krishna's family relationship to Arjuna), speaking carelessly, though with affection,—

(11:42) and for any irreverence I may have shown Thee, O Unshakable Lord! lightheartedly while eating, resting, walking, when we were seated together whether by ourselves or in the company of others—for all such unintended slights, O Illimitable Lord, I beg Your forgiveness.

(11:43) Father of all beings Thou art: of animate and inanimate alike. None is worthy of worship but Thee, O Guru Sublime! Unequaled by anyone in the three worlds, who can surpass Thee, O Lord of Incomparable Power?

(11:44) Therefore, O Thou Infinitely Adorable! I cast myself humbly at Thy feet, imploring Thy pardon. As a father to his son, as a friend to a dear friend, as a lover to his beloved, do Thou, beloved Lord, forgive me!

(11:45) Overjoyed I am by this cosmic vision, never beheld before. Yet, I confess, my mind is not free from terror. Be merciful to me, O Lord of gods and Shelter of the worlds! Show me Thyself once again in Thy (limited, human) form.

And so came to an end the Vision of visions. I have—craving the reader's indulgence and forgiveness—offered here a very free paraphrase, considering it more important to convey the feeling of awe and majesty than to preserve the exact words of the original—even those, indeed, of my Guru's translation. Many books contain literal translations. I have long felt there was a need for something more poetic, in contemporary language.

Paramhansa Yogananda wrote a great mystical poem, "Samadhi," conveying his own experience of this supernal experience. It seems fitting here to quote that poem also:

Vanished the veils of light and shade,
Lifted every vapor of sorrow,
Sailed away all dawns of fleeting joy,
Gone the dim sensory mirage.
Love, hate, health, disease, life, death,
Perished these false shadows on the screen of duality.
Waves of laughter, scyllas of sarcasm, melancholic
    whirlpools,
Melting in the vast sea of bliss.
The storm of *maya* stilled
By magic wand of intuition deep.
The universe, forgotten dream, subconsciously lurks,
Ready to invade my newly-wakened memory divine.
I live without the cosmic shadow,
But it is not, bereft of me;

As the sea exists without the waves,
But they breathe not without the sea.
Dreams, wakings, states of deep *turia*, sleep,
Present, past, future, no more for me,
But ever-present, all-flowing I, I, everywhere.
Planets, stars, stardust, earth,
Volcanic bursts of doomsday cataclysms,
Creation's molding furnace,
Glaciers of silent x-rays, burning electron floods,
Thoughts of all men, past, present, to come,
Every blade of grass, myself, mankind,
Each particle of universal dust,
Anger, greed, good, bad, salvation, lust,
I swallowed, transmuted all
Into a vast ocean of blood of my own one Being!
Smoldering joy, oft-puffed by meditation
Blinding my tearful eyes,
Burst into immortal flames of bliss,
Consumed my tears, my frame, my all.
Thou art I, I am Thou,
Knowing, Knower, Known, as One!
Tranquilled, unbroken thrill, eternally living, ever-
    new peace!
Enjoyable beyond imagination of expectancy, *samadhi*
    bliss!
Not an unconscious state
Or mental chloroform without wilful return,
Samadhi but extends my conscious realm
Beyond limits of the mortal frame
To farthest boundary of eternity
Where I, the Cosmic Sea,
Watch the little ego floating in Me.

The sparrow, each grain of sand, fall not without My
    sight.
All space floats like an iceberg in My mental sea.
Colossal Container, I, of all things made.
By deeper, longer, thirsty, guru-given meditation
Comes this celestial *samadhi*.
Mobile murmurs of atoms are heard,
The dark earth, mountains, vales, lo! molten liquid!
Flowing seas change into vapors of nebulae!
Aum blows upon vapors, opening wondrously their
    veils,
Oceans stand revealed, shining electrons,
Till, at last sound of the cosmic drum,
Vanish the grosser lights into eternal rays
Of all-pervading bliss.
From joy I came, for joy I live, in sacred joy I melt.
Ocean of mind, I drink all creation's waves.
Four veils of solid, liquid, vapor, light,
Lift aright.
Myself, in everything, enters the Great Myself.
Gone forever, fitful, flickering shadows of mortal
    memory.
Spotless is my mental sky, below, ahead, and high
    above.
Eternity and I, one united ray.
A tiny bubble of laughter, I
Am become the Sea of Mirth Itself.

Arjuna, overwhelmed with the majesty of what he has
just beheld, asked Krishna (above) to reveal himself
again in a more human form—as beloved Teacher,
Friend, and Guide. Here Arjuna repeats that request,

somewhat more surprisingly (to modern minds)—asking
Krishna to appear not as a man, but (probably to satisfy
traditional tastes)—as Vishnu.

(11:46) I long to see Thee (O Krishna!) in the form
that is familiar to most: as four-armed Vishnu,
diademed, his mace and discus held aloft. O Lord of
a thousand arms, for the reassurance of many appear
to me now in that known shape.

(11:47) The Blessed Lord said: By My grace, exercising
My yoga power, I have revealed to you—as to none
other—this Supreme form of Mine: radiant, infinite!

(11:48) No mortal man—save thee alone, great hero
of the Kuru dynasty!—has looked upon My universal
form; not by sacrifices, nor by gifts in charity, nor by
noble works, nor by pious study of the Vedas can that
vision be attained.

(11:49) Be not fearful, nor bewildered by this vision
of the wholly impersonal aspect of My being. Take
comfort; be glad at heart, and behold Me in this, My
(humanly speaking) reassuring aspect.

(11:50) Sanjaya said: Having thus addressed Arjuna,
Vasudeva (Krishna) appeared once again, comfort-
ingly, to his disciple in his own (human) form.

(11:51) Arjuna said: O Granter of all Boons (Krishna)!
Viewing You once again in the human form I love, my
mind is pacified and I feel I am once more myself.

(11:52) The Blessed Lord said: Very difficult is it to
behold, as you have done, the vision of the divine universe. Even the gods yearn to see it.

(11:53,54) Its revelation, however, is not attained by

penances or by faithfulness to scripture or by chari-
ties or by formal worship. O Scorcher of Foes
(Arjuna)! only by single-hearted devotion, achieved
through deep yoga practice, is it possible to behold
Me, and to become one with Me, as you have done, in
My cosmic form.

(11:55) He who serves Me alone, who makes Me his
only goal, who lovingly surrenders every thought of "I"
to Me, who releases all attachment to aught else, and
who (beholding Me in all) bears no ill will toward
anyone—he, O Arjuna!, enters My vast being.

Thus ends the eleventh chapter, called "The Divine
Vision," of the Upanishad of the holy Bhagavad Gita,
in the dialogue between Sri Krishna and Arjuna
discussing yoga and the science of God-realization.

CHAPTER TWENTY-FIVE

THE PATH OF BHAKTI YOGA

(12:1) Arjuna said: Between those who worship You with steadfast devotion, and those who concentrate on the Absolute, which is better versed in the yoga science?

(12:2) The Blessed Lord answered: Those who, with minds fixed on Me, are ever united to Me in pure devotion, are in My eyes the best versed in yoga.

(12:3,4) Those, however, who aspire to the Indestructible, the Indescribable, the Unmanifested, the All-Pervading, the Incomprehensible, the Immutable above all vibration, who have subjugated the senses, are even-minded, and devote themselves to the well-being of all—verily, they, too, attain Me.

IT SHOULD BE NOTED HERE THAT KRISHNA IS NOT saying that devotional love is higher than yoga (union) with the Absolute. He is, as always, being practical. Most human beings are accustomed to seeing themselves as individuals, living in ego-consciousness. They cannot simply banish that self-awareness and worship an abstraction: the Unmanifested Spirit. They must begin realistically where they are now on the spiritual path. Dwelling in bodies, it is very much easier for them to worship God in an I-and-Thou relationship, and even to visualize Him as possessing a form: as Vishnu, Shiva, forms of the Divine Mother, Krishna, or Jesus Christ. People can visualize love in a human form: It is difficult for them to visualize it as an abstraction. As my Guru once put it, "How can the little cup hold the whole ocean?" They need to expand their consciousness by degrees. Yoga is the "down-to-earth" spiritual science which lifts people from the ground, with which they are familiar, into the vast, unknown skies of Spirit.

(12:5) Those who make the Unmanifested their primary goal make the path more difficult for themselves. Arduous for embodied beings is that path.

It should be added, for those of intellectual and philosophical temperament, that heartfelt devotion even to abstract truth, is an absolute necessity. Without love—which must be childlike, innocent, and pure, and not some brow-furrowing, carefully formulated theological attempt at exact definitions—one cannot set one foot before the other on the path. He lacks the necessary urgency of desire to reach the goal.

It should also be said, for those lovers of God who find it offensive to practice techniques, which to them seem mere mechanisms that intrude on the flow of devotion, that undisciplined inspiration has always been the mark of the amateur and dilettante. No art is needed to *feel* inspiration, but to *express* that inspiration requires self-discipline and a focus of energy, which come only as a result of much training and effort. The true artist is never one who, feeling uplifted by what he sees, makes wild brush marks on his canvas that can have meaning for no one but himself.

(12:6,7) **For those who venerate only Me, offering to Me all their actions, with their minds concentrated on Me by yoga practice, and their hearts' feelings uplifted to Me in devotion: Such devotees I rescue from the ocean of mortality.**

(12:8) **Immerse your consciousness in Me alone; direct all your discrimination toward finding Me: Then, beyond any doubt, you shall come to Me.**

(12:9) **O Dhananjaya (Arjuna), if you cannot absorb your thoughts in the contemplation of Me, then practice the techniques of yoga, which are intended to help develop concentration.**

(12:10) **If, however, you find yoga practice too difficult, then perform all actions in the thought of Me. By this means, too, you shall achieve final success.**

(12:11) **But if even, during activity, you cannot think of Me, then give Me your *intentions*. Ever striving to discipline your mind, offer to Me the fruits of your every labor.**

Sir Edwin Arnold puts it beautifully in his much-loved (and deservedly so) paraphrase, *The Song Celestial*. His translation of this passage is, "But, if in this thy faint heart fails, bring Me thy failure!"

As Yogananda gave the counsel, earlier, to give God even one's mistakes, so he would give the counsel to give one's failures to God. It is the *intention* that counts. Every thought that is uplifted to the Lord becomes purified and strengthened in time. No amount of restlessness can define anyone as he is at the present.

Regarding attunement with the guru, also, Paramhansa Yogananda said, "If you shut me out, how can I come in?" The glass that is turned upside down cannot receive the drink that might fill it. The first step toward receiving divine blessings is to hold oneself in readiness for the moment when those blessings are poured. Indeed, the blessings are there, ever waiting, if the vessel of our consciousness is "upturned" to receive them.

(12:12) Perseverance in pursuing Self-knowledge, and (sincere) aspiration to (experience) it through meditation, is better than the possession of theoretical knowledge. Offering up to Me the fruits of action, moreover, is better than one-sided but restless meditation. Action, coupled with renunciation of the fruits of action, brings inner peace, which makes it possible to meditate deeply.

This passage is often translated to suggest that the "easier" path of devotion is more suitable than meditation for *bhaktas*, who tend rather to sing and chant devotionally to the accompaniment of drums and cymbals. At no time in the Gita has Krishna recommended outward practices as *preferable* to silent, inner communion. What he offers in this stanza is encouragement to those who cannot yet take their devotion inward. Devotion is always paramount. When it is offered *only* outwardly, however, there can be no question of merging in the actual *experience* of God's love. It is like being at a banquet: The one who eats best, and with the greatest enjoyment, is he who eats in silence, not he who keeps on loudly and repeatedly exclaiming how delicious the food is!

Prayer and chanting may be described as either talking or singing to God; meditation means listening for His answer. Could the Lord possibly be pleased with someone who doesn't want to hear His reply? And could He possibly be *even more* pleased with such noisy, self-centered devotees? Absurd!

(12:13,14) He who bears no ill will toward anyone, who is kind and friendly to all, who has no consciousness of "I" and "mine," who is even-minded during pain and pleasure, forgiving toward all, inwardly contented, steadfast in his (yoga) meditation practices, self-controlled, who tries faithfully (through yoga practice) to unite his soul to Me, who is firm in determination, and whose mind and discrimination are surrendered to Me—such a one is dear to Me.

(12:15) One who doesn't disturb others, and is not disturbed in return, who never exults in anything, is never jealous, fearful, or worried—such a one is dear to Me.

(12:16) One who is free from worldly expectations, pure-minded, prompt in action, unconcerned and unafflicted by circumstances, who is without ego-motivation—he, My (true) devotee, is dear to Me.

It should be specified here once again that to be without ego-motivation is not the same thing as to view the world with bland indifference. Indifference, unless it is accompanied by inner freedom and joy, can be tamasic. Sometimes people pride themselves on "being above it all," when in fact they are only apathetic. The true yogi is intensely aware at all times. He is *interested*, also, not in the sense that he is emotionally involved, but in the sense that he *gives* energy, rather than waiting to be entertained.

(12:17) He who neither rejoices in good fortune nor grieves when things go wrong, who judges matters as neither good nor evil, who is devoted only to Me—such a one is dear to Me.

(12:18,19) He who treats friend and foe alike; who is even-minded whether (receiving) honor or dishonor; who calmly, without attachment, accepts warm and cold, pleasure and pain; who is the same under praise or censure; who is inwardly tranquil and contented; who is attached to no abode and is ever calm and devout—such a one is dear to Me.

(12:20) But those who, filled with devotion, pursue the deathless dharma I have described, ever engrossed in Me, are above all dear to Me.

Thus ends the twelfth chapter, called "The Path of Bhakti Yoga," of the Upanishad of the holy Bhagavad Gita, in the dialogue between Sri Krishna and Arjuna discussing yoga and the science of God-realization.

CHAPTER TWENTY-SIX

THE FIELD OF BATTLE

Preamble:
Arjuna said: O Keshava (Krishna), I long to know the (mystery) of Prakriti and Purusha (Intelligent Mother Nature and transcendent God, the Father); of *kshetra* (the body) and *kshetragya* (the inner perceiver); of knowledge and its object (that which is known).

THE ABOVE STANZA IS USUALLY UNNUMBERED, with a view to keeping the number of stanzas in the Gita to exactly 700.
Arjuna, after hearing Krishna's discourse on divine union through devotion, wants to know more about the eternal struggle (the war of Kurukshetra) between good and evil in the self and in the cosmos. One cannot help wondering, given the sequence of these two chapters, whether he is not (on the behalf of all seekers) asking Krishna these deep questions to help clarify for the reader the fact that the relatively easy path (at least, so

it appears) of devotion must be paired with the deep, extremely practical teachings Krishna has been giving him. The Gita begins with Arjuna showing himself reluctant to fight at all. The reader's need, now, is to be shown that *bhakti* (devotion) does not render that fight after all unnecessary. Only at the end of the Bhagavad Gita does Krishna, in the proper context and at the right time, explain divine love in such a way as to contrast it properly with all other considerations of the spiritual path. People might otherwise seek a shortcut, through devotion, and end up becoming superficial in their spiritual search.

(13:1) The Blessed Lord replied: O Son of Kunti (Arjuna), those who know truth perceive this (human) body as kshetra (the "field" where good and evil karma are reaped), and the knower of the field (the soul) as kshetragya.

There are two forces at work in the body: the outward- (and downward-) flowing energy, and the inward- (and upward-) flowing. Although the scene of the Bhagavad Gita is set on an actual, outer battlefield, the setting is primarily allegorical, as this stanza makes very clear. The *body*, and not the outer field of Kurukshetra (which still exists geographically in northern India), is what is really intended by the field of battle. The "knower of the field" (kshetragya) is the indwelling soul, which, like Krishna on the legendary battlefield, takes no active part in the war. The soul observes, but remains inactive. It is not the soul which incarnates and dies with the body.

Paramhansa Yogananda defined ego as "the soul attached to the body." The body—the bodies, actually: physical, astral, and causal, the first two of which are subject to birth and death—may be described even on the physical level as only ideas of the soul. All three bodies are unreal in eternity, and endure only as long as the idea of them is activated by desires. That idea is fueled in the astral and physical bodies by the concept of individuality. Ego-consciousness is, indeed, an "element" of the astral body.

The human intellect, presented with the problem of the knower and the known (kshetragya and kshetra) says, "To know something is, in fact, to differentiate *three* distinct things: the knower, the thing known, and *the act of knowing*." So long as the act of knowing (that is to say, of perceiving) is directed outward, the energy in the body will flow outward also through the senses, and man will be sucked into a downward vortex, as it were, from which escape will become increasingly difficult.

The true war of Kurukshetra is the struggle between upward aspiration, which causes the energy in the body to flow upward, and the downward pull toward lower awareness which brings man's expectation of fulfillment outward to the senses. The mere things he hopes to enjoy are themselves inanimate, and can never satisfy him in any way except in his own reactions to them.

What defines the downward direction as being evil is that, in its outwardness from the inner source, it disappoints what everyone in *samsara* (*maya*) really wants: ego-fulfillment, emotional happiness, and the enjoyment of life through the senses. It takes man also in the direction opposite to what he wants ultimately: divine bliss. Were it possible for human nature truly to be fulfilled outwardly, as man mistakenly believes, what person in good conscience could consider it evil to seek such fulfillment? Society might be outraged by actions it considers contrary to custom, but what others want of one is not really their business! Everyone has his own life to lead. What makes certain behavior wrong—and sometimes, indeed, evil—is the fact that desire deceives people into behaving against their own higher interests.

Habit and desire separate one from soul-awareness. Added to that initial separation is the fierce hold the ego exerts on his awareness. The host of negative qualities that develop from ego-consciousness—pride, for example, and guilt, and a fancied need for self-justification—though integral to man's dance with delusion, bring false satisfactions which, in the end, cause him suffering. These qualities wrap themselves around his ego, binding him quite as tightly as Gulliver was bound by the many threadlike "cords" that tied him down when he was shipwrecked, and stretched, unconscious, on the sands of Lilluput.

Because the memory of the soul is never lost, man begins slowly to tire of forever-disappointing dreams, and longs to dispel them. The process of wakening is what is termed good, since it draws man's energy and consciousness up the spine again, and, in bringing him back to himself, brings him also greater happiness and, eventually, the state of oneness with Spirit.

Rising energy and consciousness in the spine eventually bring about both inner and outer unity. Knowing, knower, and known become one. Devotion rises in response to the magnetism of divine love. Material desire, on the other hand, pulls people down in response to the magnetism of the downward-moving Kundalini, which manifests in the body as the outward pull of *maya*, called, in some religions, by the name, Satan.

In this chapter Krishna details the cosmic verities, both inward and outward, by which Spirit created the universe, and the soul of man which is caught in that creative vortex. When the soul ultimately escapes that vortex, it reclaims its oneness with the Spirit.

(13:2) Know Me also, O Bharata (Arjuna), as the silent Knower (Perceiver) in all kshetras (bodies evolved out of the cosmic creative principle and Nature). I consider true wisdom to be the understanding of kshetra, the field, and of its relation to kshetragya, the perceiver of the field.

A young man named Naresh met a saint. The saint asked him who he was, and the youth answered, "I am Naresh."

"Who are you?" asked the saint again.

Naresh, thinking perhaps the saint hadn't heard him, said, "My name is Naresh."

"Yes, but who are you?"

Naresh, puzzled, replied, "My father's name is Ram Dutta. I live in Delhi. I'm an accountant."

"Yes, but who are you?" persisted the saint.

The young man puzzled over this question. Was the saint hard of hearing? Was he, perhaps, growing old and a bit senile?

"Well, if you don't know," said the saint with a smile, "maybe it's good you came to me."

By now the young man was thoroughly bewildered! Still, he felt a certain peace in the saint's presence, and returned to him many times—he didn't really know why. Gradually, however, he came to think, "Can I really define myself in such a limited way as to say that I'm an accountant?" He began to think, "I'm not what I *do*. I'm a young man with many interests, including that of visiting this saint—though I do so for reasons I don't fully understand."

"Who are you?" the saint asked him again one day. By now the older man seemed to the younger not only perfectly normal, but even wise.

"I don't know who I *really* am," said Naresh.

"That's better!" exclaimed the saint. "Now then, think about it again. Who are you?"

Well, thought the young man. I have a name, a family, a domicile. But am I really any of those things? Suddenly it dawned on him: "I'm a soul in search of itself!" His body was still young, but he knew it would age in time. Even now he was the same person inside that he'd been as a little child. The body had changed, but he hadn't. Therefore, he realized, he was not the body.

He introspected further. His understanding had changed since he'd met the saint, but he was still the same person, inside. His personality had changed, but something in his consciousness had remained the same. Slowly he came to realize that he, himself, was a point of inner perception from which he merely observed these changes, but didn't define himself in terms of any of them.

That which changes, he realized, cannot be what I am.
I am that something within that remains unchanged—
that simply observes every change. Thus, he came to
identify himself more and more with his soul.

One day he said to the guru, "I know who I am, but
there are no words with which to speak of it." The saint,
hearing those words, only smiled. Later on, the saint
said, "Now that words fail you, there is much that we
can communicate!"

Wisdom begins with the knowledge that we are not
this body or personality. We are the immortal soul.

**(13:3,4) Hear now briefly about the field, its attrib-
utes, its cause-and-effect principle, and its distorting
influences; also what He (the kshetragya) is, and the
nature of His powers—truths which have been sung by
sages in many ways: in chants of the Vedas and in well-
reasoned, conclusive aphorisms of the *Brahmasutra*.**

Krishna states that he is expounding truths already
declared in the scriptures.

**(13:5,6) Succinctly stated (quoting scripture), the
kshetras are composed of (both) undifferentiated and
differentiated Nature, their differentiated nature being
the gross "elements" (earth, water, fire, air, ether), the
ten senses (the five organs of knowledge: the ears, skin,
eyes, nose, and tongue; and the five "objects" of sense—
hearing, feeling, sight, smell, and taste), and the five
organs of action (the hands, feet, mouth, anus, and
generative organ); the one sense-conscious mind,**

intellect, ego-consciousness, the distortions of chitta (attraction/aversion, pleasure/pain), the body itself, consciousness, and persistence.

These principles have their cosmic, undifferentiated aspect as well as their differentiated, individual aspects. The cosmos itself is a conscious entity, self-aware (though not egoically so, since ego—the soul *identified* with the body—becomes an "element" only with the astral body). As Swami Sri Yukteswar stated in the chapter on his resurrection in *Autobiography of a Yogi*, causal beings have vast powers, which enable them even to create universes. (Perhaps he meant, "galaxies.")

Krishna himself offers these extraordinarily intricate details as a quotation from the Shankhya scriptures. His intent is to lead Arjuna, the universal devotee, from the consciousness of complexity to the simplicity of non-identification with any of them, and therefore to non-identity with the thought of the ego as being in supreme control of anything.

Persistence, or fortitude (*dhriti*), is manifested physically first of all by holding the body and consciousness together. The body is an aggregate of the twenty-four "elements" of creation (expounded in the Shankhya system of India), combined with the aspects of consciousness arising from them. On this "field of battle" the war constantly rages between passion, desire, attachment, and other human delusions on the one side, and their opposite aspirations: devotion, non-attachment, and all virtuous qualities. The goal of yoga practice is to resolve this complexity in the simple, all-unifying awareness of changeless soul-consciousness.

(13:7) The true insight bestowed by wisdom is revealed in the following qualities: humility; unpretentiousness; harmlessness; forgiveness; integrity; service to the guru; purity (of mind and body); steadfastness; self-control;—
(13:8) indifference to sense-objects; lack of emphasis on one's own self; perception of the sufferings and evils inherent in birth, illness, old age, and death;—
(13:9) non-attachment; non-identification of the ego with one's own children, wife, and home (and with everything that these entail); equal acceptance of both fortune and misfortune;—
(13:10) unswerving devotion to, and identity with, Me through yoga practice; love of solitude; disinclination for worldly society;—
(13:11) perseverance in the pursuit of Self-knowledge; aspiration toward true wisdom, which is the goal of all learning. Qualities that oppose these virtues are the signs of ignorance.

The above-listed qualities speak for themselves. They are the mark of one who is intent on absorbing his little self in the Self of all. Whatever duties he has on earth—the examples listed here are duties to one's children, wife, and home—must be fulfilled without ego-identification. The yogi must perceive God as equally present in all. Living in this world, he must constantly remind himself that birth, life, and death are passing phenomena, and are fraught with suffering and pain—paired, inevitably, with earth's pleasures and fulfillments. He should not identify himself, therefore, with anything outward.

Whenever possible, he should seek seclusion—for one or two weeks a year, or for longer periods—to immerse himself in the thought of God. He should not *dislike* worldly company, since to dislike anything is to create a disturbance in his chitta, or feeling. He may not always find it convenient to avoid such society, but he should be conscious of, and accept as the right attitude for a devotee, an inner *disinclination* for it. Thus, if he must sometimes attend worldly gatherings, he should relate to people from a firm center of calmness within himself.

Intellectual knowledge for its own sake is not a worthy pursuit for anyone who seeks wisdom. Knowledge is the possession of a mere catalogue of facts: Wisdom is the understanding of how to use facts in the quest for enlightenment in the Self.

(13:12) I will now tell you what knowledge one should pursue: true knowledge, which bestows immortality. Hear (what I have to say) about the Supreme, Beginningless Brahman: He who cannot be said either to exist or not to exist (since existence implies coming into being).

(13:13) He dwells, however, omnipresent in the universe, pervading all: heads, eyes, ears, faces everywhere;—

(13:14) shining in all the sense faculties, yet transcending them; the mainstay of everything, yet

attached to nothing; above the (three) gunas (qualities), yet experiencing (everything) through them;—

(13:15) within and without all that exists, both animate and inanimate; the "nearest of the near," yet so subtle as to be imperceptible;—

(13:16) He, the indivisible One, appears divided into countless beings—maintaining, then destroying their forms, then manifesting them anew;—

(13:17) the Light of lights He is, beyond all darkness; all knowledge, (whether) knowable or aspired to: He is (forever) seated in the hearts of all.

(13:18) I have briefly described here the field (kshetra); the nature of wisdom, and the object of wisdom. Possessed of this insight, My devotee enters into Me.

It is amazing to contemplate the infinity of truth—all of it united by the one consciousness of God. The sum of all these facts listed by Krishna is the overarching realization that God is not only *in* everything, but *is* everything. Nothing could have come into existence without having been dreamed into being by Him.

Yet the second amazing point to contemplate is that even the universe, in all its vastness, is not *directly* the product of His will. He is removed afar from everything, vibrationless, immutable, untouched. He conveys His power, love, and wisdom to universal, conscious forces (manifested by Him) who produce the universe we know.

(13:19) Know that both Purusha and Prakriti are without a beginning. Know also that all the modifications and qualities (gunas) of Nature are born of Prakriti.

Purusha and Prakriti—Spirit and Nature: Paramhansa Yogananda described them as dancing together in an eternal divine play, or lila. The Lord Transcendent (the kshetragya, or observer) and Prakriti (Mother Nature): These two are not separate, but one essential Reality. As the ocean is ever the same, whether with or without its waves, so the ocean of spirit, whether with or without the waves of cosmic manifestation, is ever one and the same reality.

Prakriti might be described as the storm which produces the waves. She is the product of Spirit's "desireless desire" to manifest His bliss outwardly: to "enjoy Himself through many," as the scriptures put it. The storm produces the three gunas, or qualities, which are degrees of manifestation. Sattwa is like a low wave, closest to its Source in the ocean; it most clearly reveals the truth of its being. Rajas is the agitation which begins to manifest itself in a gale, rather than in a light breeze. The higher the wave, the more it is removed from its Source. Thus, its height distorts the truth more completely. Tamas, finally, is the result of extreme violence in the shape of a storm, which produces towering wave crests. The crests seem to obliterate any sense of oneness as they disintegrate into innumerable bubbles. Being farthest from the Ocean Source, they also give no hint of the ocean's calm depth and majesty, but rather conceal every suggestion of vastness.

It should be emphasized that "closest, more removed, and farthest" are figures of speech and not literal facts, since God, or Prakriti, is *equally* present everywhere. Thus, this image needs to be balanced against another:

Sattwa guna casts only a thin veil over Eternal Reality. Rajoguna may be described, in this second image, as casting a blanket over that Reality, rather than a flimsy veil. And tamoguna, finally, may be described as enclosing that reality in concrete, seeming to separate it from God and from all godly qualities altogether. As violence often ends in exhaustion, so the quality of tamas also sinks the mind into utter dullness, despair, and hopelessness.

Satan—a common theme in Judaism, Christianity, and Islam, especially—is not, and could not be, such a separate or different reality from the Divine Lord of the Universe. Satan is a manifestation of the outward-moving force of *maya*—away from Spirit, and toward creation. It should be clearly understood, however—we made this point earlier also—that Satan is a *conscious* force and *will*, an ever-further manifestation of consciousness into matter. Thus, Satan is—determinedly so—the source of all disharmony and discord. He is "at the bottom of" every disease or distortion of what might otherwise have been a relatively carefree existence on earth. Plagues, illnesses, poisonous and otherwise noxious insects, the intrusion of ugliness with the deliberate purpose of disturbing whatever is beautiful and uplifting: These things are not the products of higher entities, but of that force which *wills* disharmony to exist on earth.

In the higher astral spheres, such nuisances do not exist. In material worlds where sattwa guna predominates, those nuisances either do not exist or are not a problem. In worlds, and in whole galaxies, on the other hand, that are more tamasic than our own, these "nuisances" enormously exacerbate the general misery.

This subject will be treated at greater length later on, but for now it is important to clarify the fact that Nature, in her aspect of Cosmic Mother, is not responsible for human suffering. It is Prakriti in her outward-manifesting aspect, as Aparaprakriti, that (from a relativistic human standpoint) is so frightening.

Modern science has prepared people for a less deistic, but at the same time more fundamentally spiritual, outlook on reality. It is necessarily—considering what is known now of the vastness of the universe—a much more impersonal view than people held in the past. No longer can people view themselves so confidently as being watched over by an ever-benevolent, fatherly God who concerns Himself intimately with human affairs— a loving Personage who *wants* everyone to succeed in his life ambitions and to be humanly happy; one who really *hopes* that Joe will make up with Mary, and that Bob will get that diploma for which he and his parents have been praying so earnestly.

Some people in the past have viewed God, alternatively, as a God of wrath and jealousy—again, very personal in His concern for the human scene, but angry enough with sinners to condemn them to eternal hell— even though (this has to be said) He gives people all the incentive they need to sin, and to sin exuberantly! These incentives are often overwhelming, and cannot be blamed on man alone.

God *is* impersonal. He is willing to let people suffer who ignore Him, or who turn against Him, or who betray their own erstwhile dedication to Him. But to those who love Him, He is also personal *through* their love.

The view of things people held in the past made life into a sort of football game, with satanic and angelic forces vying together—often evenly matched, alas—each side fiercely battling for eventual victory. God is said to be all-powerful, all-knowing, all-caring, all—well, all-everything—except there's always that insidious "serpent," Satan, who manages somehow to interfere with every good plan, and to keep everyone wondering whether God really has in Him the stuff that it takes to win. If anyone resolves to play on God's side, that person's chances for success are improved, but still it helps to have the guarantee of a few miracles to push things along.

The cosmic view that is now evolving out of science's revelation of how things really work is not friendly to the concept of divine favoritism. Yet science, too, is veering toward a view of reality that includes a universal consciousness, rather than an inert, material sludge. Old-fashioned religious concepts are being undermined by the discoveries of the very impersonal nature of everything. At the same time, so also is the traditional scientific outlook being transformed from complete materialism into an increasingly spiritual—indeed, Vedantic—perception of reality.

Without conscious evil, there could be no conscious good. Without duality, there could be no cosmic manifestation of anything. On the ocean's surface there would be no waves, nor any compensating troughs to keep the over-all ocean level unchanged. Creation would never have come into being. The gradually evolving model people are forming of ultimate reality, and which the Bhagavad Gita firmly declares, suggests no final, objective victory for either good or evil. Final victory is reserved only for individuals. Usually, in this world of duality, any victories are transient; they are necessarily balanced by defeats (owing to the nature of duality). Individual seekers of truth must dive, one by one, beneath the agitation of the storm at the surface, and find peace in the depths. Liberation is achieved singly, not by group effort. Though groups can at least provide a supportive environment for the individual aspirant, the exercise of conscience must be done personally— and often solitarily: It is ever a matter between the individual and his Maker.

In God's eyes there are no favorites. However—strange to say—His law does seem somehow to favor those who seek Him earnestly. For the sincere seeker, the cosmos is like the sounding board of a musical instrument. It resonates with his consciousness, and greatly enhances his power. For such a soul, miracles do indeed happen, though never in the sweetly sentimental, smilingly supportive way many orthodox worshipers envision. What does happen is more like what happened at Kurukshetra, when Krishna agreed to be Arjuna's charioteer on the condition that he himself would take no active part in the battle. Arjuna gladly accepted this condition, for he realized correctly that, whether active or not, Krishna's mere presence would in some way guarantee victory in the end. That, indeed, was what finally happened. And it is what happens in the private "war of Kurukshetra" within every individual.

Amazingly, the shift from belief in an intensely personal God to One who is sternly aloof and impersonal is not giving us a stone-carved, solid statue, rock-firm in its absoluteness. Exceptions occur constantly: The statue keeps cracking, and is in constant need of repair. Who, really, can fathom God? He is impersonal—yes, clearly so. Yet He dwells in every one of us, and He *does* care for each of us very personally, if we give to Him our hearts. His impersonality consists in wanting nothing from us, except, indeed—since in each of us, through our human feelings, He is also very personal—He longs for our love!

Sweet, foolish sentiments don't win Him. Earnest, complete self-offering does. True miracles are a constant feature of the spiritual life. By appealing to the Mother of the Universe, people do receive Her loving response. The condition for forming this relationship with Her is utter, childlike trust, and a total absence of selfish desire.

Let me finish this discussion with a very little, but true, story from the life of Paramhansa Yogananda.

Living as he did in California, he often traveled back and forth between his headquarters on Mount Washington, in Los Angeles, and his oceanside hermitage a hundred miles to the south, in Encinitas. In Laguna Beach, a little town on the way, he found a shop that made delicious Scotch shortbread. A true master like him is not attached to pleasures, and isn't driven by the slightest desire for them. Nonetheless, he can *enjoy* the things of this world. When he is strong in his non-attachment, he doesn't need to remain always grimly aloof from everything.

With that preamble, we may relate that he sometimes broke his journey between Los Angeles and Encinitas by stopping at that little shop. In the car, afterward, he would share with his companions the pleasure of eating this shortbread. It was something that he enjoyed sharing especially with the Divine Mother.

One day they stopped at this shop, and a disciple went in to buy a small supply of the shortbread. She came out to report regretfully that all the shortbread had been sold. The Master, as he told us later, was not disappointed: He was only surprised. He never did anything without first consulting the Divine Mother. Had She, this one time, led him awry?

"Divine Mother," he prayed for an instant, "what happened?"

Just then he saw a shaft of light descend onto the roof of that shop. A moment later the proprietor came running out, bearing in her hand a little package. "Wait!" she cried. "Don't go away! This package is for you. I was saving it for another customer who had ordered it, but I can make him another batch."

Strange to say then, in this vast, impersonal universe, where God is so remote, untouched, immutable, and apparently unconcerned, the old truths are being reinforced and with a vengeance! Young people, nowadays especially, want a religion that will answer the demands of common sense. When all the sound reasoning has been done, however, and the final tally is in, we find that in spite of everything the universe is more loving, more caring, more interested in us than even our forefathers believed!

(13:20) Material cause and effect are the product of Prakriti. Joy and sorrow (the mental experience of those effects) are the product of Purusha (the soul) in man.

Divine consciousness filters down into human consciousness. As the soul, that divine consciousness is the
impartial observer. Yet the soul provides us with our
very awareness and gives us the capacity to enjoy, or to
grieve. In order to become more conscious of the soul,
we should tell ourselves, "It is not I, in my true Self, who
rejoice or grieve." The bouncing ball of emotional reaction is what keeps people's attention focused outward
on the game of life. My Guru gave this advice: "Always
remain in the Self. Come down a little to eat or to talk
as necessary, but when the opportunity comes, withdraw
into the Self again."

**(13:21) Purusha, acting through Prakriti, and the
soul acting through the body: Both experience (impersonally) the gunas, born of Nature. It is _attachment_ to
the gunas which causes men to return (to earth) in
good or in evil wombs.**

The three gunas, or qualities, are an omnipresent feature
of Nature. Their constantly varied mixture produces the
vast differences that exist among human beings. As a
diamond's luster is not dimmed by any pouch containing
it, whether it be diaphanous, translucent, or opaque, so
the soul is unaffected by the gunas in man. Whether a person is saintly, worldly, or evil in no way affects or defines
him in his soul, which is the presence within him of the
ever-changeless Spirit.

**(13:22) The Supreme Spirit, manifested in each
body as the soul, is the detached witness; it is**

(through man's conscience) the counselor who, though accepting all, offers guidance, if asked. The soul is the Sustainer, the one who experiences (without reacting with feelings of either pleasure or pain), the Great Lord and Supreme Self.

God, in other words, *is* the soul of man—individualized but ever perfect. The soul is the witness. Through the ego, its consciousness experiences the joys and sorrows of life. Through intuition, it offers wise guidance when it can—that is, when people ask it, or when the ego shows itself in other ways or on other occasions open to it.

Sometimes the devotee, through spiritual absent-mindedness, or through not sufficiently guarding himself against temptation, slips momentarily from his devotion. If his normal openness to divine grace has not been closed off by present delusive directions, the soul may be able to enter the scene and prevent him from slipping any further. This hope, however, should not—*obviously* should not!—give him the impudence to presume on its kindness. Still, the thought may help to keep one hopeful, when the way before him seems dark. Grace is an all-important feature of the spiritual path. It is never imposed, but it can be *won*.

Sometimes, indeed, it happens that a person in great danger of a spiritual fall, whose karma from the past is essentially good, may for a time be granted high spiritual experiences—his deserved blessing from right effort in past lives—to encourage him to return with a good will to his spiritual practices. Other devotees on the path, aware of his deep experiences, may imagine him to be highly advanced, but in truth his soul, invited to do so by his good karma of the past, is offering him a special grace. Sad it is, when people reject that offer.

(13:23) Whatever his mode of life, one who (by realization) understands the relationship between the Spirit (also, his individual soul) and Nature (and, on an individual level, the body) with its threefold gunas, even though he engages outwardly in the activity of this life, need never again undergo rebirth.

It may be helpful, here, to reiterate that what is intended in this passage is intuitive, not intellectual, understanding.

One day my Guru scolded a disciple for some shortcoming. The disciple, although resisting mentally, replied as if patiently, "I understand, Master."

"You do *not* understand," retorted the Master. "If you really understood, you would do what I say!"

(13:24) To behold the Self in the self (the purified ego) by the self (the clarified mind), some seekers follow the path of meditation, some that of knowledge, and some the path of selfless activity (service).

Described here briefly are the three main approaches to God (which is to say, to Self-realization). The first is meditation—the path of inner action, which we've described as the science of Kriya Yoga. The second is Shankhya Yoga, the path of discrimination, or Gyana. The third is Karma Yoga, the path of right action.

One may ask, "Why has Krishna not mentioned also the path of Bhakti Yoga—devotion?" The truth is that without devotion *no other path* will work. Krishna frequently, in the Gita, stresses the importance of devotion. In this chapter he is emphasizing the need to wage inner war in the cause of truth. (Hence the repeated references to kshetra, and to Kurukshetra, symbol of the struggle involved in advancing spiritually.) Whether meditating, discriminating, or acting, a devotional attitude must underlie everything one does. Devotion is the bowstring that shoots the arrow to its mark. Without it, all spiritual effort is merely gathering good karma. It cannot bestow liberation.

(13:25) Some men, ignorant of these three paths, heed the instructions of their guru; accepting what he teaches as their supreme refuge, they approach the truth worshipfully, and thus cross over (the river of) death.

Few people understand the importance of the human guru. No scripture can fulfill his function. As my Guru put it, "You can argue with scripture, and it won't answer you. But a living guru can set you straight on anything you misunderstand." What he mentioned above all, however, was the guru's subtle assistance inwardly, whether in the form of guidance or of needed inner strength and blessings. Many people misunderstand the role of the guru, imagining that he needs only to be a wise teacher, competent in spiritual matters and familiar with the common pitfalls on the way. As we said earlier, it is not uncommon for true gurus in India to preserve *maun*, or complete silence. A true guru's teaching is, above all, by transferral of consciousness. His main "job" is to uplift the disciple by his spiritual magnetism.

The disciple's role is to listen, not to argue. If he has doubts or questions, of course, it is important that he express them. The way to do so, in that case, is not challengingly, but with an earnest desire to learn. In this case, indeed, it may be that the more questions he asks, the better. What often happens instead, however, is that the disciple enters the room where the guru is seated, full of questions, but finds in the guru's presence that all his questions have evaporated. The reason is that questioning is often of the intellect, whereas the guru emanates vibrations of superconsciousness. Those vibrations often satisfy the disciple's questions by silently giving him the answers he wants, or by nullifying the very desire to question, since he finds the joy and peace he feels in his guru's presence completely fulfilling.

Gradually, as the disciple tunes into his guru's consciousness, he finds his own consciousness changing, old habit patterns being erased, and new ones being created that open him to superconscious inspiration and guidance. Tendencies that the disciple himself desires intensely to eradicate, but has not been able to by his own efforts, may disappear suddenly, in attunement with the guru, as if they had never existed.

Paramhansa Yogananda said, "The spiritual path is twenty-five percent the disciple's effort; twenty-five percent the guru's effort on his behalf; and fifty percent the grace of God." Because the guru is a channel for God Himself, it may even be said without error that God,

both in and through the guru, accounts for seventy-five
percent of the disciple's spiritual journey.

In every true guru's ashram there are disciples in many
stages of spiritual maturity, from struggling beginners to
those who are highly advanced. One may learn from
their various examples how best to tune in to the guru's
help, inwardly. Those "green" disciples whose focus is
outward follow the guru around as if hoping that his
least word or gesture will somehow be of help to them.
Those who are spiritually more developed tune in
inwardly, and bathe their consciousness in the uplifting
vibrations the guru emanates.

Service to a guru is not the busy fussiness of a restless
person, whether playing the role of nurse or that of
a petitioner eager to catch his attention. It is primarily
inward. Service to the guru means primarily to offer one's
energy and devotion up for cleansing in his fountain-flow
of grace. One serves him more with the right consciousness than with outward actions, though both, depending
on circumstances, can be appropriate. The important
thing is that one's *attitude* be respectful and receptive.

Is it important to be physically with the guru? Not necessarily. Mental attunement is everything. My Guru told
me that even one physical contact may suffice to seal
that bond. There must, however—so he told me—be at
least one outward contact. That contact can occur
through an advanced disciple. Those, however, who
think to form it only by mental acceptance on their part
do not get the same results. The truths here stated are
visible and tangible, and can be tested. They do not
depend on blind faith.

Physical proximity to the guru is, certainly, a great blessing. It carries the disadvantage, however, (unless one is highly advanced) of making the disciple think that he knows the guru well through mere familiarity with his personality. A master needs a body, and therefore also a personality, in order to function in this world at all. He is *not*, however, either that body or that personality.

What will his personality be like? It should go almost without saying that it will be radiant, magnetic, loving, joyful, and overflowing with divine power. Apart from that, however, it will be very individual. Nevertheless, to know and love that personality does not necessarily mean that one is in tune with his inner spirit. Inner attunement is the supreme necessity for receiving to the fullest degree his true grace.

Long-time disciples often cling to attitudes of their own, which may not reflect the guru's attitudes. They may not even be aware of such a discrepancy, since they feel fulfilled, personally, in their attunement with him. They deserve no blame for what might otherwise seem in them a deficiency. Their reason for coming to him in the first place was to find God. Nevertheless, it is unwise to keep *any* door in one's consciousness closed to him by thinking, "This much only will I accept. Beyond that, I have my own ideas, and believe that I must develop my own strength."

(13:26) O Best of the Bharatas (Arjuna), whatever is in existence, know it to have been born of the union of kshetra (Nature and the body) and kshetragya (Spirit and the soul).

(13:27) He sees truly who perceives the Supreme Lord present equally in all beings, the imperishable within the perishing.

Mahatma Gandhi put it beautifully: "In the midst of death, life persists." Life itself, born of Spirit through Nature, is the imperishable principle.

(13:28) Beholding the Divine Presence everywhere, he no longer harms himself by Self-ignorance. (Thus,) he attains the Supreme Goal.
(13:29) That man sees truly who perceives that all actions are performed by Nature (Prakriti) alone, not by the Self (which is above all action).

This last stanza can be given a secondary meaning: The yogi needs to offer all his actions up to God (or Nature), and feel that God (Nature) alone is acting through him. Although this concept is not literally true, since it eliminates the reality of the ego altogether, it helps in the exercise of expanding ego-consciousness from the little self to the infinite Self.

(13:30) When (the yogi) sees all beings as contained in the One, having expanded his consciousness (and sympathy) to include all living beings, he merges into Brahman.

A practical aspect of the teaching in this stanza is something Yogananda said: "Don't think you can love God purely and entirely if you are able to treat even one human being unkindly. The one Lord is equally present in all. To mistreat or to feel ill will toward any of His creatures is, at least to that extent, to separate yourself from God."

(13:31) Arjuna, the Supreme Self, having no beginning and no attributes, even though it dwells in a body (as a realized master), neither acts nor is touched by any action.

(13:32) As the subtle, all-pervading ether is unaffected (by what moves through it), similarly the Self, though pervading the whole body, is never affected by it.

(13:33) O Bharata (Arjuna), as the sun illuminates the whole world, so does the Lord of the Field (God and His reflection as the soul) illuminate the whole body (of Nature, and of man).

(13:34) They go to the Supreme who perceive with the eye of wisdom the distinction between the kshetra and kshetragya, and understand how beings can become liberated from (involvement in) Prakriti.

Thus ends the thirteenth chapter, called "The Field of Battle," of the Upanishad of the holy Bhagavad Gita, in the dialogue between Sri Krishna and Arjuna discussing yoga and the science of God-realization.

CHAPTER TWENTY-SEVEN

TRANSCENDING THE THREE GUNAS

(14:1) The Blessed Lord said: I will declare to you once more that supreme wisdom, higher than any knowledge, in the realization of which all sages, after death, have attained the Final Perfection.

(14:2) Those who attain this wisdom and become established in Me are never reborn again, even when creation itself is re-manifested. Nor are they troubled at the time of Pralaya (cosmic dissolution).

THIS STANZA IS A COMFORT TO THOSE IN WHOM the doubt lingers that, at some future time when the universe is remanifested, they may have to go through the long struggle for liberation all over again!

(14:3) The great Prakriti is My womb in which I plant the animating seed which gives birth to all life.

(14:4) O Son of Kunti (Arjuna), whatever form issues from any womb, its (true) womb (and cosmic source) is Great Prakriti's, and I am its seed-implanting Father.

(14:5) O Mighty-armed (Arjuna)! What binds the

imperishable soul to the body are the three gunas, brought into manifestation by Prakriti.

(14:6) O Sinless One (Arjuna)! Of these gunas, the pure quality of sattwa bestows health and understanding, but (still) causes bondage to the body by making man attached to happiness and (intellectual) knowledge.

Even sattwa guna, though elevating, does not free one from the thought of "I." He thinks, "I am happy. I am insightful. I am healthy." Ego-consciousness is the final limitation; it lingers on after every other bond has been severed. "Chains, though of gold, still bind." To be happy is not binding in itself, of course. What binds one is the thought, "I." It binds to the degree that it separates oneself from others, and becomes more and more limiting to the degree that it doesn't include their happiness, and makes one clutch his own happiness to himself rather than offering it up into the joy of God.

Happiness, in its highest form, is the goal: bliss. Attachment to the thought, however, "I, John, am happy" keeps that thought from expanding to infinity. It is like those disciples we mentioned a few pages back who feel personal fulfillment in whatever progress they have made so far, and are not urgently motivated to climb higher toward spiritual perfection. Thus, although they continue making the right efforts, they always act with the thought, "I have the happiness I struggled so long to reach."

Intellectual knowledge also is a trap, or let us call it, rather, a cul-de-sac on the spiritual voyage. Many spiritually inclined people feel fulfillment in the vicarious knowledge they get from reading and discussing spiritual truths. Intellectual knowledge, however, does not touch a person inwardly. It is not based on direct experience, but only on the thoughts, opinions, and experiences of others.

(14:7) Know (the quality of) rajas to be imbued with passion, which activates strong desires and attachments, and binds one to the body by the intense expectations it develops in him, through his restlessness.

A good example of rajas is the excitement shown by the crowd at a football game: wild exuberance when the "right" team scores a point; rage when the referee makes a "wrong" decision; muttered oaths when scoring is done by the "wrong" team; joyful exhilaration when the "right" team wins; despondency and gloom when victory goes to the "wrong" team. What makes this an especially good example is that it doesn't really matter one way or another who wins or loses. It is only a game.

So also is life itself: only a game! Yet people take it with great seriousness, and invest all their hopes, or all their fears, in certain outcomes that, as far as the soul is concerned, don't even exist!

(14:8) O Bharata (Arjuna)! Know the (darkening) quality of tamas to produce (spiritual) ignorance, which deludes the mind and makes people lazy, heedless, and excessively attracted to subconscious sleep.

Drunkenness is tamasic. Drug addiction is tamasic. Dull-mindedness is tamasic. Stupidity is tamasic. Anything—whether wrong food, habitual inactivity, lack of proper exercise, unwillingness to puzzle anything out or to face any challenging reality, passive acceptance of things as they are however degrading they may be to one's consciousness, and not caring to see them improved: anything that keeps one from mental clarity may rightly be called tamasic.

Tamas is that quality in human nature (born, however, of cosmic nature) which attracts misery of all kinds. It creates such a thick wall around the ego that it causes one to view himself and his own interests as quite unrelated to anybody else's.

In the analogy of the ocean and the waves, tamas represents that part of the wave which protrudes farthest from the ocean bosom. The action of tamas is generated by the "rajasic" middle part of the wave. Tamoguna, in itself, has no power, and only disintegrates to foam after it reaches the peak of its self-expression. In the flow of energy in the spine, tamoguna is the downward pull of matter-attachment, after it reaches the point where it no longer seeks anything actively, but rather clings blindly to whatever material thing or condition the ego insists on as being "mine, and no one else's."

(14:9) Sattwa attaches one to happiness; rajas, to activity; and tamas, by stifling discrimination (which gives "solution-consciousness"), submerges one in difficulties.

Sattwa guna uplifts the consciousness. Rajas keeps it involved outwardly. Tamas dulls it to the point where questions of right and wrong don't even arise. Sattwa guna, however, if it hasn't at least a touch of rajas, may make one passively happy, and therefore too susceptible to falling again from its elevated state into relative inertia. And so the wheel keeps turning. There are three aspects to rajas: upwardly directional, non-directional except on the same plane, and downwardly directional. Though rajas spurs one to activity, that activity can be self-raising or self-debasing. To fulfill one's duty conscientiously is to act under the influence of sattwa-rajas.

Action, on the other hand, that is directed only toward self-fulfillment, under the influence of desire and attachment, may lead in any direction. If one learns, by such action, to see and appreciate that others, too, have their needs, then even selfish activity can lead upward, toward a freer consciousness. But if one determinedly *excludes* the needs of others from one's own struggle for self-fulfillment, his consciousness will shrink inward upon itself, and his energy will move downward in the spine into the lower chakras.

(14:10) In some persons, sattwa is predominant, holding in abeyance rajas and tamas; in others, rajas prevails rather than sattwa or tamas; and in still others, tamas obscures both sattwa and rajas.

All men, it must be understood, are a mixture of the three gunas, even as a wave has three parts: that which is closest to the ocean bosom; the middle part, which pushes the wave higher; and the crest, at which point the ocean itself may not seem even relevant.

Saints, who of course manifest primarily sattwa guna, nevertheless demonstrate the tamoguna aspect of their nature when they draw the curtain of sleep over their consciousness, or when resting briefly from sattwic activities. Saints show the rajas in their nature, also, when they strive for the well-being of others, or when they simply relax by telling jokes and laughing.

Worldly people, intent on their own ego-fulfillment, nevertheless show signs of sattwa when they help others—even their own children, perhaps, to grow up and seek success in their lives. They show tamas not only when they sleep or rest excessively, but also when they shun any duty as "too much trouble."

Dull-minded, *tamasic* people show the rajas in their nature when they bestir themselves to accomplish *anything*. They show sattwa when they express appreciation for *anything*—or even when they ask themselves idly, concerning life, "Is it really worth it?" (For in the very asking they tend to hold their minds upward, however briefly, and even if only in exasperation!)

When trying to help people, or to teach youngsters, it would be well to remember that one can only advance by stages. To urge sattwic attitudes, for example, on someone who is basically tamasic would be a waste of energy, and would be absurd. If one tried to get him to meditate, he would only sleep or drift off into a subconscious torpor. Meditation is not for everyone. Nor is even selfless virtue. Ask a tamasic person to do something selfless, and he won't do anything at all! Ask a rajasic person to "live more in the Self," and he'll look around to see what he can grab for himself.

A seed cannot suddenly become a tree. Every human being needs to grow from whatever stage he has reached at present. Instead of expecting overnight perfection on the spiritual path, one must work realistically with the tools he has at present. The seed will grow if it is regularly watered. That watering process, for a devotee, is daily meditation and constantly practicing the presence of God.

(14:11) When the light of discrimination shines through all of a person's sense gates, it is clear that sattwa predominates in him.

The sattwic person hears goodness and purity in all things, sees it reflected in all things, finds reminders of God in everything that he feels, tastes, and smells. What he is in himself, that he projects outward onto the world around him.

(14:12) When a person shows greed, restless activity, and selfish motivation, rajas predominates in his nature.

The rajasic person views everything in terms of what he might get out of it for his own fulfillment. The "gates of his senses" are clogged with the mental toxins of desire. He sees a beautiful mountain brook and thinks only, "how much electrical power could I harness from this flowing water to make me rich?" He sees a beautiful painting and asks only, "Monetarily, what is it worth?" He hears beautiful music and thinks only, "It needs a more sensual beat." He tastes delicious fruit, and thinks, "It needs more spicing." And so it goes for him with every sensory experience.

(14:13) When a person's consciousness is dark, lazy, neglectful of duty, and inclined to understand nothing rightly, tamas is his dominant guna.

The "gates of the senses" in such people are blocked with impurities. Everything, to them, has sexual or gustatory or other grossly material innuendoes. They see, hear, and speak only evil. To tell them to be better than they are would be an exercise in futility. The best that can be done for them is to try to get them into good company. Otherwise, the best one can do *about* them is simply to avoid their company.

(14:14) A person who, at death, has sattwa predominant in him rises to those high regions where dwell the knowers of truth.

The moment of death is all-important in everybody's life. Therefore Krishna devotes many stanzas of the Bhagavad Gita to that sacred moment. One's thoughts at that time reflect the kind of life he has lived. He must, however, make an extra effort then to keep his consciousness uplifted. Even masters, who always know the hour of their death, quite commonly experience a certain trepidation in the stark awareness that everything they have known in this life will soon be snatched away from them irrevocably. This doesn't mean they are attached. It would be truer to say that they have simply become *accustomed*.

My Guru told me that when he last saw his own guru in the flesh, shortly before that great master's death, someone said something to him like, "I'll see you shortly in Kidderpore." For a moment the Master's hand shook, and he cried with unaccustomed force, "I go to Kidderpore no more!" A moment later he was once more inwardly calm and non-attached.

The veil cast by *maya*, however, is heavy. Even masters must make a conscious effort to cast off its last lingering traces in their consciousness.

When death comes to you, therefore, make a serious effort to sever the cords of attachment that bind you to this life. With the thicker cords, mentally apply a sharp axe to them. With the thinner ones, mentally use a sharp knife to slice through and discard the knots they've formed in your heart. Cast them away from you vigorously, and try not to think of them again.

Begin with the most tamasic-seeming of your desires and attachments. Give them firmly to God, and tell yourself, "All I've gained from this attachment is misery. I gladly give it away!" Affirm then, mentally, "I am free in myself!"

Proceed upward to those bonds which, being rajasic, are thinner and less able to hold you down, keeping you from rising.

Even spiritual people may find a sudden surge of regret at the thought of leaving behind them places and people they've loved, or at least have grown used to. Keep in mind that love is a link between people; it draws them together repeatedly, until their affection merges at last in the great ocean of divine love. However sincere a devotee you've been, however, make an extra effort, when death comes, to focus on God alone.

(14:15) A person who has rajas predominant in him at death is reborn among those with strong egoic attachment to activity. One who at death, however, is permeated with tamas is reborn in the womb of someone who is steeped in delusion (and in the family, environment, and objective circumstances that promote delusion).

There are many grades of people, of course, in all of the three categories. A sattwic person may be a saint, but even saints are of different grades ranging from those who have dedicated their lives to the spiritual search to those who have realized its goal. Only those saints who have transcended ego-consciousness become *jivan muktas*—freed, that is to say, while still living in the body, even if that freedom comes only at the moment of death. Others must return to earth, bound by the cords (silken, in their case) of past karma.

Rajasic people also may be categorized as being of many types. Essentially, there are upward-moving and downward-moving people, as well as those, of course, who are horizontally motile: neither good nor bad, but merely restless.

Tamasic people, finally, come in categories ranging from the merely stupid to the actively evil. Souls who descend from higher levels of expression to actively expressing evil may even indulge in dark practices like black magic and Satanism.

We mentioned earlier that there are worlds, and even whole galaxies, where one or another of the three gunas predominates. People may ask with seeming reasonableness, "How can even a master know anything about distant galaxies?" The answer is, in samadhi, he is already **there**! Once the ego has been transcended, the only real barrier to omnipresence is demolished.

The residents of sattwic galaxies live an ideal, though still material, existence. They live long lives amid beautiful surroundings. The veil between the material and the astral universes is pierced easily.

The rajasic galaxies are like our own, filled with beings who strive incessantly to fulfill their desires. Such galaxies abound with restlessness, dissatisfaction, and anxiety. Their inhabitants "have it good," however, compared to those in the tamasic galaxies, where ferocious beasts prowl in ceaseless search of prey, and cannibalism is common among human beings. There, all is warfare, conflict, violent emotions, primitive conditions, and dullness of mind.

A question naturally arises: Are beings on other planets similar in appearance to ourselves? Biologists would say, "Impossible! Evolution is completely accidental." Paramhansa Yogananda explained, however, that this world is an imitation, on a grosser level, of the subtler astral world. The shape of the human body is determined at an even subtler level: the causal. It is reminiscent, in gross form, of the star in the spiritual eye with its five points. In man's case, when he extends his arms to the side, stands with his legs outspread, these four limbs, plus the head, form a replica of that star. Self-aware beings, far from being the outcome of pure accident, follow a prototype established already in the astral and causal universes.

Another question arises: Does each different material world *necessarily* reflect *only* one of the three qualities? The answer is, Of course not! The gunas appear everywhere mixed—always, however, in the same relationship to one another. Were not great masters, for example, born on Earth, who, here, would be inspired to seek spiritual development? The longing might exist, but spiritual hope would be crushed by the all-too-evident, grosser realities of life.

Souls are drawn back to earth—that is to say, of course, to the material plane—to places where the conditions reflect whatever consciousness they've developed so far.

People in this world express the doubt—as many have indeed done—"But if reincarnation is a fact, and the soul is not created for the first time with every new baby, why is it that the Earth's population is increasing? Where do all those souls come from?" The answer is, of course, "From everywhere!"

(14:16) It is said (by sages) that the fruits of sattwic action are harmony and purity (of heart and mind); that those of rajasic action are pain and suffering; and that the fruits of tamasic action are the various manifestations of spiritual ignorance (dullness of mind, slothfulness, stupidity, and general helplessness in confrontation with life's difficulties).

These results of the various kinds of activity, born of the diverse qualities, act as spurs toward eventual enlightenment. Alas, man's inventiveness in protecting himself against self-improvement amounts almost to genius! Rajasic people often—instead of working out rajasic complexes in themselves—hate sattwic people merely for their very harmony and purity. Tamasic people resent those with high energy, seeing their energy as a personal insult to their own lack of it. Tamasic (as well as rajasic) people, again, cannot bring themselves to believe that there really are sattwic people. They attribute to those who are good every imaginable shifty motive. If they fail in the attempt to bring good people down, they persecute and even slay them, as the Jews treated Jesus Christ in his time.

(14:17) Wisdom arises from sattwa; lust and avarice, from rajas; and (the darkness of spiritual) ignorance, from tamas.

It is important to realize that although each person is unique as an individual, the *qualities* he manifests are universal. The words of a sentimental song that was in vogue some years ago in the West managed somehow to express a truth that is eternal: "There will never, ever be another you." It is equally important to realize, however, that the "*you*" (the personality) about whom the song was written had nothing to do with the truly eternal "you." The qualities, or gunas, belong to no one. They are simply manifestations of Prakriti, and can attach themselves to anyone, seeming verily for a time to define him.

The wisdom of sattwa can become in time, *in the same person,* the lust and avarice of rajas or the dark ignorance of tamas. No quality is or can be anyone's *possession*, and is never his definition. The qualities, or gunas, only reside in people temporarily. One might describe the gunas as eternal wanderers. Any quality a human being manifests can be increased, diminished, or eliminated altogether, but it can never, in any way, be identified with who he really is, inside.

And—the question begs to be asked—who is he really, inside? He is Satchidananda!

The war of Kurukshetra, and Krishna's counsel to Arjuna to fight, is founded on this eternal truth. On the Pandavas' side, it is a war against qualities that cannot ever in any case—since they are universal and eternal—be slain, for they cannot be identified with anybody. On the Kauravas' side, it is a war to protect territory seized by trickery and held onto with arrogant contempt for the well-being of the populace. When lust and avarice are transformed into wisdom, they are "slain," in a sense, but nothing has been lost. The transformation has made use of all the same "materials"—energy and consciousness—and has simply dressed them up in new clothing.

Thus, the best persons, if they live wrongly, can acquire worse, then the worst attributes. And the worst persons can in time, if they live rightly, acquire the best attributes. The qualities, or gunas, themselves are abstractions. The individual they attack, harass, or bless is the host reality, and therefore is more permanent. He too, of course, is only a dream-actor in the cosmic drama. His existence as an egoic self is, in eternity, impermanent—except as a memory, which remains even after he has achieved final union with

God. There is nothing permanent or self-defining, however, about any quality.

What the Gita is pointing out here is that the gunas can be manipulated. If you act in a certain way, you will attract the guna belonging to that kind of activity. If you act in another way, you'll attract the guna belonging, again, to that different kind of activity.

The less you allow your ego to identify itself with any quality, the more you can pick and choose the qualities you'd like to manifest, and can thus learn to act appropriately under any circumstance. If you want to be happy, work at developing sattwic qualities. Remember, no quality is "you." That deeper "you" never changes inside, and can never be identified with anything—least of all with that little self, the ego.

Happiness, if you manifest it by living a sattwic life, is real, though it doesn't define you. It should inspire you, however, to rise above even that satisfaction into the supernal bliss of the Spirit. Otherwise, if you become satisfied *with* yourself, you'll only fall—once again!— owing to the fact of having reaffirmed your ego. True joy is not tied to the petty thought, "I." It is possible to have it only in perfect freedom. There is no possibility of a fall from the state of complete ego-liberation. This state comes with full Self-realization.

The way to transcend the gunas is different for each guna, and different for every individual also, depending on the particular mixture of gunas that manifests in him. It is useless to try to shrug off the dark and heavy manifestations of tamoguna. They cannot be transmuted: They must simply be endured, and gradually worn down in contact with other people—like the rounding of pebbles in a riverbed by constant friction against other pebbles. It is at the other end of the spectrum that transcendence becomes truly possible, though rajoguna can at least make people *want* to be calmer, more peaceful, and happy *in themselves*. One can ascend the ladder of spiritual evolution only by patience, and by accepting what *is* as a present reality. The almost-transparent veil that covers delusion with sattwa guna can, like an illustration used in the Gita earlier, be blown away like smoke by a mere puff of wind: A little meditation soon uncovers the bright fire of wisdom behind its smoke screen.

We see here the importance of having a true guru. He alone, from his level of highest wisdom, with—in addition—his clear insight into your nature, and with his commitment to helping you as his disciple to find God, can be relied upon to show you the way through the minefield of the bewildering mix of qualities you manifest. With his help you will emerge onto the plateau of wholly sattwic qualities, and then will understand how to pass beyond even those elevated qualities to perfect freedom from the last traces of ego-consciousness in infinite consciousness.

Even to be in tune mentally with the guru can help you to understand, every time you come to the point where you might make a mistake. What you will feel will be a certain nervousness in the heart's feelings. When you are doing right, on the other hand, you will feel the guru's calm inner endorsement and approval in your heart.

We see here again the utter importance, on the spiritual path, of having a true guru. Few people even appreciate that need. And few, even after getting a true guru (which means also being accepted by him), have the faith needed to follow him implicitly. True faith in the guru is not passive, nor is it an indication of ignorance. Disciples blessed with that faith soon emerge from the confines of ego into the spotless skies of divine consciousness.

In the annals of spirituality, there are a few outstanding examples of obedience. It must be said, on this point, that a true guru makes every effort to ensure that his disciple's obedience will be both deliberate (free-willed) and intelligent, and will not be a matter of blind or merely submissive acquiescence.

Swami Shankara was standing on the other side of a river from a close disciple of his. My Guru once described to me what happened. I still remember his understated facial expression, the subtle hand gesture, and the quiet tone of voice with which he related this part of the story.

Shankara called gently to his disciple, "Come over here." Most people would have looked around for a boat. This disciple, however, placed a foot unhesitatingly on the water. The moment he did so, a lotus leaf appeared beneath his foot and supported it. With each successive step another leaf appeared. The disciple quickly reached the other side. From then on, he became known as Padmapada ("Lotusfeet").

Sadashiva (who was mentioned earlier in this book) was another case. Both these stories indicated perfect obedience, and the grace of the guru. As a young man in his guru's ashram, Sadashiva was a brilliant conversationalist. He often bested in discussion men much older than he. One day, he discomfited an older man by pointing out the inadequacies in his arguments.

His guru demanded somewhat impatiently (or so his words seemed), "When will you learn to hold your tongue?" His disciple's penchant for showing off his intellectual brilliance was a manifestation not only of intelligence, but, less laudably, of ego.

"Instantly, Master, if I have your grace!" came the response. From that day forward, Sadashiva never spoke another word. He became widely known as a *mauni* of unbroken silence.

(14:18) Those established in sattwa rise upward; those immersed in rajas remain in the middle regions; those steeped in tamas sink to the lower spinal centers.

We have already discussed the gunas relative to the direction of energy and consciousness in the spine. In yoga, the energy is inward. In people who live in ego-consciousness, filled with desire and attachment, their flow of energy is outward. The consciousness of sattwic people, being focused more at the point between the eyebrows (the frontal lobe of the brain), is more centered in the clarity of the intellect and understanding. That of rajasic people being centered primarily in the emotions, is ruled by likes and dislikes, hopes and disappointments, ambitions and devastating failures. The consciousness of tamasic people, being centered in the lowest three chakras, is focused exaggeratedly on physical enjoyments and "rewards": cruelty, complete sex-addiction, drunkenness, and the pleasure of telling lies for the sole purpose of creating confusion.

(14:19) The seer who perceives no other active agent in the universe but the three gunas (that is, who sees human action as motivated by the gunas rather than by individual choice), and perceives that (motionless consciousness) which is higher than the gunas, enters My being.

(14:20) Having transcended the three qualities of Nature, which are the cause of physical embodiment, one is released from the suffering (attendant upon) birth, old age, and death, and attains immortality.

(14:21) Arjuna said: What signs distinguish one who has transcended the three gunas? What is his behavior? In what ways does he reveal his transcendence?

(14:22) The Blessed Lord said: O Pandava (Arjuna), he neither dislikes nor longs for any manifestation of the gunas, whether illumination (upliftment), unceasing activity, or dull ignorance;—

(14:23) unconcerned either way, unshaken (by any expression he sees of the qualities), viewing them as active throughout the universe, he remains ever centered calmly in the Self.

(14:24) Unaffected (personally) by joy or sorrow, praise or blame, appraising equally a clod of earth, a stone, and gold, he doesn't distinguish among others (according to) whether they treat him well or badly.

(14:25) Uninfluenced by honor or dishonor, equally (gracious) toward friend and foe, free from any motivation of personal ambition: these signs accompany one who has transcended the (three) qualities of Nature.

(14:26) He who serves Me with undeviating love and

devotion transcends the gunas, and is qualified to become (one with) Brahman.

(14:27) For I am the basis of everything there is: the Imperishable Brahman, in whom reside the eternal Law and unending Bliss.

Krishna has been speaking of himself as personal. How can the personal be the basis (or, as some have it, the abode) of the Infinite Brahman? Only in the sense, surely, that the devotee perceives the Divine first through the guru, as if through a window: personal first, then impersonal.

Thus ends the fourteenth chapter, called "Transcending the Three Gunas," of the Upanishad of the holy Bhagavad Gita, in the dialogue between Sri Krishna and Arjuna discussing yoga and the science of God-realization.

CHAPTER TWENTY-EIGHT

THE YOGA OF THE SUPREME PERSON

(15:1) The Blessed Lord said: They (the wise) speak of the imperishable Ashvatta tree, with its roots above and its branches below. Its leaves are the Vedic hymns. Whosoever understands this tree of life knows (the meaning of) the Vedas.

THE MYTHICAL-SEEMING TREE DESCRIBED HERE IS the human body. Its trunk is the spine. Its "roots above" are the rays of energy both emanating from and nourishing the brain and body through the *sahasrara*, the "thousand-petaled lotus" at the top of the head. The tree's branches, "below," are the many-branched nervous system.

The "Vedic hymns" are the vibrations of sensory knowledge transmitted to the brain from the senses by way of the nervous system. As the sap of a tree nourishes all its parts, including the leaves, so the life force flowing outward from the spine through the nerves to the senses thereby enlivens their fluttering "leaves" of response to the vibrations of sight, hearing, smell, taste, and touch.

The soul, as has been explained before, is encased in three such bodies, the subtlest, or causal, being the innermost, the one enclosing that (the astral body) coming next, and the outermost sheath being the physical.

Why is the body called imperishable? Because its origins lie in Brahman, the Supreme Spirit, and its prototype lies in Prakriti (Nature). The physical body dies, but the conscious desires directing its creation re-form the body again and again. The astral body, too—once that world becomes one's "home"—is absorbed periodically into the causal body, and again remanifested—owing, in this case also, to conscious desires for astral enjoyments. Even when the causal body is absorbed into the Infinite, the creative principle behind the manifestation of the three bodies is eternal.

What makes man's tree of life "imperishable," beyond the fact that it manifests that eternal creative principle, is that his body, uniquely among animal forms, has a nervous system, spine, and brain refined enough to render him capable of realizing Brahman.

Krishna's use of the Ashvatta tree as an image owes to the fact that this tree, the *peepul* or fig, has an abundance of leaves. The "leaves" on the human "tree of life" are similarly abundant: the multifarious vibrations of sensory involvement (sounds, colors, tastes, smells, and touch sensations) that are available to man with his greater ability (more developed than in the lower animals) to enjoy and appreciate. The lower animals are contented with very few sensory pleasures. Man's taste for these is never-ending. Thus, even the leaves of that "imperishable" tree are large and numerous, as the delights people derive from them are never-ending.

Human hair is a condensation of rays of astral energy that surround the brain. Yogis sometimes allow their hair to grow long so as to draw more energy from the cosmos to the brain.

(15:2) Its branches extend below and above, nurtured by the gunas. Its buds are the sense objects. Small roots extend also downward into the world of men, impelling man to action.

The metaphor of the tree is beautiful. It becomes problematic here, however, in asking us to visualize the branches extending not only downward but upward, and the roots extending not only upward but downward. The mind wants visualizations to simplify and clarify. Here, the visualization is complex and somewhat confusing. No metaphor, in any case, is exact. The image of the ocean and its waves has the disadvantage that the waves, as they increase the ego and the quality of tamas, *rise* from their source in the ocean, whereas in fact to return to our source in Spirit, and to develop sattwa guna, our consciousness must rise upward, not descend. Downward movement in the spine increases negativity. Another problem—almost too trivial to mention—is that, to water the seed of spirituality with faith, the water flows *downward*, not *upward*, whereas to water our consciousness with faith demands an *upward* flow of energy. The problem, again, with making spiritual progress is that one doesn't really *progress* at all: One simply becomes whole in himself.

One might pursue this point further, but—to what avail? A metaphor must simply be accepted lightly for what it is: a mental crutch. No image will "stand up" under too-careful scrutiny!

Let us, then, focus our attention less on the upside-downness of the tree than on the function of its roots and branches. The branches indicate the extensions of consciousness as expressions of the gunas—some of them reaching back (upward?) toward their roots; others stretching sideways; still others reaching downward toward the earth, but *away from* the roots, which are nourished from above.

The leaves begin as buds, then spread out to assume their large, leafy form. As buds they symbolize the sense objects of sight, hearing, smell, taste, and touch. As leaves they bestow the full-blown, variegated enjoyment of those sense objects.

The "roots," which draw their principal energy from the cosmos, also draw life-force from the response of consciousness to likes and dislikes in the world. These secondary roots keep the life flowing ever back toward the re-creation and perpetuation of this tree of life that constitutes our humanity.

(15:3,4) The true nature of this tree—its beginning, its end, its continuity—cannot be understood by ordinary men. The sage, having felled this Ashvatta tree at its roots with the axe of non-attachment, thinks, "I seek refuge only in the Primeval Purusha,

from whom issues all creation (rather than under the protection of any tree)." He seeks the Supreme Goal, from which there is no need to return.

The wise man perceives Cosmic consciousness as the beginning, continuity, and end of the tree of eternal life.

(15:5) Those reach the eternal goal who crave no human honor, who are free from infatuation having severed the bonds of attachment, who are untouched by the pairs of opposites such as pleasure and pain, and who are established in the Self within.

(15:6) Where shines neither sun nor moon nor the light of fire, there lies My abode; those who reach it pass beyond birth and death.

The sun in the body represents the light of the spiritual eye—or, alternatively, the *sahasrara* (the "thousand-rayed lotus") at the top of the head. The moon represents the reflection of that light in the ego, or *agya chakra* (the medulla oblongata), and therefore represents the human ego itself. Ego-consciousness is, in fact, centered in the medulla. Fire is the life energy in the body, burning as self-control in the *manipura chakra* or lumbar center. In finding God one goes beyond these differentiations of consciousness into absolute oneness.

(15:7) An eternal part of Myself, manifesting as a living soul in the world of humanity, attracts to itself the six senses, inclusive of mind, all of which rest in Prakriti.

(15:8) When the Lord as the jiva (the individualized soul) takes on a body, he takes with him (into it) the mind and the senses. When he leaves the body, he takes them with him and leaves even as the breeze wafts scents away from their dwellings (as in flowers).

Thus the jiva, still possessing an astral body, carries with it its capacity for sense-perception and its individuality.

(15:9) Thus, he still (possesses and) enjoys the senses of sight, hearing, smell, taste, and touch.

(15:10) His departure from the body, like his abiding in it, is not perceived by the ignorant (who see only the *effect* of his presence: the body itself). It takes the eye of wisdom to perceive him (as he is).

(15:11) Yogis who strive for liberation see His reality in themselves, but those who, even though striving, have not purified (their hearts) and lack discipline, see Him not.

(15:12) The light of the sun, which illuminates the world, of the moon, and of fire—know that their radiance comes (ultimately) from Me.

(15:13) Permeating the earth with My effulgence, I support all beings; through the watery moon, I nourish all plants.

The sun gives energy to the world. The moon, which is its reflection, represents the sap, blood, and life fluids in all creatures, permitting that energy to flow through matter.

(15:14) I am the flame of life in all living creatures. It is I (alone) who manifest as prana and apana, and digest their food.

(15:15) From Me, seated in the hearts of all beings, come all memory and knowledge, and also the loss of these. I am the Goal of knowledge in the Vedas. I am also their Author, and He who knows them.

(15:16) Two beings (purushas) there are in the cosmos: the destructible and the indestructible. Creatures are the destructible. The Kutastha Chaitanya is the indestructible.

This stanza refers to Prakriti manifested as all creatures, and to Kutastha Chaitanya, the vibrationless consciousness at the heart of all manifestation, which informs the universe and cannot be destroyed since it remains unchanged when all creatures are reabsorbed into Spirit.

(15:17) There exists, however, Another—the supreme Self who, permeating the three worlds (the causal, astral, and physical planes), is their Sustainer.

(15:18) I (the Supreme Lord) am beyond the perishable (Prakriti) and am higher than the Imperishable (Kutastha Chaitanya). Therefore, in the (three) worlds and in the Veda (which reflect perfect, intuitive perception) I am proclaimed as Purushottama, the Uttermost Being.

(15:19) Whosoever, freed from delusion, thus knows Me as the Supreme Spirit, knows all (there is to be known), O Descendant of Bharata (Arjuna). He worships Me with his entire being.

(15:20) Herewith, O Sinless One (Arjuna), I have taught you this deepest of all wisdom. Comprehending it, one becomes a sage, having successfully fulfilled all his duties, (even if) he yet continues to perform dutiful actions (in the world).

Thus ends the fifteenth chapter, called "The Yoga of the Supreme Person," of the Upanishad of the holy Bhagavad Gita, in the dialogue between Sri Krishna and Arjuna discussing yoga and the science of God-realization.

CHAPTER TWENTY-NINE

THE NATURE OF THE GODLY AND THE DEMONIC

K RISHNA NOW RELATES TWENTY-SIX QUALITIES that ennoble the mind spiritually.

The goal of spiritual progress is, as has been repeatedly emphasized, the transcendence of ego-consciousness in the realization that separateness from other selves, and from the Absolute Self, is the one great delusion from which all other delusions derive. The sense of individuality is rooted in infinity. There is no other reality but the Self: God, the Self of all. In Himself He is ever-conscious, ever-existing, ever-new Bliss. No one created Him: He is self-existent.

A spiritually ennobling quality, therefore, is one that can lift us toward that awareness.

(16:1) The Blessed Lord said: Fearlessness; purity of heart; perseverance (in the acquisition of wisdom and in the practice of meditation); (sattwic) charity; self-restraint; the performance of holy rites (symbolic

self-offering to God and to the devas), service to holy
persons, and *agnihotra* (pouring oblations into the
sacred fire); study of the scriptures; self-discipline;
straightforwardness;—

(16:2) harmlessness; truthfulness; freedom from
anger; renunciation; tranquility; disinclination toward
faultfinding; kindness to all; non-covetousness; gentleness; modesty (not calling attention to oneself);
steadfastness of purpose;—

(16:3) radiance of character; forgiveness; fortitude;
cleanliness; absence of malice; absence of self-
conceit—these qualities, O Descendant of Bharata
(Arjuna), are the endowments of those who are
divinely inclined.

Fearlessness comes with perfect non-attachment. It is
a natural attitude for those who feel they have nothing
to protect. The instinct of self-preservation is, of course,
the fundamental reason for fear. Ego, or the sense of
having a separate individuality and of being different
from all others, gives rise to the instinct of fear. Ego-
consciousness is born of attachment to the body:
Therefore, fear arises from anxiety to protect the body,
and cannot be conquered so long as attachment to the
body lingers.

The more a person's body-consciousness expands—to
include such things as a sense of possessions, a concern
for one's reputation, a sense of personal power or
importance—the greater the likelihood of feeling fear.
Fearlessness, on the other hand, comes from releasing
those attachments—quite possibly in their reverse

order—into the infinite: the desire for personal importance; the desire for power or control over anything or anyone; the desire to be well thought of, admired, and respected above others; attachment to possessions; attachment to bodily health and well-being; and, finally, identification of one's self with the body.

The fast and sure way to develop fearlessness is to love God. By loving Him, one feels ever protected by a force far greater than any power of one's own.

Purity of heart comes when one has removed from his heart any feeling that is foreign to his true nature. Thus, purity begins by removing anything that nourishes his consciousness of ego. This includes, of course, all the motivations for fear that were listed above. Included also must be an absence of selfish or "ulterior" motive. A person who is pure of heart is guileless, and never harbors the slightest wish to make use of anyone without his willing consent. He bears no malice toward others. Indeed, with such purity alone he automatically manifests virtually all the spiritual qualities listed above: absence of malice, harmlessness, forgiveness, truthfulness (selecting these as examples, primarily).

Perseverance (in the acquisition of wisdom and in the practice of meditation) is a distinct quality, demanding the continuous re-application of will power to whatever cause one believes to be right and worthy. In its ever-newly creative outlook, perseverance is different from stubbornness. Stubbornness is a refusal to re-examine the facts or to reappraise one's position with regard to them. Perseverance means not to allow oneself to be dissuaded or diverted from any worthwhile goal, but to meet every difficulty creatively, with new solutions, until one's ends have been achieved.

Thus, perseverance means to be willing to re-examine one's position, if necessary, to correct one's first assumptions, and to seek ever-new avenues by which any worthwhile goal one has may be achieved. It means being firm in the faith that what is right and true *must*, eventually, come to pass, provided one holds firmly to high principle.

Sattwic charity means many things besides alms giving. It means being generous in one's opinions of others owing to the simple realization that all men are basically motivated by the same desire: the attainment of Satchidananda, divine bliss. Most people seek this apotheosis in wrong ways; they do so, however, only out of ignorance. Thus, a charitable attitude must be based on what someone called out from the audience at a children's recital: "Don't be nervous, Susie. We're all your friends!"

When giving alms or helping others materially, make it an important point not ever to convey the impression that you are placing the other person under an obligation. Bear in mind that he, too, must be allowed in his receiving to preserve his sense of dignity and self-worth. Give him something to do for you in exchange for what you give him or do for him. Never try to make him subservient to you. Indeed, his dignity should be placed on a par with your own. Otherwise, to receive gifts can be demeaning, creating at least a *sense* that one has been placed under an obligation, and (sometimes) creating a certain resentment against the giver.

Self-restraint means retaining always, even during times of sense enjoyment, the feeling of being centered inwardly in the Self. This doesn't mean not to enjoy good things, but to realize that the *source* of that enjoyment is not in those things, but in one's own heart. Sadhus and other religiously dedicated people sometimes recommend that one not permit himself to enjoy *anything*. This is a very dry attitude. To neutralize the *vrittis*, or vortices of chitta, as Patanjali recommends, does not mean to *deaden* one's capacity for feeling, but simply to calm one's feeling quality and make it perfectly receptive. There cannot be consciousness without feeling. Indeed, feeling *is* consciousness. Spiritual progress depends on refining the receptivity of feeling. This is possible only when the intuition is calm and therefore pure.

Thus, in any sensory experience—the enjoyment of food, or sex, or anything at all—never give in completely to the sensation. Remain somewhat restrained in every expression of feeling. In this way, self-control will gradually come easily to you, and you'll develop effortless control over the senses.

The performance of sacred rites is enjoined on all spiritual seekers. Listed as a *quality*, it must be understood primarily as an attitude rather than an outward practice. The practice of offering oblations into a sacrificial fire accompanied by Sanskrit mantras that help to attune one with subtle aspects of vibration, and especially with the Cosmic Vibration, AUM, can help one to attain certain definite outward effects, but these effects, one should realize, will be limited to the realm of *maya*; they cannot take one out of *maya* except to the extent that one's practice of them is accompanied by the *thought* of self-offering.

On the other hand, mental self-offering (of heart as well as mind) is the highest sacrifice, and need not be accompanied by any external ritual, the highest benefit of which is only symbolic.

Service to holy persons, notably to the guru, should also be done with the heartfelt intention of receiving his uplifted consciousness into oneself.

Study of the scriptures, again, is not an attitude, but can become so if one takes it to mean *reverence* for the scriptures. Reverence for them will surely lead to the study of them, also.

It is important to be discriminating, however, in one's choice of scripture, for not all writings that are purported to be scripture are founded equally in truth. People often accept as revelation the writings of some well-meaning but spiritually unenlightened person, or of persons less well-meaning but ambitious for personal glory.

Paramhansa Yogananda told the story of someone who wrote a treatise which he wanted to have people consider a scripture. He then buried his document under a tree, and began giving religious discourses. Fifteen years later, affecting to be guided by angels, he was "led," accompanied by a few followers, to that tree, where he dug. There, lo and behold! this "angel-materialized" scripture was "discovered." Thus, a new religion was founded, and although the document itself was later "lost," its copied versions continued to attract a large following.

Other false religions, similarly, have won people by methods other than scrupulous. What was appealed to was people's credulity, not their intuitive discrimination. Accept nothing that doesn't appeal to your highest sense of what is right and true. Even then, be guided by the supportive opinions of the wise. When wise persons in general agree on the spiritual authenticity of a document, that is when—so wisdom dictates—the document can safely be accepted as true scripture.

Self-discipline is included in the advice Krishna gave earlier to be moderate in all ways. Do not "flagellate" yourself, whether literally or figuratively—by depriving yourself, for example, of the sleep you need to remain mentally alert, or by denying your body the life-sustaining elements of a balanced diet.

Straightforwardness means to be completely honest and truthful in all your dealings. Any corners that you "cut" in this respect will only weaken your powers of accomplishment, and will also weaken your ability to persevere to final success in any worthwhile undertaking. Both honesty and truthfulness harness one's power to the infinitely greater power of the universe. It is—to use a simile we've found helpful before—to turn that greater reality into something like the sounding board of a musical instrument, augmenting one's own efforts by making them "resonate" with the vibration of infinity.

Harmlessness is far from being ineffectual: It results in inviting the sympathy, cooperation, and support of all who tune in to your ideals.

Harmlessness is not passive, as it may at first appear. Once one has removed his ego's natural impulse to wrest from life what it wants, he achieves his goals effortlessly, often (though not necessarily) with the help of others.

Truthfulness might be included under "straightfor-wardness." It has, however, the further connotation of not *wishing* reality to be other than it is. Be truthful with yourself. Don't try to pretend even to yourself that your motives have been, perhaps, better than they may actually have been. Only when we face reality *as it is* can we begin to *make* it what it ought to be. If, for instance, we have spoken rudely, we can only become gentler in our speech after we've faced frankly the possibility that we may, in fact, have spoken harshly on occasion.

Freedom from anger comes from not desiring any-thing, whether things or "right" behavior in others. Anger creates a disturbance and an unsettling influence in the brain. Righteous anger, of course, can be a virtue, but it is so especially if directed by calm will power through the spiritual eye. Because the point between the eyebrows is the seat of will power in the body, energy directed through there can help to set the wheels turn-ing for necessary change.

Renunciation has been defined by Krishna as being the transcendence, especially, of selfish or otherwise ego-inspired motive. Thus, it means also *nishkam karma*: action without personal desire for the fruits of action. Renunciation means giving up all one's *attachments*. The man who said, "My children died, my wife left me, I've been fired from my job, and my house just burned to the ground. I've decided to renounce the world," hadn't yet quite the right idea of renunciation. As my param-guru Swami Sri Yukteswar remarked wryly, "That man hasn't renounced the world: The world has renounced him!" Renunciation must be of the heart, primarily.

Tranquility means in all circumstances to be centered calmly in the inner Self. When others are agitated (and you might be, too), tell yourself, "Things will be quite normal again in a few hours, or days, or another week—or another month—or another year." However long the period, it *will* end. The reason hell itself is described in some religions as eternal is that when suffering comes it *seems* everlasting. Nothing is permanent, however. All is in flux. All is change. No wave remains at its peak; no wave trough remains forever depressed. The wise man, in the face of both fulfillment and disappointment, remains unaffected and ever tranquil in himself.

Disinclination toward faultfinding is, again, a willingness to accept situations and people as they are. This does *not* mean one should never try to improve things, or to help others to improve themselves. Whatever good one does in the world, however, will be more effective if all of one's efforts are directed positively, and not in mere *reaction* to anything.

Kindness to all is not compassion, as some people translate the Sanskrit word *"daya."* It would be a distortion of genuine feeling to feel *compassionate* toward someone who had treated you unkindly, for it would imply condescension, as though you were looking down on him from above. In kindness there is no pride: In compassion there might be, especially if you saw to it that others realized how compassionate you were. Kindness means the simple acceptance of others in recognition that they are all, like you, striving for self-improvement.

Non-covetousness means not wanting anything that is not yours by right.

Gentleness means not trying to force anyone to act in any way contrary to his free will.

Modesty is well expressed as not trying to draw attention to oneself. It is not the same thing as backing bashfully, so to speak, into the limelight. That is false modesty. True modesty in dress means not to appear either over- or under-dressed, but (out of regard for the feelings of others) to dress simply and in good taste. Modesty in demeanor means not to push oneself ahead of others, nor yet to exasperate others by excessive *disclaimers* of one's own worthiness. Modesty of speech means to speak only loudly enough to enable others to hear; not to speak too much about oneself; and to show respect for (and, if possible, interest in!) the opinions of others.

Steadfastness of purpose was allied, above, to perseverance. The two qualities are similar, but are also different. Perseverance (as indicated in the Gita) means not to allow anything to dissuade one from his high, spiritual ideals. Both perseverance in the quest for truth, and steadfastness in a lower purpose, are often mistaken by scatter-minded persons, or by those with different interests, for mere stubbornness. One should always be ready to consider the possibility that one may have been mistaken, and in that case to change his direction instantly. However, granted that one's purpose and ideals are right, shows virtue to stand by them steadfastly.

Radiance of character is more an attribute than a quality, but it shows in the eyes and demeanor of those who are inspired by superconscious insight.

Forgiveness is often merely verbal. One may *want* to forgive, but the thought of the offense that needs forgiveness may continue to rankle in his heart. Forgiveness should therefore be coupled with the word, *forget*. Forgetfulness too, however, can be a mistake if what is forgiven is an act that might recur. If, for example, a person's behavior has revealed a flaw in his character—betrayal, for example, or disloyalty—it would be wise to keep that flaw in mind in future dealings with him, until the flaw has been convincingly corrected. One may accept that person even as a friend, and forgive him, but one should also bear in mind his potential until adequate proof has been given of its eradication. Most people (indeed, all of them, except the wise) have flaws. It would be a bleak world if one carried always the feeling that no one could be trusted! One should also ask himself, introspectively, "And what about me? Haven't I, too, things to overcome? Let me therefore be lenient toward others." Nevertheless, when someone shows his true nature, one should accept him for what he is (forgive him, in other words), but behave toward him in future with appropriate awareness and common sense. Forgiveness means, in the last analysis, giving a person a chance to reform but also recognizing that an apology is not in itself the same thing as reform.

Fortitude, or patience (the two words are often paired), means to keep the compass of your intention ever pointed toward the polestar of high purpose, no matter how many influences intrude to deflect it.

Cleanliness is an outward reflection of an ordered mind. When someone keeps his person clean—either his body or his clothing—it is an indication of self-respect as well as of regard for the feelings of others. One time in America Paramhansa Yogananda met a man who was unkempt, filthy, and seemingly indifferent to what anyone thought of him (though quite possibly this was a pose intended to shock others, which would have shown definite interest in their opinions!). Yogananda asked him, "Why do you appear like that?"

"I'm a renunciate!" announced the other, proudly.

"But you've become attached in a new way," the Master replied, "—to disorder!"

Malice is an all-too-common flaw of those who think the world owes them something—or anything. *Absence of malice*, like kindness and forgiveness, enables us to accept—indeed, to smile upon—the world without judgment, accepting whatever is as, simply, what it is.

Absence of self-conceit may be translated as *humility*, or the *absence of pride*. Humility, however, is often taken as self-abasement, and as a consciousness of personal inadequacy—not before God, which is right, normal, and in fact obvious—-but before other people. Humility is not an inferiority complex! Self-conceit is often present, moreover, where pride is absent. It is the fertile soil in which the seeds of pride, given enough fresh circumstances, can sprout, grow, and flourish.

Self-conceit, however, means to *entertain*, and not merely to have, certain feelings about oneself. A famous singer, for example, would be deficient in something if he didn't *know* he was good at singing, and was famous for it. If he *entertains* that thought, however, and lets it feed his self-definition and make him think it *matters* in the great scheme of things: *that* is self-conceit.

Krishna now gives the nature and destiny of those with the opposite qualities.

(16:4) Vainglory, arrogance, self-conceit, wrathfulness, harshness, and ignorance—these, O Pandava (Arjuna), mark the person whose nature is demonic.

Vainglory is ostentation, boastfulness, extreme vanity, and an exaggerated sense of the importance of anything one does. It is setting oneself on top of an anthill and crying out, "I have conquered Mount Everest!"

Arrogance is an exaggerated opinion of one's own importance relative to the merits of anyone else.

Self-conceit has already been defined and explained. Essentially what it means is holding an almost-invisible hair so close to one's eye that it seems as thick as a tree trunk.

Wrathfulness is a *tendency* to lose one's temper, with or without good reason, because one lacks control over the presumption that people and circumstances ought to be other than they are.

Harshness comes as a result of insensitivity to the needs and feelings of others, and of a wish to impose one's own feelings on the world around him.

Ignorance, finally, means having no notion as to what is true or false, real or unreal. It doesn't necessarily mean lack of education, though certainly it indicates a lack of refined feelings. Ultimately what it means is to mistake what is not for what is. It means *spiritual*, not merely intellectual, ignorance.

What Krishna has outlined are the qualities of an *asura*, or demon. Such beings inhabit not only the regions of hell, but may be found in abundance, in human form, here on earth.

(16:5) Divine qualities lead to liberation. Demonic ones lead to (continued and increasing) bondage. Fear not, however, Arjuna, you are endowed with divine qualities.

It may seem strange that Arjuna should need this reassurance. No doubt he didn't. Yet every devotee who wants to be completely sincere with himself, who knows the ego's seemingly infinite capacity for self-deception, and who has discovered how difficult it is to see oneself as he really is, must ask himself sometimes, "Am I as I should be?" It may often happen that others criticize him—especially if he is trying earnestly, as they are not, to become spiritual. Thus, it is a consolation which every devotee should take to heart. "Krishna," he should reflect, "offered this reassurance even to so great a devotee as Arjuna! And he said that even an evil man who tries steadfastly to become good should be counted among the virtuous. Need I worry, really, as long as I try with all sincerity to improve myself?"

(16:6) There are two types of men in this world: the divine and the demonic. I have described at length the divine. Now hear Me, O Son of Pritha (Arjuna), on (the subject of) the demonic.

There are in the universe, as we've seen, not two but three qualities (sattwa, rajas, and tamas) in a varied mixture of expressions. There are at the same time, however, only *two* directions of movement: upward, and downward—or, more exactly, upward in the spine and downward in it. The *quality* of rajas is in between, and might be described as asking, in a vacillating way: "Where to, next?" As the sattwic qualities are the upward answer to that question, the demonic ones are the answer to the downward.

(16:7) The demonic do not know the meaning of right action, and do not know when to refrain from acting.

When moved by strong urges, whether sexual or covetous or prejudicial to others, they act without consideration for the possible consequences.

(16:8) They say: "The world is without fundamental morality. There are no abiding truths. There is no God. There is no system in the universe; it is all accidental. There is no aim in life, apart from lustful delight."

Their "philosophy," often expressed with a leering grin, is, "Where sexual passion is concerned, conscience isn't an issue."

(16:9) Feeble of intellect, such self-ruined men cling to their (darkened system of) beliefs and commit countless atrocities. They are the enemies of mankind, devoted to its destruction.

Virtuous people find it difficult to believe that such evil exists on earth. Its proponents, moreover, often proclaim (if they have a degree of intelligence) teachings that are designed purposefully to win others to their side: teachings like "the greatest good for the greatest number," and "to each according to his needs, from each according to his capacity to give." On the field of actual activity, however, they show themselves nothing but power-hungry, ruthless, and utterly cynical in the application of their so-called "ideals."

Such people appear in every age. Usually, they are more or less successful according to how many dissatisfied Shudras, and idealistic but undiscriminating intellectuals, they can persuade to fill their ranks.

(16:10) Abandoning themselves to insatiable desires, hypocrites, pretending a noble purpose, filled with self-conceit, insolent (to anyone who disagrees with them), their concepts (assuming they have any) twisted by delusion: their actions prompted solely by impure motives.

(16:11) Convinced that the fulfillment of physical passion is man's highest goal, confident that there is no world (and no life) but this one, such persons, until the moment of death, are engrossed in earthly cares and concerns.

(16:12) Bound by the fetters of hundreds of selfish hopes and expectations, enslaved by passion and anger, they strive by unlawful means to amass fortunes with which to purchase sensual physical pleasures.

(16:13) "This much," they say, "I have acquired today, (putting me in a position to) attain this desire.

I have this much money at present; my goal, now, is to acquire more."

(16:14) (Or they say:) "(Today) I have slain this enemy. Next, I shall slay more. What I've wanted, I possess. I am successful, powerful, and happy!"

(16:15) (Again they say:) "I am wealthy and well-born! Who can rival me? I will show my greatness by giving alms and making public sacrifices. I will rejoice (in my glory)!" Thus they boast, befuddled by their own lack of wisdom.

(16:16) Addled in thought, caught in (a spider's web of) delusion, craving only sensual "delights," they sink (in life, and even more so after death) to a foul hell.

(16:17) Vain, (heedlessly) obstinate, intoxicated by pride in wealth, hypocritical in whatever sacrifices they perform, careless of scriptural injunctions,—

(16:18) egotistical, ruthless, arrogant, lascivious, prone to (fits of) rage, these evil-intending persons despise Me (though for all that) I dwell in them, as in all beings.

It is the practice in some religions to decry "idol worship," which it is called when devotees make images to remind them of Abstract God or of high, impersonal ideals. The real idol worshipers, it should be pointed out here, are those who worship the false gods described in these stanzas: idols of ego, lust, pride, and the host of other materialistic goals that so many set for themselves.

(16:19) These cruel perpetrators of evil, filled with hatred, worst of the human race, I hurl again and again into demonic wombs on their return to earth.

(16:20) Cursed and fallen, filled with delusion life after life, (far from) attaining Me, they sink to the lowest depths.

It is frightening to contemplate the people one meets, or has met, in life who manifest some, or even many, of the above traits. They are human beings, and not different outwardly, at least, from everyone else. Many of them are rich, successful, publicly respected. Some of them are famous thinkers, philosophers, writers, scientists. And yet, self-declaredly, they subscribe to at least some of the views Krishna describes as demonic.

It would be convenient, and no doubt reassuring, to believe that worldly success is always the fruit of good karma, and that wealth, prominence and even fame, power, and all the accoutrements, at least, of the kind of fulfillment many people seek are necessarily proof that one has done at least something right, by any definition of the karmic law. Unfortunately, the escape route from *maya* is not so clearly defined as that! As Krishna points out—and even though happiness ought to be (and indeed is, when rightly understood) the criterion of virtue—evil people often do consider themselves happy in a dark way that does not understand true, pure happiness. This "happiness" is not unlike the "pleasure" one feels when scratching a mosquito bite, an act which hurts, yet somehow feels good at the same time! Nevertheless, those with nothing better to compare their state to may delude themselves into believing they have everything they want in life, and that all they need now is more and more of the same. (For of course they can never get enough.) The "fulfillment" they seek is like the carrot dangled from a stick and tied to the head of a donkey: It draws him forward as he pulls behind him a heavy load. Out of arrogance, moreover, such people shout down or loudly dismiss any attempt to persuade them they are wrong.

Many people of base consciousness are wealthy, powerful, and, by their own definition, "well born" (as Krishna puts it)—though that definition is, by sattwic and even rajasic standards, warped and confused. How is this even possible? It may be because karma itself is usually a mixed bag. The worldly success of evil people may be due to good karma along with the bad. There is more to be said on the subject, however. For much that passes for success in worldly eyes is not really even good karma, and may actually result in a person's eventual spiritual downfall, and immediate misery.

There are two factors to consider. One is the fact that success comes as a result of focused concentration. Energy can be concentrated by causing it to flow mostly in one direction. Complete focus occurs only when all one's energy flows up toward union with God. There may be degrees of focused energy, however, in which the focus is on one specific image—of success, perhaps, or wealth, or power. Thus, very worldly and even demonic people may be so sure of their goals, for a time, that they actually acquire the power they need to achieve lower levels of success.

The other factor to consider is an image that was mentioned earlier in this book: that of the sounding board of a musical instrument. If God and angelic forces in the universe can reinforce one's power through his attunement with them, it follows that one's power can also be increased by attunement with lower—indeed, with satanic—forces.

It may be easier, even, to achieve this kind of increase by attuning oneself with the dark forces. They are closer to the human scene—especially to scenes with low vibrations. If one invites them, they may respond instantly. It isn't even necessary to invite them consciously—that is to say, by believing in evil, and by willing deliberately to contact it. A person need only live in some of the ways described in the last stanzas. People's very disbelief in the conscious power of *maya* constitutes one of her greatest victories.

The downward spiral presumes also on the power derived from past good karma to reinforce present evil tendencies. "People," my Guru once exclaimed in exasperation, "are so skillful in their ignorance!"

Misery is, certainly, the final result of evil, and it is important to understand that such misery is self-inflicted. Indeed, the deluded mob of fallen souls may consider themselves well off, as we saw. They have what they think they wanted. Many, many lifetimes must pass before such souls awaken to their own higher truth—as all must do, in time, for divine freedom is the destiny of every soul.

The question naturally arises at this point: how far can a soul fall? We saw earlier that our potential for expansion of consciousness is infinite. This potential must perforce, therefore, include also the potential to shrink—to become, in time, infinitesimal. The upward road cannot preclude the possibility of a downward road also: indeed, it necessitates such a premise.

Krishna has spoken of the descent of evildoers into demonic wombs. It must be understood that what descends is the soul in its identification with the body— the ego, in other words. An individual may fall so far downward as to find compatible self-expression only in the body of some lower animal, not a human being. A story came out from Tibet several years ago about a lama who, because of his misdeeds, found himself in the womb of an ass. As a man, he had behaved already like an ass in his sexual overindulgence!

A fall to the level of the lower animals does occur, my Guru stated quite clearly. He also said, however, that that fate, which is a great punishment, lasts only for one incarnation at a time. After a single lifetime as an ass, a monkey, or a tiger, or as some other form, the soul, having once reached the human level, quickly returns to that level.

My Guru added, however, that if a person stubbornly perseveres in sinning, life after life, refusing to reform even after repeated forays into lower forms, he may actually be cast very far down the evolutional ladder— as an insect, perhaps, or to some even lower form.

Almost unbelievably, if one continues sinning without repentance, he may, after repeated, heavy punishment, be cast down as far as the level of a germ. From this level he must work his way slowly up the ladder of evolution again. How could there be a quick reprieve? He has brought suffering on himself by *willing* to embrace darkness and ignorance.

There are tamasic galaxies, infested with hordes of such degraded souls. Plagues and similar scourges of earth are often caused by an invasion of clouds of disease germs— fallen souls, brought here by their karma and by the earth's karma. Their destiny is to be destroyed, here, by modern medicine.

An evil-doing human being may not be fully aware of his misery. He may even successfully persuade himself, in his arrogance, that he is well off. Anyone, however, who has known a higher, more refined existence cannot but feel intense (though suppressed) suffering—at least on a subconscious level, when he finds himself submitted to the indignity of confinement in a lower, animal, existence. Some suffering surely remains, and may even be exacerbated, when he finds himself living in the body of a rat. Probably, any awareness he has of the degree of his indignity is muffled somewhat, but it cannot be quenched altogether.

What, then, of the germ? Surely some higher awareness lingers during the long, slow climb up the ladder of evolution again—enough awareness, perhaps, to keep it sensing at least subconsciously, "There's something wrong. I ought to be much more than I am." Whatever the case, some level of suffering could hardly fail be the lot of every fallen soul. The suffering would be born of an awareness that there are potentials it is not expressing.

The above realities are sobering! One would like to think of life as offering less stark alternatives. Every devotee should take heart, however, from the simple fact that, as Yogananda said, "As long as you make the effort, God will never let you down." And again the comforting words of Lord Krishna: "Arjuna, know this for a certainty: My devotee is *never* lost." One further thought remains, both to stiffen one's resolution and to brighten one's hope: Once the desire for God wakes in a person's heart, that desire *must* be fulfilled. It is already his guarantee of salvation.

(16:21) Lust, anger, and greed for gain: these are the three pathways to hell, leading to the destruction of soul-happiness. In man's own interests he should avoid them all.

(16:22) O Son of Kunti (Arjuna), by avoiding these three ways down into the realms of darkness, man acts for his own highest good, and sets himself on the (upward) way to the highest state.

A monastic disciple of Paramhansa Yogananda fell in love with a beautiful woman and wanted to marry her. When the Guru tried to dissuade him, the young man said, "But she's a *wonderful* person."

"Naturally," replied our Guru. "Satan knows best how to tempt you!"

The disciple did leave his monastic calling, and in consequence suffered greatly for many years.

The lure of "sex, wine, and money," as *maya* has often been epitomized, emits an aura of almost visible attraction. Anger ensues when the desire for them is thwarted; hence the inclusion of anger in Stanza 21 (above). The very fact that desires can lead to anger should be a sufficient indication that the desires themselves are manifestations of bondage, not of freedom.

(16:23) One who ignores the commands of scripture and follows his own ego-driven desires finds neither happiness, nor fulfillment, nor the supreme goal of life.

(16:24) Take (true) scripture, therefore, as your guide in determining what should be done and what should be avoided. With intuitive understanding of the injunctions in holy writ, perform your earthly duties.

The words, "intuitive understanding of . . . holy writ" are important, lest even true scripture be distorted by fanatics who use the scriptures to justify heinous deeds. The ways of God are ever rooted in godliness. God may on occasion be a "refining fire," destroying evil and restoring virtue to its proper place in order to bring back a balance again to the affairs of man, but His vengeance is never motivated by wrath, hatred, or vindictiveness. What seems so to men who are afflicted with these faults is only a projection of their own nature.

Krishna counseled Arjuna to fight in the righteous war of Kurukshetra, but he also urged him to fight dispassionately, without attachment to the results. This is the secret of true ahimsa, non-violence (harmlessness). Sometimes one must destroy in order to honor his higher duty. He need not, however, *wish* destruction on anything or anyone.

To the person of strong ego-consciousness, of course, destruction effected is destruction *willed*. Such a person sees only God's wrath when he himself is punished—a fate he has willed, however unwittingly, upon himself. God does not will our suffering. His will, which manifests personally in all of us, is for our eternal freedom in Him.

Thus ends the sixteenth chapter, called "The Nature of the Godly and the Demonic," of the Upanishad of the holy Bhagavad Gita, in the dialogue between Sri Krishna and Arjuna discussing yoga and the science of God-realization.

CHAPTER THIRTY

THE THREE LEVELS OF SPIRITUAL PRACTICE

Krishna, at the end of Chapter 16 of the Bhagavad Gita, recommended following the guidance of true scripture. Arjuna's next question, proceeding from that statement, marks the beginning of Chapter 17.

(17:1) Arjuna said: Those who set aside scriptural rules, yet sacrifice (to God) with devotion—what, O Krishna, is the status (of their sacrifice)? Is it sattwic, rajasic, or tamasic?

The point was made earlier that there are true scriptures, less true ones, and even false or man-made ones. Arjuna's question here is based on true, revealed scripture. His concern is twofold: Can the sincere exercise of devotion ever be wrong? And, Are there different qualities of devotion? For it is not enough to say, "He prays with devotion." There are different kinds of devotion, from selfless to self-serving. Ultimately, the effect of prayer depends not on

504

any prayer-formula, however valid in itself, but on the attitude of the person praying.

Essentially, Arjuna is setting the scene for a discussion of the different kinds of devotion, rather than of the different kinds of people practicing devotion. Most tamasic people, especially, practice no devotion at all. Many rajasic people too, may practice devotion of a type more tamasic than rajasic.

(17:2) The Blessed Lord said: (The issue involves) the quality of faith exercised—whether it is in fact sattwic, rajasic, or tamasic. Hear My words on this point.

(17:3) Each one's faith depends upon his nature. As a man is, so is his faith. As his faith is, so is the man.

We are, in other words, what we believe. All followers of a religion may declare an article of faith, and use exactly the same words day after day, week after week, year after year, but there will for all that be as many beliefs as there are adherents. Each person's understanding will be molded by what he *is*—by his experience in life, his understanding, his personal preferences and prejudices, his likes and dislikes. It cannot be otherwise, for our entire understanding is based less on objective reality than on who and what we are in our own natures. Thus, a simple word like "home" will have very different connotations for one who was raised in a happy family than for someone who was raised by unfeeling authorities in an orphanage "home." Words like "father" and "mother," similarly, have different connotations for different people, depending on the happiness, or lack of it, of their own home life. So has success. So have many other words: work, kindness, travel, sport—indeed, so have virtually all words in any language.

We may declare, "I believe in God," but that simple statement raises all sorts of images in different people's minds. Most who call themselves atheists are only rejecting some formal concept of what others they know think of as God. However, no one, surely, would reject such concepts as love, or joy.

To good people, God will seem good. To ordinarily selfish and ambitious people, God may seem a kind of "horn of plenty," or—if not that—a stern judge or perhaps a kind of "boss," more or less indifferent to human needs. To evil people, if they believe in God at all, He may seem filled with jealousy, anger, and vindictiveness—as are they themselves. To lustful people He will seem, like the gods of Greek and Roman mythology, consumed with lust. To kind people He will seem kind. To narrow-minded people, and to those filled with narrow prejudices, He will seem like themselves: narrowly sectarian and grimly disposed to judge men for their sins.

(17:4) Sattwic reverence is given to the devas; rajasic reverence is offered to the *yakshas* and *rakshasas*; tamasic "devotion" is the fascination some people feel for ghosts and (astral) spirits.

Good people revere God, of course, but they also love goodness in others, and revere it in the angels.

Worldly people bow with respect (mixed with anxiety) to anything or anyone they think may help them to fulfill their worldly desires. Thus, rajasic "devotion" is described by Krishna as being directed toward the *yakshas* (the legendary astral guardians of wealth). *Rakshasas* are reputed to be astral beings whose wrath or favor can unmake or make a person's fortune.

Tamasic devotion is not limited to the "devotion" felt by tamasic people—a sentiment which few among them actually feel—but includes the lowest levels of devotional feeling itself, even if practiced by people of higher, perhaps rajasic nature.

Of particular interest here is Krishna's description of this last kind of "devotional" fascination. Many people (not only, we repeat, those who are tamasic) are faddishly consumed with interest in communication with departed spirits, and (exaggeratedly so) in soliciting help from nature spirits—fairies, elves, and a host of beings described everywhere on Earth in "fairy tales."

It is an all-too-common mistake to think that *any*one "up there" who has passed beyond the veil that separates the material from the astral world must have insights that are denied to the people of earth. The Gita is not necessarily saying that those who make this mistake are themselves tamasic. It is the *form* their fascination takes that is tamasic, for it leads to spiritual confusion. Spiritualistic séances produce "guidance from the masters," and from a wide variety of other supposedly knowledgeable entities. What makes these phenomena, and devotion to them, tamasic is twofold. First, they are imaginary. Second, to access this "information" one must enter a passive state of consciousness in which the thought process is not transcended in superconsciousness, but blanked out to "receive" whatever impressions come. This practice shows spiritual ignorance, and is a doorway through which much mischief enters.

To contact a spiritual master, one must raise his consciousness to a superconscious level. No master would deign to come through mediums—not because he couldn't, but only because to do so would convey the false message that spiritualism is not only a simple and easy way of communing with higher beings, but also that it is a spiritually acceptable practice. It doesn't work. It is, as Krishna states, tamasic.

(17:5,6) Tamasic devotion also takes the form of trying to show off by the performance of terrible austerities, unauthorized by the scriptures; by hypocritical displays, ego demonstrations, (the expression of) lustful passions and attachments, and power madness. Senselessly (those with this kind of devotion) torture their body-elements, thereby offending Me, who dwell in their bodies.

The unnatural austerities mentioned here are practices like self-flagellation (which we've mentioned before), wearing hair shirts, piercing the body with sharp spikes, trying to achieve kumbhaka (breathlessness) by holding the breath unnaturally, and risking death by, again, depriving the body of the oxygen it needs with a view to attaining a sort of giddiness that ignorant people equate with superconsciousness. There are many methods, similarly misguided, that are indulged in by those foolishly seeking shortcuts to ecstasy: drugs, "sacred" mushrooms, and the like. These methods are not sanctioned by true scripture, and are condemned by Krishna as tamasic.

The body is the temple of God. It should be respected as such, and not abused as though it, rather than its animating ego, were the thing to be "conquered."

Another display of tamasic devotion is indulgence in lustful passion, whether in the name of falsely understood *tantra* or of trying to imitate the "lila" of Krishna, as a child, and the gopis. Gloating attachment to worldly pleasures and giving the excuse, "Oh, it's all God," and the hunger for adulation with the ulterior motive of controlling other people—all these practices, though claimed as being conducted in the name of God, have no higher motive than ego-glorification.

(17:7) Even the taste for food is, variously, sattwic, rajasic, or tamasic. So also the preferred types of yagya, or sacrifice, the penances, and the ways of almsgiving. Hear these distinctions.

Every taste in food proclaims to some degree a person's state of evolution. So also do his natural predilections regarding spiritual practices.

(17:8) Foods that promote longevity, vitality, endurance, health, a cheerful attitude, and a good appetite; that are pleasant-tasting, mildly flavored, nourishing, and agreeable to the body: such foods (give sattwic enjoyment and) are preferred by sattwic people.

(17:9) Foods that are bitter, sour, heavily salted, excessively hot, pungent, sharp tasting, and burning (give rajasic enjoyment and) are those preferred by people of rajasic temperament. Such foods produce pain, discomfort, and disease.

(17:10) Foods that are nutritionally worthless, tasteless, putrid, stale, thrown away as garbage, or (otherwise) impure (give tamasic enjoyment and) are preferred by tamasic people.

The spiritual qualities of food should not be confused with their chemical properties. Discussed above are the *vibrations* of what one eats. For this reason also, it is important that food be *prepared* in an uplifted frame of mind, and not under the influence of such harmful emotions as anger, grief, or depression.

It may be said, basically, that sattwic food helps to calm the nerves and to make them clear channels for the energy flowing into the body, and for higher inspiration. Rajasic foods are stimulating to the nerves to the point of irritating them. Even poison, if it is taken in minute quantities, can stimulate, though too much of it kills. Rajasic foods have an exciting effect on the body, whether slightly or pronouncedly, causing the flow of energy into the body to become restless. Tamasic foods, finally—lacking as they are in nutritive value—merely clog the nervous system and make a person dull and unenergetic.

Sattwic foods consist of fresh fruits and vegetables. The vegetables should be lightly cooked, or even raw. This diet includes also whole grains and legumes, fresh dairy products, nuts, and such natural sweets as honey, dates, and figs. Cooked foods should be combined and prepared in such a way as to preserve their natural ingredients. Food should be pleasing to the eye as well as to the palate—only lightly seasoned, and agreeable to the body's constitution.

Rajasic foods are, as indicated above, excessively stimulating to the life forces in the body, somewhat irritating to the nerves, and exciting in their effect on the mind. Not all such stimulation is bad, however. For someone whose life includes activity as well as meditation, a certain amount of rajas may be helpful in stirring him to action. Onions, garlic, and eggs are examples of rajasic foods that may prove beneficial for sattwic people also who need to be busily active. Eggs are mistakenly considered a meat product: In fact they are not significantly more so than milk products. Other rajasic foods include those which are excessively hot, spicy, salted, or otherwise strongly flavored. Certain meats may be included in a rajasic diet: fish, fowl, and lamb.

Tamasic foods are well described in this stanza. They include horseradish and also such meat as beef, veal, and pork, which have been validly proscribed in various religions. The slaughtering of these more highly evolved animals produces strong emotions such as fear and anger, which remain as vibrations in the meat itself and increase people's naturally aggressive and/or fearful tendencies. Beef causes cancer. Pork is an unclean food, the very sweetness of ham being due, my Guru said, to the pus it contains.

Because the food one eats has an effect on the clarity and upliftment of the mind, it plays an important role not only in bodily health but also in one's spiritual life.

(17:11) That yagya (sacrificial rite, or performance of duty) is sattwic which is offered without any desire for (personal) gain from the deed, which is performed in accordance with (the teaching of) scripture, and with firm belief in its rightness.

(17:12) Yagya performed with the hope of reward, O Best of the Bharatas (Arjuna), and in a spirit of ostentation, is rajasic.

(17:13) That yagya, finally, is declared tamasic which is not motivated by regard for scriptural injunctions, which makes no (suitable) gifts of food or money, which is performed without the offering of sacred chants or prayers, and without devotion (to God).

Sattwic self-offering has only the highest "motive" of union with God. Rajasic offerings are made in the hope of selfish gain. The advice to have regard for scriptural injunctions raises two questions: "Which scriptures?" and, "Which injunctions?" As we've seen, not every so-called "scripture" is true. Certain injunctions, moreover, even among those stated in true scripture, may have a special application to some particular time in history, to a particular culture, and to the general consciousness at the time. Jesus Christ, for example, said that a teaching of Moses (who was a true master in Judaism of earlier times) had been given because of the "hardness" of people's hearts at that time.

The universal point in Krishna's emphasis on scriptural injunctions may be explained as respect for high tradition. After all, many people in the world don't know the teachings of any religion—even that in which they are supposed to have been raised. One who egotistically flouts the worthwhile traditions of his own culture, however, ignoring them or even substituting "rituals" of his own making that reflect a disregard for general opinion, rituals performed for self-glorification, without devotion to or faith in God, without due consideration for others (which would be shown by the distribution of food or money), and without any prayer or mantra to indicate that one is invoking the aid of a higher power: Practices like these are tamasic.

There are three, or perhaps four, categories of religious tradition. The first, the sattwic, contains those which show an awareness that man can realize God. People in these traditions revere the saints. Under rajas, two categories may be discerned: the sattwa-rajas as well as the "pure" rajas. The former traditions, sattwa-rajasic, have a strong dedication to ethical behavior. The people in these traditions aspire to become morally good, but not holy.

The more clearly rajasic traditions are full of emotional displays. They encourage loud singing and exuberant physical displays such as rolling on the ground or jumping up and down in a kind of ecstasy of agitated feelings.

The tamasic traditions, finally, have a darkening influence on the mind. They contain dark rites such as voodoo, black magic and various other kinds of sorcery, and dark practices, hypnotic in their effect, that are intended to invoke evil forces for the wreaking of harm.

(17:14) Veneration of the devas, the priestly, the gurus, and the wise; purity (of heart and deed);

straightforwardness; sexual restraint; harmlessness (non-violence): these are considered the austerities of the body.

(17:15) Speech that is pleasant, beneficial, and truthful without being offensive, the repetition of *japa* and recitation of the scriptures: these are called the austerities of speech.

(17:16) Even-mindedness, cheerfulness, kindliness, serenity, self-control, purity of heart, meditative communion with the true Self—these are said to be the austerities of the mind.

(17:17) This threefold austerity (of body, speech, and mind) is sattwic in nature; it is practiced by persevering seekers (blessed with) deep devotion, who desire not the fruits of their actions.

These sattwic "austerities" are the natural products of an uplifted consciousness. "Austerity" in this context, therefore, suggests no grim efforts at self-restraint, but is a natural offering up of the mind to superconsciousness.

(17:18) Those austerities which are performed for the sake of gaining respect, honor, and a good name—done, therefore, for the sake of show—are mere ostentation, fitful and transitory. These are what are called rajasic.

(17:19) Tamasic austerities are performed without reasonable purpose—(perhaps) for self-injury, or (perhaps) to inflict harm on others.

Rajasic "austerities" are not laudable, but at least they are better than the tamasic ones. As Yogananda said,

"It is better to do good for the sake of praise than not to do good at all." Tamasic rituals of witchcraft, sorcery, uttering incantations with a view to inflicting harm: Some of these practices have been shown to be effective, but they inflict much more harm on the person practicing them than on his victims. People with sufficient awareness to know that sheer thoughts and incantations can have power should have the common sense to realize that the same force, once hurled, must perforce return, boomerang-like, to the person who first hurled it as an anathema.

(17:20) (In the matter of gift-giving) to give sattwically is to give without a thought of receiving in return; to give because it is right to do so; and to give appropriately, at the proper place and time, and to one who is deserving.

Sattwic gift-giving is of three kinds: material, mental, and spiritual. A gift of money to someone who is in need is good, but it is well also to consider Krishna's counsel to give *appropriately*. If one had a million dollars to give away, and donated one dollar each to a million people, the best they could do with it would be to make some trivial purchase like a dish of ice cream. That same amount of money, however, concentrated in a single worthwhile project could help many people significantly, over a long period of time.

In the early days of the movie industry, many actors and actresses who became wealthy handed out money indiscriminately to any friend who simply asked them for it. They ended up poor. Had their giving been sensible and appropriate, they would have been far less likely to suffer such a fate.

My Guru used to say that to give food or money to someone in need is good; to give him a job is better; and to help him to become qualified to get a good job is best of all. To give continuously to the same person would be to make him not only financially but psychologically dependent on the giver.

On a mental plane, to give good advice inappropriately, to someone who is not likely to benefit from it, would be a mistake also. Give counsel charily, when it is clearly wanted and requested, and never impose it on anybody: This is sattwic counseling.

To help people spiritually is best of all, for when they rise out of spiritual ignorance they attain the true wealth of the universe. Spiritual sharing should focus on the satisfaction one feels in giving, and not on the pleasure of being listened to (which would be a-sattwic, or unspiritual). Greater than words, however wise, is the sharing of uplifting vibrations. Those who wish to share spiritually should be conscious above all of sharing with others their *vibrations* of divine joy and inspiration.

A spiritually aware person sees everyone as an expression of God, and as *desirous*, in his heart, of the gifts which God alone can give him. He tries to help everyone according to that person's capacity to receive. Above all, however, he tries to bring people to God.

(17:21) A gift is deemed rajasic if it is given, perhaps reluctantly (in the thought of what one is losing), in the hope of getting something in return.

It is, as we've already said, better to do good—including giving gifts—than to give nothing at all. Such giving, even with an ulterior motive, may be a step toward learning to give in a truly sattwic way.

Such rajasic gifts, however, being tainted with selfish purpose, always convey a certain lack of cleanness—like giving someone a glass of muddy water.

(17:22) A gift is tamasic if it is given inappropriately: at the wrong time or place, or to an unworthy person, or contemptuously, or with ill will.

To give money or help of any kind at the wrong time is to give it where it can serve no good purpose and may even do harm. To give it at the wrong place is to give it insensitively or foolishly, without due consideration for the effect your giving may have on others. To give it to an unworthy person may be, in the case of money, to enable him to spend it for an unworthy cause; or, in the case of advice, to give good advice to someone who may turn it even to some wrong purpose. To give contemptuously is to give with the motive of slighting others by showing your superiority to them. And to give with ill will is, in a sense, to curse the other one with potentially damaging energy even while pretending to give good energy.

(17:23) AUM, *Tat, Sat*: This has been declared as the threefold designation of Brahman (God). From this power issued, in the beginning, the wise knowers of Brahman, the (holy) Vedas, and the (Vedic) sacrificial rites.

This Holy Trinity, it should be noted, is the same thing as the true Christian Trinity. Most scholars have equated the Christian Trinity with the three aspects of AUM: Brahma, Vishnu, and Shiva—the Creator, the Preserver, and Destroyer of creation.

AUM is the Cosmic Vibration. We have explained this aspect of Spiritual Truth before, but it may be helpful to explain it briefly again in the present context.

Sat stands for eternal and absolute *truth*: the Supreme Spirit, above and beyond all vibration. Out of that oceanic consciousness are projected, at the time of creation, the waves of Cosmic Vibration, AUM. The three letters of AUM stand for that vibration's three basic aspects, personalized in Hindu tradition (as the Trinity has been in the Christian) as Brahma, Vishnu, and Shiva.

In the Christian Trinity, *Sat* stands for the Father, and AUM, for the Holy Ghost. "Ghost," in this case, stands for the divine breath, or cosmic "wind" of delusion, which raises waves on the surface of the ocean.

Tat (meaning "That"—as in the scriptural declaration: "Thou art That") is the still reflection at every point of vibratory creation of the calm, unmoving consciousness of the Spirit beyond all vibration. Thus, Spirit is present everywhere, though not visible anywhere because all that God's creatures are able to observe, *as* creatures, is vibratory creation.

Everything in existence is a manifestation of Brahman, the Supreme Spirit. Spirit's first manifestation, however, is that which most perfectly expresses the highest consciousness. Thus, those (the knowers of Brahman) who most perfectly manifest wisdom, express it most perfectly (in the Vedas, and in all true scriptures), and that which shows the way most perfectly (above all, the sacrificial rite of self-offering into the fire of wisdom, and the consumption and reabsorption in Spirit of ego-consciousness, which is best accomplished by the *true* fire rite of Kriya Yoga, magnetizing the spine and raising the energy through it to the brain).

(17:24) Therefore, scripturally sanctioned deeds— sacrifice, the giving of gifts, and the practice of (the sattwic) austerities—are always (traditionally) begun with the chanting of AUM.

There is power even in the sound of AUM, when rightly pronounced. Therefore let us repeat here (as well as can be done in writing) how AUM should be uttered. The sound is like the English syllable, "OM" (but more the American than the British vowel, which introduces a third sound, "e-o," into the "equation"), because, as in American English, the "O" should be a double, not a triple diphthong. "A" in Sanskrit has two sounds, a short and a long. The short is pronounced as it is in the English, "a tree," or "uh." The long is pronounced like the "a" in "sharp." Because "OM" is pronounced in other lan- guages (most of which have pure vowels) with a single vowel sound ("o" as in the vowel sound of the English word, "gone") it should be written, as it is in Sanskrit, as three distinct sounds: "O" as in "gone," or (short "a") as, "uh"—"U" (like the "o" in the English word, "who")— and a long-drawn-out, not briefly uttered, "M" (like a short "humming" sound). Alternatively, in English, it may be written, "Uh—oo—mmm."

This sound, as we've said, has great power. It serves somewhat the same purpose as the word, "Amen," which is uttered at the end of Christian prayers. Originally, the meaning was the same.

(17:25) Those who seek (spiritual) liberation should perform all the rites of (ego)-sacrifice (true yagya), gift giving (sharing with others whatever blessings one receives), and (the sattwic) austerities while concentrated on the higher Self (the Christ consciousness, or Kutastha Chaitanya in oneself), without any wish for (specific) results.

Kriya Yoga (and all other meditation practices), sharing (especially truth, and higher inspiration), and sattwic austerities (listed in Stanzas 14–16 of this chapter): all these should be practiced with a consciousness of deep calmness, centered in the inner Self.

One of the traditional gifts performed after yagya (sacrifice) is an offering to the guru. Gifts of food and money can easily be seen as symbolizing the higher gift of truth and inspiration to the "needy"—that is, to those who can benefit from this higher gift—but some people may object, "How can such higher gifts be given, even symbolically, to the guru?" The answer is that every true disciple must mentally offer up everything that he has and is to the teacher, partly in order that he might receive still further enlightenment; partly that any error in his understanding might be corrected; and partly in that kind of gratitude which even the enlightened disciple always feels toward the source of his enlightenment. Indeed, the enlightened disciple, even more than others, offers his eternal gratitude, in the form of obeisance, to him from whom his enlightenment came.

Not to desire results does not mean not to desire enlightenment. A truly sattwic person need hardly be advised not to seek selfish fruits from his spiritual actions. He may need to be counseled, however, not to seek *specific* results, even spiritual ones, from his spiritual practices. Many meditators, for example, hope for visions and phenomena. Many who share even truth and inspiration *want* others to be helped, instead of leaving the results in God's hands, or (a very difficult thing to surrender) they *want* some outward manifestation of the Guru's pleasure or love for them. And many who practice austerities *want* (quite rightly and understandably) to see some inner consequences of those practices. All these desired results do come, in time, to the sincere seeker, but giving up attachment to those results keeps one focused on *doing*, rather than on *reaping* benefits from, his practices, and therefore on continued effort until there is no sense of doing, doer, and done because one has merged in the Infinite.

(17:26) The word *"Sat"* is the designation of the Supreme Truth (beyond vibratory creation) and of the supreme goodness emanating from it. Thus also this word refers to every higher form of spiritual action.

(17:27) Steadfastness in self-offering (sacrifice) to the Infinite, the austerities, and selfless sharing, and any

activity connected with these purposes (for the sake of realizing the Supreme Self), is also spoken of as *"Sat."*

Yoga practice leads gradually from oneness with AUM, the Cosmic Vibration, to oneness with *Tat*, the Kutastha Chaitanya (or Christ consciousness), and finally to merging into a state of oneness with *Sat*, the Supreme, Vibrationless Spirit (God the Father).

(17:28) O Partha (Arjuna)! Whatever sacrifice is offered, gift bestowed, or austerity performed, if (it is done) without devotional faith it is called *asat*— "untruth." Both here and in the hereafter, it has no (spiritual) value.

Deep, devotional faith is an utter necessity on the spiritual path. Yet there remains a simple truth: One cannot have faith *before* coming onto the spiritual path! Faith, as we saw some time back, means more than belief. It is what comes after receiving *some* spiritual insight. Indeed, perfect faith comes with deep realization.

What Krishna is referring to here, then, is that provisional faith (belief, in fact) which is born of the conviction that only in God will one find everything he has been seeking in life.

Krishna means also that one should abandon as early as possible the absurd tendency of the doubting mind which, sitting on the river bank and fearful of plunging into the water, says, "Yes, but how can I be *sure* I won't drown?"

Compare what everything else has given you— *nothing!*—with even the first peace and inner consolation you feel in spiritual practices, and even from these exalted teachings in the Gita, and decide for yourself. The only thing that makes any possible sense in life is to go ahead and take the plunge!

As long as you hold back, you will be inwardly divided against yourself, and every step forward will be canceled by another step backward.

Thus ends the seventeenth chapter, called "The Three Levels of Spiritual Practice," of the Upanishad of the holy Bhagavad Gita, in the dialogue between Sri Krishna and Arjuna discussing yoga and the science of God-realization.

CHAPTER THIRTY-ONE

YOU SHALL ATTAIN ME

THIS FINAL CHAPTER OF THE BHAGAVAD GITA IS A summation of the whole scripture, which began with the blind king Dhritarashtra, a metaphor for the "blind mind," asking Sanjaya (introspection) what had happened on the battlefield of Kurukshetra. Already in the first stanza the stage was set for spiritual reflection, not for the actual history of the epic war. It is only *after* an internal struggle, whether spiritual or psychological, that one asks, "Who won?" During the heat of battle one is too preoccupied with the struggle to ask seriously how the battle is going. That question is reserved for later: the time of introspection and calm reflection.

The Gita immediately lists the psychological warriors facing each other. And here, suddenly, the question is addressed in the present tense: who the warriors *are*, not who they *were*. For after the war, of course, many will have been slain.

In the final analysis, the entire battle is between the ego (represented by Bhishma, who is fighting for

524

Duryodhana or Material Desire) and the soul's aspiration for divine union. Bhishma has received the grace not to die until he *offers himself* up to death. Thus, though riddled with arrows, he cannot die until he himself wills to do so. Thus also with the ego: One can never be stripped of it. It must surrender itself of its own free will to the Infinite.

Renunciation (of ego), therefore, is the final message of the Gita. It is fitting that this, Arjuna's first question, should be posed at the outset of this final chapter.

(18:1) Arjuna said: I desire, O Mighty-armed (Krishna), Slayer of (the demon of ignorance) Keshi! to know the true meaning of *sannyasa* (renunciation), and also of *tyaga* (self-surrender), and the distinction between the two.

How, Arjuna is asking, can I tell the difference between renunciation and Karma Yoga, the essence of which is the renunciation of the fruits of action?

(18:2) The Blessed Lord said: The wise understand renunciation to be the relinquishing of any action performed with (personal) desire. They also declare that it is not action itself which should be abandoned, but only that action which desires the fruits of action.

Essentially, Krishna is saying, "Act, but don't consider yourself the 'doer' of action."

No one, he has explained, can abandon action. To breathe, sleep, eat, and perform all the necessary functions of the body must be classified under the general term, action. No one, therefore, can renounce action altogether unless he is so spiritually advanced that he can sit the whole day in breathless ecstasy—a possibility for very few.

The important thing, then, is to give up the sense of personal "doership." Everything the renunciate does should be done with the thought, "God is doing all this through me."

The *tyagi*, on the other hand, may have to involve himself somewhat in personal activities—wife, job, family, and social responsibilities—but for himself he must desire nothing from any activity. This is the true meaning of Karma Yoga, and certainly is not substantially different from the path of outer renunciation except insofar as, if one need not attend to such outward duties, he is certainly freer to pursue the path of giving his life to God alone, and finds it *easier* to free his ego from all limiting attachments.

Lest anyone think this easier way indicates a path requiring less courage, it would be well to point out that the path to God takes all the courage and strength one possesses. Only someone very foolish would choose the more difficult path simply to show others (and perhaps also himself) that he possesses these two qualities in full measure. *Tantra* is an approach to God that teaches one to be strong in himself in the very teeth of temptation. It is a "back staircase" to God, and spiritually very dangerous. Far wiser is one who saves his strength, instead, for the strenuous task—in every sense in any case a supreme task—of climbing up by the "front staircase" of right action, meditation, and renunciation of both the thought of "doership" and of desire for any personal gain from the doing.

Krishna goes on to explain these thoughts more fully.

(18:3) Some (theoretical) philosophers claim that all work should be forsaken as (being) tainted. Others insist that worthwhile activities (at least), such as yagya (sacrifice), philanthropic works, and (various) austerities should not be relinquished.

(18:4) Hear now therefore from Me, O Best of the Bharatas (Arjuna), for *tyaga* (non-attachment to the fruits of action) has been declared, O Lion among Men, to be of three kinds.

(18:5) The activity involved in yagya (sacrifice), philanthropic works, and the austerities (listed in 17:14–16) ought certainly to be engaged in, and should not be abandoned, for, when performed with wisdom, (they) purify the heart.

(18:6) Even these (self-uplifting) activities, however, ought to be performed without attachment (either) to them or to their fruits. This, O Partha (Arjuna), is My decided and final view.

We see here Krishna's sublime practicality. He was no abstract or theoretical philosopher. He firmly believed in doing what *works*. Theoretically, to be sure, the highest truth is to be merged in Brahman. One who can spend his whole time in samadhi doesn't need *any* teachings! Nevertheless, as Krishna points out, not to act also in ways that uplift the mind is to set a wrong example for those who want to reach that state. Thus, the highest truth, for mankind, is that which will help everyone to *reach* the absolute state.

In answer to those *vairagis* (persons of supreme non-attachment), moreover, who say that one should not enjoy *anything* in God's creation, their counsel might even be considered an insult to God! They overlook the fact that it was God who *made* everything, through his instrument, Prakriti. How can He be pleased with anyone for despising His handiwork? Surely the best attitude, and one which Krishna himself recommends, is to *enjoy all things inwardly, with the joy of God.*

(18:7) It is not (laudable, or) right to abandon dutiful action. To relinquish it when one is still in delusion is (in fact) considered tamasic.

Indeed, not to perform right, dutiful actions is to open oneself to evil—as in the saying, "The devil finds work for idle hands to do."

(18:8) One who gives up a duty because he finds it difficult, or because he fears it will cause him pain, relinquishes that action with rajasic consciousness (motivated by desire and attachment). He will never attain any reward from such renunciation.

Desire and attachment, it must be understood, relate not only to what one hopes to gain, but also to what one wants to avoid. To rise above duality means to give up *both* desire and repulsion, attraction and aversion.

(18:9) O Arjuna, one who renounces in a sattwic way performs dutiful action solely because it ought to be done, forsaking both attachment to it and the desire for its fruit.

It is common for people who want to do good in the world to *want* certain things in the personal conviction that those things are what the world needs. Such action may or may not be laudable, but a sattwic person allows God to decide in such matters. He acts to please God, and not for any other motive. Moreover, he acts in accordance with divine guidance—either what he receives from his guru, or, lacking that, from God directly. (A true disciple of a true guru will never pit one of those against the other.)

(18:10) One who is wise in his renunciation is ever calm in himself, and never doubtful. He has no aversion to unpleasant actions, nor is he attached to pleasant ones.

It is interesting that Krishna associates calm renunciation with freedom from doubt. In fact, doubts arise—obviously so—from uncertainty, and uncertainty arises from at least some degree of attachment. Where there is truly no attachment, one no longer questions whether he likes or doesn't like what he has to do: He simply does it.

(18:11) It is not possible for an embodied being to abstain from action altogether. *Tyaga* (self-surrender) is possible, however, by relinquishing the fruits of action.

This point has been carefully clarified before. Krishna is only re-emphasizing it here.

(18:12) The fruits of action (for those who are attached to them) are threefold: pleasant, unpleasant, and mixed. They accrue after death (in the astral world, or in the next incarnation) to those who have not renounced them. For the self-surrendered, however, they do not accrue (to oneself).

A question sometimes arises with regard to the *jivan mukta*, who is free from ego-consciousness: "Does he create *no* karma?" Every action, it should be emphasized, *is* karma. Action is the very meaning of karma. Yes, of course, an ego-freed being creates karma. Because he has no ego-identification with his actions, however, their good results accrue not to himself, but to his disciples and to the world generally. All action has to have a reaction, which in his case will naturally be a good one, but there is no "post" of ego to which the action is tied; therefore its karmic result either comes back to those for whose good he did it, or expands outward in blessing on the world. Indeed, all the actions of a saint are both particularly and universally beneficial.

(18:13) O Mighty-armed (Arjuna), hear from Me now the five causes of all action and its accomplishment, as chronicled in the supreme, Shankhya wisdom, and the means of eradicating (the last vestiges of) karma.

The teaching of Shankhya is based on man's need to free himself from his bondage to karma by eradicating its roots, which may be seen as the basic cause of all his physical, mental, and spiritual suffering. The teachings of Yoga give *methods* for accomplishing this eradication. Vedanta, the meaning of which is "end (or summation) of the Vedas," describes the nature of Brahman, the Supreme Spirit, union with which is the ultimate goal of all spiritual striving.

Without the eradication of karma, as taught in Shankhya, and without the techniques for controlling the mind and energy as taught in the yoga science, man would not find it possible to emerge from the suffering he undergoes in subjection to cosmic delusion.

These three systems are not distinct and separate from one another—and are certainly not mutually exclusive, as certain scholars have claimed. Each of them simply emphasizes different aspects of the same truth. Man must know *why* it is important to extricate himself from the meshes of karma. He must know *how* to do so. And he needs to know, at least intellectually, *what* the consequences will be from his doing so.

Without the right method of extrication—through renunciation, first, of the fruits of action—man will continue to flounder in his first efforts. Again, without yoga practice to help him gain control over his mind, energy, and breath, which keep him tied to body-consciousness, he can try futilely for lifetimes to reach that center of perfect calmness without which true renunciation is not even possible. Thus, although the goal of all spiritual practice is renunciation of ego-identification with that little reflection of Spirit, the body, and the realization of one's fundamental oneness with the Supreme, to proceed on this path by mental aspiration alone is inadequate.

(18:14,15) The five causes of all action—of right action as well as wrong—performed by man in body, speech, and thought are as follows: (1) the human body itself (as the seat of action); (2) the causative agent of action (the ego, or *jivatma*); (3) the various instruments of action (senses, mind, and intellect); (4) the various kinds of action (the power of speech and the motor activities of hands, feet, and rectal and genital organs); and (5) destiny, which is the influence exerted by past karmas or actions, and is the "presiding deity" of all action.

(18:16) Considering how many factors are influential in human action, anyone, lacking this awareness, who thinks of his ego as the sole doer of everything accomplished by him shows no understanding at all.

Man little realizes how much of a pawn of many influences he is when performing even so simple a task as sitting down to eat. First, the body he feeds is not the fixed, solid reality it appears to be, but is constantly changing: its cells forever being removed and replaced. It is also not even physically solid, but only a temporary wave of energy.

Second, he imagines that he, John, is eating according to his own wishes, tastes, and convenience. Apart from the obvious fact that those "wishes" are dictated by the body's needs; that those "tastes" are dictated by his upbringing and habits; and that his "convenience" is dictated by social convention, by the wishes and convenience of others, and by the influences of his own upbringing—apart from all these obvious factors, it is not even John who does the eating! John's ego, which thinks he has seated its body at the table, is only the soul dreaming a separate, narrowly confined bodily existence.

Third, the instruments of action: the senses, mind, and intellect—members of the "committee" of which he is "chairman"—are not always obedient to his wishes, but may in various ways rebel. They may, for example, see things differently, and not accept his intentions.

At a certain dinner party many years ago, the hostess, hoping to create a picturesque setting, hung green Japanese lanterns over the table. Unfortunately for her wishes, the green color shining on the meat made the meat look unhealthy. Though it tasted as good as it was meant to, all the guests became ill from eating it; for some, a stomach pump was actually required!

The ears, and their power of hearing, also may rebel— if, for example, while John is eating, a woman in the house next door is sobbing loudly and long. Various other examples might be given to show the senses of smell, taste, and touch affected similarly, and affecting his intention of eating.

His intellect, also, may be affected by a variety of unsettling factors, and his mind, though the passive perceiver, may perceive several things unclearly.

Fourth, one can imagine various adverse influences from the kinds of action—one's own or someone else's careless speech, for example—and disturbances from the other parts of the body affecting the ego's decisions. In fact, we are not, even as "chairmen of the committees" of what we think of as our own bodies, nearly so free to act as we like to imagine.

Moreover, even the chairman of the board of directors of a large company must obey the wishes of the stockholders, over which he himself has little or no control. And this brings us to the final cause of action, the fifth: Past karma can enter unexpectedly onto the scene in an infinite number of ways, rendering null and void any present decision made by the ego.

(18:17) He who is above the hypnosis of ego-motivation, and whose understanding is clear (because not distorted by false perception), is not the slayer on the battlefield (of Kurukshetra), and commits no sin in the slaying.

The truth, as pointed out heretofore, is first that no one is slain—and this for two reasons: There is no such thing as death, but only transition. Moreover (still under the first reason), what are actually being "slain" in this allegory of war are not people, but evil tendencies in oneself. Their activating energy is simply being redirected toward their opposite, virtuous tendencies.

The second aspect of this stanza's teaching (giving, as it does, a brief overview of material that came before it) is that the sin of slaying accrues to the agent of the act: the ego. When all consciousness of ego has been transmuted into a realization of God as the sole Doer of everything, no karma accrues to that ego. This does not mean that, armed with an ego-free attitude, one can do as one pleases! One doesn't "please," in that state, to do anything except God's will.

(18:18) Knowing, knower, known: these three together constitute the impulse to action: doer, awareness of the deed, and the action done.

Thus, we see here even more limitations on the ego, these being an explanation for the action itself: not its "five causes," but what happens in order to make an act possible. Subtle refinements like these serve the practical purpose of helping to convince the ego of how little freedom it has in its ego-conscious state. In divine consciousness, knowing, knower, and known are one and the same. The person *is*, in fact, the thing known; he is not only the knower. Thus, learning, for him, is no longer difficult, since he already *is* that knowledge! He is also the act of knowing, which means that, in learning, he doesn't really absorb anything new. In accomplishing a task, even a big one, one who has merged his ego in the larger Self considers no task too big for him. Must he climb a mountain? He already *is* that mountain, and therefore doesn't view it as looming high above him. Not thinking of himself as having to do that strenuous climb, the act of climbing is already a part of his own reality: climber, climbing, and the thing climbed are one. With such awareness, an arduous task like this may take, relatively speaking, hardly any time at all—although for people who lack this awareness it might take an unconscionably long time, and be accomplished only by Herculean effort.

(18:19) Awareness of an act, the accomplishment of that act, and the person accomplishing it are described in the Shankhya system as being of three types, according to the gunas involved. Hear Me now about the manifestations of these three types.

Clearly, what one does, how he does it, and the spirit in which he does it are all influenced by the mixture of sattwa, rajas, and tamas in his character. Few people are—in fact, it must be said, no one is or can be—completely one type or another, but it would be helpful to understand the factors involved in what he himself, or others around him, are seeking to accomplish.

(18:20) O Arjuna, understand that influence to be sattwic in which the one indestructible Spirit is perceived (as residing) in all beings, and not as separate in each of them ("undivided in the divided").

The image of a motion picture theater is apt here. The countless images on the screen are only changing manifestations of the one light shining steadily behind the film in the projector. Such is the sattwic view of reality. It influences everything one does by bringing a unity to what others see as disunity, and harmony, therefore, to what others see as disharmony or even chaos.

(18:21) That influence, on the other hand, which is

based on seeing the multiplicity of beings as real (in themselves) is, by nature, rajasic.

The influence of rajas on a person's nature inclines him to see himself and everyone else as being motivated by ego, selfishness, and personal motive.

(18:22) That influence, finally, is tamasic which views every effect as though it had no connection with any other, and which disregards as irrelevant the motive, whether deeply valid or trivial, behind the act.

People acting under the influence of tamas never think of action in terms of karmic cause and effect. They consider the act itself the reality, as something quite independent of whatever motivated it. If they are fired from a job, whether or not they deserved to be fired is irrelevant to them. They are only upset by what they conceive to have been their mistreatment. If they are criticized for something they've done, they turn the cannon of outrage on the criticism itself, not on the question, "Did I deserve to be criticized?" If they do a job badly, they ask, "Well, but at least I got it done, didn't I?" And if someone feeds them food that they don't like, they don't say, "Well, I know you meant well." Instead, they are simply distressed not to have been given what they liked.

(18:23) That action is sattwic which is divinely inspired, performed with complete non-attachment, without any sense of likes or dislikes, and without any desire for its fruits.

At this point we come to an explanation of the actual relationship of the three gunas to activity, rather than discussing the *influences* of the gunas on activity.

Sattwic action is motivated by superconscious inspiration. It is performed without attachment, without likes or dislikes, and without desire for any fruits accruing from it. Once again it should be pointed out that this is not being offered as new information, but is simply a review of what has been said at length previously.

(18:24) Action is rajasic if it is motivated by desires, if it is performed with ego-consciousness, and if it produces a sense of great (stress) and effort.

The more sattwic an action, the greater the sense of ease that accompanies it. On the other hand, the more rajasic it is, the greater the sense of effort because ego-consciousness cuts off higher power and inspiration, giving one the illusion that he must solve every problem and complete every labor by himself, alone.

(18:25) Tamasic action is performed heedlessly, without measuring one's ability, and in disregard of the possible consequences, (for example) failure, injury, or some other disaster to oneself or others.

It is interesting to see how often it occurs that opposites resemble one another. In this case, the attitudes described as tamasic might apply, on a higher level, to sattwic attitudes: faith, non-attachment to the fruits, and fearlessness. Yet it is not like a circle closing itself. Rather, it

is an upward spiral, as if one returned to some of the same attitudes he held in immaturity, but at a higher level of more mature understanding. The soldier who hurls himself heedlessly against an enemy line learns, with experience (assuming he lives through the event!), to be more careful, and may even become intensely fearful. One who has offered his ego up to God, however, and who feels that God alone is acting through him, may be perfectly conscious of the dangers he faces in battle, yet if he feels this is what God wants of him, he may throw himself with the same, though more conscious, courage as the tamasic warrior, completely aware of everything his courage entails.

(18:26) That action is called sattwic which is without ego-motivation, which cares not for either fulfillment or lack of fulfillment, success or failure, and which is filled with courage and zeal.

We have seen the difference in quality between tamasic and sattwic courage. In tamas, however, there is no true zeal. Zeal comes from selfless, but very conscious, dedication to an idealistic cause. Thus, the "courage" of the one is blinded and dark, and is based on ignorance of (or indifference to, which is the same thing in this case) the possible consequences. The courage of the other, the sattwic, on the other hand, is based on perfect knowledge, and on acceptance of the possible consequences. It weighs sensibly in the balance, therefore, the probabilities of its possible usefulness.

(18:27) The instrument of action (the individual performing it) is called rajasic if he is full of attachment to and longing for its fruits, if he is full of greed, impure motive, and ruthless determination, and if he is jubilant or depressed in the face of success or failure.

Even in the light of what people want for themselves, those who leap up and down in victory, or sob themselves hoarse in defeat, deprive themselves of the clear energy needed to carry to success whatever they do! Greed for gain, attachment, desire, selfish motive, indifference to the feelings of others—all these, combined with a jack-in-the-box reaction to everything, are great deterrents to accomplishing well or to completing anything in life, whether worthwhile or trivial.

(18:28) Tamasic action is vacillating, vulgarly ostentatious, obstinate, unscrupulous, deceitful, (frequently motivated by) malice, lazy, and procrastinating.

There is no point in telling tamasic people how to cure their tamas. They see nothing wrong with being as they are. If they seem to accept your advice, it will be only to "get you off their backs." You may count on their betraying you or otherwise letting you down at the first opportunity. The only reason for treating them with leniency and forgiveness will be for your own sake, to affirm your non-attachment to the fruits of what they, too, are doing. Otherwise, be warned by the above signs that tamas is at work in their nature. Such people are never to be trusted, and if, out of charity, one agrees to

work with them, one should always be aware of their dangerous proclivities. Never, for example, trust them to take the week's income to the bank!

(18:29) O Winner of Wealth (Dhananjaya: Arjuna), I will now explain, at length and singly, the threefold divisions of the gunas in their relation to people's capacity for understanding and to fortitude.
(18:30) That intellect, O Partha (Arjuna), is sattwic which understands the nature of right action and knows when to refrain from (even right) action; which knows what should be done and what should not be done; which understands the distinction between what ought to be feared (as wrong) and what ought to be embraced fearlessly (as right and dutiful), and between what constitutes bondage and what constitutes the path to liberation.

This stanza speaks its teaching clearly and well. It hardly requires any commentary except, perhaps, to point out that Krishna has said there may, occasionally, be a right motivation for fear: when the action one contemplates might put one in karmic error.

(18:31) O Partha (Arjuna), that intellect is influenced by rajas which causes one to perceive dharma and adharma (righteous and unrighteous action) distortedly, as also (any) dutiful and undutiful action.

Consider the prospect of a war between one's country and another. The drums of propaganda will be beating loudly to proclaim the righteousness of one's own country, whichever one it may be. Is that cause, however—in light of a higher law—justified, or unjustified? The rajasic influence is already fully in evidence, and will do its best to incite people to fight, through loud, self-justifying slogans that claim the justness of the cause. Sattwic people, however, should withdraw their feelings to an inner center of calm intuition, and there ask God, "Is this cause *just*? Would I be more justified in supporting it, or in refraining from involvement in it?"

Sometimes, as with the war of Kurukshetra, and as it would be were one's own country invaded by hostile forces, the cause may be adjudged right and justified. Sometimes, however, it is not karmically justified. Would one, in this case, be right to object, pleading conscience? Or, if the ethics of the situation seem mixed, would one be right to show loyalty to one's own country by accepting a draft into the armed forces? These are matters of conscience, and should be settled by the discriminating individual at that level.

For rajasic people, however—the great majority of them—the decision is quite a simple matter: launch into it, no matter how lurchingly. Activity, to the rajasic, is its own reward.

(18:32) O Partha (Arjuna), that intellect is tamasic which, enveloped in ignorance, thinks that wrong is right, and judges *everything* (not only dharma and adharma) distortedly.

Tamasic people, if they have the intelligence, use whatever dim reasoning they have to justify obviously false conclusions. They'll say (and in fact notoriously *have* said), "Well, if I steal from this unlocked car it will be a good lesson for the owner. It will teach him to lock his car next time, so he'll keep thieves like me from entering it."

They will march with self-righteous zeal in support of a dictatorial cause, and see those who resist the cause as "enemies of the people."

(18:33) (In the matter of steadfastness,) sattwic fortitude depends on steadying the mind by yoga meditation, and keeping the energy of (both) the body and senses controlled by *pranayama.*

Sattwic fortitude depends not on grim determination, but on being centered in the Self, and on keeping the breath and the body's energy calm by regulating the flow of prana and apana in the spine.

(18:34) Rajasic fortitude manifests itself in clinging fast—whether to duty, to the objects of desire, or to possessions—and demanding (for oneself) the fruit of every effort one expends.

This "clinging fast" produces tension, anxiety, and uncertainty in everything one does who acts under the influence of rajas. People under this influence loudly demand their "rights." They are often obsessed with the fear of being robbed or burgled. And even if they have a good desire, they allow themselves to be so seized in its jaws that, for them, there can be no other "cause" in the world!

(18:35) Tamasic fortitude, O Partha (Arjuna), manifests as addiction to sleep, obsession with whatever one fears, utter absorption in grief, abandonment to despair, and overweening arrogance.

The tamasic temperament tends, in other words, toward extremes—to the point where reason is completely abandoned. Unable to see beyond the horizons of one's present reality, whatever that may be, if a tamasic person sorrows, he can't imagine ever feeling calm on the subject again; if he does something well (or is praised for it, however undeservingly), he preens himself absurdly on his excellence. If he fears something, his fear is, for days, all he can talk about.

(18:36) Now hear from Me, O Best of the Bharatas (Arjuna), the three kinds of happiness, transcendent above which is Supreme bliss—the consequence of continuous inwardness of mind (through meditation). In bliss (alone) does one achieve the end of all sorrow.

It is fitting that Krishna begins his discussion of the kinds of happiness that are under the influence of the three gunas by referring to the bliss that transcends them all. All human happiness is relative. Only in absolute bliss is the end of all sorrow attained.

(18:37) That (human happiness) which is called sattwic (is attained through what) seems in the beginning like poison, but in the end is like nectar, and leads to the clear perception of the Self.

It is more difficult to climb a mountain than to slide down it. Virtue is difficult to practice in the beginning, and may, like poison, have a bitter taste. After a time, however, it becomes easy to practice and tastes as sweet as nectar. There is a certain magnetism in higher consciousness that draws the soul as it were effortlessly upward—once a certain point in one's sadhana has been reached. There is a saying that applies at this point: "When we lift up one hand to God, He reaches two down to help."

(18:38) That happiness is rajasic which arises from contact of the senses with their objects. It seems like nectar in the beginning, but in the end is like poison.

Sensory enjoyments may often seem, in the beginning, as sweet as nectar. If we consider them to be the *source* of our enjoyment, however, they soon turn bitter and, indeed, poison our happiness. Good food is pleasant, but if we consider it a source of happiness we may overeat and become too heavy, flaccid, and prone to disease. Wine may be pleasant to the taste, but if we consider it, too, a source of happiness we may drink to excess, and become alcoholics. The same must be said of anything and everything that is enjoyed through the senses: sex, drugs—everything. Surfeit never fails to end in boredom, disgust, and, sometimes, in tragedy.

(18:39) That elusive happiness is termed tamasic which begins and ends in the deluded stupor of oversleep, drunkenness, and slovenliness.

The choice to live in mental darkness comes from bad karma, reinforced by bad company. There is also the draw of the almost-familiar: We have come up from less conscious levels of awareness as lower animals. Subconsciously, that memory lingers with us, exerting the attraction of effortless ease. A comfortable alternative, it seems, to the long, steep climb up the mountain to Perfection. Having the choice eternally before us between effort and ease, it is hardly surprising that many cry out, in effect, "Stop bothering me; let me sleep!"

This tamasic tendency, though pronounced in some people, is present at least latently in everyone. It has a certain magnetism of its own, rooted in nostalgia for old, subconscious habits. Everything in Nature manifests a blend of the three gunas. Watch your own mind for any reluctance you may feel to do what you know you must do. That is the influence in you of tamoguna. Of its lowering tendency on the mind it may be said, "Give it an inch, and it will take a mile."

(18:40) There is no one in the material world (or in the material universe), nor among the gods in the astral heavens, who is free from the three qualities, or gunas, born of Prakriti (Cosmic Nature, the manifestation of God).

As my Guru put it, the fabric of creation is held together by the threads of the three gunas. Even saints manifest tamoguna (tamas), although, relatively speaking, to a very mild degree. They manifest it in the fact that they sleep, or take rest. Even tamasic or very evil people, moreover, show the sattwic quality to a mild degree when they do anything good for anyone. My Guru told a story about a very wicked woman who bit into a carrot she'd stolen, found it contained a worm, and gave it carelessly to a passing urchin. On reaching hell after death, that one "good deed" was recalled as her one and only (relative!) merit.

(18:41) O Scorcher of Foes (Arjuna)! the duties of Brahmins, Kshatriyas, and Vaishyas, as also of Shudras, are (inborn and diverse) according to the gunas uppermost in their natures.

Krishna separates the Shudras in that way (saying, "as also of") because the mentality of a Shudra is not given to taking the term, "duty," seriously.

Paramhansa Yogananda often said that the real "races" of man have nothing to do with the color of people's skin. It has everything to do, however, with their state of consciousness. The true divisions of the human race may be discerned vertically, not horizontally. They are the four natural castes.

At any congress of accountants, let us say, from many countries and from every continent of the world, the attendees will display a unanimity of basic outlook that they may not feel with their own next-door neighbors. Monks from different parts of the world will feel a greater kinship with one another than, possibly, with their own relatives. Businessmen will understand one another naturally and easily, even if they have to converse through translators. What people do, and even more so the kind of people they *are*, separates them into categories that cut across all barriers of language, nationality, and skin coloring.

Svabhava (one's own inherent nature) is the word Krishna uses here, indicating clearly that caste-distinctions depend not on heredity, but on what each person is in himself. This subject has been gone into extensively already, and need not be restated here at length. Krishna himself is merely recapitulating, for the sake of emphasis.

(18:42) The inherent duties of a Brahmin (the highest caste) are mind control (concentration), sense control (by the practice of *pranayama*), self-restraint, purity, forgiveness, integrity, wisdom, meditation to attain Self-realization, and faith in a higher truth.

The question may be asked, "Aren't all these things, being good, the duty of every man?" Krishna, and indeed the caste system itself (as rightly understood), simply accepts reality as it is. What people *should* do, and what they are capable of doing, are not always by any means one and the same thing. Even the self-restraint, purity, and integrity expected of a person of spiritual refinement differ from the best one can expect from people of less refined nature. Self-restraint in someone who is devoted to amassing riches might mean showing the "kindness" not to ruin a competitor completely. Purity might mean electing to refrain from gouging a customer even when the opportunity presents itself. And integrity might mean admitting that merchants (Vaishyas) elsewhere (in another city perhaps, and thus at a safe distance) may offer better prices on certain items.

A sattwic person, and therefore one who is by nature a Brahmin, has a duty to behave in a manner that is more refined, because his nature makes such refinement possible. He should nevertheless reach up toward the perfection of his potentiality for virtue. Where a lesser person might deserve praise for relatively generous deeds, a sattwic person, and therefore a true Brahmin, deserves none, and in any case should not desire it if it so happens that others appreciate his godly qualities. Any praise owing to his behavior should be both offered and accepted for the *quality* of goodness alone, which he merely manifests. Sattwic virtues are, as Krishna put it earlier, like smoke, which obscures a fire slightly but can be easily dispelled with a little puff of the "wind" of meditation. Since the fire can be seen through the smoke, appreciation for the light and warmth of the fire is given rightly to the fire alone, shining through the smoke. The wind which blows the smoke away is only the agent, not the end benefit.

(18:43) The natural duties of a Kshatriya are valor, vigor, fortitude, resourcefulness, skill in action, standing up firmly to the enemy (whatever kind of "battle" is involved), munificence, and leadership (of a kind that inspires others).

Kshatriya types are not always in a position to fight in battle, to show courage in the face of the enemy, or to lead others to victory. The *qualities* of a Kshatriya, however, show up under all circumstances. In one incarnation a person may be a ruler, and in the next, a monk. The ruler may not—indeed, surely will not—be always at war, and the monk may have no one over whom to rule but himself. In *character*, however, the two will be basically the same. It is the *character* of a Kshatriya that determines what he really is. A true Kshatriya stands up for what he believes, but his rectitude will be appropriate. In the home, for instance, he doesn't stand up to his wife if she wants to go out to dinner but he himself doesn't want to. In that case, he is *munificent*—within the general meaning of the term: not, that is to say, as a heroic concession to her wishes! As a monk in his next incarnation, he will probably have no enemies to fight, but he will have spiritual tests, perhaps temptations, and times of difficulty with others. In such cases, instead of fleeing he will stand up to those tests courageously. If in any difficulty with others he can practice munificence by holding an understanding attitude, he will show himself willing to see their point of view.

Thus, in many ways it may be seen that a Kshatriya is one who has Kshatriya qualities *by nature*, and who doesn't only display them under necessity.

(18:44) The duties of a Vaishya by nature are tilling the soil, cattle breeding, and business. Those of a Shudra are service to members of the higher castes.

The duties of the Vaishya must be reckoned by his own individual "reality," which begins with a rajasic, ego-centered attachment to things. Thus, even though not all societies on Earth, nor every place even within one country, concern themselves with farming and cattle breeding—cities, for example, offer few opportunities, if any, for rural activity—and though even merchandising is a fairly circumscribed activity, nevertheless there are many Vaishya types in a large variety of gainful activities, and there must have been such even in Krishna's (perhaps) simpler times, which cannot be listed in exact categories.

We must begin, therefore, with the underlying *purpose* of those Vaishya activities which the Gita lists. First, what makes any action a *duty*? Speaking of man's duty to society, it is that which will best serve society as a whole. Krishna's concern, however, is with the individual's *spiritual* progress. Therefore, the duties of a Vaishya must be those activities which can help him to rise spiritually. Activities that will help him to fulfill his own desire for gain and for ego-, or for self-, expression, and which may at the same time help him to raise his consciousness, include such things as all kinds of artistic expression. Yogananda lists artists—including composers, novelists, sculptors, musicians—in fact, as Vaishyas. Yet one can well imagine that this designation does not include those as Vaishyas who create works of art, music, and literature for the upliftment of others! Those, rather, who create such works for money, and for people's mere pleasure or diversion, are what he meant by the term, Vaishyas.

The "mere" in that last sentence is not meant derogatorily. To give esthetic pleasure to others can be a means of raising their, and one's own, awareness, and of clarifying one's own and other people's understanding.

The duty of a Vaishya is to include the benefit of others in his own activities. Thus, he will become more sensitive to the needs of others, and will develop, in time, the nature of a Kshatriya.

Shudra types can only grow spiritually by mixing with those of a higher level of consciousness than themselves. The only practical way for them to do so is by holding positions of service under persons of greater refinement.

(18:45) Each one attentive to his own duty, man rises toward the highest success. Hear now how, by devotedly pursuing his own duty, one may rise toward that final end.

Caste should be determined, not by one's parentage or by society, but by the nature of the individual himself. Indeed, without even defining a person's natural caste, one usually finds it naturally for himself. Parents may help a child to get the sort of education that is best suited to his actual needs, but when the child himself attains an age and a level of maturity to decide such matters for himself—even to move out on his own—he alone must determine, finally, what his place is. As for his duty, that can be at least suggested by others who are perhaps wiser and more mature than himself.

Always, one's duty (as distinct from one's predilection) should be determined in terms of what will help him to rise—both toward a higher caste and toward a higher influence of the gunas.

(18:46) One attains perfection by offering his own

special gifts up to Him by whom all beings were manifested, and by Whom the whole (universe) is permeated.

Whatever one's particular gift, one can advance best, spiritually, by offering that gift up to God. God, on the one hand, will perfect that offering and help the person to excel at whatever he does. He will also help that person who longs for truth to walk in the direction of inner freedom.

Here again we see, recapitulated, Krishna's advice to Arjuna to act, and not to try to reach God by abandoning all activity. The only qualification to this teaching is its balancing one: "If a duty conflicts with a higher duty, it ceases to be a duty." In other words, if there are several things one can do well, he should concentrate on that activity which will most expand his sympathies and uplift his consciousness.

Many commentators have claimed that Krishna in this stanza is saying that one should follow whatever vocation is traditional in his family. They are mistaken. In a settled society, and not one that is under transition as the whole world is today, this advice might at least be generally acceptable (though one wonders how anyone, following it, would ever become a sannyasi!). In an age, however, when society itself is in flux, this counsel could be ruinous! The truth is, everyone in this world is, simply, himself. He comes into his family as a guest. Being transient, he should take nothing outward as defining who and what he is. Every human being must follow his own star. The higher one rises toward inner freedom, the more imperative this advice becomes.

(18:47) It is better to fail attempting to follow one's own dharma than to succeed in following the dharma of another. One incurs no sin in trying to fulfill his own duty.

(18:48) O Son of Kunti (Arjuna), one should not abandon the work dictated by his own nature, even though (the work) contain some imperfection, for all undertakings (even the best) are marred by blemishes, even as a flame is (obscured) by smoke.

It should be pointed out here, incidentally, that anything done with ego-consciousness creates karma, and that any creation of karma cannot but be varied in quality and consequence. Hence, it ought not to be necessary to add: *of course* one can create bad karma, as well as good, through anything he does, even if he "only tries" to do his duty. The point Krishna is making is that in doing one's own duty one is not setting up a *new* pattern of activity (karma) to be worked through to its conclusion. If, for example, one knows it to be his dharma to help children as a schoolteacher, but responding to the advice of others he settles for a better-paying job as a truck driver, he may turn out to be a good truck driver, but he will advance no closer to fulfilling his first karmic pattern, and may in fact add a new pattern created by an entirely new set of experiences and type of companions.

Everyone's highest duty is to seek God. To pursue this duty may effectively cancel out every other karmic pattern—so that if the schoolteacher decides to go off and live with a group of people who are seeking God, and is not able in that new environment to teach children, he will in any case have chosen a higher dharma, and one which will take him up more surely to that divine "summit" where all duties end. To fail in that task will also be more liberating for him than to succeed as a schoolteacher, for it will take him eventually out of karma altogether, whereas teaching school will only aid him on the path toward good karma, but not toward liberation.

(18:49) That person comes closest to attaining perfection who keeps his intellect non-attached to everything outside the Self, who reigns in victory over the Self, and from whom (all) desires have fled.

The true rulers in this world are not those who sit proudly on their thrones, but those who rule themselves to perfection. The king or emperor can command people's outer activities, but none can tell them what to think, feel, believe, or how simply to be, in their hearts. That man, however, who has command over himself can inspire, and therefore truly lead, thousands.

(18:50) O Son of Kunti (Arjuna), hear from Me how he who attains such perfection finds the culmination (of all seeking in) Brahman.

To become perfect in one's Self is to attain Infinite Consciousness. There is no need to seek outside the Self for wisdom. To know even one atom to its depths of mystery is to possess the secret to all truth. The objective atom cannot be known this way, but the ego *can* so be known. Once one traces the ego to its "lair," by removing from it the last veil between it and God, there will be nothing else to attain. Space and time are illusions. To know one's Self is to know God! To know one's Self is to know everything!

(18:51) Absorbed in complete purity of the intellect, subjugating body and senses by resolute self-restraint, protecting oneself (as much as possible) from noise and from other sense-entanglements, relinquishing both attachment and repugnance;—
(18:52) abiding in a solitary place, eating lightly, controlling the body, speech, and mind; absorbing oneself in divine yoga meditation; dispassionate;—
(18:53) serene; self-surrendered; relinquishing (any lingering) attraction to power, vanity, lust, anger, possessions, and the consciousness of "me" and "mine": such a person qualifies to become one with Brahman.

Purity of the intellect requires, first, that one give up the tendency of the human intellect to "figure things out," as though life were only a puzzle needing intellectual solution. The yogi learns to approach any problem or question by holding his mind up to the downflow of superconscious inspiration. Wisdom comes not by careful reasoning, but by simply knowing in one's Self what the answer is. "Solution-consciousness," not "problem-consciousness," is the key to wisdom: holding the mind up to that higher aspect of knowing which already *has*, and can provide, every answer.

Protecting oneself from "noise" is more properly translated, "sound." Some sounds, however, are not intrusive. "Noise," therefore, is more readily understandable. The sounds of nature—wind in the trees, bird calls, and other common sounds—are not intrusive. If one must sit for meditation where automobile traffic and other sounds intrude on one's concentration, one continuous sound (like flowing water, or a waterfall) may suffice to block out those individual sounds sufficiently to prevent one from noticing them.

Abiding in a solitary place is, for most people, not possible. Krishna himself repeatedly advises in the Gita the performance of normal, dutiful action—a way of life that, for most people, precludes solitude. How, then, to follow the advice he gives here? The answer, for many people, is: by creating a "place of seclusion" in one's own home. Set one room aside, or even a screened-off portion of your bedroom, where the only activity allowed is meditation. Superconscious vibrations will develop there, and will effectively "screen out" the surrounding, worldly atmosphere.

The other points in these stanzas are self-explanatory.

(18:54) One attains supreme devotion to Me, and can be absorbed in Brahman, who is always inwardly calm, who never laments and is without desire, and who beholds all beings with equal mind.

A human image made of salt, if it is immersed in the ocean, will dissolve in it and become lost. The human body, by an interesting coincidence, is very similar to ocean water, in that the percentage of salt in the blood and that of salt in the ocean are the same. Were one to immerse himself in the ocean, however, his whole body would not dissolve, for it is composed of other elements besides salt and water.

What keeps man's consciousness separate from Satchidananda (divine bliss) is, of course, the fact that his consciousness is composed of other elements also. Prominent among these "elements" are restlessness; the wish that things were other than they are (lamenting the state of anything, in other words); desires (which keep him from feeling complete in himself); likes and dislikes regarding people and things (which keep him forever putting forth energy to attract and repel). Only when these "elements" are transformed into the "salt" of devotion (that one-pointed feeling which alone is capable of merging one's consciousness in the ocean of bliss) is one capable of being absorbed in Brahman.

It often happens that great yogis come out, for a time, from that great ocean in which their consciousness has been dissolved, and reassume the individuality they once had as human beings to enjoy again an I-and-Thou relationship with the Lord. Because they are now pure "salt images," however, made only of the same "elements" of consciousness as those contained in the ocean, they can merge back into Him any time they wish.

Ramproshad, a great devotional saint who lived in the eighteenth century in Bengal, India, once sang, "Oh, though a thousand scriptures declare Thee to be *nirakara* (formless), come to me in the form I love: as the Divine Mother of the universe!"

(18:55) By supreme devotion to Me he can quickly realize Me in My true nature: what and who I am. Knowing these truths, he can unhesitatingly enter into Me.

(18:56) Over and above the faithful performance of all one's duties, and taking shelter (completely) in Me, he must still be received by My grace.

It is important to understand that God, because He is above His law, cannot be won only by following His law. No mathematically exact formula can induce Him to reveal Himself. Man thinks too easily that he, himself, can *cause* things to go the way he wants if only he will make the correct effort. This is, notably, the attitude of modern scientists. It is the attitude of many doctors, who think their patients' health *depends* on them—on their correct diagnoses and on the medicines they prescribe. Yet doctors know that there are cases in which they, in their efforts, go completely "by the book," yet still have had patients who died. They know also that cases which seemed to them hopeless have recovered all of a sudden, quite unexpectedly.

The ego can intrude in so subtle a fashion that even at the last step of the journey, some people think they themselves have made it by their own effort. This simple thought is enough to keep them from merging completely in God: it is that little bit of consciousness which reveals that one has not completely taken on all the "elements of the ocean." Freely we should give of ourselves, expecting nothing in return, and only loving Him who is our very own. Will He, then, give Himself to us? Yes, certainly! The very presumption, however, implicit in that word, "certainly," is enough to prevent us from completely becoming (it is more than acquiring) that perfect state of consciousness!

(18:57) Mentally devote your every action to Me. See Me as your Supreme Goal. Uplift toward Me every discernment of your intellect. Thus, with love, absorb all your heart's feelings in Me.

(18:58) With heart absorbed in Me, you shall (also) by My grace overcome every impediment. If, however, with any (lingering) thought of ego, you do not fully heed Me (by absorbing My consciousness into yours), you may (even then) be thrown down again to your destruction.

The destruction intended here, my Guru explained, is temporary. Still it is possible even after achieving *sabikalpa samadhi* to fall again for a time into delusion, until that last *samskara* (tendency) of being a separate individual, and, to that extent, apart from God, is dissolved.

(18:59) If, indulging your ego, you should determine, "I will not fight," you would have to fight anyway, obliged to do so by Nature (your own, as well as cosmic).

That devotee who, after incarnations of struggle and effort, has acquired the nature of a spiritual warrior determined to vanquish every inner weakness, will be driven to fight anyway by that nature (and also by the help of Cosmic Nature, which his efforts have summoned), until every delusion is vanquished.

These words of Krishna's are supremely reassuring. For it does happen that the devotee, even after long struggle to perfect himself, recoils suddenly, thinking, "Oh no, not this one, *too!*" Some delusion may seem particularly dear to him, and may even persuade him to think in protest, "Why must I give up *even this (fond) idea, or this (dear) attachment?*" Fortunately for his devotion, once he has reached the firm resolve to offer himself wholly to God, even God (through Prakriti, or the Divine Mother) will protect him, and will keep his feet firmly on the path. His fleeting nostalgia for that "sweet" aspect of *maya* evaporates, and he finds himself once again determined to engage in yet another battle.

This next stanza is a reminder that, ultimately, our very strengths and weaknesses are not our own: they are the operation of cosmic forces, *through* our human nature. Here, however, Krishna is saying that Arjuna had already won those influences to side with his higher, spiritual aspiration and efforts.

(18:60) O Son of Kunti, that (momentary) delusion—the ripened fruit of a past karma—which has now made you reluctant to fight will be snatched from you by another (good) karma, and you will find that you have (no choice but) to fight anyway.

In the beginning, one's "second nature" (namely, habit) impedes his spiritual efforts. He may want, for instance, to meditate all night, but habit forces him to

sleep whether he wants to or not: He cannot keep his
mind wakeful enough to soar in superconsciousness—in
fact, not to put too fine a point on it—he simply cannot
fight off the impulse to plunge heavily into the relative
stupor of subconsciousness. (I remember our Guru
telling us monks one day, "Lying in bed last night, I
experimented going into subconsciousness. I didn't like
that feeling at all. I found myself hemmed in on all sides
by a thick wall of flesh!")

Gradually, as the devotee keeps trying, his higher
nature takes over, and a power he thought impossible
for him manifests itself, making it impossible for him *not*
to make the effort necessary to continue on to victory.

**(18:61) O Arjuna, the Lord is lodged in the hearts of
all beings. His cosmic delusion compels them to
revolve as though they'd been mounted on a machine.**

These words are uttered to show man how insignificant
is his ego in its constant thought, "I do," and, "I am."
The words are *not* uttered to discourage anyone from
trying to plunge into that stream, which will carry him to
Cosmic consciousness, but to understand from where that
power comes.

The question arises in some minds, "How free, really,
is human will?" Man is free, my Guru said, to turn
to God or to reject Him. Balancing the metaphor of
a machine—something fixed, in other words—and recognizing the final inadequacy of all metaphors, let us
consider also another: a stream down which pebbles are
rolled helplessly. There is another stream, however,

which flows in the opposite direction. Man has this much choice: He can decide, with each lifetime, which stream he will enter: the stream toward greater involvement in *maya*, or that which will take him away from *maya* to merge, eventually, in the cosmic ocean.

(18:62) O Arjuna, make Him (alone), with all eagerness of heart, your refuge. By His grace you will attain the uttermost peace, and find shelter for all eternity.

(18:63) Thus has wisdom, the most secret (and sacred) of all secrets, been given to you by Me. Reflect on it. Then do as you feel to do.

We come now to that part of the eighteenth chapter which has made the Bhagavad Gita not only the most instructive, informative, and inspiring—perhaps of all scriptures in the world—but also the best loved.

Krishna has expounded truths more clearly, exhaustively, and convincingly than divine truth—ever one and the same everywhere—has ever been explained before, and has done it so succinctly and so wonderfully that no thinking person, surely, could fail to determine to give his whole life to the quest for God.

It is marvelous that, after this exposition (so far) of nearly 700 verses, during which Krishna has set forth persuasively every human being's need for God, he still could end by saying, "Now then, do as you feel."

(18:64) Again, hear now My supreme word, the most secret (and sacred) of all. Because you are dearly beloved by Me, I offer it now for your highest benefit.

Krishna's words to Arjuna, here, are nectar-sweet. Is everyone, however, so dearly loved by God as to be deemed worthy of receiving the Lord's concern for his highest well-being? Yes! All are loved equally by God. It must be added, however, that, if one would have proof incontrovertible of that love, he must have a heart pure enough to receive it. A cup turned upside down cannot receive nectar which, otherwise, might be poured out, filling it to the brim.

Imagine a story in which a young man is born to poverty—perhaps in a city slum among degraded people, with little opportunity for schooling because he must work to support his widowed mother and younger siblings. At night he studies hard, and becomes fit at last to obtain good employment in a large company. He rises in the ranks of that company, and is finally made a vice president. At those heights he meets the boss's daughter. They fall in love, and, with the boss's blessings, get married. Later, the boss dies. The young man inherits his position and also his palatial home.

At the end of such a story, wouldn't the reader exclaim with deep satisfaction, "What a *beautiful* story!"

Now imagine another story: a young man, raised in a wealthy home, joining a large company and, without any obstacles before him, becoming a vice president and marrying the boss's daughter. Would it end by the young man's inheriting the boss's position, and moving with his wife into the boss's palatial home? Quite possibly so. But even more possibly the reader would have closed the book much sooner with a yawn, and would never find out what happened at the end!

The cosmic drama *needs* suspense, excitement, at times terror, and at other times thrilling beauty. Man *needs* to feel that the ending to it all is highly uncertain, and may, for him, prove disastrous. Only thus will his interest throughout hold him "on the edge of his seat." Every soul's journey is unique. It is filled with uncertainties, with sorrow mingled with joy, with hope mingled with despair, with triumph mingled with crushing defeat, with dark doubt as to whether life has any meaning at all followed by the discovery of human love, of success, of history-making knowledge, of undreamed-of power, of joyful laughter followed by heart-wrenching tears. If man could know, through this long journey, that God's love was always with him—deeply, eternally, unconditionally—he might well preen himself on that "good fortune," grow cocky, and never learn the attitudes absolutely necessary for entering into, and becoming one with, that love.

He must learn to empty the vessel of his heart of all pride, all selfishness, all indifference. He must learn how to hold that vessel high, in pure and unconditional devotion, to be filled with the nectar of divine love. Only then, at the conclusion of his aeons-long adventure, will he learn that God has always loved him. He may, then, hear those words, "You are dearly beloved by Me." Not—please note— "I love you," with the personal, ego-framed suggestion of an ego loved, but the more impersonal expression of love in which there is no separate individual reaching out with love toward another separate individual.

(18:65) Absorb yourself in Me; be wholly devoted to Me; worship and bow to Me alone: So shall you

undoubtedly reach Me. This I promise you faithfully, for you are dear to Me.

(18:66) Forsaking all other dharmas (duties), remember Me alone. I will free you from all sin (even from that of not fulfilling other, lesser duties). Do not grieve!

Man's highest duty is to love God. All dharma serves the highest end of developing one-pointed, single-hearted devotion to, and love for, God, the Supreme and finally the Only Beloved.

We told the story earlier of how Krishna once asked Draupadi, "Why don't you practice the techniques of yoga meditation?" Draupadi answered, "I would love to, Lord, but how can I do so, when I can't take my mind away from You long enough to practice them?" Hearing her reply, we said, Krishna only smiled.

This is what Krishna means, here, about "lesser duties." Of course, the correct practice of yoga *includes* doing it with deep devotion. One should not take his mind away from God in order to practice it. Nevertheless, if the river of energy in the spine is flowing strongly upward through the heart to the brain, what further techniques are needed? Yoga techniques have the purpose of directing that energy upward, for those who can be helped by that extra nudge.

(18:67) Never share these truths with one who is without self-control or devotion, nor with one who won't share with others in a spirit of service, nor give them to one who is indifferent to them, or who finds fault with Me.

One whose life has been changed by finding the truth, or even by finding the way to it, naturally longs to help others to find it also. He should reflect, however, that each one needs to come to it in his own way, and at his own time. Out of respect for wherever others may be now in their spiritual evolution, one should not (as Jesus Christ put it) "throw his pearls before swine."

One who has no self-control may view as offensive any teaching that emphasizes self-control. That person isn't ready to face his weaknesses and may only reply, perhaps with resentment, "Now is not the time." Nevertheless, most people know in their hearts that lack of self-control has not given them fulfillment, but has only brought them suffering. Because of this very subconscious recognition, they may resent being given advice prematurely on the subject.

One who has no devotion, whose heart's feelings are desiccated, who feels (foolishly) fully satisfied with himself, and who is accustomed to applaud such dry statements of the intellect as, "Just the facts, please," may sneer at any manifestation of devotional feeling that expresses a heartfelt aspiration toward higher truths. To him, such feelings are "mere sentiment." Why offer a beautiful chalice filled with ambrosia to someone who will merely spit in it or throw it away?

Those who serve no one, who share with no one, who—miser-like—try to hoard all their gains, their sympathies, their concern (which they lavish only on themselves), could never understand the selfless happiness of self-giving to others. Instead, their hearts shrink inward upon themselves, become dry shells of dead feeling, and turn angrily against anyone who suggests to them that they even consider the needs of others. Such people should be left alone, unless one is blessed with great spiritual power to affect everyone's life for the better. Suffering, alone, in such cases, will provide the rain to soften such hearts and make them ready to receive higher truths.

Many people are self-satisfied and simply don't want to hear about a better way of living and believing. Such people, also, must be left to their own devices, until they themselves ask to receive more.

There are people, finally, who presume to think the universe might be better arranged than it is; or who blame God for their suffering, and do so in such a way as not to "want to hear anything more about it"; or who accuse God of being "unfair." In counseling others, never try to *impose* even good ideas on anyone, even if you are sure of those truths in yourself. People need to ask, first. They must *seek* understanding. To try to force even wisdom on them would be an offense against their eternal birthright, free will.

(18:68,69) Whosoever will, with supreme devotion, impart this supreme, secret knowledge to My devotees, shall without a doubt come to Me. No one among men performs a more priceless service to Me. Nor is there in all the world anyone more dear to Me.

My Guru once told a group of us, "Pray in this way: 'Give me Thyself, that I may give Thee to all.' That," he concluded, "is the highest prayer." To broadcast high truths without practicing them oneself gains one little merit, but to seek God earnestly oneself, and, while doing so, to share one's inspirations, discoveries, and growing wisdom with others is the highest divine service any man can render to others—which is a service to God in them.

(18:70) Whoever studies and (intuitively) understands this sacred dialogue between us will worship Me by the sacrifice (self-offering) of wisdom. Such is My holy declaration.

(18:71) Even that person who, full of devotion and without skepticism, merely listens to this holy discourse, and heeds its teachings, shall become free from earthly karma and shall be blessed to dwell in the high realm of the virtuous.

Salvation is of two kinds: final liberation from all karma and union with God; and freedom from earthly karma, giving the possibility of living from then on in high astral regions, from which one can work out his astral and causal karma until he reaches final liberation. Salvation from the need for further imprisonment on this material plane is in itself a great blessing, and can be won even without (yet) achieving divine perfection.

(18:72) O Partha (Arjuna)! Have you received this wisdom with wholly uplifted consciousness? Has your delusion-born ignorance, O Dhananjaya, now been dispelled?

(18:73) Arjuna answered: My delusion has been demolished! I have, by Your grace, O Krishna, regained the memory of my soul. I stand firm now, all my doubts and questions answered and dissipated. I will act according to Your word.

(18:74) Sanjaya said: Thus have I listened to this wondrous discourse between Vasudeva (Krishna) and high-souled Arjuna. It has caused the hair on my body to stand up (so greatly have I been awe-stricken and thrilled with joy).

(18:75) Through the grace of Byasa (the author of the Bhagavad Gita), this supreme secret of yoga has been given to me, imparted directly to my consciousness by Krishna himself, the great Lord of yoga.

(18:76) O King Dhritarashtra, as I recall over and over again this wonderful, holy dialogue between Keshava (Krishna) and Arjuna, I overflow repeatedly with joy.

(18:77) And, O King Dhritarashtra, as often as I remember the cosmic manifestation of Hari (Krishna, "Thief of Hearts"), I am overwhelmed with amazement, and am ever and again renewed with joy.

(18:78) (Sanjaya concludes:) Such is my faith now that, wherever Krishna is manifest, and wherever is Partha (the true devotee, Arjuna), expert wielder of the bow of self-mastery, there (I know) will be success, victory, the attainment of (all) power (needed for any accomplishment), and the manifestation of all glory and righteousness. Such is my firm conviction.

Thus ends the eighteenth chapter, called "The Yoga of Release by Renunciation," of the Upanishad of the holy Bhagavad Gita, in the dialogue between Sri Krishna and Arjuna discussing yoga and the science of God-realization.

GLOSSARY

Adhibhuta. The consciousness immanent in physical creatures and the physical cosmos.

Adhidaiva. The consciousness manifest in astral bodies and in the astral cosmos.

Adhiyagya. The Supreme Creative and Cognizing Spirit.

Adhyatma. Brahman's manifestation as the essential soul of all beings.

agya chakra. The center of the ego, in the medulla oblongata.

ahankara. The ego.

anahata chakra. The dorsal or heart center (chakra).

apana. The descending energy in the astral spine.

Aparaprakriti. The outwardly manifesting creative force, *maya.*

asana. Firmness, erect posture in meditation.

Ashtanga Yoga. Patanjali's exposition on the eight stages of enlightenment.

Ashvatta tree. The human body. Its trunk is the spine. Its roots "above" are the rays of energy that both emanate from and nourish the brain and body through the *sahasrara* at the top of the head. The tree's branches, "below," are the many-branched nervous system.

astral body. The body of light and energy.

AUM. The vibrational sound of the cosmos.

AUM-*Tat-Sat*. *Sat* is the eternal Truth from which all of creation issues; AUM is the cosmic vibration, from which proceeds cosmic manifestation; and *Tat* is the still reflection, at the heart of all vibration, of the motionless Spirit beyond vibration.

avatar. A liberated soul sent back into manifested existence by the will of the Creator to save souls still wandering in delusion.

Bhakti Yoga. The yoga path of intense devotion, whereon all one's feelings are channeled upward in the spine toward God.

bishuddha chakra. The cervical center.

Brahma. The creative vibration; along with Vishnu and Shiva, part of AUM, the Cosmic Vibration.

brahmacharya. "Flowing with Brahma"; self-control, especially sexual.

Brahman. The Divine Absolute.

brahmanadi. The "spine" of the causal body, so called because it is the primal channel through which Brahman—the divine consciousness—descended into the body.

Brahmisthiti. Absolute oneness with the Infinite.

buddhi. Intellect.

caste system. The four castes, or "races" of man, were originally based not on man's birth but on his natural capacities and the goal of life he elected to achieve. The goals can be described as (1) *kama*, desire, activity of the senses (Shudra stage), (2) *artha*, gain, fulfilling but controlling the desires (Vaisha stage), (3) *dharma*, self-discipline, the life of right action (Kshatriya stage), (4) *moksha*, liberation, the life of spirituality (Brahmin stage).

causal body. The innermost body made of ideas.

chakras. Plexuses or centers in the spine, from which energy flows out into the nervous system, and through that system into the body, sustaining and activating the different body parts.

chitta. The feeling aspect of consciousness.

Day of Brahma. The aeons-long period of cosmic manifestation. At the dawn of Brahma's Day, all creation, remanifested, emerges from its (night) state of unmanifestation.

devas. Astral or angelic beings.

dharana. One-pointed concentration.

dharma. Virtue, righteousness, right action.

dhyana. Absorption in deep meditation.

diksha. Spiritual initiation.

dwaita. Duality.

ego. The soul attached to the body.

gunas. The three basic qualities that comprise the universe: sattwa guna, the elevating quality, that which most clearly suggests divinity; rajas, the activating element in nature; tamas, the darkening quality, that which obscures the underlying unity of Life.

guru. Teacher; spiritual savior.

Gyana Yoga. The path of discrimination.

iḍa. One of the two superficial nerve channels in the astral spine, *iḍa* begins and ends on the left side of the spine. The energy passes upward through it, and causes inhalation.

japa. The constant repetition of God's name.

jiva. The soul, individualized consciousness: the Infinite limited to, and identified with, a body.

jivan mukta. "Freed while living"—a state of freedom from ego-consciousness while still having karma to work out from past lives.

Karma Yoga. The path of right spiritual action.

karma. Action.

Kriya Yoga. The ancient yogic science reintroduced to the world by Lahiri Mahasaya in the nineteenth century. It consists of the careful, conscious circulation of energy around the spine in order to magnetize it and to redirect the mental tendencies toward the brain.

kshetra. The body, the "field," where good and evil karma are reaped.

kshetragya. The inner perceiver, the soul.

kumbhaka. Retention of the breath.

Kundalini. Located below the base of the spine, where the outward-flowing energy from the spine to the nervous system becomes "locked" in its downward pull. Kundalini awakening signifies the moment when the downward flow of energy relaxes its grip on outwardness and begins to return upward in the direction of its source in divine consciousness.

Kutastha Chaitanya. The Christ consciousness underlying creation, reflecting the motionless Spirit beyond creation.

Kutastha. The seat of the spiritual eye, which lies at the point midway between the two eyebrows.

lila. The divine play.

Mahabharata. The longest epic in the world—deeply allegorical, of which the Bhagavad Gita forms a relatively brief episode.

manas. The perceiving mind.

manipura chakra. The lumbar center.

mantra. Potent chant.

maun. Complete silence.

maya. Delusion, the outwardly manifesting creative force.

moksha. Final, perfect liberation in absolute union with Divine Consciousness.

mudras. Asanas combined with special stimulation of the flow of certain inner energies.

muladhara chakra. The coccyx center.

muni. One who has dissolved his ego-consciousness in God.

Night of Brahma. The aeons-long period during which all creation remains in its unmanifestated state.

nirvana. The extinction of individuality.

nishkam karma. Action without desire for the fruits of action.

nadi. Subtle channel of life force.

param mukta. A supremely free soul.

Paraprakriti. Immanent as opposed to overt Nature: the hidden reality behind the whole material universe.

pingala. One of the two superficial nerve channels in the astral spine, *pingala* begins and ends on the right side of the spine. Energy passing downward through it causes exhalation.

Prakriti. Intelligent Mother Nature, the outer "show" that we see through the senses.

prana. Energy; also, the ascending energy of the breath in the astral spine.

pranaba. The sound of AUM.

pranayama. Control of the senses through withdrawal of the energy.

prarabdha karma. Present tendencies, and the results of past actions brought over from former lives.

pratyahara. Interiorization of the mind.

Purusha. Transcendent God, the Father.

purushakara karma. Actions generated in this life under the influence, not of habit or desire, but of soul-guidance.

Raja Yoga. The royal yoga, which takes the meditator to the central river to enlightenment, the pathway of the spine.

rajoguna. The activating element in nature.

rishi. Seer or sage.

sadhana. Spiritual practice.

sadhu. Holy man.

sahasrara. "Thousand-rayed lotus" at the top of the head; union with this point produces Cosmic consciousness.

samadhi. Divine ecstasy. *Sabikalpa samadhi* is conditioned ecstasy. *Nirbikalpa samadhi* is unconditioned: one's consciousness has become so established in oneness with God that there is no possibility of a return to the limitations of the ego.

samsara. The outward play of *maya* or delusion.

samskaras. Past tendencies.

Sanaatan Dharma. The "Eternal Religion."

sannyasi. A renunciate.

Satchidananda. Ever-existing, ever-conscious, ever-new Bliss.

satsanga. Good (and especially spiritual) company.

sattwa guna. The elevating quality, that which lifts one toward divinity.

Shankhya. One of the three main systems of Indian thought, or revelation, along with Yoga and Vedanta, Shankhya underscores the need to escape from *maya,* or delusion.

Shiva. The destroying or all-dissolving vibration; along with Brahma and Vishnu, part of AUM, the Cosmic Vibration.

siddha. A perfected being.

sloka. Scriptural passage.

smriti. Divine memory.

spiritual eye. The Kutastha, a reflection of the medulla oblongata: a field of dark blue light surrounded by a golden halo, in the center of which is a five-pointed star. The golden aureole represents the astral world; the blue field inside it, the causal world and also the omnipresent Christ consciousness; the star in the center, the Spirit beyond creation.

sushumna. The deep spine, through which Kundalini, being magnetized to flow upward, begins its slow ascent toward enlightenment.

swadisthana chakra. The sacral center.

tamoguna. The darkening quality, that which obscures the underlying unity of Life.

tyaga. Self-surrender, non-attachment to the fruits of action.

tyagi. One who is self-offered to the Divine.

Upanishads. Indian scriptures that present the essence of the Vedas.

Vedanta. One of the three main systems of Indian thought, or revelation, along with Shankhya and Yoga, Vedanta describes the nature of Brahman, the divine consciousness.

Vedas. India's oldest scripture.

Vishnu. The preserving vibration; along with Brahma and Shiva, part of AUM, the Cosmic Vibration.

vrittis. Eddies or whirlpools (of feeling).

yagya. A religious rite, the symbolic offering of the ego-self into the sacrificial fire for purification. The true yagya is Kriya Yoga.

Yoga. One of the three main systems of Indian thought, or revelation, along with Shankhya and Vedanta, Yoga tells the sincere seeker *how* to escape from *maya*, or delusion.

yugas. Ages or cycles of time; the four ages are Kali (dark), Dwapara ("second," an age of energy), Treta ("third," an age of awareness of the power of mind), and Satya ("Truth," also called *Krita*, an age of high spiritual awareness) *yugas*.

LIST OF INDEXES

INDEX OF STORIES

Index of Bible Quotations

ABOUT THE AUTHOR

PARAMHANSA YOGANANDA

"As a bright light shining in the midst of darkness, so was Yogananda's presence in this world. Such a great soul comes on earth only rarely, when there is a real need among men."
—The Shankaracharya of Kanchipuram

Born in India in 1893, Paramhansa Yogananda was trained from his early years to bring India's ancient science of Self-realization to the West. In 1920 he moved to the United States to begin what was to develop into a worldwide work touching millions of lives. Americans were hungry for India's spiritual teachings, and for the liberating techniques of yoga.

In 1946 he published what has become a spiritual classic and one of the best-loved books of the 20th century, *Autobiography of a Yogi*. In addition, Yogananda established headquarters for a worldwide work, wrote a number of books and study courses, gave lectures to thousands in most major cities across the United States, wrote music and poetry, and trained disciples. He was invited to the White House by Calvin Coolidge, and he initiated Mahatma Gandhi into Kriya Yoga, his most advanced technique of meditation.

Yogananda's message to the West highlighted the unity of all religions, and the importance of love for God combined with scientific techniques of meditation.

"Swami Kriyananda is a man of wisdom and compassion in action, truly one of the leading lights in the spiritual world today."
—Lama Surya Das, Dzogchen Center, author of *Awakening The Buddha Within*

SWAMI KRIYANANDA

A prolific author, accomplished composer, playwright, and artist, and a world-renowned spiritual teacher, Swami Kriyananda refers to himself simply as "a humble disciple" of the great God-realized master, Paramhansa Yogananda. He met his guru at the young age of twenty-two, and served him during the last four years of the Master's life. And he has done so continuously ever since.

Kriyananda was born in Rumania of American parents, and educated in Europe, England, and the United States. Philosophically and artistically inclined from youth, he soon came to question life's meaning and society's values. During a period of intense inward reflection, he discovered Yogananda's *Autobiography of a Yogi,* and immediately traveled 3,000 miles from New York to California to meet the Master, who accepted him as a monastic disciple. Yogananda appointed him as the head of the monastery, authorized him to teach in his name and to give initiation into Kriya Yoga, and entrusted him with the missions of writing and developing what he called "world brotherhood colonies."

Recognized as the "father of the spiritual communities movement" in the United States, Swami Kriyananda founded Ananda World Brotherhood Community in 1968. It has served as a model for a number of communities founded subsequently in the United States and Europe.

In 2003 Swami Kriyananda, then in his seventy-eighth year, moved to India with a small international group of disciples, to dedicate his remaining years to making his guru's teachings better known. To this end he appears daily on Indian national television with his program *A Way of Awakening*. He has established Ananda Sangha, which publishes many of his eighty-six literary works and spreads the teachings of Kriya Yoga throughout India. His vision for the next years includes founding cooperative spiritual communities in India, a temple of all religions dedicated to Paramhansa Yogananda, a retreat center, a school system, and a monastery, as well as a university-level Yoga Institute of Living Wisdom.

ABOUT THE PAINTER

DANA LYNNE ANDERSEN, M.A.

The cover illustration was commissioned for this book. It is titled, *"The Divine Vision."* The original oil painting was based on Arjuna's vision of the Infinite Form, described in Chapter Eleven of the Bhagavad Gita.

Dana Lynne Andersen, the creator, is an American artist of growing renown, acclaimed for the insight she brings to the function of consciousness in the arts. Her thesis is that there exists in our times an outstanding need, which becomes therefore the spiritual duty of artists of every kind (painters, sculptors, composers, musicians, and writers of both prose and poetry) to help inspire an upliftment of consciousness on Earth. Hundreds of people, in response to Dana's pioneering efforts, are developing an awareness of the importance of higher consciousness—not only to the arts, but to every human activity.

Dana Lynne Andersen is the founder of Awakening Arts Institute centered in Nevada City, California, U.S.A., a worldwide network of artists, patrons, and friends of the arts who believe in the need for art not merely to entertain, nor—darkly, in the name of "stark realism"—to degrade human consciousness, but to inspire in people everywhere an acceptance of, and need for, higher vision.

FURTHER EXPLORATIONS

I F YOU ARE INSPIRED BY *The Essence of the Bhagavad Gita* and would like to learn more about Paramhansa Yogananda and his teachings, Crystal Clarity Publishers offers many additional resources to assist you:

Paramhansa Yogananda's best-known and most widely beloved book is *Autobiography of a Yogi*. This book has sold millions of copies worldwide and is considered one of the masterpieces of 20th Century spiritual literature. It is a considered a must-read for sincere seekers of all paths.

Autobiography of a Yogi
Original 1946 Edition
Paramhansa Yogananda

Yogananda's *Autobiography* has entered the homes and hearts of millions of people all over the world. Reading it, one feels hope and finds peace. Many readers have given it to their friends and families, who in turn have given it to others. This Crystal Clarity publication is a verbatim reprinting of the original 1946 edition. Subsequent editions reflect revisions made after the author's death. The few thousand originals have long ago disappeared into the hands of collectors. Now it is possible to read the first edition, with all its inherent power, just as the great master originally intended it.

"In the original edition, published during Yogananda's life, one is more in contact with Yogananda himself. While Yogananda founded centers and organizations, his concern was more with guiding individuals to direct communion with Divinity rather than with promoting any one church as opposed to another. This spirit is easier to grasp in the original edition of this great spiritual and yogic classic."
—David Frawley, Director, American Institute of Vedic Studies

There are two different collections of the sayings, stories, and wisdom of Yogananda, each covering a diverse range of spiritual practices and topics, presented in an enjoyable, easy-to-read format.

Conversations with Yogananda
Edited with commentary by Swami Kriyananda

This is an unparalleled, first-hand account of the teachings of Paramhansa Yogananda. Featuring nearly 500 never-before-released stories, sayings, and insights, this is an extensive, yet eminently accessible treasure trove of wisdom from one of the 20th Century's most famous yoga masters. Compiled and edited with commentary, by Swami Kriyananda, one of Yogananda's closest direct disciples.

"Not many theologians can speak of Conscious bliss from a place of personal experience. Paramhansa Yogananda, a renowned twentieth-century spiritual teacher . . . can. His personal authority lends dramatic credibility to concepts and methods for spiritual aspirants from any tradition, from uncertain agnostics to fervent believers."
—*ForeWord* Magazine

The Essence of Self-Realization
Edited and compiled by Swami Kriyananda

A fantastic volume of the stories, sayings, and wisdom of Paramhansa Yogananda, this book covers more than 20 essential topics about the spiritual path and practices. Subjects covered include: the true purpose of life, the folly of materialism, the essential unity of all religions, the laws of karma and reincarnation, grace vs. self-effort, the need for a guru, how to pray effectively, meditation, and many more.

"A wonderful book! To find a previously unknown message from Yogananda now is an extraordinary spiritual gift. Essence *is wonderful to read in bits and pieces, before bed or to open up at random for an encouraging word from one of this century's most beloved spiritual teachers."*
—*Body, Mind, Spirit* magazine

If you'd like a succinct, easy-to-understand overview of Yogananda's teachings and their place within ancient and contemporary spiritual thought and practices, we suggest:

God Is for Everyone
Inspired by Paramhansa Yogananda, written by Swami Kriyananda

This book outlines the core of Yogananda's teachings. *God Is for Everyone* presents a concept of God and spiritual meaning that will broadly appeal to everyone, from the most uncertain agnostic to the most fervent believer. Clearly and simply written, thoroughly non-sectarian and non-dogmatic in its approach, with a strong emphasis on the underlying unity of all religions, this is the perfect introduction to the spiritual path.

"This book makes accessible the inspired pursuit of Bliss in simple, understandable ways. Written as an introduction for those just starting on the spiritual path, it is also a re-juvenating and inspiring boost for experienced seekers. Clear, practical techniques are offered to enhance personal spiritual practices. The author maintains that "everyone in the world is on the spiritual path" whether they know it or not, even if they are temporarily merely seeking pleasure and avoiding pain. Sooner or later, "They will want to experience Him (God)." Experiencing God—and specifically experiencing God as Bliss—is that underlying goal of this work, based on the teachings of a self-realized teacher. It hits the mark for contemporary spirituality."
—ForeWord Magazine

During his lifetime, Yogananda was famous for being a powerful speaker and riveting personality, and an awe-inspiring presence. If you'd like to experience a taste of this, we suggest:

Paramhansa Yogananda: Rare Film Collection

This DVD contains three short film clips of the world-renowned spiritual teacher, Paramhansa Yogananda, recorded in the 1920s and 1930s. Thrilling and utterly riveting, the unique combination of both seeing and hearing Yogananda is a life-changing experience. Also included is a video slideshow depicting many of the places that Yogananda himself wrote about in *Autobiography of a Yogi*. Narrated by his close disciple, Swami Kriyananda, this video retraces Yogananda's footsteps throughout India, recounting his visits with many great saints and sages. Filled with many rare and precious photographs,this is a must-have for anyone who has ever been touched by this great master.

Yogananda has many direct disciples, individuals that he personally trained to carry-on various aspects of his mission after his passing. One of the best known of these disciples is Swami Kriyananda, the founder of Ananda and Crystal Clarity Publishers. Kriyananda's autobiography contains hundreds of stories about Yogananda, culled from the nearly four years that Kriyananda lived with and was trained by Yogananda. It offers the unique perspective of a disciple reflecting on his time with a great Master.

The Path
One Man's Quest on the Only Path There Is
Swami Kriyananda (J. Donald Walters)

A continuation of Yogananda's *Autobiography*, Kriyananda's story gives a firsthand account of life with Yogananda, through the eyes of a disciple who lived and worked with him during the last four years of his life. Whereas Yogananda recounts stories of the remarkable saints and sages that he met during his youthful years of spiritual seeking, Kriyananda gives us a view of Yogananda himself as a spiritual sage and master, whose work in the West created a revolution in the way that people perceive themselves and their life's purpose. Kriyananda tells over 400 stories about Yogananda, including rare accounts of times spent with him at his desert retreat and of the days proceeding, and the moment of, his passing.

"The Path *is a deeply moving revelation of one man's poignant search for truth. With this book, Walters provides us with a rarely seen portrait of the joys and the problems of the spiritual path. The Path is filled with profound insight and practical advice for the novice and the more advanced seeker. I cannot conceive of anyone not deriving value from reading Walters' life story."*

—Michael Toms, Founder and President,
New Dimensions Radio

"This book let me see inside the life and teaching of a great modern saint. Yogananda has found a worthy Boswell to convey not only the man but the spirit of the man."

—James Fadiman, author of *Unlimiting Your Life*
and *Essential Sufism*

Crystal Clarity also offers two additional biographical resources about Swami Kriyananda. These are:

The Story Behind the Story
My Life of Service Through Writing
Swami Kriyananda

This is a warm, personal account of the inspirations which motivated seventy-two of Kriyananda's books, and the significance which he perceives in them. A delightful "behind-the-scenes" glimpse into the private world of an inspired author.

Faith Is My Armor
The Life of Swami Kriyananda
Devi Novak

Faith Is My Armor tells the complete story of Swami Kriyananda's life: from his childhood in Rumania, to his desperate search for meaning in life, and to his training under his great Guru, the Indian Master, Paramhansa Yogananda. As a youth of 22, he first met and pledged his discipleship to Yogananda, entering the monastery Yogananda had founded in Southern California.

If you would like to learn more about the spiritual heritage of India, the highest meaning of Hinduism, Yoga, and Christianity, including the deeper, underlying unity between Eastern and Western spirituality, you will enjoy reading:

The Hindu Way of Awakening
Its Revelation, Its Symbols: An Essential View of Religion
Swami Kriyananda

In a scholarly and thorough manner, Kriyananda brings order to the seeming chaos of the vast symbols and imagery one encounters in Hinduism, and clearly communicates the underlying teachings from which these symbols arise. Sure to deepen your understanding and appreciation of the Hindu religion, this book also helps establish the transcendent unity of all religions.

"Swami Kriyananda's inspired, entertaining, energetic writing style makes this book delightful reading for Hindus and non-Hindus alike. He brings order to the seeming chaos of the vast symbols and imagery one encounters in Hinduism and brings forth the underlying teachings from which these symbols arise . . . Kriyananda does a superb job not only in deepening our understanding and appreciation of the Hindu religion, but of encouraging us to expand our awareness to include an appreciation of truth in all religions."
—Yoga International

The Promise of Immortality
The True Teaching of the Bible and the Bhagavad Gita
J. Donald Walters (Swami Kriyananda)

Destined to become a classic, *The Promise of Immortality* is the most complete commentary available on the parallel passages in the Bible and the Bhagavad Gita, India's ancient scripture. Compellingly written, this groundbreaking book illuminates the similarities between these two great scriptures in a way that vibrantly brings them to life. Mr. Walters sheds light on famous passages from both texts, showing their practical relevance for the modern day, and their potential to help us achieve lasting spiritual transformation.

"While Walters' study speaks to an urgent need for understanding and compassion, his book also brings both the Bible and The Bhagavad Gita vibrantly to life. The Promise of Immortality is the most complete

commentary available on the parallel passages in these two texts."

—Bodhi Tree Book Review

If you would like to learn how to begin your own practice of yoga postures, meditation, Kriya Yoga, and more, as taught by Yogananda and Kriyananda, we recommend:

The Art and Science of Raja Yoga
Swami Kriyananda

Contains fourteen lessons in which the original yoga science emerges in all its glory—a proven system for realizing one's spiritual destiny. This is the most comprehensive course available on yoga and meditation today. Over 450 pages of text and photos give you a complete and detailed presentation of yoga postures, yoga philosophy, affirmations, meditation instruction, and breathing techniques. Also included are suggestions for daily yoga routines, information on proper diet, recipes, and alternative healing techniques. The book also comes with an audio CD that contains a guided yoga postures sessions, a guided meditation, and an inspiring talk on how you can use these techniques to solve many of the problems of daily life.

"It's tough to do a good yoga book, because a number of variables have to converge: substantive integrity, clarity in how-to explanations and quality visuals. By those measures, this book succeeds. Walters' long teaching record shows his ability to discuss key yogic concepts and practices in simple terms. . . . This

comprehensive guide has an extra medium to distinguish it on the crowded yoga bookshelf: an accompanying audio CD that contains a vague lecture as well as more helpful sections of guided meditation and posture instruction. All things considered, it's superior to books that reduce yoga to a series of physical exercises taught by this year's guru."

—Publishers Weekly

Meditation for Starters
J. Donald Walters (Swami Kriyananda)

Meditation brings balance into our lives, providing an oasis of profound rest and renewal. Doctors are prescribing it for a variety of stress-related diseases. This award-winning book offers simple but powerful guidelines for attaining inner peace. Learn to prepare the body and mind for meditation with special breathing techniques and ways to focus and "let go"; develop superconscious awareness; strengthen your willpower; and improve your intuition and increase your calmness.

Awaken to Superconsciousness
Meditation for Inner Peace, Intuitive Guidance, and Greater Awareness
Swami Kriyananda

This popular guide includes everything you need to know about the philosophy and practice of meditation, and how to apply the meditative mind to resolving common daily conflicts in uncommon, superconscious ways. Superconsciousness is the hidden mechanism at work behind intuition, spiritual and physical healing, successful problem solving, and finding deep, and lasting, joy.

"A brilliant, thoroughly enjoyable guide to the art and science of meditation. [Swami Kriyananda] entertains, informs, and inspires—his enthusiasm for the subject is contagious. This book is a joy to read from beginning to end."

—Yoga International

Ananda Yoga™ for Higher Awareness
Swami Kriyananda (J. Donald Walters)

Ananda Yoga™ is the system of postures that Kriyananda developed based on the training and instruction he personally received from Yogananda. This handy lay-flat reference book covers the basic principles of hatha yoga, including relaxation poses, spinal stretches, and inverted and sitting poses, all illustrated with photographs. Includes suggestions for routines of varying lengths for beginning to advanced study.

Affirmations for Self-Healing
J. Donald Walters (Swami Kriyananda)

This inspirational book contains 52 affirmations and prayers, each pair devoted to improving a quality in ourselves. Strengthen your will power; cultivate forgiveness, patience, health, and enthusiasm. A powerful tool for self-transformation.

Swami Kriyananda has also written extensively on philosophy, science, and the humanities:

Out of the Labyrinth
For Those Who Want to Believe, But Can't
Swami Kriyananda (J. Donald Walters)

Modern scientific and philosophical claims that life is meaningless and merely mechanistic are refuted by Kriyananda with his fresh approach to evolution and directional relativity. Hailed by scientists and religious leaders alike, this book is essential for everyone who is struggling to find answers to existential dilemmas.

Hope for a Better World!
The Small Communities Solution
Swami Kriyananda (J. Donald Walters)

In proposing what he calls "the small communities solution," the author expands Yogananda's vision of "world brotherhood colonies," which offer hope and promise for building a better world by example, rather than mere precept.

"Walters takes us on a fascinating journey backward in time in order to explore the future of human relationships. He guides us through the history of Western thought to arrive at a deep understanding of our evolutionary moment—the expansion of human consciousness. Like a good storyteller, Walters keeps us waiting breathlessly to hear more, and how we can put ourselves on this path to a better world."

—Louise Diamond

Books by Swami Kriyananda on Arts and Education:

Art as a Hidden Message
Swami Kriyananda (J. Donald Walters)

With insightful commentary on the great musicians, artists, and creative thinkers of our time, this book offers a blueprint for the future of art, one that views both artistic expression and artistic appreciation as creative communication.

"Kriyananda's predictions for Art's future are enlightening. They include a return to simplicity and a renascence of beautiful melodies. This book is, I believe, the most important book of our time on this vitally important subject."

—Derek Bell

Space, Light, and Harmony
The Story of Crystal Hermitage
J. Donald Walters (Swami Kriyananda)

Space, Light, and Harmony—containing 70 beautiful color photographs—is an adventure in design, building, and living. It is the true story of the evolution of a home—from initial planning to interior decorating—that serves as a powerful metaphor for personal development.

Education for Life
Preparing Children to Meet the Challenges
Swami Kriyananda

This book offers a constructive and brilliant alternative to what has been called the disaster of modern education, which, according to the author, derives from an emphasis on technological competence at the expense of spiritual values. Based on the pioneering educational work in India by Paramhansa Yogananda, the Education for Life system has been tested and proven for over three decades at the many Living Wisdom schools located throughout the United States, and will provide the basis for The Yoga Institute of Living Wisdom in India.

"The author makes clear that 'education for life' begins in the home. The moment people become parents, they become the primary teachers. Through reading this book, parents will be learning more

simple and effective methods of leading their children into becoming happier and more successful human beings. They will also be learning from their off-spring. The author's techniques will help produce a much less stressful home-life for all."

—Jim Doran, Education Consultant, *Joyful Child Journal*

Higher Consciousness in the Workplace:

Material Success Through Yoga Principles
A twenty-six-lesson study-at-home program
Swami Kriyananda

This new course by Swami Kriyananda condenses the experience of nearly sixty years of work—organizing, building, and creating out of "thin air" seven of the largest, best-known, and most successful communities in the world today.

These lessons compellingly communicate that spirituality and material success are not separate, unrelated aspects of life. These two fields of endeavor can indeed help each other. By following yoga principles, you can have all the benefits of true success: happiness, inner peace, understanding, true friendships, and life's normal comforts without the suffocation of meaningless luxury.

Each of the twenty-six lessons is packed with information, examples, stories, inspiration, and solutions to common problems that face every person seeking success.

By applying the principles and practices taught in this course, business, government, and educational leaders will be better prepared to guide our future directions with dignity, right-action, and success. It is also of immense help to the millions who suffer from symptoms of stressful business rhythms, and who seek a more balanced approach to personal satisfaction through their work.

"[This] is a significant contribution to the transformation of human awareness . . . . This course provides the platform on which ethics and practicality meet, each strengthening the other. I sincerely recommend that business and government leaders who want to be morally, psychologically, and practically prepared for the challenges that face our world study this course and apply its lessons with all due urgency, making it part of their training program for leaders of tomorrow."
—Professor Ervin Laszlo, Nobel Peace Prize Nominee, Founder and
President, Club of Budapest

The Art of Supportive Leadership
A Practical Guide for People in Positions of Responsibility
Swami Kriyananda

Here is a new approach, one that views leadership in terms of shared accomplishment rather than personal advancement. Drawn from timeless Eastern wisdom, this book is clear, concise, and practical—designed from the start to quickly produce results even for those who don't have huge amounts of time to spare.

Used in training seminars in the United States, Europe, and India, this book gives practical advice for leaders and emerging leaders to help them increase effectiveness, creativity, and team building. Individual entrepreneurs, corporations such as Kellogg, military and police personnel, and non-profit organizations are using this approach.

"We've been looking for something like this for a long time. We use it in our Managers Training Workshop. This book is very practical, very readable, and concise. Highly recommended!"

—Kellogg Corporation

Money Magnetism
How to Attract What You Need When You Need It
Swami Kriyananda

This book can change your life by changing how you think and feel about money. According to the author, anyone can attract wealth: "There need be no limits to the flow of your abundance." Through numerous stories and examples from his own life and others', Swami Kriyananda vividly—sometimes humorously—shows you how and why the principles of money magnetism work, and how you can immediately start applying them to achieve greater success in your material and your spiritual life.

"A thoughtful, spiritual guide to financial and personal prosperity. This book has timeless wisdom and practical solutions."

—Maria Nemeth, author of *The Energy of Money*

Crystal Clarity also offers many music and audio resources by Swami Kriyananda and others. Some of our most popular selections include:

Kriyananda Chants Yogananda
Swami Kriyananda

This CD offers a rare treat: hear Swami Kriyananda chant the spiritualized songs of his guru, Paramhansa Yogananda, in a unique and deeply inward way. Throughout the ages, chanting has been a means to achieve deeper meditation. Kriyananda's devotional chanting is certain to uplift your spirit.

AUM: Mantra of Eternity
Swami Kriyananda

This recording features nearly 70 minutes of continuous vocal chanting of AUM, the Sanskrit word meaning peace and oneness of spirit. AUM, the cosmic creative vibration, is extensively discussed in *The Essence of the Bhagavad Gita*. Chanted here by Kriyananda, this recording is a stirring way to tune into this cosmic power.

Mantra
Swami Kriyananda

Discover the ancient healing chants of India. For millennia, the Gayatri Mantra and the Mahamrityunjaya

Mantra have echoed down the banks of the holy river Ganges. These mantras express the heart's longing for peace, wisdom, and ultimate freedom from all earthly limitations, embodying the essence of every prayer. Both mantras are chanted in the traditional Sanskrit style, accompanied by the sound of 120 tambouras.

Metaphysical Meditations
Swami Kriyananda (J. Donald Walters)

Kriyananda's soothing voice leads you in thirteen guided meditations based on the soul-inspiring, mystical poetry of Paramhansa Yogananda. Each meditation is accompanied by beautiful classical music to help you quiet your thoughts and prepare you for deep states of meditation. Includes a full recitation of Yogananda's poem, "Samadhi", which appears in *Autobiography of a Yogi*. A great aid to the serious meditator, as well as those just beginning their practice.

Ananda Sangha

Ananda Sangha is a fellowship of kindred souls following the teachings of Paramhansa Yogananda. The Sangha embraces the search for higher consciousness through the practice of meditation, and through the ideal of service to others in their quest for Self-realization. Approximately 10,000 spiritual seekers are affiliated with Ananda Sangha throughout the world.

Founded in 1968 by Swami Kriyananda, a direct disciple of Paramhansa Yogananda, Ananda includes seven communities in the United States and Europe. An eighth community is presently being established in India. Worldwide, about 1,000 devotees live in these spiritual communities, which are based on Yogananda's ideals of "plain living and high thinking."

"Thousands of youths must go north, south, east and west to cover the earth with little colonies, demonstrating that simplicity of living plus high thinking lead to the greatest happiness!"

After pronouncing these words at a garden party in Beverly Hills, California in 1949, Paramhansa Yogananda raised his arms, and chanting the sacred cosmic vibration AUM, he "registered in the ether" his blessings on what has become the spiritual communities movement. From that moment on, Swami Kriyananda dedicated himself to bringing this vision from inspiration to reality by establishing communities where home, job, school, worship, family, friends, and recreation could evolve together as part of the interwoven fabric of harmonious, balanced living. Yogananda predicted that these communities would "spread like wildfire," becoming the model lifestyle for the coming millennium.

Swami Kriyananda lived with his guru during the last four years of the Master's life, and continued to serve his organization for another ten years, bringing the teachings of Kriya Yoga and Self-realization to audiences in the United States, Europe, Australia, and, from 1958–1962, India. In 1968, together with a small group of close friends and students, he founded the first "world brotherhood community" in the foothills of the Sierra Nevada Mountains in northeastern California. Initially a meditation retreat center located on 67 acres of forested land, Ananda World Brotherhood Community today encompasses 1,000 acres where about 250 people live a dynamic, fulfilling life based on the principles and practices of spiritual, mental, and physical development, cooperation, respect, and divine friendship.

At this writing, after nearly forty years of existence, Ananda is one of the most successful networks of intentional communities in the world. Urban communities have been developed in Palo Alto and Sacramento, California; Portland, Oregon; Seattle, Washington; and Rhode Island. In Europe, near Assisi, Italy, a spiritual retreat and community was established in 1983, where today nearly one hundred residents from eight countries live. The Expanding Light, a guest retreat for spiritual studies visited by over 2,000 people each year, offers courses in Self-realization and related subjects.

Ananda Sangha Contact Information

mail:

14618 Tyler Foote Road
Nevada City, CA 95959

phone:

530. 478.7560

online:

www.ananda.org

email:

sanghainfo@ananda.org

CRYSTAL CLARITY PUBLISHERS

WHEN YOU'RE SEEKING A BOOK ON PRACTICAL spiritual living, you want to know it's based on an authentic tradition of timeless teachings and resonates with integrity.

This is the goal of Crystal Clarity Publishers: to offer you books of practical wisdom filled with true spiritual principles that have not only been tested through the ages but also through personal experience.

Started in 1968, Crystal Clarity is the publishing house of Ananda, a spiritual community dedicated to meditation and living by true values, as shared by Paramhansa Yogananda, and his direct disciple, Swami Kriyananda, the founder of Ananda. The members of our staff and each of our authors live by these principles. Our worldwide work touches thousands around the world whose lives have been enriched by these universal teachings.

We publish only books that combine creative thinking, universal principles, and a timeless message. Crystal Clarity books will open doors to help you discover more fulfillment and joy by living and acting from the center of peace within you.

To request a catalog, place an order for the above listed products, or to find out more information, please contact us:

mail:
   14618 Tyler Foote Road
   Nevada City, CA 95959

phone:
   800.424.1055 (toll free in USA and Canada)
   530.478.7600

fax:
   530.478.7610

email:
   clarity@crystalclarity.com

For our online catalog, complete with secure ordering, please visit us on the web at:

   www.crystalclarity.com